The State of Loyalism in Northern Ireland

Also by Graham Spencer

DISTURBING THE PEACE?

OMAGH: Voices of Loss

THE MEDIA AND PEACE

The State of Loyalism in Northern Ireland

Graham Spencer
Senior Lecturer in Media Studies
University of Portsmouth, UK

© Graham Spencer 2008

All rights reserved. No reproduction, copy or transmission of this publication may be made without written permission.

No paragraph of this publication may be reproduced, copied or transmitted save with written permission or in accordance with the provisions of the Copyright, Designs and Patents Act 1988, or under the terms of any licence permitting limited copying issued by the Copyright Licensing Agency, 90 Tottenham Court Road, London W1T 4LP.

Any person who does any unauthorised act in relation to this publication may be liable to criminal prosecution and civil claims for damages.

The author has asserted his right to be identified as the author of this work in accordance with the Copyright, Designs and Patents Act 1988.

First published 2008 by
PALGRAVE MACMILLAN
Houndmills, Basingstoke, Hampshire RG21 6XS and
175 Fifth Avenue, New York, N.Y. 10010
Companies and representatives throughout the world

PALGRAVE MACMILLAN is the global academic imprint of the Palgrave Macmillan division of St. Martin's Press, LLC and of Palgrave Macmillan Ltd. Macmillan® is a registered trademark in the United States, United Kingdom and other countries. Palgrave is a registered trademark in the European Union and other countries.

ISBN-13: 978–1–4039–8975–8   hardback
ISBN-10: 1–4039–8975–3   hardback

This book is printed on paper suitable for recycling and made from fully managed and sustained forest sources. Logging, pulping and manufacturing processes are expected to conform to the environmental regulations of the country of origin.

A catalogue record for this book is available from the British Library.

Library of Congress Cataloging-in-Publication Data

Spencer, Graham.
  The state of loyalism in Northern Ireland / Graham Spencer.
    p. cm.
  Includes bibliographical references and index.
  ISBN-13: 978–1–4039–8975–8 (alk. paper)
  ISBN-10: 1–4039–8975–3 (alk. paper)
  1. Northern Ireland—History. 2. Unionism (Irish politics) 3. Paramilitary
    forces—Northern Ireland—History—20th century. 4. Peace
    movements—Northern Ireland—History—20th century. 5. Northern
    Ireland—Politics and government—1994– I. Title.

DA990.U46S674 2008
320.54094109416—dc22   2007050065

10 9 8 7 6 5 4 3 2 1
17 16 15 14 13 12 11 10 09 08

Printed and bound in Great Britain by
CPI Antony Rowe, Chippenham and Eastbourne

In memory of David Ervine

Contents

Acknowledgements ix
Glossary x
Brief Chronology xi
Introduction 1

1 The Unionist Imagination 7
   Unionism and nationalism 8
   Unionism and tradition 12
   Unionism and religion 13
   Containment and change 19

2 The Identity of Loyalism 29
   Paisleyism 29
   Paramilitarism 39

3 Violence and Politics 54
   Motivation and structure 54
   The UVF 61
   The UDA 64
   Politicisation 68

4 The Peace Process Part 1: Early Stages and Key Players 74
   Initial developments 74
   Clergy 80
   Chris Hudson: an intermediary 90
   The Irish government 94

5 The Peace Process Part 2: Talks 112
   Ceasefire 112
   Exploratory dialogue 119
   Ministerial dialogue 139

6 Towards the Good Friday Agreement 153
   Multi-party talks 153
   Final stage negotiations 161

7	After the Good Friday Agreement	180
	The decline of the UDP	180
	Omagh	188
	Feuds and intra-Loyalist violence	191
	The Loyalist Commission	200
8	The Media	206
	News and negotiations	207
	Media as conduit and platform	212
	Signalling and advancing positions	214
	Framing and interpretation	217
9	Recent Developments and the Way Ahead	224
	Political background	224
	Internal consultation and change in the UVF	227
	Internal consultation and change in the UDA	234
Conclusion		246
Afterword		251
Bibliography		257
Index		263

Acknowledgements

This book would not have been possible without financial support from the British Academy and teaching sabbaticals provided by the AHRC and the Centre for European and International Studies Research at the University of Portsmouth. Nor would it have been possible without the help of the following individuals who I wish to thank: Peter Brooke, Stephen Leach, John Steele, Michael Ancram, Patrick Mayhew, Albert Reynolds, Dick Spring, Fergus Finlay, Brian Fitzgerald, Eamon Delaney, Sean Duignan, Martin Snodden, William 'Plum' Smith, (the late) Billy Mitchell, Paul Murphy, Tommy Kirkham, David Nicoll, Jackie McDonald, John Dunlop, Ken Newell, Roy Magee, Robin Eames, Gerry Reynolds, Mervyn Gibson and a number of others from the UVF and UDA who cannot be named, but know who they are. Particular thanks to Chris McCabe, David Adams, Gary McMichael, Billy Hutchinson, Quentin Thomas, Tom Roberts and Frankie Gallagher, and a special thanks to Chris Hudson. This book is dedicated to David Ervine, who was supportive throughout and died in January 2007.

Glossary

CLMC	Combined Loyalist Military Command
DUP	Democratic Unionist Party
EPIC	Ex-Prisoners' Interpretative Centre
INLA	Irish National Liberation Army
IRA	Irish Republican Army
LINC	Local Initiatives for Needy Communities
LVF	Loyalist Volunteer Force
NIWC	Northern Ireland Women's Coalition
PUP	Progressive Unionist Party
UDA	Ulster Defence Association
UDP	Ulster Democratic Party
UFF	Ulster Freedom Fighters
UKUP	United Kingdom Unionist Party
UPGR	Ulster Political Research Group
UUP	Ulster Unionist Party
UVF	Ulster Volunteer Force

Brief Chronology

1966	Formation of modern UVF
1971	Formation of UDA
1973	Formation of UFF
1974	Ulster Workers' Council Strike
1979	Formation of PUP; formation of New Ulster Political Research Group, UDA document *Beyond the Religious Divide* published
1981	Formation of Ulster Loyalist Democratic Party
1985	*Sharing Responsibility* document published by the PUP; Anglo Irish Agreement
1987	UDA document *Common Sense* published
1989	Formation of UDP
1991	Formation of CLMC
1992	Loyalist ceasefire to facilitate Brooke Talks
1993	Irish government meet PUP
1994	IRA ceasefire; Loyalist representatives meet British officials; Loyalist ceasefire; start of exploratory dialogue with British officials; *Joint Declaration* published by British and Irish governments
1995	Publication of *Frameworks Documents*; start of ministerial dialogue; Loyalists meet British Northern Ireland Secretary Patrick Mayhew; publication of *Building Blocks* document by British and Irish governments; Drumcree stand-off
1996	Mitchell Report; Sinn Fein document *Building a Permanent Peace* published; IRA end ceasefire with Canary Wharf bomb; elections for multi-party talks; start of multi-party talks; UDP and PUP visit Downing Street
1998	The Good Friday Agreement

Introduction

In early 2007 the autobiography of the Loyalist paramilitary Johnny Adair was published (Adair 2007). Imaginatively titled 'Mad Dog', the cover of Adair's book in a single image confirmed a number of dominant narratives and stereotypes about Loyalist paramilitarism. On that cover Adair is photographed dressed in black, sporting a diamond stud earring and wearing dark glasses. He is photographed from side on, holding a revolver with both hands in an elevated position, as if about to fire. And he is positioned without a context to be in, except for a blood-red background, which seems to reinforce a pornographic fascination with violence. The image of Adair is that of the paramilitary as pathological gangster. There he stands as an individual with no apparent political aspiration, motivated by his own individuality and a desire to acquire status only by his ability to inflict fear through violence and murder. Brutal, callous, selfish, thuggish, ruthless, calculating, emotionless, detached and ultimately uncontrollable is how he appears.

Nobody could suggest that the characteristics which this image evokes are without foundation in relation to Loyalist paramilitarism and keep a straight face, just as one cannot deny the picture's resonance in highlighting much of the sectarian hatred and horrific violence which has emanated from Loyalist paramilitaries during the history of the Northern Ireland 'Troubles'. But, taking this into account, it is important to recognise that for at least the last 20 years there have been influential figures within Loyalist paramilitary groups who have sought to bring violence to an end and contribute to building a lasting peace. Their attempt to try and create an articulate and politically motivated loyalism, which stands in contrast to the enduring myths as captured in an instant by the cover of Adair's autobiography, is the subject of this book.

What this study sets out to do, is to explain how paramilitary loyalism in Northern Ireland has shifted and responded to challenges brought about by the peace process which began in the 1980s. Through interview material with key players within loyalism, along with officials and representatives from Irish and British governments, the clergy and other intermediaries, this book provides a political history of loyalism and the peace process from the perspectives of direct dialogue. Charting the trajectory of the peace process through the chronology of events, negotiations, documents, experiences and contestations, this narrative shows that bringing violence to an end in Northern Ireland has been dependent on the theatre of political interaction and dialogue (Dixon, forthcoming), of which loyalism has been a necessary part. What the interview responses perhaps indicate most is that the composition of the peace process is determined by the work of actors, responding to the script of political change and operating as performers in a play (some might say a tragedy). The direct dialogue used in this book, not only illustrates the role of such performers, but highlights the complexity of this play (which is called the 'peace process') and the risks associated with being part of it. Significantly, a number of individuals at considerable personal risk have undertaken to try and move others away from violence towards discussion and debate as a more effective and desirable way of addressing the threats and fears posed by political change. Those risks, how they were facilitated and opposed and ultimately what they have meant for those who define themselves as Loyalist and live as part of the imagined Loyalist community form the substance of this book.

The material used in this study challenges the impression that political direction and debate is peripheral or incidental for those involved in Loyalist paramilitarism. Unlike republicanism, which tends to acquire political legitimacy and purpose among significant sections of the Nationalist community, loyalism receives little sympathy or credence, let alone support, among the Unionist population in general. Rather, the actions of Loyalists are invariably seen by much of unionism as criminal, motivated by a lawless siege mentality, without credible reason and entirely lacking in political legitimacy. What interrupted this perception however, was the emergence of articulate political Loyalist spokespersons in the early 1990s, who began advocating a need to recognise loyalism as an essential element in the developing peace process which had a serious contribution to make in bringing conflict to an end. David Ervine and Billy Hutchinson (of the Progressive Unionist Party (PUP)) and David Adams and Gary McMichael (of the Ulster Democratic Party (UDP)), who represented the paramilitary Ulster Volunteer Force (UVF) and Ulster Defence Association (UDA) respectively, are now seen by many who participated in the negotiations and politics of the peace process as being the more progressive voice of unionism in terms of working towards a peace settlement. Contrary to the popular view of loyalism being reactionary and defensive, these participants were actively promoting positions which were in opposition with the intransigence of traditional unionism and played a constructive and purposeful role in the talks which led to the Good Friday Agreement. That process of engagement, the problems the representatives were up against, how their respective organisations reacted and where those organisations have come to by the summer of 2007, are all questions, which over nine chapters, this book seeks to examine and interrogate.

In Chapter 1, I begin by outlining some of the characteristics and complexions which are seen to underpin the Unionist worldview, particularly in relation to imaginations about nationalism, religion and social and political change. The conventional approach of unionism to political change has historically been to try and prevent it, in as much as change is associated with a weakening of the Unionist position. Though the peace process has shown that there are exceptions to this approach, this nevertheless hardly invalidates the traditional stance of obstruction which unionism has displayed in relation to the transformation of political and social life in Northern Ireland. The influence and interrelationship of nationalistic and religious experience within unionism provide the interpretive framework which shapes communal attitudes and themes of self-definition and meaning. This chapter examines these areas in order to provide some background understanding of how the Unionist sense of belonging is conceptualised and applied to life in Northern Ireland.

Chapter 2 looks at the construction of Loyalist identity through the two categories of Paisleyism and paramilitarism. The concept of loyalism is historically depicted as an extreme version of unionism, where the theology and politics of Rev Dr Ian Paisley (as conveyed through his political party the Democratic Unionist Party (DUP)) function in the same social and political space as paramilitarism, which uses violence as an expression of defiance. Although each of these groupings have obvious differences in that one relies on the psychological projection of fear and insecurity as a basis for public support and attention, while the other chooses violence as a way of dealing with such fears and insecurities, both also exhibit a certain rigidity and devotional attachment to defending and preserving the Union with Great Britain and are seen as extreme because of the extent of that conviction. The ideological influences of Paisleyism, with its apparent inflexible opposition to change (at least until very recently), can be seen to intersect with the attitudes of paramilitaries in that it underpins and reinforces the hard line resistance which is seen as necessary to confront the anxieties and dilemmas brought about by the constant presence of nationalism and republicanism. The violence of the paramilitaries is the physical manifestation of resistance which is itself shaped, and some would say even legitimised, by the extreme articulations of Paisleyism and its emphasis on the dangers of change. Having said that, there have also been challenges to the potency of this relationship, brought about both by the peace process and the emergence of politically motivated representatives from within paramilitary loyalism. This chapter highlights those challenges and suggests a need to rethink the associations between Paisleyism and paramilitarism in the shift from war to peace and the development of conflict transformation in Northern Ireland.

Chapter 3 examines the relationship between violence and politics in loyalism and the debates which took place inside paramilitary organisations towards developing a political position and voice in response to ending conflict and engaging with the peace process. This chapter provides a short history of the two main Loyalist paramilitary groups – the UVF and the UDA; it then deals with aspects of motivation and structure inherent to Loyalist paramilitarism. It concludes by looking at the key consultations and proposals which formed the backdrop for interaction with politics and peace and which became the basis of negotiating positions adopted by the PUP and the UDP once involved in peace talks.

Chapters 4 and 5 describe the background developments and moves which led to Loyalist representatives engaging with Irish and British governments, and map the dialogue process which provided the necessary foundation for later substantive negotiations. In Chapter 4 the role of the clergy, who were operating as initial contacts and conduits between governments and the Loyalist representatives, is considered alongside the work of intermediaries and the Irish government. A number of Loyalist representatives dealt with the Irish before they met the British and it is apparent that in the formative stages of contacts, it was the Irish, rather than the British, who put most effort into constructive engagement with loyalism. The structure and order of Chapters 4 and 5 therefore also reflects the chronology of interactions. I should also point out here that although there is inevitable interdependence between all the participants, which intensified as time progressed, I have provided a separation of the roles performed by the participants with respect to the timing of meetings and dialogues for reasons of narrative cohesion and to provide the reader with a clearer picture of developments and intentions.

Chapter 5 takes us through the period when the Loyalist paramilitaries called a ceasefire, so fulfilling the request of both governments to end violence as a condition for entering exploratory and ministerial dialogue with the British. Drawing from interviews with the officials involved in these interactions, this chapter explains the nature of those dialogues in relation to the broader political strategy of trying to draw the paramilitaries further into the political process so as to avert a return to violence. During the exploratory and ministerial dialogue phase it was the British who most actively controlled the parameters and purpose of discussion, rather than the Irish, and it is the comments of British officials which inform this section.

Chapter 6 examines the talks and negotiations leading up to the Good Friday Agreement of 1998 and details the intensity and substance of the final stages before the Agreement was reached. To date, this would appear to be the high point for political loyalism in terms of negotiating Unionist and Loyalist concerns and principles into the agreement and working to secure the protection of the Union through the principle of consent. Yet, after the Agreement, that political influence began to decline, leading quickly to the dissolution of the UDP and where PUP representation was reduced to one seat at the Assembly by 2003. Chapter 7 charts the trajectory of this decline, describing the events that ended the UDP, the turmoil created by the Omagh bomb and the rise of feuds and intra-Loyalist violence which served to effectively reinforce the negative stereotype of loyalism as being driven by little more than irrational violent impulses, and standing in complete contradiction to the efforts of those working to bring about political development and progress.

In Chapter 8, the public perception of this image and its negative consequences are assessed as part of a brief discussion on the media's role in the peace process and its association with loyalism in general. Here, attention is given to the part played by the media in negotiations and the media's role as a conduit for messages and communications throughout the peace process from the formative stages until the Good Friday Agreement. The media is seen by those who took part in the negotiations as integral for exerting pressure on opponents and important in the process of trying to gain negotiating advantage. It is also recognised as a necessary influence in the presentation of party positions and framing and interpreting messages in order to shape and influence public attitudes and relationships with emerging issues and events. How the Loyalists viewed the significance of the media, how it was used in association with political aspirations and how it came to impact on what the Loyalists were trying to achieve, are the questions which this chapter addresses.

Chapter 9 describes how the UVF and the UDA moved into a phase of internal consultation from 2004 and 2005 respectively, to cope with the challenges of political transformation and respond to a power-sharing Assembly which was agreed by the two dominant parties, Sinn Fein and the DUP, and set up in May 2007. By that time, the UVF had effectively ended its existence as a paramilitary organisation and the UDA had become preoccupied with community development and the potential difficulties of managing loyalism in transition. Realising that the threat of political violence can no longer be justified in the absence of physical armed conflict, both organisations have reacted (albeit differently) to a broad public consensus on the need for political stability in Northern Ireland and have either moved, or are moving, in response to that consensus. The difficulties and issues which this shift has created for Loyalist paramilitarism are considered in relation to criminality and politics, and the implications which each might have for where loyalism is heading.

Importantly, this book traverses between the broader political context of the peace process and the internal workings and actions of the paramilitary organisations in response to that process. It highlights the many difficulties that the UVF and UDA have experienced around the issues and dilemmas thrown up by moving from a violent to non-violent society and how they have tried to deal with struggles over self-definition and legitimacy in the wake of such change. Not surprisingly, because of a tradition and history which has emphasised violence for dealing with social tensions and fears in Northern Ireland, many have viewed the peace process as detrimental to an identity which has been necessarily formed by the communication and expression of violence. However, a significant number have also constructively engaged in the ambitions and momentum of the peace process, presenting ideas of substance and purpose and are seeking to demonstrate that Loyalist paramilitarism is not just motivated by the desires of sectarian, pathological and criminally motivated gangsters, who lack political awareness or the ability to make any relevant or positive contribution to society and peace. What this study shows is that Loyalists have played an important and necessary part in helping to reach an agreement about ending political violence in Northern Ireland, and it is because of this, that their role should be acknowledged alongside the efforts of Republicans and others who have worked to facilitate the slow but deliberative transition from conflict to peace in Northern Ireland.

1
The Unionist Imagination

The Unionist experience in Northern Ireland appears to be shaped by both consistent and contradictory outlooks. Consistency is maintained by the desire to remain committed to the Union with Britain, while competing desires and interests influence contradictory reactions to political life and change (Cochrane 1997: 35). What appears noticeable in much of the literature which examines the nature of unionism is the complex interrelationship between varying religious, cultural and political perspectives, which inform difference and resist definitions that emphasise a generalised characterisation of political life (Coulter 1994).

On the subject of political identity, Aughey views unionism as concerned primarily with the role of the state and citizenship (1989: 19), where the rights of citizens are prioritised and where convictions about state values converge with debates about the Union, which is itself idealised through notions of individual liberty and citizenship (ibid.: 24). But, given that such concerns are expressed towards a Union that already exists and, because of that, are actual rather than aspirational, it is perhaps unsurprising that political positions towards the Union are routinely articulated around themes of preservation and defence, which are used to maintain pre-existing structures of political control and resist the potential decline of unionism through the threatening presence of Irish nationalism (ibid.: 202). By emphasising unionism as diverse and concerned principally with the rights and responsibilities of citizens in relation to state institutions and structures of power, Aughey appears to suggest that anxieties about the union are ostensibly matters of democratic principle, which cannot be realised through the rather monolithic nature of Irish nationalism and its seemingly homogenised approach to politics and society. However, Aughey also hints at a key problem when he mentions that unionism 'conveys little meaning beyond its own narrow confines, for its contradictions reveal it to be essentially self-serving and particular' (ibid.: 21), since it is the particularism of unionism which poses problems for the credibility of democratic argument and which displays a noticeable lack of consideration for those who operate outside its 'imagined community'.

Unionism and nationalism

Aughey's argument that unionism should not be seen as nationalism, but as a construct for identity which is concerned with citizenship and the state, is resisted by others such as McGarry and O'Leary, who view the Unionist outlook as a 'variation of British nationalism' (1995: 92). Cochrane expands this point further when he observes that concerns about the preservation of identity, religion, culture and history, which are so keenly asserted by unionism, are also shared by Nationalists (1997: 80), and that imaginations about the state tend to be closely linked with concepts of the nation (ibid.: 77). Moreover, since the protracted conflict between unionism and nationalism relies on oppositional concepts of national identity, where Nationalists want to be part of a united Ireland, while Unionists want to remain part of the United Kingdom (generally speaking), it is apparent that nationalistic perceptions are linked in that they inform and sustain notions of irreconcilable difference (Whyte 1990: 172). Just as Nationalists construct self-definition around histories and imaginations of Irish nationality, so Unionists seem to 'feel themselves of British nationality' (ibid.: 149), with each position reaffirmed and legitimised by the threat of the other. As O'Dowd notes, the distinction between Nationalists and Unionists is routinely articulated via two separate yet interrelating discourses, where 'Unionists speak the language of universal rights and citizenship while Nationalists are mired in the insular language of identity and self-determination' (1998: 81). Here, unionism constructs this discourse within constraints that 'operate with highly exclusivistic and traditional notions of national sovereignty' (ibid.: 89), where citizens are foremost sovereign subjects and where citizenship means adhering to national duty and responsibility (ibid.: 82). To indicate the centrality of the Nationalist outlook within loyalism, it is worth referring to east Belfast UDA leader 'Charlie's' comments, which are typical of many paramilitary figures interviewed for this book:

> To me this conflict is not about religion, but nationality. The splits and divisions which I have encountered have always been about differences in attitude towards nationality and how it is perceived.

The expansive range of circumstances and conditions which are permeated by the influences of nationalism indicate its scope and elusiveness as an ideological construct. However, one of the more impressive attempts to grasp the rather slippery nature of nationalism is provided by Anderson, who views the nation as an 'imagined political community' (1983: 6), where those outside the community are perceived as a threat to integrative values and shared experience. Aughey's attempt to downplay the role of nationalism in Unionist thinking, on the one hand, neglects its associations with British nationality, and on the other hand, highlights how identity is shaped by, and inextricably linked to, fears and anxieties about Irish nationalism. Indicating how these distinctions also sustain relations between the two traditions, O'Malley makes an important point when he notes how 'one of the anomalies of the conflict is the fact that the Northern Ireland question is to a large extent a tale of two minorities. Catholics see themselves as a minority in Northern Ireland, while Protestants see themselves as a minority in the whole of Ireland. They both look at things the same way; it is the things they look at that are different' (1997: 138). This difference is both preserved and conveyed by Catholics, who embody a culture which 'has developed into a clearly national consciousness' (Wallis et al. 1987: 301), and by Ulster Protestants, where identity is a mix of Ulster and Irish and where the Northern Ireland problem is seen as 'a conflict between a nationality on the one hand and a dominant ethnic group on the other' (ibid.). Conflict is supported by Catholic and Protestant categorisations where 'one is homogenous and the other mixed' (Whyte 1990: 163), but where both are 'operating within the same paradigm' (ibid.: 172).

That Protestants may tend to define themselves more in terms of what they are not (Wallis et al. 1987: 301) is no less powerful a force in shaping identity than those who confidently express what they are (exclusion and inclusion both being essential for the construction of identity and self-definition). Indeed, this distinction is imperative to the politics of division and the ideological separation of the two communities in Northern Ireland. In trying to emphasise the diverse and democratic nature of unionism by concentrating ostensibly on citizenship and the state, Aughey seems to put distance between unionism and nationalism by stressing a diversity and pluralism which, he suggests, nationalism lacks. However, by not recognising the nationalistic connotations of Unionist belief, he is also overlooking an important influence on the Unionist imagination. Significantly, one needs to recognise that unionism is bound by the same institutions and practices which help form 'a national identity constituted in opposition to Irish identity' (Todd 1988: 11) and acknowledge that there may be parallels between the different historical traditions in Northern Ireland, in terms of both territorial claims and stories about siege (Brown 1985: 8). Furthermore, the conflicts which exist between unionism and nationalism can be seen to derive from 'ideologies of communal assertion and defence' (Ruane and Todd 1996: 91), where for unionism, 'the contemporary language of British political identity, economic progress and liberal human rights' has been used to challenge the Nationalist position while entrenching Protestant claims and interests (ibid.: 88). As McGarry and O'Leary contend, addressing the interlocking interests of Unionists and Nationalists, 'conventional Unionist discourses mirror those of traditional Irish Nationalists. Each blames exogenous agents for the conflict. Unionists blame the Republic, Republicans Britain; both Unionists and Nationalists also blame their own patron-state for being insufficiently committed to their national cause. Just as Nationalists argue that Unionists are really Irish and are manipulated into thinking themselves British, so Unionists argue that northern Catholics are really capable of being British, and are externally or educationally manipulated into thinking of themselves as the lost tribe of Erin' (1995: 137).

As Billig argues in his book *Banal Nationalism*, the ability of nationalism to shape social attitudes derives essentially from its power to manufacture and sustain differences between 'us' and 'others' (1995: 17). In relation to each, 'loyalty' and 'identification' are constructs which Billig believes are loaded with nationalistic tendencies and underpin the reproduction of ideologies and meanings that sustain common sense images of home and nationhood (ibid.: 16). It is a familiar occurrence, Billig suggests, for nationalism and its extremist implications to be used primarily in order to separate 'us' from 'them', where all imagined communities rely on such categorisations to a greater or lesser extent. The idea that unionism is not nationalistic but Irish nationalism is may be seen as a false differentiation, because as Billig observes, not only is nationalism 'simultaneously obvious and obscure' (ibid.: 14), but in established nation state-type societies, it 'is the endemic condition' (ibid.: 6).

A further complication arises if we think of nationalism not as a single entity, but as one which encompasses a range of influences which change in connection with differing vantage points (Mandle 2006: 36). We might wish to stress that a general view of nationalism needs to be weighed against the specific traits and characteristics of a more specifically focussed and individualistic form. Mandle argues that we can think about the construction of both such types if we use the concepts of 'particularistic nationalism' or 'generalized nationalism'. Particularistic nationalism 'is the thesis that one particular nation or people are specifically chosen and valuable from the moral point of view itself', while generalised nationalism 'says that each individual properly has a morally weighty attachment to his or her nation, whatever it happens to be. On this view, the moral point of view itself does not single out any particular nation for special treatment; rather, it authorises individuals to do so themselves, based on their own identification' (ibid.). Both these definitions may be usefully applied to understanding unionism and cater for fundamentalist as well as more pluralistic determinations of identity and self within the Unionist community. The extent of social solidarity among members of the imagined community clearly has room to shift and incorporate extreme as well as moderate positions, and indeed it is necessary to accommodate such differences in order to maintain the image of democratic freedom which helps distinguish community members as different from those of other less democratically inclined communities (ibid.: 37). Further, since individuals are typically absorbed into a 'national culture', by sharing the constitutive tastes and characteristics of that culture as well as expressing differences within consensual boundaries (ibid.: 38), Unionists can be seen to display Nationalist tendencies just as other imagined communities do.

There are other considerations we might also want to take into account when thinking about how nationalism functions. Firstly, as cultures and communities come into conflict with one another, individuals tend to cling to experiences of ethnicity and nationality in order to (re)define identity and a sense of self (Volkan 1985). In that instance, communities seek to reinforce common notions of territory, history, language and religion, the intensity of which fluctuates in relation to time, place and circumstances of threat (ibid.: 223). The shifts and movements of nationalistic expression at such moments also become necessarily adaptive in order to deal with the boundaries of communal life, which both enter a phase of flux and are subsequently reasserted in order to confront the dangers of change. In relation to loyalism, it is clear that this fear of change is a central factor in shaping ideological attachment to self and defining the Catholic threat (Todd 1994: 69). Intersections between ethnicity, religion and nationality influence the shape of both communal cohesion and ideological resistance to opposing communities (ibid.: 71). The exercise of nationalistic sentiment acts as a response to the perceived violation of communal existence and may be reawakened or recycled through the symbols of songs (Finlayson 1996), marches (Roshwald 2006: 111–20), murals, sport or commemorative occasions, as part of a process where concepts and images of belonging and nationhood are strengthened. Within loyalism, the historical tendency has been to defend communities rather than address class-based inequalities and segregation (Finlayson 1996: 109–10), and strive to maintain social integration and systematically facilitate that integration (Mason 1985: 411) by drawing from a combination of other influences (social, historical and cultural) and ideas that collectively help contribute to the politics of memory and group formations (ibid.: 416). Moreover, Protestant associations with Britain have historically not only provided the reason for defending Ulster, but shaped the conditions under which that defence takes place (ibid.: 418). And, systematic activities which have allowed for the reassertion of symbolic expression have functioned to influence both the patterns and preferences of communal formation, as well as provide boundaries within which movement and change take place (ibid.: 423).

Arguments which bring into question unionism's relationship with a nationalistic intent show a distinction with Irish nationalism which stresses ethnicity over concerns about nation (Bruce 1998). Unlike Catholicism in Northern Ireland, which may be seen as inextricably linked with nationalism (Wallis et al. 1987: 302), there is no homogenised sense of nationality within Ulster Protestantism, and it is this comparison which perhaps explains why, for some, unionism is seen to be lacking in nationalistic character and orientation (ibid.). Yet, it could also be argued that unionism should not be seen as less nationalistic than Irish nationalism because it exhibits a greater diversity of identity, since it is precisely this diversity which is used to recycle and maintain the values of nationalistic belief and emotion, and it is precisely this perceived diversity which is emphasised and defended as part of the nationalistic discourse. Frankie Gallagher – a representative of the Ulster Political Research Group (UPRG), which is the political wing of the UDA – illustrated the potential for variation in identity by describing himself as an 'Ulster-Nationalist' before elaborating:

> What you will find is that the majority of England see us as a bunch of Paddies, where we're all seen as Irish. We also have a problem in Ireland where the majority of people think we're all Irish as well, but that we haven't come round to understanding that we are. They are two very problematic ways of thinking because we don't see ourselves as Irish and we don't see ourselves as English. We're certainly not all Paddies. I see myself as British-Ulster.

Unionism and tradition

The belief that one is connected to both Britain and Ulster indicates that there are two traditions which impact on Unionist culture. For Todd, those traditions are Ulster Loyalist and Ulster British (1987). For the Ulster Loyalist, northern Irish Protestantism becomes a focal point for identity, with British influence a secondary consideration. Todd observes how this tradition 'derives its intelligibility and power from the Evangelical fundamentalist tradition. Its core assumption is that the only alternative to Ulster Loyalist dominance is Ulster Loyalist defeat and humiliation' (ibid.: 3) In contrast, for the Ulster British, it is Britain which becomes the centre of influence, with less significance attached to Northern Ireland. This position 'shares many characteristics with liberal ideology but within a social and political context where it is constantly challenged by the realities of Loyalist sectarianism, the policies of the British state and Nationalist grievances and achievements' (ibid.: 11). Here, Britain 'is conceived not as a nation but as a sphere of influence which encompasses diversity within it' (ibid.: 14). In separating the functions of the two traditions, Todd highlights how differences may be best summarised in terms of how each approaches the possibilities of change. Particularly resistant to any moderation, the Ulster Loyalist ideology is seen as 'a self-contained, closed system', where the 'binary structure of thought – purity vs. corruption, domination vs. humiliation – does not allow for any gradual move towards compromise with or understanding of political opponents' (ibid.: 20). In comparison, the Ulster British ideology also has problems with change and conceptualises ideas of the liberal in narrow and self-interested ways, but offers some scope for a critique of the Union and, potentially at least is more open towards transition (ibid.: 21).

The two traditions which Todd outlines demonstrate a joint approach to perspectives about the Union which McGarry and O'Leary prefer to theorise as *devolutionist* and *integrationist*. Devolutionists argue that 'Northern Ireland must have extensive devolved self-government' designed to act as a 'bulwark against British treachery', whereas integrationists believe that 'union is best maintained by legal, political, electoral and administrative integration of "the province" with the rest of the UK' (1995: 93). While integrationists want to promote British electoral practice and the idea of a pluralist democratic state which legally binds Northern Ireland into the Union, devolutionists prefer the idea of local majority control and tend to support the principle of devolved power to regions of the United Kingdom (ibid.: 94–5). The contrasting attitudes inherent to these positions may be discerned in relation to the Ulster Loyalist tradition (notably the DUP), where a propensity to declare a loyalty to the crown but less so to parliament exists alongside Ulster Protestants who see themselves in terms of 'no precise national identity' because of oscillations between Britishness and Irishness (ibid.: 112). The scope for (re)interpretation of identity, which these formulations offer, hints at the potential for other discourses of unionism to emerge, which become especially pronounced when changing political and social circumstances come into view. Then, other considerations of how unionism should react may emerge, opening the field of contestation to allow alternative articulations to take place. The development of the PUP and the UDP can be seen as a response to challenges posed by the peace process and introduced debates to the political/public sphere which were critical towards dominant unionism and its preoccupations with the Union, as well as standing in contrast to those obsessed with defending conventional aspects of national identity.

Unionism and religion

Along with the powerful influences of tradition and national identity, the values and meanings which influence and sustain Unionist identity have an interpretive basis that historically draws from the theological traditions of Presbyterianism and Protestantism, and more particularly from principles of order and control which have roots in Calvinism, which emphasises the individual's relationship with God. A system of theological principles developed by John Calvin, a leader of the Reformation from the mid-sixteenth century, Calvinism presents a moral framework for social order by way of dividing society into 'the elect', who are seen to represent God's will, and the 'non-elect', who are both inferior and a threat to the social order supervised by the elect. This order is a product of 'predestination' where social life is a manifestation of God's will, which must be maintained and defended. The idea of change therefore sits rather uneasily with those who strive to adopt a Calvinist approach to life. The relationship between the individual and God is at the centre of Calvinism, where, as Weber observed when addressing the linkage between Calvinism and individualism, the focus is on self-reliance and where the individual 'himself creates his own salvation' in order to achieve 'the systematic self-control which at every moment stands before the inexorable alternative, chosen or damned' (1930, 2005 edition: 69). The moral certainty which supports this outlook poses obvious problems for compromise since this would mean a dilution of moral goodness and a negation of theological principle. While it is by no means the case that all those who consider themselves as Unionists adhere to such theological orthodoxy (indeed, it is important to recognise how Protestants have played a constructive and moderating role in the Northern Ireland problem (Gallagher and Worrall 1982; Taggart 2004; Power 2007)), Protestant and Presbyterian traditions nonetheless continue to exert influence on the Unionist imagination and reinforce a view of the world which is both introspective and exclusivist. Not surprisingly, efforts to modernise are invariably seen as 'threat or betrayal, performed either through ignorance or with malevolence' (Cash 1996: 139) and stand to violate the fixedness of belief which provides security and clarity.

Paradoxically however, the emphasis on individual conscience, which is particularly dominant among Conservative Protestants, means that interpretation of the orthodoxy is subject to contestation and schism. This disagreement is reflective of Protestantism's association with theological rather than institutional principles (unlike Catholicism), and its adherence to a set of beliefs which shift with individual interpretation, creating inevitable fissures and disputations in the process (McGrath 2007: 15). The certainty and authority of the Protestant tradition is underpinned by changing fears and concerns based on individual responsibility and judgement before God. Although more liberal Protestants are seen to favour reason over faith, Bruce argues that shifts in traditions are largely bound by interpretative differences over the Bible and the lessons of scripture (1985: 599). Constrained by the authority of God, Bruce believes that such contentions demonstrate the importance of 'free thinking', which is highly democratic, if also prone to schism. It is this schism, Bruce suggests, which allows for heterogeneous expression within the Protestant tradition and facilitates the articulation of difference. And it is this articulation of competing interpretations of the world which accounts for the rather contradictory nature of Protestantism and the problem of trying to provide any single or agreed definition of the tradition (Elliott 1985: 21). The sense of superiority which infuses Protestantism and Presbyterianism is underscored by a distrust for authority (ibid.: 4), which, more often than not, is seen as a threat to the purity of principle and theological obligation (ibid.: 20). Clearly, the certainties of such belief make it much harder to move those who are under its influence towards change and compromise. Even if the individualistic emphasis of Protestantism means that there is perpetual contestation about meaning and conviction, it seems that such discrepancies are bounded by the orthodoxies and expectations of the tradition, and that potential difference does not extend to an imaginative comprehension of the human condition beyond well-established parameters of acceptability (Brown 1985: 8).

The emphasis on individual conscience, which draws from the struggle over civil and religious freedom (Miller 1978), means that Presbyterianism prides itself on the idea of a radical nature. Stewart summarises the Presbyterian as 'happiest when he is being a radical. The austere doctrines of Calvinism, the simplicity of his worship, the democratic nature of his Church, the memory of the martyred Covenanters, and the Scottish refusal to yield or to dissemble – all these incline him to that difficult and cantankerous disposition which is characteristic of a certain kind of political radicalism. His natural instinct is to distrust the outward forms of civil government unless they are consonant with his religious principles. On the other hand, his situation and his history in a predominantly Catholic Ireland have bred in him attitudes which seem opposite to these, making him defensive, intolerant and uncritically loyal to traditions and institutions' (1977, 1989 ed: 83).

Stewart showed considerable foresight when, writing in the 1970s, he predicted that DUP leader Rev Dr Ian Paisley's support would grow as 'Ulster Protestants became more and more threatened, either by Catholic nationalism or the British Government' (ibid.: 100). In contrast to the English assumption that 'compromise is the answer to all disputes', Stewart maintains that 'Ulstermen believe the opposite' (ibid.: 101), where the rigidity and certainties displayed by the fundamentalism of those such as Paisley have historically reaffirmed a sense of security, through resisting compromise or moderation in political attitude (ibid.: 100). In relation to the conflict in Northern Ireland, this way of thinking means that the struggle for political control and authority has been aligned with the 'moral and spiritual battle' of religious belief, where 'in the face of violence and chaos, people are driven back to the comfort and knowledge of righteousness and order' and where 'traditional religion offers both immediate comfort and the hope of triumph' (Morrow 1997: 56).

The ability of Protestant fundamentalism to connect with fear of change and a 'siege mentality' derives from 'its ferocious attachment to the division into sinned against and sinning' (ibid.: 58), and its 'relative durability and reliability as myth sustaining the fundamental division between good and bad' (ibid.: 62). During moments of perceived threat, this more extreme version of Protestant belief becomes the reference point for defiance and throws into relief the symbolism of identity which it aspires to protect and preserve. Moral assurance thus operates as a key component within the emotive power such a position exerts (ibid.: 70). To enter into a process of change ostensibly contributes to a weakening of the fundamentalist position and the admission that the idea of righteousness is not as it seemed. What could be achieved from negotiation with others which will advantage this position? Indeed, to be part of such an interaction can only be disadvantageous and destabilising for the rigid certainties of belief. Only concession and a relaxation of the purity principle can occur here. To negotiate on what is seen as absolute is a contradiction in terms, and it is precisely this tension which sustains the Protestant fundamentalist resistance to interaction with those outside the tradition. This is why throughout the duration of the Northern Ireland 'Troubles' the question of negotiation has tended to be an anathema for the more extreme religious elements of Protestant unionism, and why this community has shown a propensity to obstruct dialogue even when compromise offers the best chance of a positive social outcome (Dunlop 1995: 101).

Although it is important to point out that Presbyterian beliefs are not held within the wider Unionist population with equal conviction, it would still be fair to say that such beliefs continue to exert influence over popular perceptions of civic values (Dunlop 1995: 12). Moreover, there are certain characteristics which are seen to be indicative of the Presbyterian which shape dealings with others and relate to such values. For Dunlop, the Presbyterian defence of individual freedoms and responsibilities (ibid.: 12) tends to produce a certainty about such ideals which correspondingly inspires a lack of tolerance towards difference, or dealing with those not of 'the people'. As Dunlop observes here, 'Presbyterian language does not have too many layers to it; it does not possess too much flexibility. Presbyterians may not be very good negotiators. Their opening statements tend to contain an analysis of the situation along with the bottom line. There is no movement either contemplated or even possible, unless you can convince them that their analysis is wrong. If you can't convince them of that, the bottom line will not move, on principle' (ibid.: 101). At the fundamentalist level of religious belief, this has led to a 'political and philosophical rigidity within radical unionism where politics is seen as a struggle to maintain socio-cultural hegemony and liberty', where 'the way to achieve political success is seen in terms of what worked in the past' (Cochrane 1997: 40). There is little room for modification or reflexivity in such an imagination.

One cannot talk of the religious influences on loyalism in Ulster without referring to the fundamentalist Presbyteranism as practiced by the Rev Dr Ian Paisley and his party the DUP, since this party traditionally epitomises the importance of politico-religious ideology within Ulster politics (Smyth 1986). For Bruce, to understand the appeal of Paisley (which will be examined in greater detail in chapter 2) one needs to look at the role of Evangelicalism within Ulster unionism (1986: 249), for it is here one finds 'the core beliefs, values and symbols of what it means to be a Protestant' (ibid.: 264) which mark out the distinct and evidently incompatible differences between Protestant and Catholic. It is here too, as Mitchel notes, that one tends to find 'in essence an ethnic, particularist ideology, defined in negative terms and practising exclusion through a combination of means' (2003: 99). These means are supported through intersecting fundamentalist and nationalistic emphases which demand clear separation from opponents by exaggerating the need to respond to the call of defending Ulster (ibid.: 204).

A consequence of this calling is the exclusion of those who are seen to betray the Ulster cause by not responding to the sense of 'belonging, uniqueness and emotional commitment' under threat, or by disputing the isolation and exclusivity which such a response requires (ibid.: 206). This particularism logically resists the tendency towards positive interaction with others and, as Mitchel contends, works to maintain 'an insecure identity that needs enemies, fears and conspiracies to sustain its dynamism'. Because of this, Mitchel continues, 'It belongs outside the establishment in that it is inherently incapable of dialogue or compromise – the language of democratic politics' (ibid.: 210).

The emotive power of such extreme religious belief enables it to exert considerable influence over moral values and identity (Mitchell 2006). This sense of projected moral correctness and the obligations of the self which derive from that sense, invariably draw from 'the capacity of biblical discourse', which provides the interpretative framework to 'evaluate political conflict as good versus evil' (ibid.: 96) and perpetuates the narratives and myths which surround notions of righteousness. In order to maintain clear demarcations which insulate the imagined community, it is necessary to develop and perpetuate stereotypes. As Mitchell points out,

> Truth versus deceit, honesty versus hypocrisy, clarity versus hidden agendas: these ideas form part of the cultural vocabulary of many Protestants in Northern Ireland today. They are pronounced amongst Protestants with strong theological beliefs, but they also exist amongst many non-churchgoing Protestants, especially those who have been raised in religious families. The constructions of the differences between Protestants and Catholics generalize and simplify; however, they are effective in reproducing class stereotypes of straightforwardness versus sneakiness. They also provide moral evaluations of the communal boundary' (ibid.: 103).

Mitchell goes on to explain that 'religious ideology often sets the boundaries within which politics operates' and that the potency of such belief tends to rise and fall with changing political circumstances, when the possibility of threat or loss is more or less evident (ibid.: 115). She refers, for example, to where Protestants' feelings about loss after the Good Friday Agreement, coincided with a rise in anti-Catholic feeling, and when Sinn Fein failed to make expected moves on decommissioning, so feelings about Catholic dishonesty also increased. In comparison, as conditions are seen to improve for Catholics, so perceptions of victimhood become less prominent within that tradition (ibid.). In explaining key differences between the Protestant and Catholic outlook, Mitchell identifies how oppositions are constructed and carried through concepts of 'communalism versus individualism'. For Protestants, it is ideas about liberty and individualism which have political resonance, whereas for Catholics it is ideas about the community which have particular salience. It is because of these differences, Mitchell contends, that Protestants and Catholics have 'different understandings and expectations of certain political policies and processes' (ibid.: 139). Elaborating further on how approaches to politics are shot through with historical and religious meaning, Mitchell observes how

> the insecurity of Protestant settlement was imbued with religious notions of siege and contractual loyalty. Many Catholics gave meaning to social and economic consequences of invasion through religious ideals of suffering and victimhood. The role of the Catholic Church was enhanced by experiences of struggle as a faith community, as it built alternative social structures to British and Protestant power, and provided resources for identification ... In this context, Protestant fears of going under politically as a community were infused with religious ideas of freedom and individualism versus a seemingly authoritarian Catholicism (ibid.: 139).

It is because Protestants draw from 'religiously informed concepts and ideas, rather than separate religious practices', that the self takes on particular importance in the processes of identification and belonging (ibid.: 135), unlike Catholicism, which views church and communal responsibilities as the foundation of social stability and belonging. The idea of community obligation within Protestantism is constructed through the individual and the preservation of freedoms through an adherence to individual responsibilities. Thus whereas for Protestants the individual provides the focus for ideas about the community, for Catholics it is the community which provides the focus for ideas about the individual. Because of the potency of these differences in relation to social life, it is not surprising that the imaginations which they create have also been constitutive of political separation both in attitude and reason.

One of the dilemmas which arise in relation to this mix of political and religious belief is that if certainty is at the centre of faith, and political change indicates uncertainty, then faith becomes problematised when confronted by shifts in political circumstances. For dedicated Evangelicals (those most dedicated to the fundamentalist expression of Protestant faith) and those who adhere strongly to the more extreme aspects of Protestantanism, this brings about confusion which all too often turns into a negation of self and security (Jordan 2001: 140). The tendency at such moments is to turn away from the process of change and return to the predictable security of isolation (ibid.: 172). Moreover, this outlook extends beyond the convictions of those who practice fundamentalist Protestantism or adhere to the restraints of the Evangelical tradition (a tradition which relies on a strong historical link to the Reformation, authority of the scriptures, the cross and resurrection, direct individual encounter with God, conducting belief through the details and routines of daily life and communication of the gospel (ibid.: 19)), by providing the historical backdrop which has historically defined Ulster unionism, functioning to exclude or hinder tolerance for alternative outlooks and maximising difference in relation to opposing traditions (Bruce 1998: 73).

Containment and change

It is therefore a regular feature of Unionist discourse to equate religious faith with cultural identity and to view the potential erosion of political influence as a threat to religious belief and values (Cochrane 1997: 67). The resulting effect of this mix is invariably one of negativity towards moderation and a tendency to conceptualise any such development in terms of loss, weakness and a violation of the Unionist cause. A fixation with identity differences also means that even community-based projects can be looked upon suspiciously, as evidence of Republican sabotage. As Billy Hutchinson, former PUP politician (now community worker) who represented the paramilitary UVF in the peace talks, put it, when explaining the linkage between religious and political perception:

> I would make a distinction between the conflict here being a religious problem and where people's religious beliefs and background impact on conflict attitudes. One of the problems with Protestant communities is that they are very individualistic and that's something that goes back to the Reformation. They practice religion as a very private and individual activity, unlike Catholicism, which is more communal. This also creates problems for trying to involve people in community work and community development, because it's seen as communism and they equate that with republicanism. Protestants think very individualistically and they don't forgive easily; they don't have this sense of confessional as Catholics do. For Protestants, the thinking is very much that nobody but God will forgive you. There is also a tendency to have two birthdays; the day you were born and the day you gave yourself over to Jesus and became born again. It's then that you are no longer a sinner. Even for those who don't go to church or follow devoutly, there is a strong sense of attitude which comes from religion. The religious connotations of the old testament are about thinking in absolute terms. For Protestants, the influence is that nothing is a grey area and everything is black or white, it's either yes or no, with us or against us, I'll believe it when I see it, that kind of thing.

For PUP colleague David Ervine, this kind of thinking is illustrative of a general negativity in the Unionist imagination which impacts badly on confidence within communities and which obstructs movement towards progressive political positions:

> People are very much tribal and if you step outside of that tribe you are labelled a traitor. But the perception that whatever is happening can only be bad news for Unionists is always there. Everyday I hear people saying

that if it's good for them then it must be bad for us. There is a mindset in the Unionist community that if all the bad people would go away this would be a wonderful place. But that also helps with the process of denial and keeping morality in place. It is evident that if there were such a thing as a single overarching morality, there would have been no conflict here in the first place. All Protestants are clairvoyants and it's never good news and because of our experience of the malaise of the troubled mind we seem incapable. There are considerable contradictions with the way we see the world. We call the British government 'betrayers' and then demand that those betrayers look after our interests and the reason for this is because we see ourselves as too moral to deal with bad people. We let the Brits deal with the bad people and it gives us a get out clause because we can then always claim it wasn't us, but the evil betraying government that did it. We want to stand back and say we didn't do it. The celebration of individualism within Presbyterianism is an important reason for why we seem to have more leaders than followers but it also marks us out as people. I remember as a kid shouting 'We are the people' and I had no idea that somebody else wasn't. The deviance we expected or wanted of the 'enemy' was a reaffirmation of the things we were taught. Being told, for example, 'You can't trust them, they're a fifth column, they're devious, the priests sleep with the nuns', these were the stories we were told; always about denegration.

Gary McMichael, who was a representative for the now-defunct UDP which represented the Loyalist paramilitary UDA in talks which led to the Good Friday Agreement, conveyed a similarly critical response in his evaluation of unionism and politics:

The whole demeanour of Unionist politics over the last 30 years has been not about how we achieve X, Y and Z, but how we seek to resist losing X, Y and Z, or at least minimise the threat. It's a very negative ideology in that respect. The paranoia is partly to do with a lack of conviction and there's nothing to work towards. We're continually looking back at something and are unable to unify. The nature of Protestantism is to continue breaking down into smaller factions and in trying to find ways of how different we are to each other. Unionism certainly has a mentality that it can never win, so it's about trying to minimise the damage. It's a very negative view where the glass is almost empty as opposed to even half empty. Even those who support agreements see them in terms to trying to stop the rot. You can never move forward but you can control how much you move back. Within unionism any sign of moving forward or compromise is seen as negative and weak. It's win or lose, where loss is somebody else's gain. In a time of crisis, most will automatically follow Paisley's rhetoric because it very much provides them with the protection that they need. There's no reaching out and no accommodation. It's easier to put people back in their trenches when they feel under threat. Calming voices and moderation are generally seen as a weakness.

To a large extent, this perspective was also shared by McMichael's UDP colleague David Adams, who in outlining the limitations and problems of unionism argued:

> We talk of unionism as if it's this homogenous block of people, but it really isn't. Unionism isn't an actual political philosophy at all; it's just about a constitutional choice. It's not a political philosophy in the same way republicanism, or socialism, or liberalism, or conservatism is. There is a real problem with the idea of change which is self-defeating and to a large extent it's self-imposed. We are encouraged to act like losers, so it's no surprise that outcomes are seen in that way. You have political leaders who present every victory as a defeat, telling you that you are being hard done by, accentuating the negative whilst ignoring the positive. This creates nihilism and erodes confidence. Whilst this wins votes for Paisley it does nothing for the wider society. Unionism needs to stop acting like the football chant 'Everybody hates us and we don't care'. There is certainly a maxim that if it's good for them, then it must be bad for us. Whilst Republicans have successfully worked to sell defeat as victory, unionism does the opposite. There's also a continual jockeying for power within unionism which reinforces its fragmented nature. There is always a clash on issues and this relates to the centrality of individualism within the Protestant tradition. There is a deeply held belief about making up your own mind and voicing your own opinion. On the one hand, the ability to disagree and not follow the crowd is a democratic positive, but continual disagreement makes it impossible to move forward and undermines confidence in the community. It seems that constitutional preference is the only commonality between all the different strands of unionism.

Unionism's tendency to fragment is augmented when confronted by the prospect of political change, when intransigence and disagreement become familiar responses (Cochrane 1997: 35). Under these circumstances, traditional positions and imaginations often become intensified, making the potential for any kind of collective response highly unlikely (ibid.: 83). Yet, although the peace process in Northern Ireland and the challenges it poses have brought into relief disagreements within unionism, reflecting the tensions and fragmentations around the problem of how to respond and what to resist, we should remember that through the emergence of Loyalist politics and the more imaginative approach of the Ulster Unionist Party (UUP) under David Trimble's leadership, there has also existed a willingness to seriously engage with the idea of change and even to promote it. The development of this pragmatic approach reveals the start of a progressive unionism which stands in contrast to the conventional posturing of resistance which has served to effectively segregate unionism into 'yes' and 'no' camps in relation to the problem of change. Indeed, the development of the peace process has created a situation where unionism has been forced into deciding whether to support those intent on preserving expressions of Protestant Britishness, or work towards a deal with those traditionally seen as enemies (Tonge 2005: 65). The issues raised by this transformation invite two distinct categorisations within unionism which Tonge calls 'rational civics' (those willing to do a deal which recognises Irish involvement in Northern Ireland) and 'orange sceptics' (those resistant to any diminution of Britishness) (ibid.). And what has become increasingly evident as the peace process has progressed is that although the latter of these two categories has conventionally dominated Unionist approaches to change in Northern Ireland (particularly with the DUP), it is now the former category which is gaining currency and presenting challenges to the Unionist imagination.

The sense of negativity which pervades the Unionist imagination can be witnessed across the range of political representations in Northern Ireland. As stated, the uncertainties which pervade this thinking derive from a desire to preserve symbols and expressions of identity while promoting fears and anxieties about the constant and growing threat to both. What is apparent, even among politicians of mainstream Unionist parties, is the sense of insularity which is reinforced by the weight of religious influence and its projected values. One representative of the UUP described the Unionist worldview as based on a simplistic 'if you are not with us, you must be against us' outlook (Spencer 2006a: 52). For another UUP respondent, this belief draws heavily from the assumption that 'if God be for us who can be against us?' (ibid.: 53). Elaborating further, the respondent continued, 'There's a verse in the Bible which says "Come out from amongst them and be ye separate" and Protestants have taken that to extremes. I represent the Shankill in Belfast and there are about 24,000 people there, but there are something like 27 different congregations. That's 27 brands of Protestantism on the Shankill struggling for recognition. That's the paradox of unionism, together yet divided' (ibid.). Such division is further underscored by a distrust of all those who are seen as outside the imagined community and who exert a threat to identity and its preservation (ibid.: 53–4). Not surprisingly, this leads to a fear of interference from those with alternative political objectives and creates a situation where obstruction to reform becomes adopted as a central component of political strategy (ibid.: 58).

Problematically, the individualism which is espoused as integral to the Unionist psychology operates within narrow limits of acceptability which are defined by the conventions and characteristics of what it means to be a Unionist. As David Adams explained this process of definition:

> Individualism is both a strength and a weakness. It's very hard to get a collective or agreed position, but the flipside of that is that the parameters for disagreement are very narrow because when anyone speaks outside the consensus they are traitors or naïve fools. This contradicts the notion of civic Protestantism where there should be as many disparate voices as possible. The tendency towards individualism doesn't allow an agreed Unionist position to be adopted. Of course, there are a range of individual approaches to a range of issues, but they broadly operate within a consensus about the Union and nobody is allowed to stray very far from that. At the same time, this consensus makes sure that Catholics are not going to be attracted to it. It also sets up a position where if somebody differs from you politically, then they are also likely to be an enemy of your religion as well. The obvious problem here is if you believe you stand for the unadulterated truth then you are not going to move from that position. Compromise is a dirty word. It's seen as moving from the truth. It's a prime example of the indivisibility of religion and politics and it's the centre of hardline support. On the one hand, the Unionist community is very democratic in that there is always room for the voices that are opposed and who are moving to the right, but, there is very little room for the moderate voice, which tends to get stymied. If you are preaching a harder message, you will always find an audience and an acceptance. If you are preaching a progressively softer line, you are an outsider. It's a very specific part of unionism and it's always been there.

Paradoxically, the certainties of the Unionist imagination are held against a growing sense of marginalisation and alienation, and contained by a dominant perception that 'within Northern Ireland, the social and constitutional bulwarks and defences for Protestants are being steadily and persistently eroded' (Dunn and Morgan 1994: 20). This disaffection, for some, is reflective of deeper anxieties around identity which invariably keep the Protestant/Unionist community in a perpetual state of uncertainty and disquiet. For Bowyer Bell, this unease creates a situation where

> The Protestants of Ulster, residents of an imagined British Ulster, united in not being Catholics, fearful that they will be melded into the national majority, are still not sure of their identity but only their distastes. Being Protestant is crucial but somehow not enough. What more is there that makes them them? They know not so much themselves as their perceived enemy and their unifying religious commitment. Yet, if they do not know exactly who they are, they know all too well what they do not want to be.
> (1996: 115)

Others, such as Finlay, go further than this and suggest that the defeatism which permeates the Unionist community is indicative of a lack of identity: 'contemporary Protestant defeatism is less a product of a pre-existing identity than symptomatic of the absence of a northern Protestant cultural identity and, perhaps, of an ongoing attempt to get one' (2001: 4). His reasoning for this is that identity within Protestantism lacks collectivity, and although there may be the potential for such an identity to emerge, it is hindered by the hegemonic identity politics of sectarian division and fragmentation.

But, from another perspective, these fragmentations may be seen as politically strategic and not inherent to meanings which shape Unionist identity. The divisions within unionism, Tonge argues, should not be read as a crisis of identity, but require us to recognise the need to separate 'national identity' from 'political strategy' (2005: 63). In contrast to Bowyer Bell and Finlay, Tonge insists that Unionists do not suffer confusion about identity because 'they know who they are and where they want to be. What concerns Unionists is where they are being taken, however groundless the concern' (ibid.: 64). Whereas for Bowyer Bell and Finlay, Unionists are seen to suffer from an identity crisis, Tonge views this identity as somewhat assured, until confronted with the problem of political change and how to handle it. The fragmentations of unionism therefore *are* its identity and should not be taken as evidence of its absence. Fragmentation is the predictable mode of reaction when unionism is confronted by change, with each party attempting to assert its own determination to defend the Union. Invariably, such change presents an opportunity for unionism to not only resist its opponents, but other Unionists, who also struggle to assert their status as defenders of Ulster. It should be no surprise then that the development of the peace process in Northern Ireland has resulted in growing fragmentations and ruptures in the 'existing social order', which has 'brought about a political ideological and discursive crisis within unionism' (McAuley 2003: 69).

But, what is particularly relevant here is that the perceptible dislocation of unionism from traditional security and dominance has also created a space for new articulations about what unionism should do in response to the challenges posed by the shifting political environment. Significantly, the introduction of new voices which critically and constructively engaged with the dilemmas brought about by the peace process has highlighted that unionism at certain moments is not merely a static political monolith, but a 'social movement constantly subject to processes of redefinition and renegotiation' (McAuley 1999: 106). As an example of this, the emergence of the PUP and the UDP might be seen both as evidence of creating a 'context of negotiating the ideological terms within which contemporary unionism seeks to re-express and redefine ideas of a British identity' (ibid.: 112), and as offering a progressive politics which promoted the need for addressing concerns of working-class unionism, which had previously been absent.

Of particular interest here is the emergence of pluralistic approaches to the constitutional question and the problem of Unionist receptiveness beyond predictable cultural and liberal expressions, towards civic transformation. A key text which addresses this problem is Porter's *Rethinking Unionism* (1996), which looks at Unionist preoccupation with cultural and liberal thinking (defined by Porter as the cultural emphasis and the liberal emphasis) as an obstruction for dealing with the political realities created by the peace process. For Porter, unionism needs to embrace the concept of civic responsibility in order to play a positive role in the process of political change and realise that obsession with preserving cultural and liberal traditions is not helpful in meeting the difficulties faced by broader debates and shifting arrangements about social life (1998: 52). As a response to such difficulties, Porter asserts it is necessary to address the preoccupation with 'institutions and practices reflecting a Protestant-British ethos' (ibid.: 72), which has little in common with how British citizens see the world, and to re-examine articulations about liberty which are consistently expressed as a form of defence and used to reinforce an identification of loyalty (ibid.: 126). Attending to the challenge of liberal responsibilities, Porter stresses the need to provide a more rational interpretation of political perceptions by recommending 'inclusiveness and plain contractual arrangements' (ibid.: 127), and overcoming the Unionist tendency towards conceptualising the possibilities of political movement on its own terms. As Porter concludes, a re-imagining of liberal and cultural attitudes is necessary in order to confront the 'no compromise' approach to change which unionism generally follows (ibid.: 167). To do this, Porter puts forward a case for articulating a civic unionism which 'comes perilously close to committing the most unpardonable of sins: compromising the Union in the name of unionism' (ibid.: 170). Civic unionism, Porter insists, does not draw from a starting point where preservation of the Union is everything, but seeks to use arguments about that Union as one among others. What takes priority for the civic Unionist is 'the quality of social and political life in Northern Ireland – a Northern Ireland that includes not just Unionists but also Nationalists and non-Unionists of other prescriptions' (ibid.). Here, Porter introduces the idea of a 'thick' conception of citizenship as the basis for engagement with political and social issues. The civic Unionist differs because he/she views 'the North not merely as a site of the Union but as a site of a co-mingling and clash of British and Irish factors all of which have to be accommodated and reconciled' (ibid.: 183). In trying to emphasise the importance of 'difference through openness' via the civic model, Porter aims to get Unionists to look outside of their own immediate and tightly contained worlds, and to recognise that conventional cultural and liberal definitions deny the possibility of co-operation precisely because they determine the possibilities of interaction on their own terms.

However, Porter's emphasis, fresh as it is, is ultimately aspirational and to date, has failed to find significant support within the confines of Unionist politics. Even the emergence of what was termed 'new unionism' – which attempted to re-define the development of a potentially more progressive politics and sought to convey a more positive representation of unionism, as exemplified by Trimble's leadership of the UUP (Walker 2004: 252) – failed to embrace any reciprocal shift from established Unionist positions and principles. Indeed, as O'Dowd argues, the development of 'new unionism' signified alignments with British nationalism as a response to the gains being made by Irish nationalism, where articulations about the value of citizenship were made through the 'universalisation of a particular view of the British experience' (1998: 79). Efforts by the proponents of 'new unionism' to create a more positive public image of unionism, according to O'Dowd, relied on promoting 'a revitalised British nationalism' (ibid.: 70), where notions of citizenship and sovereignty were constructed on the basis of identity themes and the politics of belonging (ibid.: 79). The role of Trimble's UUP in the negotiations which led to the Good Friday Agreement, as well as indicating the possibilities for a flexible and pluralistic approach to dialogue, also reflect attempts to preserve traditional interests by reducing the scope of talks and trying to limit areas for negotiation (ibid.: 91). The intention to obstruct and limit was especially evident in the selection of ministries after the Assembly elections in 1998, when the UUP selected posts in order to contain and obstruct the progress of Irish Nationalists (Spencer 2006a: 58). The end of Trimble's leadership is a clear sign that for other party members and supporters his new approach had failed to halt the advance of Irish Nationalists and, therefore, had failed to prevent a weakening of Unionist power.

Nevertheless, we need also recognise that if the peace process brought pressures and problems to mainstream unionism, it also led to the development of a working-class Unionist politics through the PUP and the UDP, each of which served to move the religious and ethnic preoccupations of traditional unionism towards a 'secular and civic' model of political engagement (Walker 2004: 253). Further, although we can see that such a transition ultimately failed to move unionism away from fixed positions (as the election of the DUP as the biggest Unionist Party from 2003 demonstrates), it is important to view the arrival of the PUP and the UDP as evidence of the possibility for a diverse Unionist response to the challenges posed by the political changes of the peace process. Because of this, we should not assume that mainstream Unionists are not highly critical of the shortcomings and disadvantages for progress which established approaches impose. Research for this book reveals a considerable awareness among Unionist politicians and political representatives of a need to move away from the negative, obstructive siege mentality which has continued to pervade Unionist politics (Spencer 2006a), towards a more forward-thinking model of political engagement constructed around themes and issues of democratic renewal.

The contention that unionism tends to define itself negatively through what it is not and what it does not want, relates in particular to its relationship with Catholicism. If we need to acknowledge that varying degrees of tolerance towards Catholicism which connect with different social and economic contexts are evident within unionism (see 'A Citizens' Inquiry', The Opsahl Report 1993 pp. 37–47), we need also recognise the pervasiveness of an anti-Catholic ethos and how it has been exercised with some consistency (Brewer 1998). As O'Malley puts it, 'It is this inability or unwillingness on the Unionist side to see Catholics as equals that precludes them from acknowledging any dimension of the problem other than their own' (1997: 145) and which legitimises the refusal 'to examine the basis, and more important the validity, of their own negative attitudes towards Catholicism' (ibid.: 147). For O'Malley, opposition to Catholicism is both an expression of identity and a lack of confidence in that identity: 'the question of identity, particularly among Protestants, is extraordinarily complex. Because they do not have a strong sense of political identity, they fall back on their religion for symbols of identity. And because they take their cohesion in religious matters from an anti-Catholic bias that is common to all their denominations, anti-Catholicism becomes an expression of a shared identity' (ibid.: 151). The social solidarity which is created and sustained by the belief that Catholics will force Protestants to do what they don't want to do (ibid.: 139) means that fears about Catholicism are vital for both maintaining the exclusivist approach to political life and shaping contestations about democratic principles (i.e. being forced to accept changes to political and social order). Although in relation to the latter point, resistance to change may be voiced far less in terms of overt anti-Catholic rhetoric among many mainstream Unionists today, but more through 'a general appeal to the idea of democracy' (Bourke 2003: 273), the perceived dominance of Catholicism still remains synonymous with a democratic deficit and therefore continues to be imbued with anti-democratic credentials which stand in opposition to Unionist principles. If there are differences among Unionists about the extent of threat posed by Catholic dominance in Northern Ireland, it would still be fair to say that such a prospect would be strongly resisted and considered destructive towards the imperatives of a Unionist-determined democracy.

Along with this overwhelming sense of resistance to any suggestion of Catholic control, it is also worth noting that the idea of a united Ireland and a resulting Catholic domination is something that a minority of Protestants during the early stages of the peace process seemed willing to accept (Ruane and Todd 1992: 76–7). The practical disappearance of this position as the peace process has gone on, where for many it is Republicans and Nationalists who are seen to have gained, while Unionists see themselves as having lost (seen as loss precisely because of perceptions about Republican progress), once more highlights how the Protestant/Unionist imagination is subject to differences and shifts, as well as overriding similarities and commonalities (ibid.). The contrast between individualism and consensus, which inform the sense of crisis and certainty towards change, finds credibility with Aughey's assertion that 'unionism may lack a definite coherence but its identity is multi-layered and variegated, with cross-cutting patterns of experience and emotional attachment' (1990: 193). These layers are particularly notable in work carried out by Ruane and Todd, when examining the possibility for a political middle ground in Northern Ireland. Categorising self-definitions of Protestant identity as British, Ulster or Northern Irish and Irish, the authors concluded 'enormous variation in the positions held by individuals'(1992: 79) towards religious, political and cultural views. This research identified common themes and responses around questions about division and diversity, but also identified that there are three Protestant groups which have political organisation in Northern Ireland: 'Loyalists', 'Unionists' and 'Reconciliationists'. While 'Unionists' are seen as drawn towards mainstream Protestant values and identify with Britishness, and 'Reconciliationists' are viewed as pragmatic on issues of constitutional importance, 'Loyalists' are categorised as those who are drawn to fundamentalist Protestant positions and identify more with the idea of an insular Ulster (ibid.). What is of particular interest with this definition of Loyalists, however, is that it was concluded at a time when working-class loyalism was just beginning to cohere into a progressive force within Northern Ireland politics. It is this transformation and the challenges it posed for conceptualisations about loyalism to which we now turn.

2
The Identity of Loyalism

Paisleyism

Debates concerned with mapping the characteristics of Loyalist identity highlight two interrelated, but distinct, groupings which fall under the category of loyalism. Those groupings are what Bruce calls 'gunmen and Evangelicals' (1994) and the presence of each reflects territorial and theological interests which can be most readily witnessed in the Loyalist motto 'For God and Ulster'. The slogan, which is rooted in the convictions of the UVF in 1912, is an expression of the importance of religion and nationality, and for the early Loyalists signified 'aligning their religious piety with their patriotism' (Kennaway in Thomson 1996: 71). The meaning of the motto was used by the Loyalists to legitimise 'their God given responsibility to do all in their power to retain their allegiance to their national British identity' (ibid.) and provided a theological basis to Nationalist intentions. If many working-class Loyalists now resist the certainties of Evangelical belief and see it as an identity construct which hinders the development of a pluralistic society (Mitchell in Thomson 1996: 87), it is nevertheless the case that theological principles still exert some resonance among such communities (and indeed unionism generally) and continue to impact on meanings of self-definition. Though there are differences in the level of support for the religious perspectives as expressed through the fundamentalist Evangelicalism of Rev Dr Ian Paisley, it remains apparent that even those who do not share the potency of these perspectives are often happy to be represented by those who do, for it is the Evangelical's view of the world which is seen to best encapsulate and represent the true nature of Protestantism (Bruce 1987: 647). At the heart of this nature is the idea of betrayal and the concept of a true faith which is seen as most fervently articulated and defended by the Evangelical tradition. For DUP politician Gregory Campbell, the slogan 'For God and Ulster' is 'properly used in the context of a beleaguered, embattled people having been so vilified and so misrepresented that they must seek a refuge which will not betray them' (in Thomson 1996: 36). The term,

Campbell continues, 'is a powerful affirmation of belief in a sovereign God who disposes that which puny people propose. Those who shun it completely in the belief that it sectarianises the gospel either do not understand or do not accept the essential nature of the dispute between Protestantism and Roman Catholicism' (ibid.: 37). It is clear from Campbell's message, which is also a reflection of religious influences on DUP ideology, that fear of betrayal is a key consideration in the party's thinking and that by resisting any such betrayal it can position itself as the sole and proper voice of Ulster loyalism. What is also built into this assumption is the idea that since the party represents the truth, it is therefore the *only* party which can legitimately articulate the meaning of that truth. As Finlayson notes in relation to the DUP, truth and its associated themes of integrity, crisis, and purity are key organising principles of the party's message (1999: 59). Enshrined in this concept of truth is the very image of Ulster, and thus because of the indivisibility between territory and belief, in order to defend Ulster, it is necessary to talk about defending the truth (ibid.). By using the rhetoric of religious fundamentalism, the DUP, Finlayson asserts, 'generates an image of Ulster as Christ, destined to be victim to Judas but to emerge victorious at the final conflagration. The DUP then become the true defenders of Ulster because they are the only ones who know the truth' (ibid.: 63).

This argument, that the fundamentalist orthodoxy (as practiced by Paisley) is about truth, requires a rejection of other religious denominations which, in comparison, are seen as deceitful and untrustworthy. This not only includes Catholics, but other Protestant/Unionist denominations which, once more, can only be potential betrayers because they are not of the true faith. The reference point for such belief is a fundamentalist position concerned with 'the absolute sovereignty of God over the entirety of the universe and the need to submit to His authority' (ibid.: 61). Founded on the ideals of seventeenth-century Scottish Presbyterianism which expresses contractual obligation, and twentieth-century American fundamentalism which advocates strong emotional attachment to homeland (Smyth 1987: 116), Paisleyism seeks to reinforce the tradition of Ulster Protestantism through identification with the symbols and emotional resonance of Ulster's Orange and Loyalist history (ibid.: 127). At the heart of this expression is a defensiveness and anti-intellectualism which is indicative of fundamentalist performance and which seeks to exploit anxieties through populist sentiment (ibid.: 135). Adopting an apocalyptic world view from the Reformation and drawing from the theological influences of those such as Knox, Paisley relies heavily on anti-Catholicism as the basis of constructing and legitimising the notion of a catastrophic end. For MacIver, it is important to appreciate that Paisley's association with the Reformed Tradition means that 'The precedent for faithful political action that Paisley finds in Scottish and Ulster history is the formation of covenant – the banding together of faithful Protestants to resist the threat of papal dominance in the political community' (1987: 361).

Paisley's reliance on the Bible as history and as the foundation of political belief means that church history is seen 'as a series of battles against apostasy, so he perceives secular history as consecutive conflicts between liberty and tyranny. The Roman Catholic Church's role in Paisley's apocalyptic world view aligns her totally with the forces of tyranny, so that history necessarily involves for him a perpetual conflict between Romanism and Protestantism' (ibid: 365). In turn, Protestants who do not resist efforts to unite Ireland are seen as rejecting their inherent responsibility to protect the 'Protestant nation' and have failed to adhere to their religious duty of preventing the Protestant community from being 'corrupted by idolatry' (ibid.: 373–4) (although 'For God and Ulster' seems to have a somewhat idolatrous tone to it).

According to O'Malley, Paisley is 'the personification of the "fearful Protestant"', as well as standing for 'the embodiment of the Scots-Presbyterian tradition of uncompromising Calvinism that has always been the bedrock of militant Protestant opposition to a united Ireland' (1997: 170). The manufacture and recycling of fears about the treacherous nature of Rome means that central to Paisley's vision is the omnipresent and unchanging threat of Catholicism, which must be met and resisted by an equally unchanging Free Presybterian orthodoxy. The prospect of reconciliation is invariably seen as surrender and capitulation to the 'pervasive, indivisible, clandestine, sinister, ruthless, perverse and insidious' controls of the Catholic church (ibid.: 174).

The superiority of the Protestant tradition is obvious because it offers the prospect of 'being saved' and being given 'access to the Truth', whereas in comparison, Catholics are 'damned and in darkness' (ibid.: 178). The possibility of concessions or moderation with Catholicism is an anathema to this position and can only lead to the erosion and eventual destruction of the Protestant state. The need to maintain demonisation in order to reinforce the need for fear and resistance also relies on simplistic stereotypes, which depict Protestantism as good and Catholicism as bad. Thus actions by Catholics to engage with politics and change are read as attempts to subvert and wreck Protestant strength, the very idea of change seen as an attempt to destroy rather than reconcile. The 'siege mentality' this creates, as O'Malley observes, invariably leads to a situation in which 'Protestant fears therefore tend to be self-fulfilling: the more Protestants behave as though they are threatened by Catholics, the more Catholics behave in a way that reaffirms Protestants in their view that they are in fact threatened. At which point Protestant perspectives polarise, the hard line becomes the only line, and Paisleyism comes to the fore. The source of its allure is its power to convince many that their particular positions depend on the maintenance of Protestant power, whether they do or not' (ibid.: 182). Importantly, the strength of Paisleyism is drawn from an anti-Catholic ethos which is used to sustain and exaggerate the constant threat of Catholic advancement. In relation,

Paisleyism articulates a heightened need for defence against such advancement and strives to address fears about this happening by emphasising and reinforcing the need to return to the security of past authority and certainty (ibid.: 188).

Perhaps one of the most succinct and cogent explanations of the values which shape Paisley's religious world view can be found in John Carroll's work *Puritan, Paranoid, Remissive* (1977), in which he details the forces that help condition what he calls the 'Puritan character'. For Carroll, the idea of election, where some men are selected for salvation while others are not, is also, for those who are chosen as the elect, a process 'hounded by doubt' (1977: 3), and this is so because of the perpetual presence of sin, which makes the privilege of election 'a constant burden, not to be taken on lightly' (ibid.: 4). Indeed, it is the presence of sin and righteous justification which both permeate the outlook of extreme Protestantism and shape associated political attitudes (Mitchell and Tilley 2004: 587). The individual's commitment to the Puritan idea is ultimately an exchange between individual conscience and God, where the struggle over morality is an introspective affair and not something that is a matter for wider social or communal conversation (Carroll 1977: 4). The binding nature of sin also means that forgiveness cannot be forthcoming and that 'penance, not penitence is all that is available to the Puritan as a means for assuaging his guilt'. Moreover, because 'in real psychological terms, their [Puritans] guilt was never expiated, their salvation never assured: there was no effective repentance' (ibid.). The burden of guilt is therefore an omnipresent weight which cannot be relinquished and must be carried as a reminder of the dangers present in deviations from the strict moral code. In order to demonstrate individual commitment to this code, the Puritan has an obligation to present his worth through public works.

Referring to the issue of social class, Carroll points out how Puritanism 'undermined the traditional social hierarchy, which had decreed that human worth and godliness was a function of the prestige of the station into which a man is born' and has been achieved through emphasising the individual's relationship with God. Here, Puritanism prioritises the opportunity for individual salvation and provides a responsibility for the individual to 'publicise his spiritual experience of redemption'; so proving his commitment to the Puritan ethic in the process (ibid.: 5). Significantly (and this highlights why for Paisley intransigence has historically been a preferable social response to change), 'for the Puritan nothing is forgotten' (ibid.) and there is the constant fear of God's judgement from which there is no 'absolution or remission' (ibid.: 6). Given that guilt is a debt that can never be paid off, it is not surprising that exactness or rigidity tend to determine responses and actions, and that vigilance to the threat of potential guilt is relentless. Not only does this mean that the 'Puritan character can be viewed as a structure whose most important function is to protect itself from despoliation', but it also means that such a character relies on emotional isolation from theological difference and moral threat (ibid.: 7). To not do so is to risk failure, and as Carroll makes clear, the Puritan ethic is 'nowhere as merciless as in its attitude towards failure' (ibid.: 8). One especially notices the Puritan character at work in Paisley from Carroll's description of the Puritan's reliance on 'qualities of intensity, inwardness and self-control combined with the inability to forgive or to repent', also 'marked by its independence, its capacity to stand alone, its command both over its inner self and its public performance of vocation. This character's stature was one of authority. It was not to be lightly swayed, not to be easily crushed' (ibid.). It is also not difficult to see why the idea of engagement with Catholicism would represent a violation of the moral code which Puritanism espouses and, by association, why anti-Catholicism has been integral to Paisley's world view.

Arguably, the most comprehensive discussion of how anti-Catholicism (as exemplified by Paisley) feeds into Northern Ireland's social fabric and body politic can be found in John Brewer's book *Anti-Catholicism in Northern Ireland, 1600–1998*. Brewer provides a detailed analysis of how the demonisation of Catholicism is supported by historical perceptions which not only seek to preserve the past, but use it in order to limit options and understanding of future ideas and developments (1998: 89). By referring to symbols and myths of ascendancy which support the orthodoxy that Protestantism is God's will and Catholicism is necessarily imbued with an inferiority which is in dangerous opposition to the perceived exceptionalism of the Protestant tradition. For Paisley, support comes from seeking to augment fear and polarisation among Protestants, but not from within the mainstream of unionism. Indeed, Paisley's strength comes from being outside of Conservative positions, which he is able to attack and ridicule as out of touch with fundamentalist principles and detrimental to the purity of his extreme Presbyterianism (ibid.: 107). By projecting blame on Unionists who are seen as seeking to dilute the strength of the Union, Paisley is able to readily criticise the idea of moderation as little more that a process of concessions towards Catholicism, which is itself most potently exemplified by the advance of republicanism and the meddling Irish state. Even after the Good Friday Agreement of 1998, which Paisley attacked as intolerable and unacceptable, he was clear in his criticism of those Unionists who could dare to tolerate Dublin's involvement in Northern Ireland's affairs (Paisley 1999: 1278), and saw the Agreement as little more than Unionists 'being asked to commit an act of collective communal suicide by voting themselves out of the Union' (ibid.: 1284). Not surprisingly for Unionists, Paisley saw the Agreement as 'a crime against their fundamental liberties' and saw Nationalists as acting out of bad faith. Using Lord Carson's 1912 definition of Nationalists as a 'dark conspiracy' of people who strive to use 'crime and incitement to outrage maintained by ignorance and pandering to superstition' (ibid.: 1295), Paisley viewed the Good Friday Agreement as little more than 'a conspiracy hatched against Unionists by a great consistent movement of pan-nationalism, which embraces within it gains made at the expense of law and order, while undermining the democratic process that feeds an unjustifiable hatred of all that is British in its expression of identity and claim of loyalty in Ulster within the Union'(ibid.). What is noticeable here is that any perceived diminution of the Union is coupled with the perceived advancement of Catholicism and the inherent dangers within it.

Paisley's militant rhetoric, as Brewer points out, 'offers continuity with tradition' and the consistency of 'no surrender' provides a resilient articulation 'that resolves the ontological anxiety of Protestants who see the Janus connection between their Britishness and Protestantism being prised apart by Irishness and Catholicism' (1998: 111). Given the continuous threat of Catholicism, it is necessary that Paisleyism offers a form of resistance which look backwards, since there can be no amendments or changes to the supremacy of this extreme Protestantism and so little reflexivity or flexibility in what it promotes, or what it is prepared to tolerate. Note also that the idea of civil liberties cannot be conceived in terms of freedoms from which Catholics might gain. Indeed, the very idea that Catholics may gain power through civil liberties, for Paisleyism, would be seen as civil liberties being eroded or subverted, since civil rights can only be understood as a Protestant construct, designed to reinforce and underpin Protestant supremacy and legitimacy.

O'Malley makes clear that although a distinction needs to be made about what is considered the true representation of Protestantism and the real voice of unionism, since Protestantism is concerned primarily with resisting a united Ireland, whereas unionism is more concerned with maintaining Union with the UK (1997: 200), and that there are Protestants who resist the orthodoxy of Paisleyism (indeed many who were interviewed for this book are critical of Paisley's rhetoric), there is nonetheless a tendency for the anti-Catholic intimations which underscore the symbols and myths of Protestant identity, to be quite broadly accepted in the Protestant community (Brewer 1998: 131). The idea of covenant and a contractual obligation to act as a 'chosen people', translates into a resistance towards any potential transition which may destabilise civil and political liberty, parliamentary democracy or 'the socio-political arrangements which God blessed' (ibid.: 137). Political conditions are therefore inseparable from the religious vantage point which prescribes what is politically acceptable or not. Since 'social and political arrangements have to be viewed in terms of their conformity with this tradition' (ibid.), it is most likely that the principles of covenant exert moral guidelines and controls which provide a focus for the conditions of social and political life. The idea of civil and political liberty is therefore an extension of Protestant claims for God-given rights that must be defended from the perpetual threat of Catholicism, which has no grounds to challenge this dominance since 'claims of injustice are either denied in the covenantal view or seen as irrelevant because Catholics are outside the political contract' (ibid.: 142). Anti-Catholicism is thereby intrinsic to the exclusivity of the covenantal obligation as historically practised by Paisley, whose DUP has functioned as a 'politicoreligious movement' (Gallagher 1981), using religious principles to inform and justify political positions. Significantly, the scope for political interaction and the possibility of political relationships is controlled by the theological principles which Paisleyism promotes (Brewer 1998: 145). It is the extremism of religious interpretation which supports Paisley's perception of unionism and which, in turn, informs his vision of DUP politics (Cooke 1996: 221).

Within the DUP itself, Paisley has traditionally exerted influence and control over the selection of party members and isolated those considered to be critical or unsympathetic to his views (Moloney and Pollak 1986: 278–9). But, perhaps most notable about his reputation is a determination to attack other Unionists who violate his principles of religious extremism and so stray from the ideal of Protestant purity. Over the years Paisley has successfully split Protestants from each other and contributed to fragmentations in churches and Orange lodges (ibid.: 265). Defining his actions in terms of an allegiance to Protestantism and Ulster, Paisley has continuously criticised successive British governments about what he perceives as their lack of commitment to the Union, and has routinely taken a hostile stance against Protestants who are receptive to the idea of changing political arrangements in Northern Ireland. Since the 1960s, Paisley has been quick to condemn any sign of moderation in Protestantism, and his protest against former Northern Ireland prime minister Captain Terence O'Neill in the early 1960s because of an attempt to communicate with Catholicism, is illustrative of the outright rejection towards any possible interaction with 'the enemy' (Hennessey 2005: 1–35). Seeking to exaggerate concerns and anxieties about loss of identity, Paisley has strategically and purposefully built a fearsome reputation around themes of loyalty and disloyalty which has been used more often than not, as a destructive force against other Unionist politicians (ibid.). Even among the more liberal elements of Protestantism, Paisley's fundamentalism exists as a constant pressure and threatening presence, poised to accuse such elements as traitors and subversives. On the one hand, Paisleyism may be seen by some Protestants as commitment to the 'true faith' and the origins of Loyalist identity, but it has also existed as a destabilising force within Protestant society, able to undermine symbols and gestures of reconciliation and maintain the preferred segregation and exclusivity of social and political life.

The work of Bruce looks in detail at Paisley's presence in Northern Ireland politics and examines how his extreme Evangelicalism seeps into the Protestant community, even shaping the attitudes and experiences of those who would not identify with its religious extremism (1986). Bruce is right to ask why Protestants who do not share Paisley's theological convictions continue to vote for him, and seems to conclude that this is because Paisley is able to access and manipulate the interrelationship of Unionist politics and Protestant belief far more effectively than other parties. Even those who might think of themselves as 'secular' Protestants, for Bruce, 'are not far removed from an Evangelical religious commitment' (ibid.: 263). This is so, Bruce argues, because 'Evangelicalism provides the core beliefs, values and symbols of what it means to be a Protestant' (ibid.: 264). In times of perceived crisis (which tends to be associated with change), two positions are made available to Protestants: first a move away from the fixed principles of identity, or, second a resurgence of support and commitment to those principles (ibid.: 265). Paisley has successfully managed the latter of these two positions and become the reference point for established modes of Protestant identity in the process. His popularity derives essentially through his articulation of historical certainty and his presence as the physical manifestation of the Protestant tradition. The fears which he strategically promotes relate ostensibly to the potential deviation from such a position.

Having said that, there is notable movement within Protestant/Unionist politics in Northern Ireland and a growing 'secularisation' which presents a challenge to the myths and symbols of Protestantism as articulated through the religious fundamentalism of Paisley. For Thomson, the Protestantism which Paisley asserted in the 1960s and the reputation he subsequently acquired from his adherence to Evangelical purity, has been haemorrhaging support in recent years (2002: 63). The idea that Protestant politics can remain self-serving and insular in relation to the political world which surrounds it seems no longer tenable and there is a significant collective recognition for Catholics and Protestants to interact, as public endorsement of the Good Friday Agreement indicates. Indeed, it has even been suggested that public support for the Agreement could be read as a sign of 'collective identity', signifying a need 'to find space to compromise in favour of a plural sense of belonging' (McSweeney 1998: 95). Though the growing fragmentation of unionism and Protestantism is a response to the turbulence created by the shifting plates of Northern Ireland politics (which has more recently resulted in dwindling support from within Protestant/Unionist communities), it is also apparent that conventional definitions of religious Protestantism are no longer powerful enough to withstand the pressures for change. The success of the DUP in the 2003 elections and its presence now as the dominant Unionist party has indeed been achieved by easing away from hardened opposition to the Agreement, to a softer more strategic anti-Agreement position, as much as deriving from an ability to capitalize on public dissatisfaction within unionism generally (Farrington 2006: 176).

The politics of the DUP has been a key factor in gaining support from a Protestant community which is increasingly secularised and this has occurred, as Southern points out (2005: 141), because an approach to social and political life which relies on religious extremism would be more likely to alienate than attract votes from that base of support. In order to explain the DUP's public support from the secularised Protestant community, Southern describes the party as consisting of two camps, which he describes as 'pragmatic' and 'fundamentalist' (ibid.: 129–30). Whereas the fundamentalists are seen to derive their approach to politics through Evangelicalism, which seeks to remain aloof from political life, the pragmatists seek to distinguish religion from politics and develop party policy in relation to the political environment, rather than religious doctrine (ibid.). For the fundamentalist, the reference point for political action and tolerance is morality, and the acceptance of political change is conducted through a moral framework which is constructed from theological ideals (ibid.: 132). But, in order to survive within the changing political climate, it is essential for those ideals to offer some degree of adaptability, which is best achieved through articulations that rely less on overt religious doctrine and more on moral judgement and conviction (ibid.: 137). It is also noted that the influence of Evangelical belief within Northern Ireland politics is being reshaped because 'Evangelicals have begun to channel their political energies into interest groups' and that this has happened because there has been a 'restructuring of civil society' which has necessitated a move away from extreme religious doctrine towards a morally focussed frame of discourse (Ganiel 2006: 138). This means that the possibility of movement has emerged alongside the traditional position of intransigence and that there has been a growing recognition that the secure 'no' position has become less acceptable in social and political terms. For Ganiel, what such change requires is the realization that 'Rather than agitating for a Calvinist political order, traditional Evangelicals are adapting to the emerging pluralist structures of civil society. They are willing to take a position alongside other civil society groups, even if they continue to draw on discourses that link the causes of 'God and Ulster" (ibid.: 144). It is a moral orientation towards issues, rather than an obsession about Catholicism or a united Ireland, Ganiel insists, which is now beginning to determine the Evangelical's approach to politics (ibid.: 149), and it is the ability to agree or disagree about issues which has now become the central concern, rather than being preoccupied with fixed positions towards violence which no longer exerts such a strong hold over public attention (ibid.: 150).

Support for the more pragmatic elements of the DUP is reflected in the comments of one former UDA and UFF commander referred to as 'Alan' who explained:

The kind of things one often reads about Loyalists hating Catholics does not apply to me. I come from a mixed family and I was reared by a Catholic aunt. I have no hatred towards Roman Catholics at all and I have cousins who are Catholic. I am a Loyalist in the sense that I see the defence of my country and the British crown as the number one concern. Although I have no wish to be part of a united Ireland, I certainly want friendship, economic ties and as best a possible life with our neighbours in Ireland. Although Paisley's view has been consistently anti-Catholic that is his personal position, which I do not share. I vote for the DUP, as I have done in the last two elections, because of the work people do on the ground not because of their anti-Catholicism. It's the work they do in terms of community development and regeneration that wins my vote, not their views on religion and most of the people I know would agree with me on that. It's the work they do for you from the grassroots up. We understand where Paisley is coming from and we all know his past. He has to say these things to keep Sinn Fein at bay, but the up and coming DUP people speak to all the people on the ground. They know we are paramilitaries and they know our past and influence, but still they come and talk with me others knowing this. Although Paisley says he won't speak to us, he's probably about the only one who doesn't.

This lack of interest in religious conviction was also shared by the UDA's west Belfast commander, who will be referred to as 'Charlie', who saw the DUP's growing support as an inevitable result of adapting to political change and commented:

The last MLA and Westminster elections took place against a backdrop where Republicans were seen to be getting a lot of concessions and Protestantism was being left behind. Flags being stopped, marches being obstructed with residents' groups springing up all over the place, watchtowers being taken down, security being downgraded, the Patten report and so on, were all seen as part of a gradual attempt to erode people's way of life. Although I voted yes to the Good Friday Agreement I would now vote no. This is not because I don't want peace because I do, but it reflects a widespread concern about change and the growth of protest voting. People would vote for Paisley not because they share his religious views but because they see him as the best option for resisting republicanism. The Ulster Unionist Party are now seen as the ones who did not argue forcibly enough for Protestants or resist the concessions that Sinn Fein have won. Growth in support for the DUP is an inevitable result of the perception that Protestantism has been usurped. It is a political rather than religious problem.

Interestingly, although there is a preference for identity to be conceived and articulated in terms of religious i.e. 'Protestant' rather than political i.e. 'Unionist' labels within studies which chart public reaction to the peace process, which itself 'reveals the salience of Northern Ireland's sectarian differential as the key fault-line in society' (Mac Ginty 2004: 88), it is notable that the growing politicisation of the DUP and its increasingly integrated role in the politically changing landscape of Northern Ireland is also reflective of other established institutions within Protestantism undergoing change. The Orange Order, for example, is now beginning to see itself as a religious organisation being shaped by politics rather than the other way round, and having to reflect secular Protestant interests because of wider social and political transformations (Kennaway 2006: 43). This signals a re-negotiation of Protestant attitude and identity which is now both widespread and a growing response to changes in political life (Mitchell 2003). For Paisley, it indicates a shift from the rigidities of oppositional Evangelicalism towards a more inclusivist form (Mitchell and Tilley 2004: 587), and points towards a reorientation in political and social awareness, where the uncertainties of political life now appear to exert greater influence on the DUP than the certainties of religious and theological conviction (as Paisley becoming First Minister in the Northern Ireland Assembly alongside Sinn Fein's Martin McGuiness as Deputy First Minister in May 2007 made clear). This shift is itself illustrative of a decline in the influence of extreme Evangelicalism on social attitudes within Protestant culture, and coincides with a growth in the perceived importance of moral conservatism as a foundation for political action and success (Mitchell and Tilley 2004).

Paramilitarism

Picking up further on Bruce's suggestion that the convictions of Loyalist paramilitarism and Evangelicalism are linked because of a commitment to defend the Protestant tradition, and that the connotations of religious belief are influential in shaping the 'Loyalist vision' (1994), it can be seen that within Loyalist paramilitarism today, this relationship is not as solid as Bruce seems to suggest. Perhaps the one real exception to this is the Loyalist Volunteer Force (LVF), which formed as a breakaway grouping in 1996 as an oppositional force to the role which Loyalist paramilitarism was playing in support of the peace process. Consisting of disenchanted UVF and UDA elements and led by the notorious Billy 'King Rat' Wright (murdered by the Irish National Liberation Army (INLA) while in prison in 1997), the LVF articulated its hostility to the peace process through discourse which evoked many characteristics of Evangelical resistance. Drawing from the fundamentalist rhetoric of Evangelicalism and expressing Wright's strange predilection for both murder and religious extremism (Dillon 1998: 67–98), the LVF objected to the idea of any perceived weakening of Loyalist unity, which proved attractive for some within the DUP, as demonstrated when one of its representatives Rev William McCrea shared a public platform in support of Wright in 1996. Reiterating Paisley's idea of betrayal, the LVF articulated its defence of the Loyalist/Protestant tradition by emphasising how loss of territory and concessions would exacerbate a 'weakening of social solidarity' (Shirlow 2000: 89). Seeking to distance itself from the emerging political loyalism of the PUP and the UDP, who were receptive to change and the need for moderation, the LVF relied heavily on promoting the image of 'besiegement' and the God-given right to defend the spaces and institutions associated with the Loyalist experience. This discourse, as Shirlow points out, constantly referred to 'the ontological security and comfort of righteousness, moral order and potential triumph' (ibid.: 91), and sought to reinforce the myth that the Northern Ireland conflict was ultimately a struggle between 'Protestant civility and Irish barbarity' (ibid.: 92). Insisting that Protestant Northern Ireland must completely refuse to engage with those who do not share its communal interests (ibid.: 94), the LVF particularly stressed the dangers of secularisation and moves towards a rights-based agenda which was seen as a Nationalist/Republican conspiracy to permeate and undermine Protestant religious and political life (ibid.: 99). In its efforts to sustain the image of 'good' and 'bad' through the myths and stereotypes of communal division and perceived Protestant superiority (morally, religiously, politically, etc.), the LVF effectively restated the themes and arguments of Paisleyism, and sought to justify its paramilitary aspirations from the standpoint of Evangelical fundamentalism.

The connections and commonalities between the LVF and the religious extremism of Paisleyism is not typical of Loyalist paramilitary groups however, and many working-class Protestants vote for the DUP out of political rather than religious conviction. In an Internal Discussion Paper which set out the *'Principles of Loyalism'* produced by the PUP in 2002, it is argued that 'The Protestantism of modern loyalism is secular rather than spiritual' (2002: 91) and that 'there are few within loyalism who are deeply concerned about the state of religion or about the claim of God on their lives' (ibid.: 93). While the document recognises that adherence to religious values still exist and that such belief is intrinsic to the history of Protestant faith, it also acknowledges how such belief is held within a growing secularised space (ibid.). One explanation why many working-class Protestants vote for the DUP, while not sharing its explicit religious views, is given by UPRG representative and former DUP Press Officer David Nicoll, who describes Paisley's political appeal within poorer sections of the Protestant community as emanating from the DUP's engagement with working-class concerns during the 1960s and early 1970s:

> As a child I can remember listening to Paisley's bluff and bluster. His 'not an ounce' and 'keep your powder dry' speeches would have found resonance with my family who felt isolated in a rural area. But the working class were better represented by the DUP than the Ulster Unionists who basically consisted of army captains and establishment figures and used their titles in the community as if they were over and above the locals.

They had masses of land and owned most of the businesses, but provided bad pay and living conditions. Things for us were every bit as bad as what Nationalists complained of at the time. People used to say that the Ulster Unionists had prostituted themselves for positions in power; 'fur coat and no knickers', that was the populism. But Paisley motivated people into a cause of calling for tighter security on borders and protection of families, which the Ulster Unionists were not seen to be doing. They weren't on the ground, going from door-to-door. Paisley was able to animate through his church what he was doing and his own constituents got out to see what the feelings of people were. People were able to articulate their problems and get the DUP to do something about it. It could have been trying to get a bathroom built onto a house, or a sewage problem or whatever, which the Ulster Unionists would never have done. I recall seeing a DUP man spat on by an Ulster Unionist who was outraged that the authority of his party was being challenged. The UDA vote has consistently been for the DUP because they are seen as having come from the working-class, whereas the Ulster Unionists are traditionally seen as having little interest in what is happening on the street and maintaining their privileged position as authoritative figures.

For fellow UPRG representative Frankie Gallagher, the submissiveness of working-class Protestants is something which he believes still suppresses aspirations and achievement and presents a problem of perception which a developing Loyalist consciousness must address:

Most of the UDA membership are ordinary down-to-earth people but they are to extent victims of their class. There is still within the working class a view that you should tip the cap to the councillor and the MP, many of whom still conduct themselves with an aristocratic air. In a sense it's a time capsule where people are locked in the past and it's what we call the 'historical deficit'. We have a Unionist leadership fighting to maintain the status quo and when the status quo can't be maintained you have problems, but invariably to deal with this, unionism fights with itself. The exclusion that we experience is with Unionists and politically motivated Unionists. From my perspective, right-wing Catholicism and right-wing Protestantism need each other to exist. The DUP don't really need policies to get votes, they just need Sinn Fein and vice versa. Fear plays a big part in keeping people in their place and fear is reinforced by Unionist politicians who keep saying that the enemy has not gone away. loyalism needs to re-define itself and to get away from this imperial legacy, where people are expected to tip their caps to the landed gentry. Modern loyalism for me, is about challenging this kind of historic burden and to start a debate about changing ideas and attitudes. I see loyalism as being about the social and economic issues which impact on the quality of life within working-class communities. Certainly, my loyality is to Ulster and the people I live with, but that does not mean that things should not change.

Former UDP representative Gary McMichael saw the attraction of Paisleyism within poorer Protestant areas as deriving from a mistrust of authority, which serves to complement an identity of second-class citizenry and legitimises the need for resolute defence:

> Since paramilitarism has seen itself as a means for doing what other people wouldn't do, it therefore saw itself as the underdog and more anti-establishment as a result. This resonated at a political level with Paisley and the wider working-class community and it is evident that at a time of crisis the community will tend to follow Paisley's rhetoric because it very much provides them with the protection that they need. There's no reaching out and no accommodation. Even though the paramilitaries would often criticise Paisley and say that he was prepared to fight to the last drop of everybody else's blood, they still gave support when a crisis emerged. It's also important to realise that Loyalist engagement with the peace process was a threat to Paisley because if the hardmen were saying that things weren't so bad, it undermined his credibility. But a problem with many Loyalists is that they give their political allegiance to those who are not interested in them, like the DUP. They also seem to take an opinion of themselves which is not based on how they view themselves, but on how others view them and they often accept and confirm such views by behaving in ways that others expect of them.

David Adams, also a former UDP representative, supported this view and saw Paisley's influence over working-class Protestants as a successful manipulation of fears:

> When I was in the UDP one of our biggest dangers was the DUP and how they appealed to the lowest common denominator in terms of accentuating people's fears and concerns. The problem is although Loyalist communities are very political in many ways, they are also very open to simplistic and emotionally based arguments. That is of course, partly about being frightened of what the future might hold, but it's also the old adage of going for a solid bat and the hardest line. The DUP play on the old fears and anxieties which are already built into the psyche. It is important though to see that loyalism has to be judged in the context of unionism; it's not a separate entity and it's by no means a homogenous lump. If the paramilitaries disappear many will direct their energies into community work and will serve broader Unionist concerns and problems. Protestantism today is more tribal than religious and there is less of the

hats off to the religious elements of Protestantism. The definition of loyalism is problematic and I don't see it as any different from unionism. It was used as a pejorative term by the media for a long time and referred to Unionists behaving badly. If Paisley held a rally which was about kicking the Pope and anti-Catholic, then he was described as a Loyalist, so it became a negative term associated with the working-class and as the paramilitaries are almost entirely working-class it just stuck. Although the issue of class in Northern Ireland is lost in the mix of sectarianism and constitutional politics, it's more of an issue than people understand. But really, people vote for the DUP because of constitutional fears and sectarian preferences. No matter how nicely packaged, it's ultimately sectarian and that trumps the concerns of many working class people.

Though the above views are indicative of a growing critique within working-class Protestantism about the influences of Paisleyism, which developed a particular focus in the context of the peace process, it is important to note that serious thought about cross-community relations and power-sharing was taking place within Loyalist paramilitarism much earlier. The UDA's discussion paper *'Beyond the Religious Divide'* published in 1979 is indicative of serious engagement with the idea of a constitutional arrangement that would be tolerated by both Protestant and Catholic traditions. The document argued that before 'there is an evolution of proper politics in Northern Ireland, there must be a Constitutional settlement which is acceptable to both sections' (1979: 1) and even spoke (albeit not in detail) about 'stability and reconciliation' through 'the development of a common identity between the two communities regardless of religion' (ibid.: 2). Such words stand in stark contrast to the politics of Paisleyism, where interaction with Catholics is traditionally seen as leading to a road to Rome and the ruination of Protestant life, and highlights recognition of a need for joint-authority based on a Bill of Rights, a proposed constitution and political structures designed to facilitate any settlement. A second document *'Common Sense'* published in 1987, argued again for a settlement by proposing mechanisms for a negotiated devolved legislative government, political structures devised through 'consensus government, proportional representation and shared responsibility', a Bill of Rights and a supreme court with powers to 'uphold constitutional law and safeguard the rights of the individual as represented in the Bill of Rights' (1987: 2). Although these documents would have been received by Nationalists with some trepidation at the time, they reveal a pattern of thinking within the UDA which embraced the idea of interaction with Catholics and which set out a process of reform constructed from a political rather than religious viewpoint.

The argument for a need to develop pluralist politics in Northern Ireland, can be seen more specifically in the actions and intentions of those Loyalists involved in the talks and negotiations which led to the Good Friday

Agreement of 1998. In particular, those connected with the PUP sought to create a political voice for loyalism which was seen as unrepresented and ignored by Paisley and the DUP, and not surprisingly there is considerable criticism towards Paisley because of this. In making reference to Paisley's popularity, David Ervine commented

> Movement from the status quo is a fear process for those who value it. The most fundamental requirement for unionism is an internal debate and we have tried to get that debate going. It's reasonably obvious that only when we come to terms with ourselves are we going to have the confidence to deal with others. But to use a football analogy, we seem to play with more defenders on the field than attackers. Unionism is brilliant at playing the zero-sum game for the political class but not for its people. Fear of republicanism is so strong it acts to exclude other more pressing issues and concerns. A further problem is that there has been a tendency for loyalism to be a catch-all phrase for bad behaviour within the Unionist community. There are many of us who believe that the modern concept of loyalism was really invented by Unionists to distance themselves from the excesses of what they perceived to be the Protestant working-class. Actually, I think Sinn Fein have it right when they talk of 'Unionist paramilitaries' who tend to be working-class Unionists. As for why people vote for Paisley, it's important to remember that we never vote for who we want, we vote against what we don't want. We vote for the bulwarks against those we don't want. What this also indicates is that unionism only really talks to itself. Remember that when the tribe feels threatened the tribe is quite capable of opting for bad leadership. My experience is that when unionism becomes homogenised through fear, it's driven by the lowest common denominator and the debate then becomes fixed on 'us' versus 'them'. Paisley has been very good at increasing tribal tensions and it's easier in a tribal battle to keep your head down and tell people what you think they want to hear. Demand that which you know you can't have and then get upset when you can't have it; these are the kind of games that go with a divided society and the games which Paisleyism has exploited very well.

Billy Hutchinson of the PUP provided a similar assessment of Paisleyism, but also identified the Protestant/Catholic antagonism which Paisley has used as a distraction from the concerns and conflicts of Irish/British politics and culture:

> One of my earliest recollections of any politician was Ian Paisley in 1966–7 when he was talking about the road to Rome and popery. I remember him telling us that Terence O'Neill was taking us into Rome and he was using the same language to describe David Trimble 30 years

later. But the problem of alienation comes not from republicanism, it comes from unionism itself. Republicans are not responsible for the social and economic problems in our communities. Unionist leadership tends to re-affirm a lack of self-belief and a lack of understanding about what needs to be done. Again and again we have Unionist leaders tell us that there is no capacity in the Protestant community, and because they don't self-reflect, they continue to make the same mistakes. The difficulty is that you tend to get back from Loyalists the kind of answers you get from Paisley, which is that the most important thing is the Protestant culture, but for me, the conflict that has been going on here is about Irish and British identity rather than Protestant and Catholic and that's where people get stuck. Obviously the term Loyalist has been used as a derogatory term in Northern Ireland. The word seems to apply to either Unionists who take up arms, or those politicians who embarrass unionism. My view is that if you are a Loyalist, then you will do anything to make sure that Northern Ireland remains part of the UK. Bear in mind that a lot of people are afraid of change and Conservative with a small c in this country. That's one of the key reasons why Paisley has been around so long, because he plugs into that fear. Paramilitaries are no different and that's what comes into their heads at the ballot box.

Former UVF paramilitary, now mediation and conflict resolution worker Martin Snodden explained the relationship between the DUP and paramilitaries in the following way:

> The DUP were never friends of the UVF. Historically they would portray themselves as law-abiding people and that anybody who broke the law should have been locked up and the key thrown away. We were people who stepped over the line, we broke the law in defence of our community, so the DUP were not friendly towards us either privately or publicly. However, a lot of things that the DUP have said would have motivated young people in working-class neighbourhoods to actually join a Loyalist paramilitary group. There was always the view that Ian Paisley was like the Grand Old Duke of York, leading people to the top of the hill and then standing back as they marched off the end of it. In terms of the psychology the difference between the DUP and the paramilitaries is quite fine. The key difference is that the paramilitaries believe that they have to take the law into their own hands in order to defend their community. The DUP has threatened and rattled and hummed about doing that but never actually have. Those in Loyalist communities wouldn't be that interested in politics and are more concerned with getting jobs, trying to get by. They don't gravitate towards politics and political parties, although Protestant culture is important to many. The old identity was much more about military activism, taking up arms and defending the

community. It was more let the politicians get on with the politics and we will get on with the war. Although that thinking is no longer suitable for the context in which we are now living, it still pervades. One reason why so many from Loyalist communities vote for Paisley goes back to the strong sense of law and order which many Protestants uphold. Generally, Protestants will vote for the law and order and constitutional type parties before they will vote for the PUP, who is associated with the UVF. But there is clearly a need for a political voice within the Loyalist areas to carry on different types of struggles within the community and to fight for the needs of those who live there. I would say that over recent years, there has been a shift in what loyalism means. Initially it meant loyalty to the British Government, to the monarch and a general sense of Britishness, but because of the different slaps that have been given by the British Government to the Unionist community, there has been a shift in relation to identification in loyalism, which is now much better expressed in relation to local concerns and issues. Loyalty is now spoken about in relation to the Protestant working-class rather that the British state.

Billy Mitchell (who died in 2006) also a former UVF paramilitary and then community worker for the organisation LINC (Local Initiatives for Needy Communities), saw the political classes of unionism as disinterested in working-class communities and highlighted loyalism's lack of involvement in politics as a condition from which dominant unionism has benefited:

> There's a real political neglect of working-class Loyalist communities and some of that is down to the politicians who don't represent us. There is no real effort by our politicians to get to grips with the social, economic and educational deprivation within the working class. Republicans who were involved in armed conflict can understand ex-paramilitaries like myself better than civic unionism can. There isn't the same social solidarity within the Unionist/Protestant communities and as people move up the social ladder they tend to forget where they came from, whereas within the Nationalist community there's a bond and solidarity. During the course of the conflict, the Unionist political leaders, both DUP and UUP, have used the paramilitaries as a sabre they could rattle. They were always threatened by a possible backlash from the paramilitaries, who by and large were cannon fodder. So when it came to negotiating a ceasefire the Unionist politicians tried to distance themselves from the paramilitaries. Indeed, some of the constitutional parties actually opposed the ceasefire. There has been the constant message of doom from Paisley and the DUP, which we call the 'Ministry of Fear'. He was constantly telling people they were losing this and losing that and this had the effect where

people thought that because of the repetition it must be true. There's a belief within the UVF that you can't influence political ideology amongst the volunteers. They joined up to resist the IRA and maintain the Union, not to oppose privatisation, water rates and get involved in political issues. Most UVF men would say that if the Union is safe and there is no threat from republicanism then it's time to go home. They would say let the people vote for the politician of their choice. There's a big difference between the UVF and the IRA. Generally speaking, most of the membership would not vote for the PUP but would go for the DUP. There is this problem of voting for a party with links to those breaking the law, but it's also important to see that most would not share the PUP's socialist politics; they would be more conservative in outlook. The ongoing criminalisation of loyalism is also a problem and makes it harder for the PUP to reach a wider audience. All these issues are factors in shaping the Loyalist experience in working-class communities.

William 'Plum' Smith a former UVF volunteer who works for EPIC (Ex-Prisoners' Interpretative Centre) a Loyalist ex-prisoners' group, underlined the lack of support within unionism for those associated with paramilitarism and continued

> There is no history in the Loyalist community or the Unionist community of actually voting for ex-prisoners or even accepting ex-prisoners. Most of us come from working-class communities and are recognised as ex-prisoners from that background, but once you go outside to middle class unionism we would be treated like a Republican prisoner. Unionism doesn't really accept those outside of the law and so we have been unable to turn military strength into political strength in the way Sinn Fein has. The Unionist community basically don't want us about the place, whereas in Nationalist communities they vote for ex-prisoners. A prison record has a very different meaning within nationalism. Because unionism supports law and order and doesn't go outside that bracket, we are seen as criminals and just as bad as the IRA. But part of that is also due to loyalism not being proactive politically. Loyalism has been a reaction to Republican violence and because of that has created no political ambitions, whereas for Republicans political ambitions have been central. Whereas Republicans were saying we want a united Ireland and the British out and were working towards that end, loyalism was saying no, you're not going to do that and so was driven by a reactive approach. But efforts to develop a political front for loyalism during the peace process have been hampered by the negativity of Paisley and the DUP. They have hammered home negative messages about the police being disbanded and prisoners getting out etc. and sensationalised the issues by stoking fears. That has done a lot of damage.

Fellow EPIC worker and former UVF paramilitary Tom Roberts provided a quite detailed analysis of the Loyalist experience in terms of how it is perceived within unionism, how it defines itself and the problems that political loyalism faces:

> Within the Protestant working-class there has been a tradition that politicians are born to lead and Loyalists have always been very subservient to this point of view. I can remember my own father being reluctant to have anything to do with trade unions because to criticise your station in life was seen as a criticism of the state and a sign of disloyality. That loyalty is also extended towards Catholicism which is seen as something to be avoided. Paisley's big vote is very much a reaction to that feeling. This also partly explains the reactionary nature of loyalism which has been good at telling people what it doesn't like but not very good at explaining what it does like. There is also a lot of hypocrisy amongst middle-class Unionists who were quite happy for Loyalist paramilitaries to be carrying out violence but did not want to form any association with them to help them on a journey away from that violence. The obsessions with law and order are also problematic. I had a brother who was in the B-Specials and my family had no real difficulty with him slaughtering people because he had the legitimacy of the state uniform. But they had great difficulty with me because I went outside the law. My view about the term Loyalist is that it was a name used by middle unionism to distance itself from the more unsavoury elements of unionism. At the start of the conflict 30 years ago, I don't recall anybody being called a Loyalist. Most UVF people would still vote for the traditional Unionist parties rather than the PUP which is a socialist party. There is certainly a view in Northern Ireland that unionism and socialism are incompatible. But there is no real conviction within the Loyalist paramilitary groups for involvement in politics either. Most of the people I was involved with when we were active in the UVF just went back to what they were doing. It was a case of the war is over go home and shut the door. But, in my opinion, you have another difficulty, which is that those within loyalism and unionism don't actively think for themselves. They're content to listen to what the vociferous leaders tell them. Many think that Paisley is right and they don't question what he says. The DUP have risen to power giving people a diet of 'You've lost everything' and the voting trends seem to confirm that. That unionism has made endless concessions to nationalism and republicanism. The irony here though is that if you pin people down and ask them what it is that they can't access but that Republicans and Nationalists can, they can't be specific and tell you. It's just a sense, a perception of loss. The DUP have manipulated that situation and projected itself as the party most able to resist the things that they fear, but in order to do that it has to exaggerate the fears as well.

The sense of loss that Roberts talks about is a central feature in Protestant disillusionment about the outcomes of the Good Friday Agreement. Increasingly, Protestants have tended to view the Agreement as providing benefits for Nationalists which have been won at the expense of Protestants (McAllister et al. 2005: 2). No doubt that the zero-sum political atmosphere of Northern Ireland has intensified this perception, along with fears about loss of power and influence, which have exacerbated concerns about political co-operation and cross-border bodies that provide an Irish interest and input to Northern Irish affairs (ibid.: 3). The collapse of the Northern Ireland Assembly in 2002 served to augment Protestant anxieties about the potential dangers of power-sharing and it seems that only when institutions are operating efficiently might those anxieties start to be assuaged (ibid.: 4). The DUP's political strategy of asserting that the Agreement 'had institutionalized a Nationalist agenda' which could only lead to the 'marginalization of Protestant and Unionist values and culture' (Patterson 2006: 347), confirmed the perception of loss which many Protestants have come to feel and intersects closely with the negative outlook which the DUP has successfully perpetuated in order to overtake the UUP as the biggest Unionist party in Northern Ireland (ibid.: 353). That negativity has derived from a consistently focussed DUP campaign which set out to magnify fears felt by Protestants and constantly 'depicted the peace process and the Agreement as an exercise in 'appeasement' that was structurally biased against Protestants and the Union' (ibid.).

Even if the respondents who have spoken in this chapter have political aspirations and convictions which are not typical of most working-class Loyalists, since many show no real interest in political involvement and resort to supporting the dominant Unionist parties come elections, they still constitute a significant voice within loyalism which is distinctly oppositional to the intolerances of Paisleyism and the severity of religious fundamentalism. They also interconnect strongly and consistently with the leaderships of the two dominant paramilitary Loyalist organisations the UVF and the UDA. Jackie McDonald, the UDA's brigadier for south Belfast, acknowledged Paisley's influence over the thinking of many within working-class Protestant areas, but showed reservations about that influence:

> Paisley's motto that 'Ulster says no' finds an awful lot of support amongst the Loyalists I know. A lot of pensioners, in particular, will slap you if you say a bad word about Paisley, because he's their man. His support from the old members is solid, even though Paisley hasn't spoken to the leadership of the paramilitaries for a very long time. But you also have to realise that historically, Loyalists have voted for almost anybody who displayed the Union Jack. They just voted for the Union Jack and it didn't really matter what that person did for the community. The realisation now though is that you can't just say 'Ulster says no', it needs to be

'Ulster says not that way but maybe this', there has to be an alternative. Going back to the start of the 'Troubles' when Paisley was making his blood and thunder speeches, he would motivate young people who ended up in prison and he washed his hands of them. He has been involved with paramilitaries on the edges where he has a certain amount of influence, but once the police become involved he has washed his hands. He's denied inciting people or pointing people in the wrong direction and won't take any responsibility for it. He uses the argument that he can't be seen talking to Loyalist paramilitaries because he won't talk to Sinn Fein and he is aware of Sinn Fein capitalizing on that if he did. But for most of us now, religion is the least important aspect of the conflict, it's more about tribalism. It's also becoming less about the Union and how loyalism will deal with itself. The big problem in recent years has been fighting within loyalism, which has reinforced the idea that it is little more than criminality.

Stronger criticism of Paisley came from the leadership of the UVF. As the UVF's Brigadier General (from now on referred to as UVF's Number One) put it

Paisley's message has been entirely negative and about how we are heading towards a united Ireland. His approach has been very much about undermining situations. The Christian right here believe every word he says and that has had a knock-on effect on our membership. Paisley seems to say things about Gerry Adams and Adams confirms those words so it's a difficult situation to move away from. There has certainly been no positive contribution from the DUP towards the Agreement. The party has also been against the ceasefire and there have been certain figures within the DUP who have fed the press that many UVF people were against it, trying to destabilise the situation. In the three or four feuds which we have been involved with in recent years, we believe that MI5 or the DUP were behind that. This is also because the PUP is a major worry to the DUP, cutting into working-class support. The DUP's support for Billy Wright was another example of the party trying to assist anti-Agreement elements within loyalism. Ironically, Loyalists would have preferred the DUP to have been involved in the talks at Stormont because they would have been less giving, but it is clear that Paisley is not a Carson, which is what is needed. You also need to remember that although the UVF membership has had DUP Unionists in its ranks, it has no political structure as Sinn Fein does, therefore its political influence is slight.

For the UVF's second-in-command (from now on referred to as the UVF's Number Two), the DUP's obstruction to the organisation's cautious support for the Agreement is also indicative of the party's disdain for working-class

Loyalists who want peace and who see the Agreement as a suitable framework for achieving it:

> When the UVF was created it was middle-class people that tended to form the membership, unlike now. These days the middle-class political Unionists distance themselves from the working-class and the word loyalism has helped them do that. Loyalist was not a term commonly used in the 1960s and has emerged with the present conflict. Loyalists are not particularly political in a party political sense. There is still a strong belief that the DUP or the UUP are better to lead the working-class, but as far as the peace process has been concerned there is no peace dividend in social and economic terms for the business classes and so many resist it. But a lot of people vote for the DUP because it's a hardline party. A lot of working guys would not understand politics. If you asked them about the DUP's policy towards education or the economy, they wouldn't be able to tell you. Most only get the rhetoric. A lot of voting is anti-voting, meaning voting for those who will best resist what you are against. Only over recent years has the DUP started dealing with working-class issues. They, along with the UUP, set up advice centres here only when the PUP gained in popularity and strength. On the point of religion there is less of a conviction about that now. We would continue to use the 'God and Ulster' slogan for purposes of continuity and tradition, but whether people pay so much attention to the God bit anymore is open to debate.

Perhaps one clear example of the UVF's disparity with the DUP's approach to the peace process came about in April 2006, when a UVF man wearing a balaclava appeared on local television in Northern Ireland to publicly state support for a power-sharing dispensation. As the UVF Number Two explained the reasoning behind this event:

> We were offered a chance to publicly state our position and took it. We wanted the chance to explain ourselves and it took two weeks of organisation to set up. There were no prepared questions, only broad subjects were given. We were trying to make the point that we were not an obstacle for the DUP going into government. It was the first public appearance of a UVF volunteer in this way in years and we wanted to address the image where we are always portrayed as bad boys. We were saying quite clearly that we weren't stopping the DUP and that we wanted to engage in discussion with Republicans.

These views suggest a departure from the contention that religious conviction plays a central role within the Loyalist experience. Particularly within the UVF and its political arm, the PUP, there is a noticeable hostility to Paisley and the theological rhetoric which he espouses (at least at leadership level). To a lesser extent, a similar discomfort is also visible within elements of the UDA and the UPRG, where criticisms are forthcoming about middle-unionism's disregard for working-class communities and those associated with paramilitarism generally. Significantly, the development of political representation by paramilitary representatives indicates that within paramilitary loyalism there is an opposition towards Evangelical loyalism and a growing reconfiguration of Loyalist identity (Graham 2004) towards what Brewer calls a 'secular mode' (1998: 153). In the case of the PUP, this shift is manifest through the articulation of ideas which have 'socialist or social democratic bases not theological roots' (ibid.). Moreover, as the UVF's Number Two highlights when talking about the television appearance of a volunteer in 2006, there is a desire to engage with Republicans which at that moment was clearly resisted by the DUP (publicly anyway). Indeed, the UVF's desire to meet with Republicans is evident in an internal document called *'Engagement with Republicans'*, which is constructed from the viewpoint that talking with Republicans would be beneficial and sets out a series of questions that would come into play should such talks take place (Rowan 2005: 172). The UDA's growing emphasis on community development and the UVF's attention to a political voice, both highlight forms of action which are constructed from the basis of 'secular loyalism' (Brewer 1998: 153) rather than 'theological loyalism', and each signal challenges to the dominant religiously based representations of Paisleyism and the DUP (especially so in the case of the PUP/UVF).

Another phrase which has been used to explain the movement of paramilitarism towards the political sphere and a more openly critical articulation of mainstream unionism is 'new loyalism'. For McAuley, the meaning of 'new loyalism' lay in its ability to represent the views of the Protestant working-class from a position of 'growing political and economic marginalisation' (2001: 9). In doing this, the PUP has attempted to locate the Unionist experience within a different historical context than that recycled by traditional Unionists, and has concentrated on the class structure of unionism as an obstruction to progress (ibid.: 11). McAuley contends that this emphasis has served to create an ideological space within Unionist discourse which has disrupted the perception that the DUP are the best party to address working-class concerns (ibid.), and though the detail of this articulation may not be sufficient to sway most voters from the protection of the DUP vote, it has provided an opportunity for alternative perceptions about Unionist representation to be more openly expressed (ibid.: 12). It has, McAuley suggests, brought about a shift away from a 'discourse of perpetuity', towards a 'discourse of transformation', where the central fears and anxieties of Unionists are debated in relation to unionism itself. By adopting 'an all-embracing discourse' which favours interaction with Republicans, this articulation argues for a distrust of traditional Unionist representation and talks about paramilitaries being 'used' by mainstream unionism to protect entrenched interests, while offering the possibility of a left-wing Unionist project (McAuley 2004: 528). As a central player in this transformation, the PUP has attempted to encourage the Loyalist working-class to engage in a 'renegotiation of the ideological boundaries within which they seek to express their identity' (ibid.: 18), and in the process, has used class in order to move unionism towards a more secularised politics (ibid.: 530).

Even though many members of the UVF and UDA would vote for Paisley, it is more likely this is a decision based on a desire to protect and preserve Protestant culture and society through resistance, rather than because of religious conviction, making such a vote politically rather than religiously motivated. As recent debates between paramilitary loyalism and its political representatives highlight, a discernible and coherent discourse of unionism has developed outside traditional positions which offers the potential for an alternative and pluralistic form of Unionist representation. In order to understand how this came about, it is important to consider the role of the UVF and UDA in some historical context, for this will enable us to better comprehend how violence has been used, how it has shaped thinking about the Northern Ireland problem and to understand the background from which recent changes have evolved.

3
Violence and Politics

Motivation and structure

Examination of the role and structure of Loyalist violence has been particularly concerned with the problem of how violence functions as 'pro-state' terror. That is, terror which aspires to defend and preserve the authority and legitimacy of the state. Existing in competition with state security agencies, pro-state terrorism tends to arise when those agencies are seen as unable to resist the forces of anti-state terrorism (in this case militant republicanism), and while anti-state terror networks do not compete with state agencies in terms of logistical and public support because of their obvious opposition, pro-state terror groups do (Bruce 1992b: 74). This happens because the pro-state group is not only exposing the inability of state agencies to contain or overcome anti-state terror, thus undermining the public perception that such agencies are able to operate effectively against state enemies, but because recruitment for pro-state terror groups invariably comes from the same communities that serve state agencies (ibid.: 76). In a pro-state terrorism environment, recruitment for pro-state terror groups is an additional problem for state agencies to deal with because the very process of recruitment is reflective of state agencies being seen as ineffective in defending communities against the attacks of anti-state groups. In that instance, by representing themselves as an important component in the realm of defence, pro-state terror groups are thereby able to gain some credibility and legitimacy from their actions and widen their base of support as a result (ibid.: 86). Although, pro-state terrorism clearly contradicts the idea of respecting norms of state security and control, in the case of Loyalist paramilitarism, there is a perception that such violence has been needed to help enforce the institutions of state control and security which the law-abiding majority require (Aughey and McIlheney 1984: 74). Moreover, because Loyalist paramilitary groups see themselves as needing to exist 'only because successive governments have not been resolute enough to defeat the IRA', they legitimise their existence and actions in terms of 'military self-help', seeing themselves as doing 'what the security forces should be allowed to do' (ibid.: 73). In the sense that Loyalist paramilitarism is seen as a reaction to anti-state terrorism which state agencies seem unable to defeat, Loyalist terror may also be seen as counter-revolutionary rather than revolutionary, and so conservative in orientation, with a dedication to that it is dedicated to 'the preservation of the existing political and social order or, if necessary, the restoration of an order which has gone'. To put it another way, such terrorism acts as a reactive force against those who threaten political and social order (Drake 1996: 41). This reactive presence, which lacks a specific political dimension and relies on violence for imposing internal order, as well as resisting external pressures, means that such terror may also be acted out as a form of vigilantism; imposing control over crime and organisation in ways which lay outside the remit of law enforcement agencies (ibid.: 31). When state agencies are seen as ineffective in preventing threats to the existing state order, it is likely that vigilante groups will step into this gap and carry out actions to try and regain control (Silke 1999: 3).

For Loyalists, an increase in vigilantism is particularly notable after the Anglo-Irish Agreement in 1985, when it became clear to many that state institutions would be unable to prevent a dilution of Protestant authority and that the forces of law and order could not be relied upon to stem this decline either. The period following the Agreement saw a rise in clashes between Loyalists and the security forces and a policing vacuum developed in areas where local populations began refusing to co-operate with the police (ibid.: 4–5). The intention of this vigilantism was not just to act as a response against perceived police incompetence, however. It became a focus for the organisation and control of Loyalist organisations themselves, providing a means of discipline and purpose, as well as a structure for standards of criminality, violence and internal order (ibid.: 8–9). As Silke points out in relation to (Northern) Irish terror organisations, 'vigilantism is a result of their efforts first, to contain victimisation among their own ranks and second, to contain victimisation among their communities' (Silke 1998a: 122). In order to exert control over both these areas, vigilantism is seen to cover warnings, curfews, fines/victim restitution, acts of public humiliation, punishment beatings, punishment shootings, expulsions and assassinations (ibid.: 124), and the impact of these activities is used not just to deter political enemies such as the IRA, but to control (or at least restrain) other pro-state terror groups and thus influence their actions (ibid.: 134). The strategy of using violence as a deterrent therefore applies to the internal workings and structure of the paramilitary organisation as much as it applies to wider social and political effects of paramilitary activity. Groups that use violence as a justification for existence, invariably use that violence as a means of responding to a variety of potential internal threats and incidents. As is evident with Loyalist paramilitarism, the many feuds and struggles for control which have occurred throughout the 'Troubles' between different groupings (Bruce 1992c; Cusack and McDonald 1997; McDonald and Cusack 2004, Woods 2006), demonstrate only too well that potential enemies exist both within and without organisations and that historically there has been a tendency for Loyalist paramilitarism to transmute into intra-communal violence while also carrying out actions of pro-state terror. Such conflict is also made increasingly likely by competition for logistical support which is acquired through criminal financing practices such as extortion and blackmail (Silke 1998b).

The reactive nature of Loyalist paramilitary groups (most notably the UDA and the UVF, respectively the two biggest organisations) indicates why traditionally they have not been as politicised as their Republican opponents, who, because of a deep hatred of state security forces, have operated efficiently as vigilantes themselves (indeed probably more so (Silke 1999: 27)). A lack of political direction within loyalism means that the focus of control has tended to be concerned primarily with internal order, commitment and monitoring criminal activity (ibid.: 14–16). Without a political goal beyond reacting to Republican violence and resisting a diminution of Northern Ireland's Protestant status through vigilantism and terror, violence for many Loyalists was legitimised in terms of self-defensive action (Bairner 1986: 643), and seen as necessary (especially given the weakness of state agencies) to resist and avert Republican attacks.

Certainly the view that Loyalist paramilitarism was both vigilante and defensive in orientation (particularly throughout the early and intermediate years of the 'Troubles') was shared by a number of respondents with UDA and UVF backgrounds. As 'Alan' a former UDA and UFF commander explained it:

> I became a Loyalist paramilitary in 1973 at the age of sixteen and basically we were vigilantes. That was our assigned role, which was defence of the area where I lived. That area would have been a predominantly Protestant/Loyalist area, but at the time we had incursions from Republicans and Nationalists, who were doing security runs to seek out off-duty security force members, as well as Loyalists if they could be targeted. The majority of young people would have been involved. It was a small rural town in County Down and because it was solidly Protestant/Unionist/Loyalist there was no real problem in the sense of having a fifth column amongst us. But we were vigilantes who did night patrols because the police and soldiers couldn't cope. In fact, there were no police in our area. They were drafted elsewhere. In areas where paramilitaries were not seen as a threat to the state, as Republicans were, the police were largely absent. People who worked did the night patrols and those who didn't carried out day patrols. It was a matter of walking

about in groups of four with radios, stopping people and cars, checking people's identity and finding out why they were in a certain area at a certain time. Basically we were policing the area. At that time we saw our role as strictly defensive. We saw it as the role of the police and armed forces to be pro-active and were formed as a defensive response to the Republican/Nationalist threat. I saw my job as very much being a protector of the community.

The UDA's west Belfast commander 'Charlie' referred to his early experiences in the following way:

I lived in an interface area and we were under attack. I was about thirteen at the time. We were quite disorganised and the UDA started a young militant squad 'Ulster Young Militants' to harness the energies of young men and I joined. At that time there was no real ethos beyond defending the area. It was an adrenalin rush as much as anything else, especially for a young man. Having said that it was obvious that the community was under attack left, right and centre and we were trying to stop that as best we could. Basically the organisation was reactive, so if there was an atrocity in the area we would react to that. Things became more pro-active from the mid-1980s around the time of the Anglo-Irish Agreement. The document *Common Sense* was floated around that time as well, so along with an increase in activity there was also a realisation that power-sharing would be necessary at some point. But during the mid-80s most of the organisation would have seen that idea as surrender and the militarists were dominant.

The UDA's east Belfast Commander 'Billy' similarly stressed the retaliatory and defensive nature of the organisation:

For me personally, it's not about the Queen, but about reacting to IRA violence. I see myself as a Loyalist in that I would respond to that. Many people would see it in terms of breaking the law, but reaction in this way is the only way I could see the IRA being dealt with. Having said that as soon as the IRA said the war is over it was over as far as I'm concerned. Now I see myself as a community-based Loyalist trying to improve things within the community. The problem for Loyalists is that they are seen as gangsters and bullies and that perception has stuck since the 1970s, whereas for the IRA, their paramilitaries are seen as heroes and are part of a broader political strategy. People joined the UDA to defend their communities and it always comes back to that. It's not so much about defending the Union today, but it's always about protecting communities. That will always come first.

UPRG representative Tommy Kirkham described his early experiences as instrumental in influencing this decision to become a paramilitary and highlighted the UDA's community role as important in terms of defence and security:

> I got caught up in the 'Troubles' as a sixteen year old because we believed that our area was under threat by Republicans. I signed up to the Youth Wing of the Tartan Gang as it was then, which was 1971. Our house was wrecked when Republicans blew up a mill which was behind it; part of their strategy of hitting 'economic targets'. Fortunately my brother and I were at school and my parents were at work and the UDA got us a replacement house. I was arrested and served a prison sentence in Long Kesh at the age of sixteen and came out at nineteen. For me the main goal was to combat the IRA and stop the Republican drive for a united Ireland. In the early days resistance existed mainly through a number of different defence organisations such as the Woodvale Defence Association, Rathcoone Defence Asssociation and Glengormley Association. Each of these units signed up to one command structure in the Inner Council of the UDA and they had a supreme commander, they worked very much on their own. Although there was no real cross-movement of people in north, west or south Belfast people would still go to where they were needed. If people were needed to go to an area to engage in rioting they would. Just as if they were asked to go to Londonderry at the weekend to man barricades and control the streets they would. At that time the UDA was involved much more in street violence and saw itself as a defender of communities.

This explanation was further reinforced by UDP representative Gary McMichael who commented:

> Essentially paramilitaries were seen as people who would do what many people were thinking but wouldn't do. The vigilantes who emerged in the UDA in the 1970s sought to provide some order of protection to communities under attack and although there was some attempt to organise in order to protect streets, there was no overall sense of organisation or agreed strategy. Protection was almost carried out on a street-by-street basis, with residents forming groups who were patrolling at night and putting barricades up at the end of streets. There was very little weaponry involved to protect from attack, but that is how people saw themselves, as protectors against Republican violence.

Defence of local communities gave particular legitimacy to paramilitary organisations operating in those areas, where paramilitarism was often accepted as an expression of communal loyalty, as UPRG representative David Nicoll explained:

> When I was growing up the UDA had an acceptable face in the community. In childhood I recall dressing up as a UDA man for fancy dress at church parties and winning prizes for being a UDA lookalike. Clergymen would give us prizes and stand with us to have photographs taken. The pictures would appear on the front of local newspapers. I remember me and my brother getting first prize for dressing up in the dark glasses and combat fatigues and this was about 1975–6. The village where I lived was 90% Protestant and every Catholic was put out because of a perceived security risk. Local members of the security forces had been targeted and fingers were pointing at local Catholics. People very much saw themselves as defenders and protecting their area.

The perception that Loyalist violence was essentially defensive and reactive in character was one shared by those who joined the UVF. For former UVF paramilitary Martin Snodden:

> I lived in a small Protestant community in south west Belfast which was surrounded by Republicans and Nationalists. We were experiencing attacks on a daily basis. They were attacking pensioners dwellings, churches, social clubs, shops and people and it was purely sectarian. We had a siren system on our estate and if it was let off people would be out on the street. There was a lot of vigilante duty at this time as well. Republicans were trying to take over Protestant homes after intimidating people out of them and people felt that the security forces were not protecting us. My decision to join the UVF was one prompted by a need to defend the community. At that particular time (early 1970s) it was a military organisation and its sole purpose was to try and defeat the Republican movement. Certainly, it was to match what they were doing in our community and to hit back in the same way. As far as I was concerned, my role was to protect the community from experiencing the aggression that I was witnessing both in the community and in the media every day. For me, it was to protect the Union, the Protestant people and Loyalists, of which there was no separation at that time in my mind. The diversity that exists in unionism today wasn't that evident in those days.

The UVF Number One added to the discussion about loyalism's reactionary tendency, contributing:

> We saw ourselves as counter-terrorists, watching the state and how it reacted to the IRA. A void was left by the state not being able to cope, so

Loyalists started counter-attacks against Republicans and arose as a reactive force. Today without that counter-violence we would certainly be in a more precarious position. We have clearly strengthened constitutional unionism's negotiating position, so in that sense counter-violence has worked. Since 1968 there has been a real awakening about different issues for us. When Republicans talk about British withdrawal they mean us. The IRA's anti-state position meant they were more organised and intense in their campaigns. Republicans were at it 24/7, but Loyalists were not. There was a lack of guns in 1969 and it was only once there was an escalation of involvement that the objective of military engagement seemed realistic. There is no doubt that loyalism can be and has been preventative, but actions tend to be seen as reactionary.

Agreeing with the emphasis on violence as reaction, the UVF Number Two then proceeded to expand on how the UVF operated from the late 1960s and how the structure of the organisation developed:

The function of the UVF was primarily as a defender of the community. The UVF reformed in 1965 but it grew from 1921–22 and developed further in the 1940s and 1950s, whereas the UDA formed in the early 1970s. The UVF is a proscribed organisation which kept people in the background, whereas the UDA was not and has had numerous divisions. In the early days I viewed the UVF as equivalent to the old IRA, who I mistakenly saw as morally upright people at that time. The UVF was totally clandestine and wives, mothers and other family members would not have known about the involvement of loved ones. I joined in 1966 at the age of seventeen. We were under attack and thought that we were going to be burnt out of our homes. I can even remember a Church of Ireland minister saying to us 'prepare to defend yourselves'. I joined to defend the Woodvale area, but I did not know who was in the UVF or who the leaders were. We also infiltrated the UDA to find out what was going on. Unionists were telling us in 1965–6 that there was going to be an insurrection and that the IRA would use the forthcoming 50th anniversary as a catalyst to resurrect itself. Even at that time everybody could make a bomb and we had weapons training. But, nobody knew about the weaponry of other units. There was huge secrecy. This changed from 1975 onwards and this was because the organisation got too big to sustain such secrecy. Most people who joined the UVF and the UDA did it to hit back. There was no real political direction or strategy. That emerged only from going to prison and reflecting.

Former UVF paramilitary and PUP representative Billy Hutchinson viewed the reactive nature of Loyalist paramilitarism as being less about a desire to protect the Union through defending symbols of religious and royal traditions, and more about defending and preserving the state and state institutions:

> Loyalists have tended to respond to what the Provos have done. There was a period in the late 1980s when they started to shoot Sinn Fein members and Republicans themselves and some say that this was a factor which led to the IRA ceasefire. That may be an example of Loyalists being proactive because they concentrated on that strategy regardless of what the Provos were doing, but historically, the use of violence was about protecting the community. UVF people in particular saw their loyalty as necessary for community protection. For the likes of Paisley, loyalty was to the Queen, but for me and many others, it was about the local community and the Union. One of the difficulties with being a Loyalist is that it's about what the state actually delivers rather than changing the state. It's not necessarily trusting the government but wanting to be part of what they deliver, even if that does not mean having a loyalty to them directly.

These comments reveal some underlying similarities in the aims and convictions of UDA and UVF paramilitaries as defenders of communities dedicated to the preservation of the Union (however that is conceived), but as the separate organisations indicate, there are important structural differences between the UVF and UDA which require some elaboration if we are to understand their respective approaches to violence and the emergence of the peace process.

The UVF

The UVF which was formed in 1912 as a movement to resist Irish 'home rule', developed as a popular and illegal army which sought to defend the Protestants of Ulster (Bruce 1992a: 2). As a mass movement, the UVF was controlled by 'the Ulster aristocracy, and trained by retired British army officers' and many joined the British army to fight in World War I (ibid.). Although UVF members were stood down at the end of World War I (Cusack and McDonald 1997: 37), the organisation continued to take part in sporadic violence between the 1920s and the 1950s and it was not until the 1960s that the organisation developed into a disciplined military network. As a consequence of resisting reforms forwarded by Northern Ireland prime minister Terence O'Neill, which were seen as concessionary towards Catholics (Boulton 1973: 186), the modern UVF publicly announced its existence through leader Gusty Spence in 1966 (Nelson 1984: 61). Initially, the organisation took little interest in politics (described by Bruce as 'ultra-Unionists' (2001: 27)) and 'were essentially followers rather than leaders', who were more 'content to be the instruments through which other Loyalists would assert control in government' (ibid.: 64). Unlike the UDA, which developed a reputation for 'brutality and racketeering', the UVF was seen as a more militaristic and disciplined organisation for confronting republicanism and because of this, a more attractive prospect for idealistic recruits (ibid.: 171). By the early 1970s, senior UVF paramilitaries were beginning to question the legitimacy and purpose of warfare and starting to think about a more constructive contribution towards social life (ibid.). Although the emergence of the modern UVF in 1966 coincided with the sectarian murder of Catholics (Cusack and McDonald 1997: 5–35), this kind of violence, which dominated Loyalist paramilitarism, was challenged within the UVF from as early as 1974 (Nelson 1984: 174), as part of an attempt to engage with political ideas about conflict. Failure to develop a political project was compounded by the UVF's existence as an alternative to political representation and its 'disillusionment with politicians and constitutional methods'. But, as Nelson notes, 'the training which they [the UVF] received did not equip them with political skills, their ethos, practices and even their language opened up a gap between themselves and politicians and, indeed, the Protestant electorate' (ibid.: 178). Attempts to develop an alternative to armed conflict therefore remained exploratory and were hindered by the aspirations and actions of the organisation itself. The structure of the UVF as ostensibly a 'self-recruiting, working-class movement' (Bruce 1992c: 26), functioned to keep military strategy as the focus for existence and minimised the potential for political development, which was seen as largely the responsibility of mainstream unionism.

The main aim of the UVF from the late 1960s, until the late 1980s, was thus essentially to exert military force. Indeed, in a brief 14-point internal document entitled '*U.V.F. Policy*' published in 1974, the emphasis is almost entirely on military activity as a necessary means of self-defence. Describing itself as 'a military organisation composed of loyal Ulster patriots who are pledged to uphold and support the maintenance of the Union of Great Britain and Northern Ireland', the UVF stresses its overriding intention as being for 'the preservation of our Protestant faith and liberties and the restoration of peace, contentment and stability to the people of Ulster' (1974: 1). To do this, the document determines how 'Attack is the best means of defence' and that the 'military policies of the UVF are designed to destroy the forces and resources of the enemy by means of counter-terrorism'. In order to implement such policies effectively, the document continues, 'we must employ the same tactics as our enemies, but we must be more ruthless and determined' (ibid.). However, a concerted and singular objective of military resistance was not the only motivating factor for recruitment. As Bruce notes, membership of the UVF is a process which draws from a number of aspirations: 'First, some people joined the UVF to defend the state. Others joined because they wanted revenge. Some simply wanted the thrills. Nobody joined for political lessons' (2001: 28).

As the UVF's Number One put it in an interview when talking about how the organisation has tended to perceive itself historically:

> It was obvious that from a conflict point of view the Loyalist combatants had no clear objective to achieve beyond defence. There was no strategy for changing the role of the state and so military action was seen as a reactive necessity. The UVF's function as essentially a military force is demonstrated by reaction to the ceasefires of 1994 where there has been no real desire to develop politically and many people chose to go back to their jobs. Two things have tended to control the mindset of the UVF, first the armed aggression of Republicans and that if it stops you must respond to that; and two, to ensure that birthright is not taken away. The defensive nature of loyalism has been compounded not only by Nationalists and Republicans but also the British as well, because the forces of the Crown have been used against us. This may have been alleviated if there had been proper political leadership from 1969. Having said that, there has always been a belief that there is a grand plan by Republicans and that is still a concern.

The structure and control of the modern UVF is centralised but also has 'a loose federal structure' (modelled on the British army, the organisation consists of four leaders, under which follow battalion commanders, company commanders, platoon commanders and the remainder of the organisation), which enables individual units to carry out actions with some independence (Cusack and McDonald 1997: 311). This independence may well have been a significant contributory factor in the contradictions of a military strategy which, on the one hand, emphasises the importance of targeting known Republicans, but on the other, allows the murder of Catholics (as demonstrated in the attacks carried out on Catholics as a response to the Shankill bomb in 1993, when the IRA planted a bomb in a fish shop on the Shankill Road, killing 10 people and injuring 57 others) (ibid.: 310). Actions against political targets and those of Catholic faith indicate that the UVF has adopted a policy of sectarianism in its military campaign, and that movement from Republican to Catholic targets has occurred even though there have been attempts to disguise the fact through the shifting circumstances of violence both suffered and inflicted (ibid.). Although there appear to be no definitive reasons why recruits join Loyalist paramilitary groups, it is clear that for some, sectarianism has acted as a motivating force for membership (McAuley 2004: 526) and that sectarian attacks have been integral to military strategy. This sectarianism has brought with it volunteers who have been driven by the allure and atmosphere of violence and who have used the image and reputation of 'the paramilitary' to pursue criminal activity at personal gain. Such involvement with criminality has also inevitably hindered the potential cohesion of a peace strategy and has been a problem which as Tom Roberts points out, invariably arises when recruitment comes from a base of support which has chosen not to join state forces:

> In the Loyalist community you really had two choices which were either to join the security forces or the paramilitaries. A lot of able people were attracted to the security forces and that left the paramilitaries with the problem of attracting the criminal fraternity. That criminal fraternity has been able to destabilise loyalism and feuds have been instigated by gangsters who have created real problems for bringing the conflict to a close.

The more disciplined and secretive nature of the UVF, for UPRG representative Tommy Kirkham, influenced choices made by volunteers in the early days of conflict as to whether they joined the UVF or the UDA:

> In the 1970s the UVF were quite mysterious to me. Most of the members were in their late twenties or thirties and they didn't recruit young people at that stage. The UDA took those youngsters who were running around fighting Republicans and tried to harness their energy. The UDA instilled in those youngsters that attacks had to be co-ordinated and not random. The UVF were more disciplined with their targets and what they were trying to achieve. They were hitting back whereas the UDA was more involved in street violence. However, the UDA had greater community involvement. People became involved in community and welfare work and were not just militarists.

The military focus of the UVF has therefore provided the organisation with a specificity of purpose and strategic presence which is different from the UDA, for whom violence has taken place alongside community and welfare-based activities which have helped the organisation acquire public appeal and legitimacy in communities where those activities have been carried out.

The UDA

Like the UVF, the UDA emerged as a community-defence group which grew out of cross-communal riots and resistance from the late 1960s. Officially formed in 1971, the UDA's involvement in community affairs provided the organisation with a social role which paralleled its paramilitary activity (McAuley 1995: 137). While the UVF became concerned primarily with military defence, the UDA membership became involved in a range of social affairs as well as paramilitary activity and has 'continued to develop strong networks of informal social welfare' (McAuley 1991: 63). The public support which the UDA achieved because of its involvement in social programmes goes some way towards explaining why the UDA was not proscribed (the modern UVF has been proscribed since its inception apart from 1974–5 when it tried to develop as a credible political alternative) until 1992, when it became apparent that the UDA's cover organisation the Ulster Freedom Fighters were engaged in campaigns of sectarian murder (Tonge 2006a: 153). However, alongside this involvement in social welfare initiatives, the organisation has been discredited by a constant lack of control, power-struggles, feuds, drug-running, racketeering and criminal activity (ibid.: 155). Notably, the UDA has continued to attract and confirm the popular image of the Loyalist terrorist as a gangster who lacks the political 'legitimacy and status' of Republicans (Cusack and Taylor 1993: 2), and has been embroiled in allegations of collusion with British intelligence services (ibid.: 5), as highlighted in 1989 by the Stevens Inquiry and subsequent television reportage (ibid.).

In the formative stages of its development, the main goal of the UDA was to discipline volunteers into a coherent fighting network and synchronise the rather random actions of disjointed military factions who operated as separate Defence Associations. Comprised of some 40,000 members in 1972, the UDA came to prominence in the Ulster Workers' Council (UWC) strike of 1974, when paramilitaries formed mass resistance, along with the UWC, to the Sunningdale Agreement, which sought to set up a power-sharing Executive with an 'Irish dimension' and therefore provide a new political framework for Irish involvement in Northern Ireland's affairs (for an overview of the UDA's role at this time, see Woods 2006: 28–54). The strike's impact led to the Agreement's collapse before it could be formally ratified. Trying to exploit its success with the UWC strike, the UDA sought to develop political credibility, but this was undermined by mainstream Unionists who were determined to prevent paramilitaries acquiring political influence (McAuley 1995: 141). The perceived strength of the UDA in the 1974 strike and its ability to defend Protestant interests was discredited in a further strike led by Rev Dr Ian Paisley in 1977. Notably divided by this time in comparison to the coordination of volunteers in 1974 (Woods 2006: 66), as well as being faced by increased tensions with Paisley and challenged by the security forces, this attempt at civil disobedience ended quickly and with it the UDA's ability to defend Protestant interests was seriously weakened (ibid.).

Unlike the centralised command structure of the UVF, the UDA consists of six autonomous units (north, south, east and west Belfast, south east Antrim and north Antrim/Londonderry) with six commanders, six outer councils, six welfare officers and six political representatives. The units tend to work individually, and until recently, actions carried out in each area were seen to be the sole responsibility of the unit occupying that area. The six areas reflect very different ways of dealing with issues which have created problems for consensus or collective decision making, and tended to exacerbate the likelihood of splits. Although the lack of a centralised command structure in the UDA and the local autonomy of its units have been key factors in the organisation's linkage with local communities, it is evident that a lack of central authority has also contributed to criminality and power-struggles (Tonge 2006a: 155). Unlike the UVF, whose origins are founded on a collective and organised approach to community defence (and where its leadership has been unchanged since 1982), the UDA operates as 'a series of paramilitary fiefdoms which sometimes acted in unison but more often than not did their own thing' (McDonald and Cusack 2004: 315) Explaining this potential divergence of decisions and interests in the UDA and how it might impact on organisational operations, south Belfast Commander Jackie McDonald commented

> The organisation has always consisted of different identities and cultures. The UDA in south Belfast extends from Sandy Row to Newry and to areas around the border. But in other areas like north Belfast the area is about six streets. People outside of Belfast have a different opinion and a different way of looking at problems from people in Belfast and Sandy Row do. Sometimes people in the country feel as if people in Belfast see themselves as superior. The likes of north Belfast, which is only a few streets, means that there are only so many pubs and places to go, so there are less people to talk with and so range of opinion is less. They have a small area. Similarly, west Belfast down the Shankill and Woodvale is a small area by comparison to the likes of north Antrim, or south Antrim which goes through to Ballymena. There are also different problems to contend with in different areas. Interface violence is a classic example. North Belfast has interface problems all the time which people in south Belfast do not face. Similarly there are seasonal problems around marches etc which are worse in some areas than others. North Belfast has serious problems and so they are on the alert all the time. This means that violence will come to the fore there far quicker than in other places. At an organisational level this can clearly cause problems in terms of trying to get consensus. The history has always been one of internal problems and ongoing difficulties. If people feel more threatened in one area and less so in another they will react according to that fear and that's why attitudes are different.

From its early days in the 1970s, the UDA has functioned as 'an organisation of distinct and disparate elements' (Crawford 2003: 27) and developed no real consensus about how to conduct war until the late 1980s, when there was some agreement about a need to intensify violence as part of a strategy of 'taking war to the IRA' (ibid.: 37). The structural problem of 'hierarchical control undermined by local control' (ibid.: 24) has meant that historically, UDA units have adopted individualised approaches to violence which has led to disjointed reactions that have been factional and sectarian in nature (ibid.: 35). In turn, sectarianism has served to create both 'common identity and high levels of social segregation' among communities (McAuley 1991: 47) which has continued to reinforce divergent social relations and produce fragmentary rather than collective approaches to defensive violence. Not surprisingly, the autonomy of different UDA units has produced differing ideological positions which have caused internal dissent and a shifting focus on military or criminal objectives (ibid.: 49). Furthermore, this friction has resulted not only in internal violence, but numerous feuds with the UVF over territory and perceived military superiority (see Bruce 1992c; Cusack and McDonald 1997; McDonald and Cusack 2004; and Woods 2006 for an overview of feuds and internal struggles).

Recognising the problem of disparity within the structural design of the UDA, UPRG representative Frankie Gallagher explained:

> The UDA has been a bottom-up organisation and is very much a confederate based on community protection. Unlike the UVF, which operate in a totally militaristic way, the UDA was never solely a military organisation. The six units does create problems however in that sometimes votes on an issue can be split in terms of three for and three against, which makes it very difficult to move. There's no doubt that for the UDA to get stronger and more influential it has to centralise.

But, former UDA and UFF Commander 'Alan' saw the problem of controlling the UDA as largely logistical and emphasised the freedom of individual units as necessary for maintaining organisational commitment:

> There is no organisation as big and it's nearly impossible to keep everybody happy. But all paramilitary organisations have problems and splits. The UVF and the IRA have experienced their share. The autonomous nature of the units does give people a bit of leeway and because of that helps keep us together.

Though the distinctions and priorities of different units have created problems for leadership and control in the UDA, this has been less apparent in the actions of its elite military wing the UFF, formed in 1973 at the time when the UDA was becoming a significant player in the Northern Ireland conflict (Bruce 1992c: 77) in order to provide 'a balance of terror' (Crawford 2003: 25). The introduction of the UFF, which paradoxically was formed in order to keep the UDA together, also sought to intensify fears by claiming responsibility for killings (Woods 2006: 109). Its presence 'confused the security sources, initially at least, and protected the

UDA from being proscribed' (ibid.: 101). Performing a similar function to the UVF's elite military grouping the Red Hand Commando, former UDA and UFF Commander 'Alan' explained the role of the UFF in the following way:

> The distinction between the UDA and the UFF is quite simple. The UDA at one time had up to 40,000 members. Today we have about 10,000 members. The UFF to my knowledge only had a range of 200–500 members. My experience of the UFF was that you couldn't go and ask to join, but were actually chosen. You were always approached. The UFF was the cutting military edge of the UDA. When I was a UDA commander I had 250 people under me, but as a UFF military commander, it was 16–20 men. Those 16–20 men were operators, drivers and intelligence gatherers. We also operated with people from different areas. Initially, if I lost one team of 4–5 people that was a third of my cutting edge taken away. It took two years to get a team up and going. If that team was lost it would take another 12 months to operate again. So we shipped people in from different areas. People didn't know until the night before an operation who they were going with. Teams began to cross-switch so if a person was lost it was only one person from an area and not a whole team. With sixteen men you could do a lot of damage over a long period. There was a military commander for an area and a commander who selected targets. Even to this day I don't know some of the members' names. Information was tight and based very much on a need-to-know basis.

Politicisation

Though the UVF and the UDA have existed to use violence as a means for resisting Republican and Nationalist political and social advancement, it is important to note that both organisations have engaged with political ideas and envisaged a role for loyalism beyond the realms of pro-state paramilitary violence. A further point to note is that the traditionally more military oriented of these two organisations, the UVF, has been more consistently successful in advocating and promoting political discourse throughout the duration of the peace process than the UDA. Yet in both cases, each has produced internal documents which attempt to address the divisive political circumstances in Northern Ireland, even if the ideas and debates which emanated from those documents have been undermined by violence and criminality. In order to properly comprehend how political representation for both the UVF and UDA emerged and impacted on Loyalist politics as part of the peace process, it is necessary to look at some of the main points raised in those documents and acknowledge their attempt to articulate a way out of the violence.

The origins of political development within the UVF are evident from the early 1970s, when the organisation formed the Volunteer Political Party in 1974 to try and gain electoral support and acquire political legitimacy. A failure to gain the necessary votes and represent local communities meant that the VPP was a brief and failed venture into the realm of electoral politics. Even a suggestion made by the VPP that militant loyalism and republicanism should engage in dialogue failed to find credence among local communities, where the emphasis on paramilitarism was reinforced (McAuley 2000: 176). Involvement in political ideas continued however and out of a desire to offer representation to Loyalists which was being denied through mainstream unionism, leading figures within the UVF worked to create a new political wing which became the Progressive Unionist Party. The inception of the PUP can be charted back to 1977 (McAuley 2004: 528), but it formally began in 1979, taking on a more solid political trajectory after the Anglo-Irish Agreement of 1985 (ibid.). From the beginning, the PUP presented a strand of political thought which was socialist in orientation and particularly receptive to the social conditions of Loyalist prisoners (ibid.: 179). Critical of the intransigence within mainstream unionism, the PUP saw a potential end to the conflict in terms of responding to a need for all communities to accept their social responsibilities and produced a key document *'Sharing Responsibility'* in 1985, which later became the basis of the party's negotiating position at the peace talks (represented particularly by David Ervine and Billy Hutchinson). The document, which had origins that began in 1972 under the auspices of Gusty Spence and senior UVF personnel while in prison, was adopted by the PUP as a statement of its political identity in 1977 and held support among senior UVF members because although its formulation had offered a political direction, this direction had been constructed from the vantage point of paramilitary commitment (Sinnerton 2002: 116). The 1985 document (which was substantiated further in the 1997 version *Sharing Responsibility 2000: Into the new Millenium*) spoke about a need to concentrate on widening a social commitment to responsibility rather than power, and argued against power being used to assist regional or sectarian political aspirations. Stressing a need for consensus politics, *Sharing Responsibility* also argued for cross-border interaction, as long as such interactions were transparent and open. The emphasis of the document was on moving power away from regional political interests towards political structures which would serve all communities regardless of interests, and underscored 'core ideas of anti-sectarianism, equality and pluralism among all of Northern Ireland's citizens' (McAuley 2000: 183). As David Ervine described the intentions of the document:

> *Sharing Responsibility* was a document which goes back some years and affirms a number of ideas that we were advocating some time ago. The

notion of sharing responsibility is not that different from the concept of power in that it is about making decisions which impact on authority. It's just different language which connotes a different attitude and atmosphere. Essentially our attitude was that we didn't think an Executive Authority was something we would get at the time *Sharing Responsibility* was released, and we advocated a process of Heads of Committee taking authority, as opposed to an Executive. The concept of responsibility rather than referring to power, from our point of view was about not having to sign up to each other. We suggested that the Chair would have to be a Unionist and that the Deputy Chair a Nationalist and it was our intention that everybody's fingerprints should be on this process. From the very start our intent was underpinned by the idea that you can't enjoy this society unless everybody enjoys it. The sense that one side is superior to the other is to guarantee a problem. The only way ahead then, is to share it and to deal with responsibility or power in a shared sense. Obviously, if exclusion is at the core of the problem then inclusion is going to go some way towards addressing that. Don't forget that we emphasised cross-border relationships and were regarded as traitors for this. But it was important to recognise that as part of an inclusive process. If you look at the documents of all the parties who entered negotiations and compare those with the Agreement we ended up with, I think you will see that ours is not too far away from that.

For the UDA, attempts to develop a political front for the organisation can also be traced back to 1970s and specifically 1979, when the New Ulster Political Research Group (NUPRG) was set up after discussions between senior UDA members Andy Tyrie and Glenn Barr, stressing the need to recognise how 'negotiated settlement was the only settlement acceptable to both sides of the community' (Elliot and Flackes 1999: 478), but also that this would be best achieved through an independent Ulster (McAuley 1996a: 169). Soon after in 1981, the Ulster Loyalist Democratic Party (ULDP), headed by John McMichael, was formed in succession to the NUPRG and sought to build political credibility by arguing for 'independence in the Commonwealth and EEC' (ibid.). Its electoral appeal was negligible though, and the ULDP did not survive to compete in the 1986 by-elections (ibid.). This lack of electoral success, which reflected the UDA's lack of political impact (Cusack and Taylor 1993: 21), did not stop the fermentation of political ideas however and the 1987 *Common Sense* document was produced, which became the basis of the later-formed UDP's negotiating position in the peace talks (represented largely by David Adams and Gary McMichael). The document proposed a devolved legislative government for Northern Ireland and a written constitution. It also stressed the need for consensus government, proportional representation and (like the PUP) shared responsibility. However, *Common Sense* also determined that potential change in the constitution of

Northern Ireland would need the consent of at least two-thirds of votes in order to 'create a new atmosphere of security and stability conducive to reconciliation and political development' (1987: 8). Curiously, this formulation (clearly designed to protect a Protestant Ulster) was seen as necessary to 'dispel the fear of exclusion felt by the 'Ulster Catholic' community and create a 'new pluralist society'. The two-thirds consent principle was forwarded so as to 'remove the need to constantly defend the psychological border' and to make sure that 'constitutional change may achieve its objective if it commands a broad consensus of support for change' (ibid.). The general thrust of the document therefore was that for Catholics to be accepted into power-sharing, they should recognise the legitimacy of the Northern Ireland state and accept what Bruce calls 'institutionalized power-sharing' (2001: 35).

Wider appreciation for how *Common Sense* might be used to facilitate further discussion on the theme of power-sharing was hindered for two reasons. Firstly, its main proponent John McMichael was murdered a year after the document was released, and secondly, there was a blatant contradiction between the UDA talking about sharing power with Catholics while killing them at the same time. UPRG representative Tommy Kirkham explained the problem:

> John McMichael, Ray Smallwoods, Harry Chicken, Glen Barr and myself worked for months and months on *Common Sense* and we were supported by the Inner Council at that time. The main intention behind the document was to feed the ideas into the political arena so existing political parties, rather than us, would take it up. The problem was that by having the document rubber-stamped by the Inner Council it became untouchable by mainstream parties. You couldn't have people who were out killing people putting their name to a document on power-sharing, so that ended it. Then it became very difficult for the political people to work towards anything.

The UDP took up the ideas of *Common Sense* again when they formed in 1989, seeking to open up political thinking at senior levels in the UDA and challenge the sectarianism, gangsterism and corruption that had dominated the organisation throughout the 1980s (Cusack and Taylor 1993: 25). A particular difficulty that the UDP faced was trying to sell the benefits of political strategy while the UDA remained committed to a programme of military activity (McAuley 1996a: 170). This divide, between the politically motivated representatives of the UDA and its rank-and-file membership, has been a constant theme of disruption since the early stages of the peace process and reflects a far more ambiguous relationship with peace politics than exists between the UVF and PUP, who have managed general and consistent support for peace politics throughout (Bruce 2001: 45).

For UDP representative Gary McMichael although *Common Sense* became the foundation of the party's negotiating position, the creation of the document was initially a response to Unionist concerns about the Anglo-Irish Agreement of 1985 and the possibility of an imposed settlement:

> *Common Sense* was talking about a shared solution, the need to recognise Northern Ireland's existence within the UK and accepting that as a starting point. It was talking about a Bill of Rights and a written constitution and it outlined shared responsibility in terms of proportionality within government. But the driving force of the document was not based on a desire to be independent. It was a desire to take London and Dublin out of the equation and to get us to cope inwardly instead of externally. There needed to be a short term view in the context of what was achievable and *Common Sense* was an attempt to do that. You need to bear in mind that *Common Sense* was driven by a vacuum because in 1985, with the Anglo Irish Agreement, there was a real need to show that unionism could take control of its own destiny. It was clear that it couldn't rely on London because London was essentially conspiring to remove Northern Ireland, that's how the Anglo Irish Agreement was interpreted. *Common Sense* and the process of devising that document was recognition of that and that it was time to start sorting out a plan B because plan A was not looking too good. It was driven by a determination to place something on the table because Unionist leaders at that time were not doing anything. So necessity forced a debate within loyalism on what might be accepted in Northern Ireland as something which would take the focus away from the Anglo Irish Agreement and give us something to rally round. That was what the motivation behind *Common Sense* was.

In the later negotiations which led to the Good Friday Agreement, fellow UDP representative David Adams explained how the document informed thinking and shaped the UDP's approach generally:

> *Common Sense* was the basic document that we worked off, but it would be wrong to describe it as a script that we struck rigidly by. As the Good Friday Agreement approached, most of us could have written on the back of an envelope the broad parameters of what the end result would be, which was a power-sharing Executive, and North–South relations. But as time went on it became obvious that there was going to be North–South and East–West relationships. *Common Sense* was not a document you had to adjourn to if a sticking point arose in negotiations, but it was basically the parameters of where we thought an Agreement lay. The document did suffer greatly from its association with the paramilitaries. If it had been a stand-alone document from one of the so-called respectable political parties, it would have been greeted with the acclaim that it deserved. The problem was there was a wide gap between the vast bulk of the membership concerned with military

objectives and those who were thinking politically in the UDA, and that was the problem.

It is the development of such political thinking which underpinned the emergence of articulate and politically motivated Loyalist representatives and which provided the foundation for a new Loyalist discourse which sought to move beyond the reactive and insular psychology of mainstream constitutional unionism. The formation of a political front which derived from thinking within the UVF and the UDA, brought a new dimension to the articulation of Loyalist and Unionist politics which proved quite vital for the negotiations and dialogues dynamic that shaped the directions and momentum of the emerging 'peace process'.

4
The Peace Process Part 1: Early Stages and Key Players

Initial developments

A number of studies which chart the emergence and development of the peace process in its formative years tend to concentrate in particular on relations between Sinn Fein (the political face of militant republicanism) and the Irish, American and British governments (Coogan 1995; O'Brien 1995; Mallie and McKittrick 1996; Mallie and McKittrick 2002). The starting point for the process has been attributed to a series of dialogues conducted between SDLP leader John Hume and Sinn Fein president Gerry Adams which began in January 1988 (Taylor 1997: 304), but signs of Sinn Fein's intention to try and build a broad-based Nationalist project, which would destabilise unionism through political means, were evident in 1984 (Moloney 2002: 238). Through a series of confidential talks between Gerry Adams and Catholic priest Father Alec Reid at the Clonard Monastery in west Belfast (which led to secret meetings between Hume and Adams at Clonard), Sinn Fein started to formulate a peace strategy based on the conviction that in both military and political terms, the conflict in Northern Ireland had reached stalemate and needed an alternative approach in order to carry the Republican agenda forward (McLaughlin 1998: 72). The secret dialogues carried out between Adams and Reid, along with behind the scenes interactions with John Hume, were seen as instrumental in laying the bedrock for eventual negotiations at governmental level and representative of efforts by the Sinn Fein leadership to slowly draw the Provisional IRA away from violence towards direct political and diplomatic exchanges with governments (Moloney 2000: 219–45). The change in strategy was attributed to a perception among Sinn Fein's leadership that Republicans would make actual gains from engaging with a peace process which would be unreachable through armed force (English 2003: 309), but was also founded on the realisation that political life in Northern Ireland (and particularly Unionist politics) was central to any eventual settlement, thereby shifting emphasis away from external forces of influence such as British involvement, to the internal forces of political resistance and difference within Northern Ireland itself (ibid.: 312).

A sign that the British government was receptive to the undercurrents going on within republicanism and that it was prepared to make gestures which would help facilitate interaction was given by British Northern Ireland Secretary Peter Brooke, who sent a number of signals to Republicans during his tenure from 1989–92. Brooke's aim, through a series of tentative steps, was to try and draw Republicans into a dialogue process and his efforts were indicative of a shift in the British position towards Northern Ireland at this time. By engaging Republicans, Nationalists and Unionists with debates on the constitutional status and future of Northern Ireland, the British worked to try and bind the parties into a broader process of negotiation. As Brooke explained his intentions:

> The central job around which everything else rotated was to honourably restore peace to the province so that we were not living in a terrorist environment. This required two principal considerations. First, there had to be a constitutional shift in order to get Unionists back into the mainstream which they had been out of between 1985 and 1989 because the Anglo-Irish Agreement had sent them into self-imposed exile, which they had to be brought out of. If they could be brought out into the open and start serious constitutional talks with the Dublin government as well as the British, then this would put pressure on Sinn Fein to engage. And the second, was to act on the information we were receiving about Adams and McGuiness who seemed to have an interest in developing an endgame. This created two separate policy strands which had to be pursued and without necessarily knowing where each would end. If we got bogged down on one front then that would give us time to advance on the other. One of the first things I did on arrival was to invite the leaders of the constitutional parties to come and see me so they could tell me about their own objectives and interests. It was vital to try and move the Unionists into 'open country' because without that there would have been no movement.

Explaining the British government's lack of dialogue with loyalism as resulting from the failure of Loyalist groupings to have a 'political arm' and operating without 'constitutional control', Brooke outlined his communications strategy:

> Firstly, I did not want there to be any misunderstanding from the Unionist side about the firmness of the British government towards terrorism itself. It was also evident that the British were seen as a monolith and in Northern Ireland for selfish reasons. But it was obvious that this was not the case. We were there on a specific policy and not trying to

milk the people of Northern Ireland. All that stuff was political garbage. I made a speech at a sixth form college in December 1989, followed shortly after by one at a Rotary Club luncheon in Northern Ireland. The second one really kick-started the process because I pointed out that we were going to have exploratory talks about whether we could have constitutional talks. But I suppose the speech which had the biggest impact, certainly with the Unionists, was one I made after one hundred days in office, when I made myself available to the press and talked with journalists on a one-to-one basis. A journalist from the Press Association stressed that there was a Mexican stand-off, where the IRA couldn't beat the British and the British couldn't beat the IRA and he asked me if I would contemplate meeting Gerry Adams. I said that I would not meet Adams as long as the IRA was involved in terrorist activity, but that I didn't rule it out. That created a greater furore amongst Unionists than the other, most widely quoted speech made in November 1990 to the British Association of Canned Food Importers and Distributors at the Whitbread restaurant in London, which became known as the Whitbread speech. I made the speech there because I was wanted to deliver a speech in my own constituency which quickly followed the Rotary Club speech where we had 'rolled the wicket' and quite deliberately made a very strong statement against the IRA to assure Unionists that my heart was in the right place towards terrorism.

It was at the Whitbread Speech where Brooke made the now-famous remark about the British government having 'no selfish or strategic or economic interest in Northern Ireland'; also a direct public message to Republicans (and made known to Sinn Fein leaders a week before it was announced (Bloomfield 1998: 54)) choreographed to follow the previous speech which sought to temper Unionist anxieties. On this now-legendary speech and the above key sentence, Brooke commented:

> I had been reading Republican News with care and it was obvious from the articles which Adams wrote that we were seen as a colonial power, which just seemed insane to me and bore no relation to political reality. That one sentence was reinforcing what I had said before, which was that if the IRA were to lay down their arms and there was a ceasefire, then there was a possibility of negotiations. The speech I had made about terrorism at the Rotary Club was preparation for this sentence. The speech was not made in London to disguise or conceal it from Unionists, because we put out press releases, but we were keen that it should be made in London because that made it a statement about a London government, and not just a comment by a Secretary of State out on limb by himself. Although in due course the Unionists asked for copies of the speech so that they could study it in detail, it did not prejudice the rest

of the conversations we were having about getting into constitutional talks, and indeed the following spring that is what happened.

Brooke's lack of interaction with the Loyalists (reflecting a general absence of interest at governmental level by the British) may give the impression that loyalism had no contribution to make to political progress at this point, but it is evident that Loyalists had been talking about political change since the mid-1980s (Sinnerton 2002: 125), and that there had been public statements from key Loyalist figures about unionism becoming more 'magnanimous' towards the prospect of change and for a need to find compromise with Republicans and Nationalists (Pollak 1985). Furthermore, the UVF leadership had formed what it termed the 'Kitchen Cabinet' in 1989 (Taylor 1999: 217), which included representatives of the PUP and two or three leading members of the UVF, seeking to provide a 'political analysis' about possibilities of change in the conflict and to assess potential responses to such change (Sinnerton 2002: 126). The purpose of the 'Kitchen Cabinet' was not to discuss strategy for violence (ibid.), but to develop ideas about how a ceasefire might be put together and consider how the conditions necessary for this to happen could be facilitated (Garland 2001: 279). As the UVF's Number One described it:

> The 'Kitchen Cabinet' was an attempt to look closely at what Republicans were doing and involved the UVF, the UFF and the PUP. It was formed out of the realisation that something had to be done and that we had to be prepared for peace, as well as be ready for war. It was also devised in order to provide a political group which could engage directly with government representatives and to discuss and assess reaction. The main objective was to seek out information from all sides. From that, we met regularly and amalgamated ideas. Things changed on a daily basis because one news bulletin could change the formula, and a core idea could be changed by one event. Out of the ideas that grew, came the ability of all Loyalist groups to call a ceasefire but that one group would carry on and the other would 'sue for peace'. There were very few disagreements and it was very much a common sense approach. There was a shared vision and we did have an idea of where we wanted to go, but this was also influenced by external events.

Discussions among members of the 'Kitchen Cabinet' quickly led to the understanding that a singular and agreed, rather than fragmented Loyalist response to debate was called for, and so contact was made with UDA representative Ray Smallwood, leading to the later inclusion of Gary McMichael and David Adams. In late 1992, this collective led to the formation of the Combined Loyalist Political Alliance (CLPA) (ibid.), which devised a political strategy based on a close analysis of Republican moves and community soundings. This analysis was then given to the umbrella Loyalist military grouping the Combined Loyalist Military Command (CLMC) (Sinnerton 2002: 141), which emerged in April 1991 to declare a Loyalist ceasefire in order to facilitate the 'Brooke talks' between the constitutional parties (the ceasefire lasted from 30 April to 4 July 1991), and provided a political dimension to the military campaign which underpinned the case for a Loyalist ceasefire that the CLMC supported and subsequently called in October 1994. The Loyalist ceasefire of 1991 which was described by Brooke as 'helpful', was an attempt to pressure the constitutional Unionist parties into making progress (Bloomfield 1998: 78), and as the UVF's Number One put it, was also about 'providing a space for politicians to talk'. For Gary McMichael of the UDP, the Brooke talks signalled an opportunity for Loyalists to try and show some commitment to engaging at a political level and he explained the thinking behind moves towards a ceasefire:

> Within the UDP we were pointing out that talks were going on and we were not involved and that as that was the case, we should be seeking to influence them in some way. We argued that we should be looking at how we could contribute beyond being directly involved and it was from these arguments that the case was made for the 1991 ceasefire. The ceasefire was designed to create space for others to fill and make things a little easier and also at some level, to test whether Republicans were willing to do that. Obviously they weren't because they were at a different stage. They wanted the talks to end because they were not involved and because it was too early in the process for them. They were looking at a longer term goal, which we weren't aware of.

Because Republicans were outside the talks, there was a continuation of the IRA campaign while the Loyalists were on ceasefire, and this became a turning point when the talks broke up without progress. As the UVF Number One explained it:

> Throughout the April to July period the IRA did not give the talks space and carried out bombing to try and break the ceasefire. When the talks failed Loyalists increased the violence. The aim was to bring about an intensification of violence in order to end it and we knew from the feedback we were getting that the Provos were looking for an endgame. There was also a general consensus and feeling on the ground that people were ready for peace. For some time there had been a conscious shift in strategy to target key figures in the Provisional movement and this had a bearing on the IRA moving forward. We tried to play down the killing against us and up the ante against clearly identified IRA leaders. For us the one key issue was an IRA ceasefire and after the ceasefire of 1991 ended we set out to create that.

Though it seems unlikely that the IRA ceasefire of 1994 was predicated on an intensification of Loyalist violence, it is nevertheless apparent that the formation of the CLMC after the Brooke talks was a key moment in terms of uniting paramilitarism as a military force. By drawing resources and organisations together, Loyalists could produce a more concentrated and effective front to counter Republicans. Gary McMichael described this development as follows:

> The CLMC was not actually created to provide for the peace process. It was created to bring about a more strategic and joined-up approach to the IRA's campaign militarily. Although it was involved in agreeing a ceasefire for the Brooke talks, it was a device to make the Loyalist war effort more streamlined and more operative. The UVF and UDA would be sharing resources, people and weapons and agreeing to take certain action, so it was more a military unification of convenience. As the situation changed to a peace process, it became a forum for dealing with circumstances as they arose, where every few weeks the leaderships came together and discussed strategic mechanisms. As it moved towards the ceasefire of 1994, it was obvious that there was no point in having two or three ceasefires, and as the process continued, we became more involved in meetings and debates that were positively political. Although the CLMC was primarily about military affairs, there was a political tier of influence there and political analysis was feeding into the military strategy. It was also through this channelling of political analysis that the UDP formed a more structural relationship with the PUP.

Alongside these internal developments it is important to note that from 1989 until the ceasefire of 1994, there was a serious and informed sequence of dialogues with clergy figures which were used to try and break down misunderstandings about the need for violence and explore the potential for creating peace. These dialogues became the first steps towards examining the credibility of moves away from violence outside the Loyalist organisations themselves, and were used to bring about Irish and British government contacts once that credibility had been established. Preliminary contacts between Loyalist representatives and the church had isolated and sporadic beginnings in 1985 (around the same time Adams commenced purposeful involvement with Alec Reid), when UDA members spoke with Clonard priests (Garland 2001: 273). However, those early contacts were carried out in some trepidation and it was not until later that Loyalist political representatives met clergy figures with the more serious intent of pushing to access British and Irish governments (as well as trying to use the meetings to assess Republican strategy). For the UVF, Gusty Spence was particularly keen to find out what developments could result from meeting the clergy and took part in a number of discussions as well as also meeting John Hume to present the UVF's concerns about the emerging peace process (ibid.: 274).

Clergy

The role of the clergy and the involvement of the church in talks with paramilitaries has been somewhat neglected within accounts of the peace process (Wells 1999), but it is significant that for Loyalists, this interaction helped to build a communications process which, if less successful, paralleled Republican activity and helped them gain access to British and Irish government representatives. Although certain elements within the clergy have had lines of communication open with paramilitaries for the duration of the 'Troubles', a more concerted and active engagement seems to have taken shape from 1990. During initial phases of this relationship, this involved Protestant ministers talking to the Republican leadership in a private capacity to try and convey the fears and concerns within the Protestant/Unionist community. John Dunlop was one such individual who, in 1991, met Republican leaders in a series of confidential meetings at Clonard. Dunlop explained his intentions:

> I met the Sinn Fein leadership in private meetings. Those conversations were an attempt on my part to explain what I was about as a person and to try and get them to understand where I and the community I represent was coming from. Previous to that, I had read a couple of books by Gerry Adams and thought this guy doesn't seem to know what people like me are about. But then again, this was not surprising since he had never met a Presbyterian minister. I listened to what they had to say, but I had to try and get across the concerns and thinking that I could see. I did this in a personal and private way. Some of them were more receptive than others. There was no set agenda, it was just discussions; very informal with a number of people in a room discussing a range of issues. I was meeting people and letting them know that I heard what they had to say, but also putting across the things I thought they had to come to terms with. They might stress to me the compromises they had made, but then I would question whether those compromises were made out of generosity, or simply because of the realisation that the armed struggle was going nowhere. I told them that it was pretty clear that the conflict had reached a stalemate and that there was no point in continuing to kill people. There was no strategy behind these meetings and I was not negotiating anything, just trying to get them to understand people like me better. What became evident is how very centralised Sinn Fein is as an organisation. Debates for them don't take place in public, they take place in private. It's an extraordinarily focussed body of people, where people

are designated to do certain jobs. It's a highly organised business and they run a tight ship.

The Presbyterian minister Ken Newell was also engaged in dialogue with Republicans at that this time (commencing in 1990) and developed a close friendship with the Clonard priest Father Gerry Reynolds. Newell's meetings were more formal than the conversations Dunlop had been involved in and he was also communicating with Loyalists across a three-year period (1990–3). Newell spoke about the beginnings of this involvement:

> I was in direct dialogue with Sinn Fein as a result of the work with Father Reynolds and Father Reid who asked me to bring a group of Protestant clergy into talks with Sinn Fein, which meant Gerry Adams and one of two of the key west Belfast Republican thinkers and activists. Usually there were three Sinn Fein representatives present. As well as working on that, it was felt necessary to open up a front with loyalism and so we entered into dialogue with Gary McMichael and David Adams of the UDP. I especially had a number of long conversations with Ray Smallwoods, who was a mediator and go-between with the UDP/UDA. Engaging the UDA/UDP in this way meant that the meetings included both Protestant and Catholic representatives. We wanted to hear what the leaders of loyalism were thinking and to convey our reflections on republicanism directly to them. Ray Smallwoods was the conduit through which we moved and made further contacts. We spoke to McMichael and Adams about our soundings within republicanism. They wouldn't meet Republicans directly, so they used us to get a sense of what the thinking was. We met the Republicans about once a month and Adams was prominent. Essentially we were trying to interpret the fluid mind of republicanism.

Father Gerry Reynolds, who worked closely with Newell, offered this interpretation of the talks and their purpose:

> Father Reid was searching for a way to try and end the violence and was very close to Gerry Adams. He tried to get Republicans to see that there was a democratic way forward and that the best way to achieve that was to build an alliance with Nationalists, involving the SDLP and the Dublin government. Meetings were also set up between Presbyterian ministers and Republican leaders with the goal of trying to develop relationships. Those meetings were about trying to understand how each saw the way forward. The Sinn Fein position was very rigid though, and a further problem was that progress was hampered by the violence that was going on. It was very difficult to argue for the need to end violence whilst it was happening, and it was difficult to make the argument in that context. The ministers were talking about the futility of the violence and how it was

driving people further and further apart. Sinn Fein tended to talk about their ideology so you couldn't call it a meeting of minds, but in some way over the few years it took place, there was a mutual understanding that grew between people from the Unionist background and Sinn Fein. This helped to facilitate some openness and engage with the problem of misunderstanding, which was very deep. We used to meet people from the PUP and would try and search with them for a democratic way forward, but always the stumbling block was violence. There was no possibility of a solution unless everybody found justice in the position of everybody else, so we tried to humanise one side to the other and give justice to one another. The main conviction driving us was to stop people getting killed.

David Adams of the UDP was extensively involved in dialogue with the clergy and saw the significance of the talks in this way:

The contacts were more conversational than specific in focus. It was about encouraging us to think broader and to plan a bit about where we actually wanted to go and how things could work in a real sense within the wider community. We were aware that in meeting the clergy we were talking to Republicans as well, but it was never a case of using them as a conduit for messages. We felt that the conversations were confidential but that others would be given a flavour of where we were at, what the ideas were and that the clergy would bring their own estimation of us into talks with others. The talks were very informal and nothing was written down. I think it was a case of tentative exploration by the clergy and don't forget that the governments needed some reassurance before committing themselves as well, so in liaising with us the clergy were also seeing if we were genuine. The clergy were careful not to draw things out of us that which we didn't wish to disclose and if they had told us chapter and verse about who they were meeting in the Republican movement and what they were saying, we would have walked away, because they would have been doing the same to us. Often it was about keeping in touch and seeing how things were going. Their role was seeing how serious people were and judging the prospects for progress. They were giving honest assessments to governments about where people were at, and they were essential for 'ice-breaking' at that time.

For some clergy members involved in the contacts, there was a notable purpose and intent in the way Republicans approached the conversations which Loyalists lacked. Ken Newell highlighted this difference:

The aim was to try and find out what Republicans were doing and to examine the grounds for the process of change they were engaged in; that was the essence of the involvement. We would look at speeches which Adams might make and look at the strengths and weaknesses of what he said. The speeches he made in 1991 and 1992 aimed at the Republican body at their Annual Convention, were assessed for signs of where republicanism was going and we would feed back our thoughts about that. It was clear that they were thinking about how to develop bridges with the SDLP and the Irish government and along with backing from America, try to put pressure on the British. It was also clear that they had a vision of where to go and how to get there. We tried to convey our reading of this transition to the Loyalists and to get across that Republicans were making positive noises about moving towards peace which loyalism needed to respond to, and to ask them what they were thinking. We met Republicans more than the Loyalists, who we saw basically at our request. It would be us knocking doors asking to talk to them, whereas Republicans were engaged and using the meetings more specifically.

Talking further about how the Unionist/Loyalist imagination tends to lack confidence and vision compared to republicanism, Newell continued

Although the political representatives of loyalism I met had a good political brain, at the grassroots the sophistication is not there. The rank and file basically lack the political awareness and rigour, as well as the hunger, to learn what politics is all about. This is engrained into Republicans, who use every opportunity to educate themselves about what is going on politically. Historically of course, Loyalists have seen the security forces as a safety net, along with the British army and Unionist domination, so there hasn't been the same hunger and as a result of that, they have not produced such focussed political thinking. Through the prison experience Republicans have sharpened their convictions, whereas although the people at the top of loyalism were thinking things through, it was mainstream unionism which sought to do most of their thinking for them. Also important is that within republicanism, there is grassroots power, where motivation at the base is strong, and unionism does not have this. It would be fair to say that unionism has nightmares but no vision, and as a result of that it lacks confidence. It goes onto the field basically trying to play for a draw. Because republicanism is fighting a battle, there is more of a commonality there which comes from a desire to win, which creates unity. But, for Unionists, talk of unity only starts to arise when they feel threatened. Unionism is like a car without petrol. It lacks energy in terms of having a unifying vision of its own.

For Newell, one of the most important moments in his work with Loyalists came when paramilitary leaders agreed to meet and converse with Catholic priests:

Generally the meetings with Loyalists were quite informal with about four or five people talking in a room. But we did have a formal meeting with a group of about 15 of the UDA's leadership in east Belfast at their headquarters. Father Reid and Father Reynolds were present at the meeting, which was set up by Ray Smallwoods. I would say their involvement with the leadership was more important than mine because here was the UDA meeting Catholic priests, who they were traditionally taught to distrust and hate. We believed this was evidence of a de-sectarianisation process which had been slowly built up through the contacts, but this was also helped by emerging political thinkers like Gary McMichael and David Adams, who did not have the sectarian baggage. At that meeting, the leadership were articulating that they were not going to be part of a united Ireland or be forced into one, which they perceived to be the IRA's main goal. For the clergy involved, we viewed the process as being like trying to deal with an iceberg. There are two things you can do with an iceberg, use a boat to ram it, in which case you will sink, or pull it into warmer waters where over time it will melt. That's how we viewed these interactions; trying to melt the iceberg. We saw the IRA ceasefire coming a year before it was announced because we saw the transition that was going on, and we were keen to keep Loyalists aware of this process, especially since it appeared that they were evolving a political voice and direction of their own.

The UVF's Number One stressed that the meetings at Clonard 'through the involvement of Adams had provided a breathing space' had 'created an opportunity for re-assessing' the conflict strategy. However, of the two main Loyalist groups it was the UDA that tended to rely most on relations with the clergy (the UVF and PUP were more advanced in engaging with intermediaries and political players). Undoubtedly, the most prominent church figure in dealing with the UDA was Rev Roy Magee. The trust which Magee gained from the UDA leadership had roots in the early years of the 'Troubles', when he challenged the Inner Council about the legitimacy of the violence the UDA was perpetrating. In particular, Magee's contact became more firmly established in the mid-1980s, when he met the Inner Council on a regular basis in order to raise critical questions about accountability. He recalls this time and the slow emergence of a political direction within the organisation:

> There were a few who were looking ahead and there was a group which was set up to try and analyse the political situation. That situation was beginning to raise its head within the organisation and they were glad of an outside voice that could be trusted to challenge them. Of course, that didn't mean they necessarily listened to what was being said, but they were conscious they were going to be challenged about what they were doing and where they were going and I think this began to focus them a bit more.

The process of dialogue which Magee became involved in was intensified in the early 1990s (around the same time other clergy figures were engaged in conversations and interactions with Loyalists and Republicans), and it was during this time that Magee encouraged Archbishop Robin Eames to join that process. Eames was able to guarantee governmental contacts and therefore bring political weight to the dialogues in ways which Magee alone could not. Magee explained the developing conditions which led to the involvement of Eames and the process of contacts which followed:

> The contact with Robin Eames came about through the CLMC, which involved the leaderships of both the UVF and the UDA. In the CLMC there were people who were unhappy about the violence and where the whole thing was going. The formation of the CLMC meant that the organisations could speak together and verbalise more strongly the need to move away from violence. They felt it was necessary to have someone who could deal with the British government and the line of communication for that was Robin Eames. They tried to make the approach themselves, which I think he turned down, so they approached me and I made the approach to him, from which we began to talk together. At this time, I became the contact with the Irish government and he became the contact with the British. It was clear that there were messages and signals which needed to be sent and interpreted with the two governments and we were doing that, trying to evaluate what was being said and what was being listened to. For the Loyalists, there was a real fear of a sell-out with any deal being done, and it was important to convince them that this would not be happening. I would travel down to Dublin perhaps twice a week and the Irish would send a representative to Belfast who I would pick up at the train station. We would go to the Stormont Hotel and talk and then he would take the results of that conversation back to the Irish prime minister Albert Reynolds. That representative was the senior Irish government advisor Martin Mansergh, and he made the approach to me. I became a very close contact with him, relaying things directly to the Irish government. It was late 1992, early 1993, when the approach was made to Robin Eames and it was also around that time when the pace of contact with the Dublin government built up.

Continuing, Magee spoke about how the Loyalists observed and interpreted the emerging dialogue:

> The Loyalists took this process very seriously. They appointed two military people, a senior figure in the UVF and one from the UDA to accompany me to meetings, to hear and express views and to get answers about what was going on. They would then report that to the CLMC, who decided at that stage that they wanted to sell it to the troops on the ground. The two military commanders would go to the different areas and answer questions on the basis of what they had heard first hand. This was a slow

process and they did it thoroughly because they stood to lose a lot of support. The meetings I had with the commanders were always determined by them, since I didn't want to be in possession of information that could be passed on. It's alright talking to people who are on the political side, but they can't really deliver. I always felt it was crucial to deal with the people who could say yes, it will happen, or, no it won't. With the UDA, I was dealing with the entire leadership of six people, but with the UVF, who I also met, it was about three or four.

Involvement with the Loyalists up until the ceasefire of 1994 was fraught with ethical and moral dilemmas for Magee. As part of an intensification strategy in order to bring the conflict to a head, the Loyalists had escalated killing from 1990–4 to exceed Republican killings (Loyalists being responsible for 144 sectarian killings during this period, compared to 29 by Republican paramilitaries (Morrissey and Smyth 2002: 52)) and Magee (as well as Eames) considered walking away from the Loyalist leaders who talked about peace, while paramilitaries carried out murders. A particularly testing period was the Loyalist response to an IRA bomb at a fish and chip shop on the Shankill Road in October 1993, which killed 10 people and injured 57. In retaliation, four days later, UFF gunmen walked into the Rising Sun bar in Greysteel, County Londonderry and killed seven customers celebrating Halloween. A further 13 were injured. October 1993 saw 27 people die in Northern Ireland, making it the largest monthly death toll since October 1976 (Bew and Gillespie 1999: 278). And although the Irish Government had sought to reduce the tension by publicly stating a commitment four days after the Shankill bomb to six 'democratic principles' which had been requested by the Loyalists to facilitate talks (to be further explored later in this chapter), this failed to deter revenge attacks, which became a cause of serious concern for Magee and Eames. As Magee recalled:

> Above Frisell's fish shop was the UDA headquarters and it was a Saturday when the bomb went off. Bodies were being carried from the rubble and one of the west Belfast commanders was standing alongside me. A couple of old ladies came over to me and said it had to stop, that the killing had to end because too many innocent lives were being lost. They said it to me so that he could hear. Those people could not go to him directly, so they said it to me, but it was aimed at him. Revenge attacks then took place and that was the time when Robin Eames nearly walked away, saying they were making fools of us. It seemed as though old scores were also being settled. After the Greysteel murders I said I was finished. But at one of the funerals I attended, Ray Smallwoods told me that the men wanted me to reconsider my decision. I told him that we had an agreement which had been violated. Then, a top military man came over and pushed for me to continue, asking me what should happen next. I told him that at meetings

things would have to be written down so we knew where we were and so there couldn't be any dispute about positions. It was important not to keep sliding back and the meetings resumed on that basis.

Archbishop Robin Eames also remembered the difficulties of this period and said to Magee, 'If they are prepared to talk with me on one day and then go out and do these things I don't want to know'. Eames had met the CLMC shortly before, when its members travelled in secret to talk with him at Armagh Cathedral. Describing that meeting, when Eames met the CLMC alone, he went on:

> They approached me to see if I could get an answer from the British government through prime minister John Major about whether there had been a private deal made with the PIRA, who they knew were working towards a ceasefire. They wanted to find out if a private agreement and concessions had been made in order to get this ceasefire. They were very worried that a deal had been done behind their backs and wanted to know if this was the case. They arrived at Armagh in their best suits and their presentation indicated the seriousness of the situation. There was about fifteen of them and nobody but Roy Magee, myself and those attending knew about the meeting, which took place at night. I started by saying that I had met them with only one condition, which was they were deadly serious about working towards peace. I also started by telling them I am totally, absolutely and convincingly opposed to the murder of Catholics because they are Catholics, and that I did not swallow the tit-for-tat justification for murdering people. I made it clear that if the thing went pear-shaped I was walking away. I then told them we had a couple of hours and to make the most of it. I kept the meeting as firm as I could; no messing about. We formulated some questions that I would put to John Major such as (1) Was there a secret deal with the PIRA? (2) Was there a deal that would in any way have ramifications for the Loyalist community? (3) Was the situation as it appeared, or were there surprises lurking? Those were the kinds of questions we put together. I told them that there was no such thing as a free lunch and wanted to know their reaction if Major's response was positive. They then told me they would take a major step towards ending the violence. I travelled to London to see John Major and he gave me a categorical assurance that there had not been a private deal. About a week later, I met the CLMC again to relay this assurance and told them that I was convinced of John Major's honesty. I also passed on my concerns to the British government that unless something was done to assuage the Loyalists' fears, they would go over the edge.

Eames considered the Loyalist threat to be underestimated by the British who, in his opinion, concentrated more on republicanism. In comparison,

Eames found the Irish government to be much more receptive to the Loyalist case:

> The British government did not see the Loyalist paramilitaries at the same level of threat as Republicans. I remember one British minister saying to me 'To be honest what drives us is the awful fear that the PIRA will do something on the mainland. I don't think the Loyalists are capable of that.' I told the minister he was in 'cuckoo land' to think that. It seemed to me as though they saw Loyalists as little more than hooligans. In contrast, and because it was seen as a much greater threat south of the border, the Irish read loyalism more carefully and clearly. Even the Americans saw the Loyalists as a 'nuisance' rather than a threat.

Summarising his interpretation of the difficulties facing loyalism at this time and how the representatives he saw compared to the Republicans he also met, Eames continued:

> With the Loyalists I was dealing with a group of men who were uncertain where they were and who wanted an answer. However, it was clear that there was an underlying consensus about why they had come to see me and that consensus emerged further as they continued to talk. The outward and most visible sign of what they were talking about was the possible dissolution of the Union. Also there was the emergence of new personalities here and the problem of authority, power and influence within the organisations was beginning to surface. But essentially, there were three causes of concern. One was the suspicion of a deal with PIRA, second was that if the peace process gathers momentum there might be a total erosion of the border leading to Irish unity, and the third was the fear of being detached from the process; being left out in the cold. loyalism is different from republicanism in the respect that republicanism has a vision and it's the long haul, whereas loyalism has an idea and it's reactionary. Also, the Republicans that I saw were very sophisticated in their preparation, documentation and the degree of seriousness with which they went about their job. They do their homework and their approach is acute. Republicanism has a depth of research, planning and philosophy which far exceeded anything I came across in loyalism. Republicans could quote without reference to notes, facts, figures, speeches and addresses. There was also a wish to understand why Protestants said or did the things they said and did. In comparison, loyalism knows what it wants to maintain, but has failed to give sufficient thought to two things. One, how to maintain itself in a vastly changed society and two, what does it do when the constitutional issue is no longer important? There was also the problem of dealing with the same people in loyalism because one would have dialogue and get to know leaders x, y and z and then x was deposed, so you had to get to know a,

b and c who had taken over from him. This problem never arose with Republicans because whoever one spoke to, one was dealing with the same position, knowing that the contact had the backing of the movement. The obstacle of instability never arose with Republicans. Although loyalism is reactive to republicanism, one could not talk about a need to react. My instinct when the IRA called its ceasefire was to tell the Loyalists to do the same, but I realised very early on that this was the wrong approach. The right approach was to say to the paramilitary figures, it's the right thing to do because it's right for you and your community, not because the IRA did it.

At governmental level Eames met the British and Irish regularly and stressed the need for both governments to be consistent in their approach towards the paramilitaries:

I made it a condition that both governments had to talk to each other closely on this. I told them how things can unravel badly because somebody puts an interpretation on something which was said on a Monday, but not repeated on the Tuesday. I also told them that I expected them to compare notes after I had spoken to each of them. This was to help me as much as them. It was vital that the governments took a complementary approach to this, because without consistency we had trouble. I also made it clear that I wouldn't be a messenger boy, but I would convey my impression of what was happening. There's no doubt that the Irish government listened to Loyalists better than the British and had a better awareness about the realities of Protestantism and loyalism in Northern Ireland. One Irish minister explained to me how he thought loyalism had happened behind the backs of the British because they never took it as a threat. The Irish deputy Dick Spring told me that the most important thing in the process of dialogue and contact was not only the trust developed, but that we did not try to convince each other without sufficient evidence for a particular path to follow. Explanation was fine, as was the idea of principle, but there always had to be factual evidence to support it.

As this interview material reveals, clergy figures helped the Loyalists to clarify their own peace strategy, raise their awareness on the value of cross-communal dialogue and establish links with government contacts. However, because the UDA were more hesitant to broaden contacts beyond the church, this also restricted opportunities for direct engagement with contacts at a higher political level. The UVF leadership and the PUP, on the other hand, realised the importance of momentum and sought to deal with the Irish government as quickly as possible. But, in order to do this they needed someone who had access to senior Irish government figures and who could be trusted as an intermediary.

Chris Hudson: an intermediary

The relationship of the former trade union official, now church minister Chris Hudson, with the leadership of the UVF since their first meeting on the Shankill Road in Belfast in November 1993 (Cusack and McDonald 1997: 295), has played a significant part in how the UVF has communicated its concerns about the peace process to the Irish government since that time. The UVF's Number Two insists that Hudson's work is responsible 'for saving hundreds of lives' and for that reason alone deserves more recognition than it has been given. Although the success of the intermediary largely depends on secrecy and confidentiality, Hudson's dealings with the UVF leadership since 1993 provide us with an insight not just into the internal workings and thinking of that organisation through the sensitive and fragile stages of the peace process, but how the concerns and aspirations of the UVF have shifted during that time. Importantly, Hudson's work is able to provide us with a perception of the UVF which is grounded in close experience of working with its leadership, and offers us a further explanation of the directions that leadership has sought to create since 1993.

Introduced to the UVF leadership by David Ervine, after meeting Ervine at a conference in Dublin during the late summer of 1993, Hudson recalled his early observations of the leadership's concerns:

> They knew there was a process going on and the signals they were getting from the Nationalist community were that there was a process in place. The problem was they didn't know how advanced the dialogue was. They also felt that every time they put out a signal to Sinn Fein and the IRA, there was an aggressive reaction which signified that the war was still on. What was scaring them was the thought that they were going to be totally out of the picture and they were unsure how to respond. The first meeting I had with the leadership was tetchy and I thought that was it, but soon after, David Ervine contacted me to say they wanted to meet again. I think they were sizing me up and making a judgement about whether they could trust me or not. They were telling me that they wanted the war to end but didn't know how to bring that about. They also wanted to know what was going on with 'the other side', and whether they were going to be included in any dialogue. Another problem was that they were getting a negative response from the British government. They saw the British as being overly concerned with the IRA and the belief that Loyalists would just follow what the IRA did. They saw themselves as being able to apply greater leverage through the Dublin government and wanted to get Dublin to recognise that they should be players in any emerging process. The bottom line for them was that the Union must be safe. I relayed their concerns to Fergus Finlay, who was special advisor to the then deputy prime minister Dick Spring (also minister for Foreign

Affairs). Both were extremely helpful and made public statements which eased concerns for the UVF. In particular, I kept in close contact with Finlay, who kept me informed of developments which I then relayed back to the leadership.

Adopting coded names for the people he was dealing with, such as 'The Grocer' for Dick Spring, 'The Grocer's Assistant' for Fergus Finlay, 'The Cricket Team' for the UVF and 'The Full Cricket Team' for the CLMC (Cusack and McDonald 1997: 295), Hudson began to inform the leadership of forthcoming public statements and events passed to him through Finlay, and by so doing, helped to create trust and confidence between the UVF, Hudson himself and the Dublin government. Although he kept the substance of his meetings with the leadership secret, Hudson nevertheless made public comments about the atmosphere within loyalism, and used the opportunity to help develop a more serious political profile for the UVF:

> David Ervine told me that it was very important to keep talking about developments within loyalism and to do as many interviews as possible [the PUP also adopting this strategy to raise its profile (Sinnerton 2002: 134)]. The purpose was to publicise that the UVF was going through its own transition, its own evaluative process and its own analysis of what was happening. I kept saying this on the radio, the purpose of which was to help convince the Loyalist community of change by creating commentary which treated them with a level of integrity. The big problem was to get Loyalists to confront their own negative perceptions about defeat and fear, and to encourage them to see themselves as players with a contribution to make. A problem for the UVF generally is that they see the world through a military perspective and find the complexities of politics difficult. One reason for this is because politics requires compromises and that generally is not part of their thinking. There is also the issue of seeing every gain for the Nationalist community as a loss for the Loyalist/Unionist community, which leads to a very negative view of what is happening. The CLMC, for example, did not strike out with a political agenda, they just wanted to preserve the status quo. Unlike Republicans, the Loyalists don't want to change society or radicalise it. They want to defend it.

Outlining the routine of the meetings and his role in relaying messages to Dublin and from Dublin to the UVF, Hudson went on:

> I would listen to what they were saying and then on the way back to Dublin try and distil the conversation into four or five key points. They made it clear early on that they could deliver the big prize of peace and that the CLMC were working towards a ceasefire. But they also reminded

Dublin that until that time came they would target Republicans as the war continued. Certainly, Dublin was looking for some indication from the Loyalists that they were moving towards a ceasefire, but the big concern for the Loyalists was that there was a secret agenda going on behind the scenes that they did not know about. They insisted that everything had to be open and that they would have to be included in any dialogue. Importantly, they knew that if the hard men were sitting around a table negotiating an end to war, then Dublin could take that as an assurance that they meant business. Over time I started to deal mostly with the UVF's second-in-command and then worked entirely alone with him. The one-to-one interaction helped to developed trust, but it also assisted clarity. It avoided the problem of numerous interpretations arising and kept communications focussed. What this involvement created was an understanding of what the UVF had in mind for the way ahead, and what their agenda would be. I tried to help them see that the political process was not a black and white affair, and I hope that for the Irish, I was able to convey the diverse and complex identity that exists within loyalism.

The period following the Shankill bombing was an especially difficult time for Hudson, leading to intense activity between Dublin and the UVF as the Loyalist leaders pressed for involvement in the talks process:

David Ervine was frantic with me after over the growing number of murders through 1994 and particularly with the Loughinisland murders where six were gunned down watching football in a pub. Much of this was seen to be carried out as revenge for the Shankill bombing and Ervine told me to work harder in order to keep the momentum going. The Loyalists were not expecting a bombing of that kind and this was because the signals they were getting from the IRA were about working towards a ceasefire. The Loyalist retaliation was severe and threatened to de-rail the whole process. However, in relation to this retaliation the second-in-command pointed out that the paramilitaries could go out and conduct this slaughter every night if they wanted. I think that although he saw those murders as revenge for the Shankill bomb, he also saw them as part of a last throw of the dice and a positioning of strength as the possibility for ceasefires increased. Their argument was that they were intensifying the violence in order to bring it to an end. They were very concerned about what they were hearing regarding a forthcoming IRA ceasefire and this was made worse because they had no knowledge of the basis for such a move. They certainly didn't trust the British government and badly needed a conduit into the Irish government. They were convinced that the British had conceded something in order to bring a ceasefire about. I showed them a note from Fergus Finlay saying this was not the case and they asked me if I trusted Finlay, which I did.

I think they had an exaggerated perception of Sinn Fein's negotiating power and they just thought Adams and McGuiness would be given everything they wanted.

Describing the psychology and motivation of the UVF further, Hudson highlighted their apprehension about dealing with the Irish and went on:

> Remember this whole process was a new thing for them. Their raison d'etre was different to the Provos who were revolutionaries. Because the Provos were trying to change society they were already highly politicised, whereas for Loyalists the process of politicisation was just starting to emerge. I had to try and get them to understand that a lot about negotiation is to do with presentation and the sound of statements. It was important that they got to grips with using effective language and positioning their arguments without sounding like backward men. I would often try to get them to re-consider their interpretation of certain statements which would come out of Dublin from time to time, and get them to see that Dublin would have to appeal to Republicans as well. Sometimes they would get very concerned about Dick Spring if he started to sound Republican. They grew to understand that compromising is sometimes necessary in order to gain a position, but early on there was no awareness of nuance in communication. I recall a planned meeting with Finlay which they were due to attend. They were talking about a ceasefire and pre-empting the Provos by calling one first. This was a positive move and Finlay agreed to meet them and start a process whereby they would be 'brought in from the cold'. However, whether they got concerned that the meeting was arranged too easily, or whether they felt they were being hoodwinked in some way, they called it off and decided to see what Republicans were going to do first. This perhaps indicates that although there was a development in strategic thinking, there was not so much strategic planning. They became good at understanding what others were doing, but got too caught up in responding to that, rather than pursuing their own agenda. They realised that they could create real problems for Dublin and early on, when they were particularly concerned about being outside talks and of a deal being done with Republicans, they talked about a low intensity campaign in Dublin, where they would hit American tourists and try to wreck the tourist market, or, pick off a chief executive of an American multi-national company operating in Ireland. This was a real consideration and demonstrated the tendency to think primarily in a military fashion. I told them I would never deliver threats and I never did. I suppose I saw my role as a 'mood-setter', interpreting and reading the mood of Dublin and the UVF accordingly. I was not negotiating anything, but playing an interpretive role. Obviously Dublin and the UVF leadership would ask me my thoughts on issues and I would

provide them. It was vital that Dublin made clear and positive noises towards the Loyalists, which they did.

Hudson's involvement with the UVF is seen by the leadership to have performed a vital role in helping to facilitate the move from war to peace and pivotal for engaging the Irish government. Working behind the scenes, Hudson gained the trust and confidence of an organisation which has traditionally been the more secretive and insular of the Loyalist groupings and the UVF leadership is adamant that the implications of Hudson's work extend far beyond the relaying of messages to the actual prevention of murder and retaliatory violence (details of Hudson's role after the Omagh bomb of 1998 further confirm this, and will be discussed later). Notably, his work performed an interpretative and educative function which assisted dialogue between Loyalists and the Irish government and helped to provide the foundations for negotiation and interaction.

The Irish government

The Irish government made contact with senior Loyalist representatives about the emerging peace process from around September 1993, and it was with the PUP and senior UVF personnel that initial talks took place (the UDA had no desire to speak with the Irish at this point and it was not until later that UDP representatives spoke to Irish officials directly). For the Irish, the contacts were effectively managed by a small team, which at the time included Brain Fitzgerald (TD for Neath and chief whip in the Labour Party), Fergus Finlay (advisor to Dick Spring in the Department of Foreign Affairs) and Dick Spring (deputy taoiseach and foreign minister). Fitzgerald and Finlay were the main conduits between the Loyalists and the Irish government and formative communications were started from a meeting which Fitzgerald had with Loyalist representatives. As Fitzgerald recalled:

> Around September 1993 I was asked to join a delegation to go to the Civic Hall in Belfast to meet a group of Unionists and community activists. During the course of that meeting I had a conversation with a man called Fred Rodgers who was an independent Loyalist based in the Shankill area and he was pointing to some men who he said were very influential in their community, but had served long jail sentences. I was at one stage sitting close to David Ervine and he said to me something along the lines of 'I don't like the way that your leader is being treated'. I asked Ervine if there was any possibility of a ceasefire being called and he told me that there were possibilities on that front. I took that as a cue and asked Ervine if he would like to meet the taoiseach, to which he said he would. He gave me Gusty Spence's phone number and I gave him my number and Ervine said that Gusty would be in touch with me soon. When I returned

to Dublin I relayed this to Fergus Finlay who was very positive about a meeting. A day or two later, contact was made and a meeting was set up in Belfast. Finlay and I travelled to Belfast and the meeting took place in a Quaker House near Queen's University. We had a frank discussion but it was also pretty informal. We closed the meeting and agreed that we would meet again fairly quickly.

Fergus Finlay offered this summary of the meeting and the thinking which surrounded it:

> The idea of a meeting seemed a good idea but it needed to be done informally. It was important that Brian came with me so that if it got out we could describe it as a party to party sort of encounter, and although Brian was a backbencher, he had no connection with the government, or the formal structures of government. Brian was therefore able to offer a kind of cover, so it wouldn't look like a government contact, or at least we could describe it that way. We realised that after the Anglo Irish Agreement took place in 1985, there was no contact made or established with unionism, and that the British told them nothing and took their reactions for granted. This was a terrible mistake and one we didn't want to make again, so we decided to keep unionism and loyalism abreast of the spirit of what was going on and what the nature of the dialogue was without breaking confidence about it. At the meeting, it was soon obvious that these were people who were committed to politics and developing an alternative to violence, but that they were very tense because they did not know what was going on. Nobody had told them anything and they were afraid that some kind of deal was being done with Nationalists and Republicans that would effectively sell the ground from under their feet. I made it clear at that first meeting that as far as the Irish government was concerned, it was totally committed to the principle of consent and that the principle of consent would be enshrined in every agreement that was made. I also stressed how it was important to build a consensus around the principle of consent and that at that level, they had nothing to fear. Principally, I think what they wanted, and what they were happy to hear about, was the fact that the Irish government had no designs on Northern Ireland as part of the process that was going on and they were always looking for reassurance about that.

Fitzgerald explained how quite soon after meeting the Loyalists, the Irish moved to pressure the British into allowing the representatives into the prisons to meet fellow Loyalists and how this helped to build trust and confidence:

> A week or two went by after the meeting when we got a phone call to say that the Loyalists we had met wanted to go into the prisons to meet

prisoners, because they were having problems with the debates taking shape. The British government wouldn't arrange to let them in and they never accepted them as having any political status. The British regarded them as criminals and that was it. Fergus and I spoke to Spring who got in touch with the Northern Ireland Secretary at that time, Patrick Mayhew, and clearance was made for them to make the visit. This was important because it wasn't just the prisoners on board, it was also their families as well. And if you had one hundred prisoners, and you had one hundred families, and you multiply that by four or five with extended families and friends, you are talking about a significant community. The Loyalists always made it clear that they wanted a re-settlement policy drawn up for prisoners coming out with nothing to do. This was a quite different from Republicans who didn't believe in re-settlement, or what they referred to as 'rehabilitation', and who made it clear they would take care of their prisoners in their own communities. The Loyalists we met were always prepared to look at what things would be like three or four years down the line for released prisoners, and didn't want them to come out and face the conditions they had faced. Getting them into the prisons certainly helped to build trust into the contacts, which, by the way, were always intimate. It was only ever Finlay and I who met the Loyalists and because of this, we quickly developed a relationship with them. They kept us informed of progress and just before the ceasefire was called in 1994, they informed us about content and when it would be announced. Spence was clearly the main influence among the Loyalists we saw and he spoke eloquently about there being one community with two traditions in Northern Ireland, rather than two communities. But it was also evident that if the conflict re-ignited they were in a position to do a lot of harm because they had a lot of information and they were well armed. It was absolutely vital that the contacts were kept confidential both for them and us because they were under threat from their own community and they had Paisley as another pressure, so they were continually being undermined and at the same time taking a huge risk in talking to us, people from the Republic. At no time did we seek to put them under pressure because we knew that these guys could do untold damage, or untold good, and it was the latter that we wanted to support.

Finlay went on to describe the relatively relaxed approach to the contacts, while also stressing that what made Irish involvement particularly important was the absence of British interest in loyalism, which he saw as being overly fixated with mainstream unionism:

Around the second or the third meeting, Billy Hutchinson attended, along with David Ervine and Gusty Spence. They had developed a set of principles which they did not present at the first meeting which we took to be more of an introduction; a feeling for the situation. I told them that I thought the principles would probably find favour with the Irish government and they were subsequently tabled for inclusion in the Downing Street Declaration by the Irish. Those principles were also revealed to taioseach Albert Reynolds when he met the Loyalists some weeks later. I was never aware of any approach by the British towards loyalism, and the Loyalists never gave me any sign that there was any kind of deep negotiation with the British. The meetings were always informal and I never gave them any paper, or had any paper with me when I met them. The only bit of paper I had was the bit they gave me with their six principles on it and we sat around in armchairs. I don't ever remember meeting them across a table, or in any kind of formal setting. It was important that we were a kind of contact point for them and that if they had a particular anxiety about a story that appeared, they could ring and we could meet. The meetings were not negotiating sessions. It was quite clear that the British never had any time for them and I don't think they were able to look beyond constitutional unionism, which also shaped their attitude to loyalism in some ways. But, I also think that when talking to the British our contacts with the Loyalists gave us an increment of confidence, which we used in the discussions. They were saying the Loyalists won't wear this and won't wear that, when we knew the opposite to be the case. There were people from the British side who would lecture us about the state of loyalism and we were supposed to see them as people whose job it was to understand loyalism, but it was obvious that they would never have them in their house and they didn't really understand them at all. I also don't think the British gave them any credit for trying to move beyond the one [constitutional] issue which divides the tribes. In relation to that issue, the Loyalists had the greatest hostility for the DUP, and frequently expressed how they thought that the DUP was prepared to fight to the last drop of their blood. They felt let down in working-class areas and that they had been isolated by their own. The fact that they were quite re-assured about the intentions of the Irish meant that they were able to continue working towards a ceasefire. If they had been completely excluded and marginalised I don't think that would have helped the ceasefire much. In fact, it was clear that the biggest single barrier to getting a ceasefire was the fear of the unknown, which was exacerbated by them being out in the cold. They were quite angry that we were giving them information and their own government wasn't, and I didn't keep much secret from them about the direction of discussions between the two governments.

When asked to describe how the Irish perceived Republicans in comparison to Loyalists, Finlay continued

> The Republicans are always on message, they always have a fallback position and they always have a technique of working towards that fallback

position. If you send one of them out of the room and bring in another, the procedure is entirely interchangeable. They never go into a television studio for an interview without being incredibly prepared and trained, and it would be the same when they attend meetings. The ice never cracks and the mask never drops. But for us, the consistent message was about an end to violence, about democracy, about the principle of consent, about mutual interest and practical concerns governing things such as North-South bodies etc. From beginning to end, we tried to be consistent with these messages, but importantly, the process of engagement required from the Irish government a commitment, where the Provos looked and felt like part of the solution and so therefore they were always at the table. The same impetus was not there with loyalism. One must also remember that loyalism would have been secondary in the very earliest stages because at that time it was not easy to open up a line of dialogue. A big weakness for the Loyalists, unlike Republicans, who were incredibly disciplined, was the problem of various factions. I could easily sit and agree something with Billy Hutchison and later David Adams, but their factions could as easily disagree and then there were factions within factions, which made it even harder still. That seriously weakened their position. They never had what you might call leadership freedom, nor were they ever able to operate on a carte blanche basis. They could never go into a room to make a deal secure in the knowledge that they could sell the deal when they got out. And this wasn't because of a lack of skill, but because of a lack of clout. I should also stress that although I had complete flexibility, this did not extend to dealing with text. I would relay messages and offer interpretations but I did not have the authority to negotiate directly.

Such authority resided much higher in the Dublin government and was exercised specifically by taioseach Albert Reynolds and through the Department of Foreign Affairs (DFA) by his deputy Dick Spring. For Spring, the main goal of the Irish was to get the IRA to stop violence in the hope that loyalism would follow:

> Our main aim was to get the PIRA to stop killing and we had certain intimations that if that happened then the Loyalists would respond in a very positive way. It was clear that the main threat to their community, as they saw it, was IRA violence, so if that dissipated it was expected that they would fall in line. The Loyalists felt vulnerable and I think they were quite surprised that we were open in approaching them. Although they were after assurances from us, we also wanted assurances from them about ending violence and were trying to find out what they wanted and needed. We saw the peace process as essentially a twin-track process, where talks with Unionists and Loyalists were operating in parallel to

talks with Nationalists and Republicans, and at some point it was envisaged that those parallel lines would meet. The meetings were tentative and there was a lack of confidence from either side on what the other wanted. The Loyalists wanted to know if we had anything to offer them, and at the same time we were a bit puzzled about whether they were serious in wanting to join the process. But it became clear to us quite quickly that these were genuine people, whose fundamental principles were far removed from obsessions about a united Ireland. Although the Unionist and Loyalist position tends to be motivated by a desire to protect the perception of what they have, and is ultimately defensive, the Loyalists were more flexible. But, there is always a difficulty with negotiating out of positions where you feel that anything you do is undermining the status quo from your point of view, and attempts to bring about resolution to an historical conflict which didn't really have a modern day context made it harder still. It is important that within a process of this kind that flexibility be built into talks and communications. This means a bit of constructive ambiguity is necessary, so, for example, the British could stand up and say something meant this and the Irish could stand up and say it meant that and the other parties could do the same. But somewhere in between all that there were common denominators that we all needed to adhere to and deal with.

Spring reiterated Finlay's argument that an absence of British engagement with unionism after the Anglo-Irish Agreement had damaging consequences, and stressed that the Irish were keen to avoid a similar occurrence:

You have to remember that the Unionists were always coming from the perception of being under threat. They felt threatened by the South, they felt threatened by various UK governments who probably would have been telling them privately that they write the cheques and that they would have to move whether they liked it or not, they were threatened by republicanism, and they were threatened by an American influence that they distrusted. But throughout, their fundamental stated position was that there was not going to be any change in Northern Ireland's status as part of the UK. We did work hard at getting the Loyalists' bedrock principles enshrined in the Joint Declaration and I think that was very important in order to win their confidence. We put many months of groundwork into working with them because we wanted to know that we weren't on a fools' errand and we certainly didn't want to be rebuffed or get a slap in the face. Of course, much of this had to be done on a 'hands-off' basis and in the end, there were nuances that had to be nuanced because I had to answer parliamentary questions. The process of engagement had to be kept fairly tight and indeed, it had no currency if we didn't keep it restricted to a tight group of people.

As with many others dealing with the Loyalists, for Spring, the Shankill bombing proved to be a particularly testing time:

> We felt that we were making good progress and then the Shankill bomb. In fact, the very day the bomb went off one of my closest allies was sitting in the drawing room of one of the top leaders in the DUP and at that time we were making progress by talking to them and opening lines of communication. Then the bomb went off and my colleague had to get out of that room and back to Dublin as fast as possible. That bomb set us back ten years and the opportunity to develop relations with the DUP never presented itself again. You can imagine the tensions at the next meeting when the Loyalists were saying to us 'You say that you are making progress and want to deal with us and meanwhile the IRA are blowing the heart out of our community'. We were absolutely stunned. I remember saying that one has to play with the deck of cards one is dealt and you could not say it was over because of such events, because that would be like saying because of the present controversy everyone stops trying to make peace. Ultimately if you're going to bring about a settlement, you have to talk to the guy who is at the other side of the gun, even though none of us in our political aspirations can ever say we're going to talk to the guys who are using the guns.

Three days after the Shankill bomb on 27 October 1993, Spring publicly announced the six principles that the Loyalists had asked for. The original principles, which were put together by the CLMC a few weeks earlier, and given firstly to Rev Roy Magee before being handed to Fergus Finlay (Finlay 1998: 200), were as follows:

1. There must be no diminution of Northern Ireland's position as an integral part of the United Kingdom whose paramount responsibility is the morale and physical well-being of all its' citizens.
2. There must be no dilution of the democratic procedure through which the rights self-determination of the people of Northern Ireland are guaranteed.
3. We defend the right of anyone or group to seek constitutional change by democratic, legitimate and peaceful means.
4. We recognise and respect the rights and aspirations of all who abide by the Law regardless of religious, national or political inclinations.
5. We are dedicated to a written Constitution and Bill of Rights for Northern Ireland wherein would be enshrined stringent safeguards for individuals, associations and minorities.
6. Structures should be devised whereby elected representatives, North and South, could work together, without interference in each others internal affairs, for the economic betterment and the fostering of good neighbourly relations between both parts of Ireland (McMichael 1999: 48).

However, those principles were somewhat modified by Spring in the 27 October announcement as

> First, the people living in Ireland, North and South, without coercion, without violence, should be free to determine their own future.
>
> Second, that freedom can be expressed in the development of new structures for the governing of Northern Ireland, for relationships between North and South, and for relationships between our two islands. For many of us, of course, the freedom to determine our own future by agreement should ideally lead to the possibility of unity on this island.
>
> Third, no agreement can be reached on respect of any change in the present status of Northern Ireland without the freely expressed consent of a majority of the people of Northern Ireland – free as I have said from coercion or violence.
>
> Fourth, let us once and for all accept here that if we talk about the freedom of Unionists to give their consent to constitutional change, we must also recognise the freedom of Unionists to withhold their consent from such change, unless and until they are persuaded by democratic political means only.
>
> Fifth, if we believe in consent as an integral part of any democratic approach to peace, we must be prepared at the right time and in the right circumstances to express our commitment to that consent in our fundamental law.
>
> Sixth, even in the aftermath of some of the most horrible crimes we have witnessed, we must be prepared to say to the men of violence that they *can* come to the negotiating table, that they *can* play a peaceful part in the development of Ireland's future – if only they would stop the killing and the maiming and the hurting. We *will* make a place, and we will develop structures, to bring in from the cold those who have lived in the shadow of their own terrorism – and we are prepared to begin that process the moment that a total cessation of violence makes it possible for us to do so.

Though the release of these principles was also timed to try and discourage Loyalist retaliation for the Shankill bomb, and although this intention failed, for the UVF's Number Two, Spring's declaration of the principles meant that 'we could go back to our people and say we basically got what we asked for', therefore helping to draw the Loyalists further into a political dialogue process. Spring's statement was taken as a public commitment to Loyalist concerns and evidence that they were being taken seriously at governmental level. It was also helpful in addressing wider Unionist perceptions that the South was only interested in republicanism.

The public communications process that the Irish were involved in was intensified as the peace process gained momentum, and produced a demand for speeches and statements from what became known as 'the script factory' within the Department of Foreign Affairs. The role of the 'script factory' was to facilitate the 'peace-speak of consensus and non-confrontation' (Delaney 2001: 335) and promote inclusive discourse (around for example, the three sets of relationships, parity of esteem and the principle of consent) which would shape the formulation and wording of documents produced (ibid.: 347). Eamon Delaney, who worked on the speeches and statements within the DFA, explains how the production of public commentary was carefully tailored to reach a specific audience (ibid.: 332) and held encoded, as well as more overt, explicitly focussed messages. In relation to the Unionists, the communications process was designed to draw unionism into the process through 'being co-opted, by language, soothed and seduced by the reasonable of the Irish' (ibid.: 336).

In an interview, Delaney stressed that the Irish interest in loyalism was not new to the peace process, but that dealing with loyalism was made problematic by its lack of electoral and communal support:

> The main thing was to get the IRA to declare a ceasefire and it was almost as if the Loyalists were secondary because their violence was reactive. But the Irish had taken an interest in loyalism for some time and this interest developed after the Anglo-Irish Agreement, when officials would travel to Lisburn and Carrickfergus to meet with Protestant clergymen who were meeting Loyalists and trying to find a way out of the impasse. These meetings took place in hotels and restaurants where the officials would not be recognised. But then, as the peace process came into focus, it was Republicans that became centre stage. The main problem was in dealing with the contradictory impulses of republicanism and loyalism, but there was also the further problem of the sophisticated political face of loyalism not being representative of loyalism generally; a difficulty which republicanism did not really have. There was some despair within the DFA early on that the Loyalists being met were not going to get a vote to match their profile. However, they welcomed the contact from the Irish who treated them with respect.

Delaney spoke further about how the DFA sought to calm the Loyalists and draw them further into the process:

> Certainly there had been a move away from the quite hostile rhetoric about unionism and loyalism which the Irish were responsible for in the early years of the 'Troubles'. Communication was measured and it was vital to balance what was being said to both sides. However, Republicans and Loyalists respond to communications very differently. For example,

Republicans like ambiguity because it suits their long term strategy and aim, whereas ambiguity frightens Unionists who want to know categorically that Northern Ireland will remain part of the UK and they want to be told it a thousand times. It was important then, to use Sean O hUiginn's expression [O hUiginn was a key architect within the Irish government for the drafting and wording of documents], to conceive of Northern Ireland as a house with two sets of foundations. Within the DFA, we would regularly draw from the romance of poetry to engage emotions and some of the phrases, for example 'turn our swords into ploughshares', became peace clichés. With the Loyalists, we looked at the strong connection with Flanders and the Somme, and references to the Ulster Division going over the top in 1916 did strike quite a resonant chord with them. The Loyalists also appreciated it when the Irish made critical comments about the IRA, which they did when moderate figures like Ray Smallwoods were murdered. The Irish were outraged by the killing of Smallwoods and they saw it as coming from a fear within republicanism about Loyalists emerging as a political force. This was appreciated by the Loyalists, who saw the Irish response in terms of their being valued as a meaningful political organisation.

When asked about how the approach of the Irish towards the Loyalists differed from the British approach, Delaney responded

> The British officialdom that I came into contact with contained upper class caricatures who were neither streetwise or affable towards Loyalists. Loyalists were often interested in football and Irish officials could relate to that, but there was never going to be any common interest from the British, which have an amorality that served them well in colonial times and continues to do so. There is a desire by the Irish to get on with people, which for the British isn't so important. The Irish like to talk and have a few pints and this kind of interaction goes back some time. It was clear that the Crown and the link with Britain was never going to have a great deal of sympathy for the grievances within working-class loyalism. Indeed, how could there be any understanding and empathy?

The isolated and more formalised approach of the British negotiating strategy, as Delaney saw it, was seen at times to contrast with the Irish approach, which Fergus Finlay described in this way:

> In all our negotiations with the British we would have endless meetings about bits of paper. There were bits of paper, there were non-bits of paper and there were bits of what was called 'angel paper', which is paper that doesn't exist unless you agree it does. Angel paper is when the British table something, but it has no existence at all unless each side agrees that

it should exist and if it's taken back at the end of a discussion, it just ceases to exist. This would happen quite a lot, with bits of text and drafts of paragraphs and proposals. The British have this reputation of being very pragmatic, interested only in outcomes, willing to do whatever is ever necessary and so on. But, my experience would have been precisely the opposite, that their psychology was one where form and process was more important than outcome. I was ticked off by a senior British official when it was discovered that I had been talking to Loyalists and who regarded this as a breach of faith, but they could not understand the Irish outrage when it emerged they had been talking secretly to the IRA. We thought that on a number of occasions their attitude resembled a colonial throwback.

Differences between the Irish and the British in the way that communications and talks were conducted and expressed were also highlighted by former press officer, Sean Duignan:

When the Irish reacted to the news that the British had been having secret talks with the IRA the British response was very much don't get hung up about these things because they happen, so let's move on and go forward. Both governments would also at times be briefing in contradiction to one another. We would be saying that there was a document on the table and the British would be saying there wasn't. Then without turning a hair, they would say that a document was now on the table and the switch didn't bother them at all. I also recall that minutes before we were to release the Joint Declaration in Downing Street, we heard from John Major's press officer that Major wanted to say in passing with the announcement of the document that he was a Unionist. This was resisted totally by Reynolds and was subsequently dropped. These differences were always there, but it is also important to remember that Reynolds and Major had a good working relationship. Reynolds used to say to Major that if he could deliver the Unionists he would take care of the Provos. At that time, James Molyneaux, who was leader of the Ulster Unionist Party, would not talk to us and we were finding it very difficult to establish contacts with official unionism.

Duignan, who was Reynolds' press officer, summarised Reynold's approach to the peace process in the following terms:

Reynolds was an impulsive and impetuous man who approached things from a business point of view and conducted his relations with people on that basis. He never stopped talking about the need for a deal and would say 'I'm a dealer, that's what I do'. He would apply a businessman's logic to the whole thing, which was talk sense to these guys [Republican and

Loyalist paramilitaries] and hopefully they would see sense as well. He had astonishing self-belief in the process. He would regularly say to John Major 'Trust me, I will look after this and I will warn you what is happening. I won't let you down and I will tell you if things are going off track. You've got to go along with me and stop listening to those MI5 people, who will screw you up and mess you around'. Before this period, if you had any kind of contact with paramilitaries, you were outside the pale completely. There are still many people who don't believe in the process because they see the paramilitaries as fascist murderers, who nobody should be talking to. Reynolds left a lot of the diplomatic stuff to the DFA and Dick Spring. He preferred to talk to people direct and sought to take personal control. He would be very secretive and the need-to-know basis was a big thing with him. He kept saying that somebody has to talk to these guys and that the reality is that we can't walk around them. It was always the deal, the deal, the deal.

For Reynolds, personal interaction was a key factor in how he dealt with participants in this peace process, and he provided this explanation of his strategy for bringing the Loyalists into the political arena:

I looked at the continuous policy which had been pursued by successive governments since 1969 and it was clear that the policy had not been very successful, so there was not much point in pursuing it. It was obvious that a different approach was required and I was prepared to take the risks necessary to change previous policy. From my first day as the new prime minister, I started to use the phrase 'Who is afraid of peace?' It was clear that first the violence had to stop so peace could be pursued, and to do this we had to change the situation so the two sides would stop using the military option to confront the problems. My objective then was to set out a formula for peace. If we could get the violence stopped, then we could proceed to the next stage, which was to try and bring people closer together and to reduce their fears of working with the other side. Through their dialogues, Hume and Adams had produced a document which was clearly one-sided in that it did not take into consideration the Unionist point of view. I told them that there was no chance of it being accepted and that John Major would have no confidence in me if I presented him with it. So, Robin Eames helped to provide me with the balance in terms of how the Protestant community would be likely to react and this was taken into account when the document was reworded. The six principles that the Loyalists had given was also added and this made the document more acceptable to John Major. Changes in emphasis on Hume-Adams within the document came from Alec Reid who had many meetings with Republicans, and Martin Mansergh, who was very aware of feelings within the Republican/Nationalist communities. My strategy in dealing with people is to sit with them face-to-face, and this was risky when talking to people who had been involved in some of the worst tragedies and murders that had taken place, but I was prepared to look at the possibility of finding another way. I told them that if we stayed and worked together we could bring about a better future. I spoke with the Loyalists about the six conditions they had drawn up, or the 'shopping list' as they described it, and said to them that if we stuck with those conditions we could proceed, but that it was better to leave the constitutional issue aside; that this would be an area we could return to later. I knew that if we started off with the constitutional issue, or became bogged down with it, it would be very difficult to proceed, and they agreed to this.

Duignan elaborated further on the Irish approach towards Republicans and Loyalists during the period from 1992 to 1994, when Reynolds was in office:

The Irish had a natural affinity and links to the Republican movement and although misguided, there would have been many who saw them as our separate brethren in the South, so we should concentrate on them. It was very difficult to understand the mindsets of the Loyalists and to start making contacts with them. There was a bit of a tunnel vision in that it was thought that if we could get the Republicans to stop then the Loyalists would follow. But Reynolds did not have any 'Republican baggage' and so was less concerned about the 'correct' way of doing things. It's hard to explain how astonishing this approach was in 1992 because to talk to the 'untouchables' was considered self-destructive. But Reynolds got his people to talk with them and there was a continual shuttling backwards and forwards to Belfast by people like Martin Mansergh and Dermot Nally. There was also deniability written into these contacts, so they could deny anything was going on. It was very secretive and we did not want to reveal our hand, because early on we would have been destroyed if it had come out that Reynolds had been talking to the top IRA Army Council people and our critics would have pushed the quite acceptable view that it was contemptuous for us to be talking to terrorists. Reynolds didn't consider the deal likely until the Loyalists were on board and he used Eames and Roy Magee a lot to help bring that about. Reynolds also met Gusty Spence and David Ervine privately.

According to Duignan's diaries, Reynolds met Spence and Ervine on 12 October 1994, the day before the CLMC announced the Loyalist ceasefire (Duignan 1996: 150). But, in Garland's biography of Spence, this meeting is said to have taken place two days after the ceasefire (Garland 2001: 291). Garland points out that Spence was highly aware of potential problems occurring if it had been leaked that the UVF had been seen talking with the

Irish before the ceasefire was announced, and so the meeting was delayed until after the ceasefire had been called (ibid.: 293). Reynolds provided his account of that meeting:

> Spence and Ervine came to the Berkeley Court Hotel in Dublin. You can drive in under the hotel to the car park and take the lift straight up without being easily detected. I told them both that I would meet them in an apartment at the top and that nobody would be likely to see us. I met them on my own and without security and we went through their list over a period of about three and a half hours. They left the hotel the same way afterwards. We addressed the various headings as we went along and I sought clarification from them about what certain things meant. I asked them what they thought was and was not achievable and I was very much guided by what their view of their own community was. Spence made it clear to me that there was no trust in the Protestant/Unionist side in relation to the IRA, and there was a fear that they would say something and not do it.

Reynold's desire to personalise the peace process and to take individual ownership of dealings as much as possible, caused some consternation within the DFA. He justified this action in the following way:

> I took full responsibility for everything I was doing. I couldn't keep the cabinet informed and if I did, any one leak was all that was needed to destroy the process. A leak would lead to a situation where the trust would go and I was working very much on the basis of trust. It was important that I deal with the military people in an honourable way, which I would not have been able to do if I was discussing everything with the cabinet. John Major had a divided cabinet which I could not afford to have. We worked on the basis that John Major would try to deliver the Unionists and I would work on the Republicans. I established a good relationship with Major and there was nobody trying to get one over on the other. I spoke to the Loyalists many times on the phone and even went to the Shankill to meet them. It was clear that one could not have a ceasefire from one side but not the other, and the Loyalists said that if I could get an IRA ceasefire, they would announce one six weeks later, which they did to the day. The Downing Street Declaration went through various drafts and in fact didn't go anywhere for some three or four months. We sat on it for a period of time to try and take some of the heat out of the process. Martin Mansergh was drafting on behalf of me and the Irish government, but I handled as much as I could on my own, because if it got out, then it was dead in the water. Confidentiality was vital and that's why many departmental officials did not know about it.

David Ervine of the PUP, who was one of the first Loyalists to have formal contact with the Irish government, gave this recollection of the meeting with Reynolds at the Berkeley Court Hotel:

> It was just Gusty and I present with Reynolds. From our point of view the issue of consent was fundamental. Prior to that meeting we had wanted to know if there were going to be any provisos around an IRA ceasefire and Reynolds laboured heavily that it would not be a three month ceasefire, or a test ceasefire of some kind. He said the ceasefire had to be full and complete, or it would be no good to him. Reynolds was keen to point out some of the conversations he had had with Republicans and some of the rejections he had made because they did have provisos. We were relatively calm about Reynolds as someone who didn't have lots of baggage, was a fixer more than a shaker, and who was ultimately a deal maker. He subsequently went on to pronounce the importance of consent and to ensure that unionism from our point of view was not left out. We were talking to people like Eames a lot at this time, but we also needed to speak to people with gravitas, in case those such as Eames were not giving us the whole picture. In other words, we needed to talk directly with people who could talk directly for the government. Bear in mind that we were constantly afraid and wanted touchstones. We were in unchartered waters in dealing with governments, intelligence services and senior civil servants, and were very much learning as we went along.

The Berkeley meeting had been preceded by a number of meetings with Finlay, and Ervine outlined the relevance and aims of those initial meetings for the Loyalists:

> What we indicated was that it was our intent to be positive, but that this would only be possible if there was integrity and openness about what we perceived may be going on. Our view, both from a potential negotiating position and from an emotional attitude, was that there was a special relationship between the Irish government and the IRA, and we made it clear that we were deeply distrustful of any such relationship and feared that we weren't seeing the whole picture. In fairness, the Irish were much more open with us than the British and they responded with incredulity to the suggestion that a secret deal was being done with the IRA. They were also much more diligent in their efforts to engage Loyalists than the British. Perhaps this was because Loyalists would be unlikely to bomb London, so the Irish had an imperative that perhaps the British did not have, and maybe that's why they were open to dialogue with us much earlier than the British. The Irish did try to reassure us, but we never listened to the opinion of an Irish minister or official without testing it in at least two or three other ways, in order as to validate what they were

saying. We always found the Irish easier to deal with and we found relationships with them much easier when negotiations did start. The Irish are much warmer and more open than the British. They are a smaller government with smaller mechanisms and there is greater latitude with their civil service compared to the British system, which is measured by the archetypal 'safe pair of hands'. There is no doubt that the Irish were more flexible in terms of attitude.

On the point of moving towards a Loyalist ceasefire at this time, Ervine added:

The first ceasefire that the loyalism created was in 1991 to facilitate the Brooke talks, but the Unionists just ignored it. What shocked everyone was that the ceasefire held against a backdrop of IRA bombings, which were clearly designed to destabilise it. At the end of that ceasefire, there was a clear view within the UVF that the war had to be escalated in order to bring it to an end and tragically that happened. But alongside that, people like me and Gusty Spence were asked to go and find out what was happening and that brought about a change within the UVF, who became receptive to exploring the options for peace. The formation of the CLMC meant that the 'ducks could be gathered in a row' and that there was a collective approach to strategy. There is also some evidence to suggest that the Loyalists would have created a ceasefire before the IRA, but for a number of killings in July 1994 [see also Taylor 1999: 231]. From that position, the IRA took the initiative by calling their ceasefire in the August, and because of that there was a strong perception that there was an agenda between the IRA and the British. We were asking at that point, what is going on here, what has been promised and what are the likely outcomes? But throughout, we still maintained that the fundamentals for us were the principles of consent and accountability.

The UDA's position, in contrast to the UVF which supported Ervine, Spence and Hutchinson in their efforts to engage directly with the Irish government, was one of opposition towards dialogue with the Irish, which meant relying on clergy figures to convey communications and positions. Gary McMichael described this relationship:

The forum for discussion involved Alec Reid on the Catholic side and Roy Magee and Archbishop Eames on the Protestant side. Monthly meetings were taking place and we would go and discuss issues. The clergy were continually trying to get us to engage with the SDLP and to sit down in a room with them, but this wasn't possible because the UDA were trying to kill people in the SDLP at that time. Loyalism at that point wasn't able to talk to nationalism, let alone republicanism. Basically, we were saying this is how we see things and Reid was saying well if I was speaking for nationalism this is how they would see it and this is what they would say. We would then convey our position towards that and so on. Eames was certainly concerned about the lack of engagement with unionism at a governmental level and tried to address that and it was Eames and Roy Magee who were talking with the Irish government on our behalf. There is always a problem in trusting someone else to argue your point, but these were the restrictions we were working under and we couldn't do much about it. Messages were being sent up to us and the UVF by Albert Reynolds. Although the UDA didn't want us to talk to Reynolds directly, they were happy for him articulate things, but such messages had to be deniable. The UDA were not happy with direct dialogue and it was the Irish who pushed that. The UDA was getting pulled into areas of dialogue and it didn't really want to be there, whereas the UVF was much more interested and pro-active. It was clear that things were going on and me and David Adams were pushing harder for dialogue internally between the UDA and the UVF. There was engagement through the Loyalist Political Alliance which involved three PUP and three UDP representatives, along with a senior member of the UDA and the UVF, which involved efforts to try and anticipate what might happen next and what the declaration we were moving towards might include. We were sharing some information about the signals we were picking up and communicating and were meeting in a place on the Woodvale part of the Shankill. That was where the six principles came from, and we discussed what the boundaries were and what would happen if any part of the process stepped outside of those boundaries. This was a serious contribution to the process and the six principles were really about drawing lines in the sand as far as we were concerned. When the Downing Street Declaration was announced in December 1993, we convinced the UDA to wait and see and not to reject it, which was a risk because it was received negatively within unionism. The fact that the paramilitaries did not reject it sent a clear signal to the governments that loyalism was serious and interested in the process.

The Joint Declaration (also called the Downing Street Declaration because of its announcement in London and providing the document with a British appeal) which was announced on 15 December 1993, reiterated that the British had 'no selfish strategic or economic interest', as Brooke had previously articulated in 1990, and sought to provide a framework which would facilitate a 'totality of relationships' through closer arrangements within Northern Ireland itself, between Northern Ireland and Dublin and between Dublin and the UK. The document consisted of 11 short sections which emphasised the importance of self-determination, the preservation of rights and identities and the need for an 'agreed Ireland' rather than unified Ireland (although as Delaney pointed out earlier in this chapter, an 'agreed Ireland' for the Irish *did* mean a unified Ireland). Archbishop Eames had been instrumental in drafting sections 6–8 of the document to meet Unionist/Loyalist concerns (Bew and Gillespie 1999: 37). Section 6 outlined the principle of consent by stressing that Irish unity could only come about if the majority of people in Northern Ireland wanted it and encouraged closer relations between the North and South. Section 7 called for 'open, frank and balanced' dialogue between the parties, and section 8 underscored the totality of relationships principle by pointing to the need for the introduction of institutions and structures that would work with areas of common interest. For the British, the document signalled a commitment to 'encourage, facilitate and enable' agreement 'through a process of dialogue and co-operation based on the full respect for the rights and identities of both traditions in Ireland'. But its role as a facilitator was qualified by the consent principle. Significantly, the document also stressed that dialogue and engagement within the process could only come about through 'exclusively peaceful methods' and that all participants would be expected to abide by the imperatives of the democratic process. The Joint Declaration therefore laid out a common set of principles which both governments adhered to and ended speculation that any consent principle would be on Republican terms, or that the British would act as 'persuaders' for a united Ireland (Hennessey 2000: 81). This, to some extent, was helpful in assuaging Unionist and Loyalist fears about the peace process being a 'pan-Nationalist' affair. As a starting point for expansive dialogue it also became the moment when moves towards an end to paramilitary violence started to take serious shape and within 10 months of its release, both Republicans and Loyalists had called ceasefires.

5
The Peace Process Part 2: Talks

Ceasefire

In the months after the Joint Declaration, Republicans and Unionists scrutinised the detail and potential ramifications of the document for signs of concession and movement. Republicans, in particular, sought clarification of the possible meanings and interpretations that the document could provide, and became embroiled with the British government about its significations and connotations. Although at first the British stressed that there would be no clarification, since this raised the possibility of pulling the specific conditions and terms of the document into increasingly ambiguous territory, the Northern Ireland Office (NIO) did generate a 21-page document in May of 1994 (which they described as a 'commentary') in response to a series of questions which Sinn Fein had put forward (Bew and Gillespie 1999: 53). The Irish further contributed to the clarification process by way of responding to a series of questions by Gary McMichael of the UDP, reiterating a commitment to democratic procedures and that there would be no coercion, or pressure, to push Northern Ireland into a united Ireland (ibid.: 55). The Irish response did little to ease Loyalist concerns about an Irish determination to create unification however, and the British government reiteration that its own position was based on 'no selfish or strategic or economic interest' towards Northern Ireland only compounded fears of isolation (McMichael 1999: 52). But, even against this backdrop of Unionist anxieties, there had been enough momentum and direction within political dialogues to convince the CLMC that it would be worth making a public announcement that if the IRA were to call a ceasefire, then its response would be correspondingly positive and that it would support a process of 'magnanimous dialogue' (Bew and Gillespie 1996: 58).

The development of a more constructive debate about the possibility of peace had been taking place between the UDP and the PUP for sometime. As David Adams of the UDP explained this dialogue:

> The PUP and the UDP had been meeting for at least eighteen months before the ceasefire of October 1994. We met once every two or three weeks on a regular basis. It was clear to us that the situation was a self-perpetuating mess and that it was going nowhere, so we began to discuss possible ways out of it. Then rumours began to fly about a possible IRA ceasefire, so the discussions shifted to the possibilities of what was happening there and how Loyalists should respond to that. There were senior Unionists who were trying to discourage the idea of loyalism calling a ceasefire, but there were others who were very supportive. We were making soundings to see if there were positive reactions and debating the implications of that and where to go next.

The UVF leadership had also been looking at moves away from the conflict and been engaged in discussions with a British intermediary given the name of 'the mountain climber', who was providing interpretations of Republican strategy. Believed to be working undercover as a Quaker and based in Derry, the UVF leadership considered the 'mountain climber' to be an MI5 operative. As the UVF's Number One described the role of the 'mountain climber':

> The 'mountain climber' was from MI5 and came from London to meet Republicans. He appeared as a Quaker, had a broad knowledge of the prison system and tended to work more with Republicans. He was a person we thought could 'open doors' and he was telling us to look closely at what Mitchel McLaughlin of Sinn Fein was saying, because his messages were the real sign of Sinn Fein's policy. We took his comments and interpreted them with other bits of information we were getting from the Nationalist community and the Catholic clergy. He tended to ask pointed questions and appeared sporadically, but he disappeared from the scene very quickly. What we were hearing made it clear that we needed to rethink IRA strategy. The 'mountain climber' seemed to assume the need for joint communications if the campaign were to be carried on. At this time, there were a number of bombs going off and we didn't want a phoney war, so we increased the ante to see if there was a desire to bring the thing to an end. For us, it was a black and white issue, it was either working for peace, or a winner takes all approach through war.

Though Loyalist paramilitaries continued to carry out violence, the IRA announced a 'complete cessation of military operations' on August 31 1994, but, just prior to this announcement, had sought to destabilise loyalism by murdering Ray Smallwoods, a key figure in its political thinking. This act, which seemed calculated to prevent the emergence of a Loyalist ceasefire, was seen as a cynical move by those working to that end. In response, the CLMC, contrary to the IRA's strategy of trying to disorientate loyalism, decided to intensify efforts to bring the Loyalist campaign to a conclusion. Just a few days after the IRA ceasefire, the CLMC produced a series of questions designed to assess the authenticity of the ceasefire and at the same time sought to impress upon both Republicans and the two governments that any secret deals which may have occurred to bring the ceasefire about would not be accepted as the basis for a progressive peace. Once again, the CLMC emphasised that the constitutional status of Northern Ireland should remain inextricably linked with the United Kingdom and that change could only come about through dialogue and agreement (ibid.: 68). Response to these concerns was taken as a reassurance that the Loyalists were serious enough players in the process, and enabled the CLMC to announce a Loyalist ceasefire on 13 October. The statement which the CLMC constructed and released to the media to announce the ceasefire stated as follows:

> After a widespread consultative process initiated by representations from the Ulster Democratic and Progressive Unionist parties, and after having received confirmation and guarantees in relation to Northern Ireland's constitutional position within the United Kingdom, as well as other assurances, and, in the belief that the democratically expressed wishes of the greater number of people in Northern Ireland will be respected and upheld, the CLMC will universally cease all operational hostilities as from 12 midnight on Thursday the 13 October 1994.
>
> The permanence of our ceasefire will be completely dependent upon the continued cessation of all Nationalist/Republican violence; the sole responsibility for a return to war lies with them.
>
> In the genuine hope that this peace will be permanent, we take the opportunity to pay homage to all our fighters, commandos and volunteers who have paid the supreme sacrifice. They did not die in vain. The Union is safe.
>
> In all sincerity, we offer to the loved ones of all innocent victims over the past 25 years, abject and true remorse. No words of ours will compensate for the intolerable suffering that have undergone during this conflict.
>
> Let us firmly resolve to respect our differing views of freedom, culture and aspiration and never again permit our political circumstances to degenerate into bloody warfare.
>
> (McMichael 1999: 66–7)

The UVF's Number One explained the build up to the statement and the events that helped to shape its formulation:

> The Joint Declaration caused major worries for us, but it also lead to a re-assessment of the inevitability of change. We knew that the policy of

consent was there and we also knew that although it was an outcome that nobody wanted, if all else failed, we could return to war. We had to convince ourselves that the IRA was serious and the war was over. We had to explain to audiences our convictions, but we also knew that until the IRA said it was over, neither could Loyalists. What led to the ceasefire was the unity of the CLMC and the ceasefire itself was managed with discipline. In a situation of change you have to educate people, but people also have to be told this is the best option and when push comes to shove, discipline is also needed. An army is not a democracy and its members have to be told what to do. Having said that, there was a broad consensus about the strategy and few people stepped outside that consensus. We often conducted the education programme in an informal manner in pubs and clubs, and there was a growing drift that brought people together. Although you always have dissidents, most were honourable to the ceasefire and realised that problems for us could only help the Provos. The escalation of violence had polluted society and reinforced a 'winner takes all' mentality, but there was a new focus from Republicans that we had to respond to and to ask where is this taking us? It was important that the CLMC spoke on behalf of the prisoners and it was they who agreed to the ceasefire statement. The ceasefire was a complex process representing many different organisations and there was intense consultation and debate. We also had to settle a number of different battles going on between the UVF, UDA and the Red Hand. The statement pressed all the right buttons at the right time. We used former prisoners doing cross-community work to give us feedback on Republicans and Alec Reid was also giving us feedback. Because of previous IRA attempts to scupper Loyalist ceasefires, we needed the IRA to go first and to consider what they were doing, and why they were doing it.

From the political perspective, David Ervine offered this analysis of the ceasefire and the factors that helped to bring it about:

Remember that the events that led to the ceasefire took place against a background where the British had declared no selfish or strategic or economic interest in Northern Ireland, and it was very difficult for Unionists to take something that was so obviously directed at the IRA. But even taking that into account, the Loyalists were considering a ceasefire before the IRA called one. One of the reasons this did not happen is because a number of people were murdered in the Loyalist community and the IRA did strange things like plant bombs in pubs, which it had not done for a long time. This was done, I think, to keep loyalism destabilised because the IRA had a vested interest in keeping it that way. The IRA had also killed Loyalists when they had been on ceasefire before and this derailed the capacity for Loyalists to go first.

But, even though they didn't call one, it was always a plus that it was being talked about because essentially those conversations amounted to them positioning themselves for that eventuality. Certainly as early as March of 1994, there were rumours that the IRA was going to call a ceasefire, but those rumours were also accompanied by a ceasefire being preceded by a 'big bang' and an awful lot of stuff, which again undermined the Loyalists taking the initiative. Against that, there was quite a bit of opposition to the CLMC which was internal to the UVF. The UDA had gone through a change of leadership and a lot of UVF volunteers thought them better left alone. They thought that getting into bed with the UDA was not a good idea. But the internal debates were well handled and when the ceasefire was called it contained all the necessary sentiments.

Ervine's assertion that Republicans had sought to destabilise Loyalist moves towards a ceasefire was also underlined by David Adams of the UDP, who commented:

The germs of the ceasefire statement had been around for some time before it was announced and there was no doubt that Republicans knew that was going on. The murder of Ray Smallwoods was a big factor in timing and development. Although it is widely believed that Smallwoods was murdered by the IRA as a last throw of the dice and an act of revenge before their ceasefire, I think its primary intention was to make sure that Loyalists didn't get a jump on the IRA by calling a ceasefire first. I think that this tactic was obvious, but it certainly didn't have the effect they wanted it to have, which was to destroy for a long time the possibility of a Loyalist ceasefire. You can imagine the kudos they would have been able to garner if they were sitting on a ceasefire and able to point at loyalism continuing to operate as per normal.

But, for Gary McMichael, the announcement of the ceasefire was a rushed affair, which had been determined by prisoners without attention to a supportive political strategy, or any idea of how political representatives would proceed to handle the situation after the ceasefire was called:

We knew that an IRA ceasefire was going to happen. For the six months beforehand, things started to change. We felt that the communication between the British and the Provos was reaching a point where a deal would be done and we were saying well if we can't stop that happening, we should at least be trying to influence it in some way. So we were trying to find out what all this would mean to us and at that point, I was involved in gathering information in order to see how we might manage the situation thereafter. But the problem with the Loyalist ceasefire was that it was taken out of our hands and there was no real commitment to the political front. The ceasefire was brought forward, even though we knew we had to wait a reasonable period of time to be sure of our standing. At the end, it accelerated over a few days because there was a meeting with the UDA's Inner Council and the UDA's prisoners in the Maze. There were also rumblings that the UVF was putting a lot of pressure on in terms of needing to make a decision. The UDA were more reluctant to make a decision, but they came out from a meeting with the prisoners saying we want a ceasefire and now. The nature of the UDA has always been that it has almost a sense of guilt in how it relates to prisoners and throughout the peace process this had a disproportionate importance and influence on decision-making. From having a lead position in the process after August, I was summoned to a meeting in north Belfast and was told it was going to happen on the Thursday, and this was on the Monday. The Inner Council of the UDA had already agreed with the UVF that it would happen on the Thursday and we hadn't been involved in that decision at all. I argued that they shouldn't do it because we weren't ready, and that once it had happened, all the focus was going to be on us. What I said was that we didn't have the tools, only to be told by the Inner Council that we would have to work with the tools we had and the decision had been made. From my point of view, it was a tactical issue and an emotional decision and I hadn't had a chance to get guarantees about anything, so we were going into it blind. We were going into a negotiations process without the necessary planning. We had no idea about how we were going to be involved, what the stages were, who else would be there, what we were going to talk about, what the safeguards against those not on ceasefire were, how to deal with that and so on. We didn't have answers to any of these questions and we didn't know what was going to happen next. We needed a longer lead up in order to put some pieces into play and have a definite strategy.

Because the ceasefire was announced within a few days of the decision being taken, it was therefore inevitable that the process of constructing the ceasefire statement would be a necessarily hurried and intense affair. As McMichael described this process:

> For the next three days after the decision was taken, myself and David Adams were working almost twenty-four hours a day with John White, Joe English, David Ervine, Billy Hutchinson, Hugh Smyth, Plum Smith, and Gusty Spence. We spoke about the management of it and how it would be delivered. We were basically living together in an office on the Shankill Road. There was a lot of argument about logistics and position playing, because you had two organisations who wanted to make sure

that nobody was seen to be in the lead and both organisations had enough problems with their own membership about what they were doing. Both within the UVF and the UDA there was grassroots dissent about prisoners dictating the pace and they felt that they had not been consulted, or involved in the decision. Gusty Spence and David Ervine were bringing a lot of wording to the table and Davey Adams, with me, did most of the wording on our side. We ended up with something like fifteen drafts. Every word was counted and re-written because of the need to balance what we were saying, namely that we are going into this with our eyes open and we are watching the enemy. There was also a lot of discussion about whether the ceasefire should be temporary, or open-ended, whether there should be an end to military hostilities, or operational activities, this kind of thing. Then there were discussions about internal discipline, which was a real fear. There were always concerns about whether we should be doing it, or whether we should be sitting back and saying nothing and let the IRA prove its intentions over time.

After the ceasefire was publicly announced, McMichael and Adams were given the task of trying to sell the positives of a ceasefire to the UDA membership and provide guidance on the meanings and intentions of the statement. McMichael continued:

After the ceasefire was announced, there were two main concerns. First, the need to have strong structures in each organisation and to make sure that people didn't jump ship, and if they did jump ship, they didn't take any hardware with them, as it were. And secondly, there had to be an extensive PR exercise throughout all of the different areas right down to the smallest company of people, where we would go through it all and try to allay fears. There were concerns about dancing to the IRA's tune and the need to keep options open. Looking back at it, I think if we had been ready and gone first with a Loyalist ceasefire it would have put pressure on the IRA to be more forthright in terms of a conflict resolution dimension. That, for us, was why the sentence about 'abject and true remorse' was included in the Loyalist statement. If you read through the statement what you will see at the start it is saying we are walking through an open door and we are doing it willingly, but at the same time, we've got principles and if this process doesn't abide by those principles, then we won't either. That's the business done and then it moves on to the sentiments. The 'abject and true remorse' bit was introduced by Gusty Spence, who used that language We knew that we had to speak to the victims and if this was about taking us out of the conflict, then the role that loyalism had played had to be recognised.

David Adams saw the ceasefire as a product of a momentum which the political Loyalists had been working on for some time, but he also remembers the significance of recognising victims in the statement:

> Regarding a ceasefire, things were always moving in that direction and for people like David Ervine, Gusty Spence, Gary, Ray and myself, as well as others, it was the natural position we were heading to. In a sense, the statement itself was the least of the problems, it was getting people to agree to the move, that was the problem. People talk a lot about the 'abject and true remorse' part, but remember that it was qualified with 'innocent victims'. Gusty wrote that. We were working on it right up to the last and were making final adjustments in line with the UVF and UDA leadership in the UVF place on the Shankill Road. I remember Gusty pointing to the 'abject and true remorse' comment and saying to me 'That's the one Davy, that's what they will hone in on', and he was right.

Exploratory dialogue

Although the Loyalists had been in contact with the Irish both directly and indirectly for some time, the British did not form any association with Loyalists until the ceasefire was about to be called. Once the ceasefire had been declared, and a period of time had passed which could be taken as a sign of credibility, the PUP and UDP were invited into a process of 'exploratory dialogue' with the British, which would pave the way for ministerial talks, and then entry to the inclusive talks which resulted in the Good Friday Agreement. Even though public statements from the British stressed that dialogue would not take place before a ceasefire had been called, a meeting did take place between senior NIO official Chris McCabe (Head of Political Affairs) and PUP/UDP representatives at a Quaker house near Queen's University a month before the ceasefire. Prior to the start of exploratory dialogue, the first meeting with McCabe occurred on 12 September 1994 and a second meeting followed the ceasefire on 1 December. At the first of the meetings McCabe met Hugh Smyth from the PUP and Gary McMichael from the UDP, and on the second occasion, McCabe met with Billy Hutchinson and David Ervine from the PUP and Joe English and Gary McMichael from the UDP. McCabe stressed that for the first meeting it was important not to engage with representatives from a paramilitary background. Hugh Smyth as Lord Mayor of Belfast had political and public credibility and Gary McMichael was 'clean' in terms of not having paramilitary baggage. However, another important and lesser known factor in this initial contact process is that between the first and second meeting, and before the Loyalist ceasefire was announced in October, Hugh Smyth, along with Chris McCabe, met privately with

Northern Ireland Secretary patrick mayhew and prime minister John Major to discuss the possibility of a Loyalist ceasefire. Smyth explained to Major and Mayhew that if McCabe were to meet other political representatives from the PUP and UDP and tell them what he had said at the first meeting with Smyth and McMichael present, then this would have a positive influence in bringing about a ceasefire. Major responded by asking McCabe to make contact with other Loyalist representatives and to support Smyth's request.

The main purpose of the first meeting was for McCabe to outline the 'bigger picture' of the British government's position and policy towards the peace process and to establish ground rules for continued dialogue. It was also a chance for McCabe to assess the convictions and intentions of the Loyalist participants and enabled both sides to consider the consequences of possible engagement. The second meeting effectively laid out the expectations for forthcoming exploratory dialogue and was used to impress on the Loyalists that the PUP and the UDP needed to work together within the dialogue process. Accompanied in both cases by an official from the political division of NIO, McCabe elaborated further on the purpose and background of the meetings:

> Those meetings which had been given heavy endorsement from Number Ten, began in September 1994 and exploratory dialogue commenced on 15 December. Roy Magee was asking us to meet them and was well briefed as to where they were at. I told them that I was there to hear what they had to say and to press them on the need for a ceasefire. The meeting was exploratory. We were not meeting the UVF or the UDA, but the PUP and the UDP, as we saw it. We wanted to make the point that the British government took them seriously. I had a bit of a script to work with, but I was also 'freewheeling'. Republicans had to wait three months after their ceasefire before they met officials, but we saw the Loyalists sooner. We were caught up in the momentum of the process and it was clear that the Loyalists did not want to be left behind. We may have given an indicative period about how long it would take before officials would meet them, but we made a working assumption that their progress towards a ceasefire was real. Questions from us were directed at the credibility and sustainability of a forthcoming ceasefire and the potential problems around that.

For Gary McMichael, the meetings with McCabe were an introduction to the expected order of moves and gestures which would be needed to facilitate entry to dialogue with British officials:

> When the Loyalists did not call a ceasefire immediately after the IRA ceasefire, they [the British] started to get nervous and then they were

keen to talk. We met over a period of about three months on and off. They would hear what we had to say and then take that back. There was no negotiation. At that point, we were trying to gather information and get assurances that would help facilitate a ceasefire, or at least no violence, and also to anticipate what the next steps were and what might be available in terms of involvement in the process.

The outcome of the meetings provided the necessary confidence that the British were seeking to set up the mechanisms for a process of exploratory dialogue with Republicans and Loyalists that would prepare the ground for ministerial meetings to begin in March 1995 (Republican teams did not formally take part in ministerial dialogue until some months later, although British minister Michael Ancram held secret meetings with Sinn Fein's Martin McGuinness in Derry on 10 May to open the way for NIO ministers to meet Sinn Fein representatives and for Gerry Adams to meet Northern Ireland Secretary Patrick Mayhew – which took place in Washington on 24 May – (Clarke and Johnston 2003: 233) and McGuinness together with Gerry Adams on 18 July 1995). The first exploratory dialogue meeting was with Republicans on 9 December 1994 and the Loyalists followed on 15 December. The PUP representatives included David Ervine, Billy Hutchinson, Hugh Smyth, Lindsay Robb and Jackie Mahood; the UDP representatives were Gary McMichael, John White, Tommy Kirkham, Joe English and David Adams (individuals from both these groups left the exploratory dialogue process and were replaced because of disagreement and/or organisational pressures). McCabe outlined the structure of the talks and gave this observation of the problems:

> Talks with Republicans were given the title XD [short for exploratory dialogue] and for the Loyalists it was LXD [Loyalist exploratory dialogue]. Essentially the purpose of both was talks about talks. It was important to deal with both sides equally and we offered them similar facilities and attention. We established two teams of officials, one to deal with Republicans and the other to deal with the Loyalists and officials at the talks contributed from their own areas of expertise, such as social/economic affairs, policing and security etc. When I met the Loyalist representatives before the dialogues started, the PUP and the UDP were happy to work together, but once LXD started they were more resistant to do so. They were distinctly different organisations and each wanted to be on a par with Sinn Fein. Each was worried about having their credibility undermined in the eyes of their respective organisations, and did not want to be seen as second fiddle to the other. Officials went through a briefing and de-briefing process before and after the meetings, and staff put out notes to experts within the NIO with requests for information about how to best address issues x, y and z, which were emerging. I also

continued to meet the Loyalists less formally while LXD was going on and was able to get a clearer sense of their mood and commitment from doing so. The meetings took place at Parliament Buildings and at the beginning there was a real fear amongst both Loyalists and Republicans that 'terms of engagement' had been agreed in advance and that dialogue would only be used to facilitate that end. Although the PUP and UDP wanted to work separately, we told them this was not possible and that there would be little hope of a positive outcome without collective action and presentation. Also, without them working together, there would have been an asymmetrical association which would have been harmful. Government teams were carefully picked for this and were well experienced at dealing with overt and confidential dialogue. The dialogue itself was about trying to see how everyone could move forward. It was about exploring positions and seeing what one side might do for the other, on both strategic and micro levels. We weren't trying to harmonise the two sides, but we did want to create a consensus and to give the smaller parties an influence in the development of that consensus. We moved through an agenda and set up workplans, but if something happened outside the talks we would also want to address that as well.

The agenda for XD/LXD worked on a rotation basis where participants would address economic and social problems and political development issues, before returning some weeks later to these themes in order to develop a more detailed examination of underlying tensions and concerns. Using position papers to provide the meetings with direction and purpose, the British gave overwhelming emphasis in the dialogues to criminality, decommissioning, policing and criminal justice issues. Since ending violence meant ending the structures which supported that violence, it is not surprising that security and criminality were issues that considerably preoccupied the British. In terms of how the oppositions of loyalism and republicanism dealt with the dialogues and how their approaches differed, McCabe explained:

> Exploratory dialogue with Sinn Fein was the big story and it had the advantage of being one, whereas the Loyalists had the disadvantage of being two. Sinn Fein had a 90-year-old history of politics and a co-ordinated approach. Everything was produced to deliver a product. Loyalists dissected information, but were more anecdotal in approach. It was more the experiences of those around the table, rather than a strategic approach. Indeed, Loyalists wanted us to go onto the streets to see what life was like, whereas, Sinn Fein were always seeing examples as symptomatic of a bigger issue. So, while for Loyalists issues were more localized, Republicans kept focussed on the bigger picture and probed

for strategic defects. Sinn Fein moved from strategic to tactical issues and they had a detailed vision attached to their strategy. They would also take tactical breaks in meetings in order to try and keep control of the pace. If we broke for lunch, unlike the Loyalists, who would have a laugh and a joke, Republicans would not eat with us, but would go away and consider their position. Meeting the Loyalists was like meeting a sophisticated set of community groups with political aspirations, whereas Republicans operated like high-level international diplomats. Republicans would greet you with courtesy, but they would also let you know that they knew what you had been doing recently, which was kind of unsettling. Sinn Fein has one personality and there was no point looking for splits or individual differences, because there weren't any. Republicans would often concentrate on books or correspondence in Irish, which were not available until the late 1980s, and street names that were in English, and point out how these examples raised 'parity of esteem' questions. A problem for the Loyalists was that they did not have strength and depth as a party and there were only a handful of political thinkers. Furthermore, Republicans thought that the British would move only after being nudged, which meant violence, but Loyalists were not able to exert any nudge and so in that sense they also lacked leverage.

The British team of five who conducted dialogue with the Loyalists was headed by Stephen Leach (now Director of Criminal Justice in the NIO), and included former Director of Policing and Security John Steele. Steele, who gave direction on policing and security, gave this summation of the purpose and aims of the dialogue:

> The talks were about us working with Republicans and Loyalists in parallel. We were talking about moving ahead after the ceasefires and building from that. There's no doubt that loyalism needed an acceptable face and the representatives we spoke to were providing that. We were clear in that we were trying to clear the ground and chart a path for negotiations involving ministers and to create substantive negotiations. The British worked to a highly formalized system, with a Chairman and comparative teams. I thought that the Loyalist leadership quickly assumed a reasonable attitude and I knew some of them from my time in control of the prisons before the peace process. I think that they had a certain amount of freedom and flexibility when dealing with us, unlike the Republicans, who had less freedom of movement. There was also an inherent assumption that if Republicans backed off, then Loyalists would follow. I recall that the PUP had a little more freedom than the UDP and that this was because the UDA were more suspicious of where this was going. Chris McCabe and Quentin Thomas [Chairman] were able

to spread support across both areas, but there was no doubt that the more senior team were dealing with Republicans. We made it clear the exploratory dialogue was not going to go on forever and that we had to be at the stage where ministers were prepared to meet reasonably quickly or it would not happen. It was important to have objectives clear in your mind and to try to understand the other's position – to see how your position can be maintained, whilst accommodating them, what movement is necessary and when to go for it. It's also a question of feeling on the day as well. Republicans were very conscious of the pace and for the need to control. I remember once when the Irish got in touch with us and said that Republicans were concerned about points a, b, and c etc. I went to a meeting with Mo Mowlam and others, and there was Gerry Kelly and others from the Republican side. I started saying to them 'We have heard from the Irish about the points you have and I think we can meet you on most of them.' That threw them completely. They started talking to each other in Irish and ended the meeting so that discussion could not go any further. I think that demonstrates that there were times when they not only expected resistance, but that they wanted it in order to exert some control.

Stephen Leach underlined the importance of crime and security issues and offered this overview of what the central concerns for the British aims were:

We very much wanted to push them down a road. The agenda was to push them as far as we could towards accepting that the disposal of all illegal weapons and explosives was essential for progress and to get them to seriously discuss the modalities of that process. The further we could get down that road, the more respectable it would make them to the other parties and the more likely that we could achieve inclusive talks. Our analysis was very much that we couldn't make progress without involving Sinn Fein and the Loyalists, but certainly Sinn Fein was the crucial element. The prize at the end of XD and LXD was meeting ministers and this was a big deal, both for Republicans and Loyalists. It was important to exert some discipline and the Loyalists were told that although they had declared a ceasefire, which was the prerequisite for dialogue, if there was a questionable incident, or an authorized paramilitary operation which took place, they would be out. We had a work programme and an underlying theory of the dialogue was that it would be used to develop relationships with them. Prisoners were very important to both Loyalists and Republicans and both were keen to get a deal for prisoners out of the dialogue. Alongside the exploratory dialogue, there were also private meetings with members of the teams on both sides. Actually, that was probably where more of the business tended to be done, since the formal meetings had a ritualistic character with less freedom for exploration.

Elaborating on his role as head of the LXD team, Leach continued:

> My job was to make sure we didn't deviate and what we said in one set of dialogues did not rebound on us in the other. We actually got the Loyalists to ministerial entry earlier than the Republicans, on about the eighth meeting, and this was a reflection of the good relationship we had established with them. We had raised the decommissioning issue and they had not rebuffed us in the way that Sinn Fein initially did. Republicans would say that the arms issue was way down the line, ahead of which was deprivation of the Nationalist people, Irish education and so on, but Loyalists were more willing to talk about arms. Although they didn't seem to mind being together, their respective organisations were pushing them to have separate dialogue. I did not want that and it would have been logistically very difficult to have separate discussions. Although there were antagonisms, both groups were also theoretically in the CLMC. I said that there would be no possibility of separate dialogue, but would respect the scope for them to express their identities and views within a single meeting, and that's how we got through it. Collectively there were about eight of them at the meetings.

Leach emphasised the necessity of procedures and discipline in the talks, and explained how Loyalists and Republicans responded differently to parameters which the British set:

> The PUP was a slightly better team in that they had worked out a bit what they were going to say beforehand. Both Ervine and Hutchinson were skilled performers, but I would also say that they benefited from being linked to a more unitary organisation, the UVF, where there was a single command structure they could relate to. The problem for Gary McMichael and Davey Adams is that the UDA is such a fissile organisation, without a single command structure, that you didn't always know where you were. Indeed, there was a moment when Michael Ancram had just entered, when a Loyalist was shot in Lisburn and I did take a strong line with Gary, that until that had been cleared up it was all off. As it turned out, that incident was looked into quite energetically and we were sufficiently satisfied about the UDA's commitment and its non-involvement. But one always saw the UDP as a bit of an artificial construct because both Gary and Davey were in a way semi-detached from the organisation. We kept trying to move them on prisoners and weapons throughout the talks and after each meeting we would issue a press release. It would be a fair account of what happened at the meeting, but we would obviously draft it in such a way that it both got our messages across and put a bit of pressure on the Loyalists. It was also important at that time to have clear and comprehensive documents on record as to where we were, so if the dialogue was misrepresented, we could point

to the documents and say that's not right and this is what we are doing. I think both Sinn Fein and the Loyalists were viewed as important because one had to recognise that if Loyalists were unhappy with what was happening and continued down a terrorist path, then that would destabilise any settlement. You couldn't have a stable ceasefire on the Republican side if Loyalists were continuing to shoot IRA men. Also, if you have the political representatives of unionism signed up but the paramilitaries opposed, then it's a very unstable situation. In terms of the politics, there was more of a priority placed on Sinn Fein for the obvious reason that Sinn Fein was going to get a significant portion of the votes in any Assembly and so therefore that had to be taken into account. With both sides we would say that there was an 'objective bar' that both had to come up to and the first to come up to that bar would be the first to benefit. And the first to do so was the Loyalists, so they were first to see Ancram.

Leach's observation about the problematic relationship between the UDA and the UDP was born out by David Adams' experiences with the organisation:

Generally speaking we did not have any significant problems with the leadership of the UDA and from my experience, leaders seldom give you problems. They might disagree, but I never sensed a personal grudge. The difficulty was always in being invited to address the troops on the ground. There were always people who just didn't see the picture at all. Some of the most difficult questions to answer are the most simplistic ones, the ones that are basically an opinion that you can't prove right or wrong, such as 'We're getting nothing out of this', or 'they're getting everything', or 'fucking Dublin are having a role in our affairs'. Where do you start on answering those kind of responses? Those meetings were always uncomfortable and were the ones where although you sense that you might have convinced the commander, he opted out of trying to convince his men and so sat silent. You worked on the basis that you didn't give people too much to bite off or chew at the one time. There were problems developing every day, but if they had been presented as like 'Oh and in a couple of years you will have to be thinking about disbanding the whole organisation and decommissioning', it would have blown the whole thing out of the water. It had to be incremental and it needed continual talks and the planting of seeds in peoples' minds, who might then come back to you with their ideas.

Gary McMichael supported this analysis and added:

Things were mostly driven by the circumstances of where republicanism was at. Loyalists had a fear of what their enemies were doing and would have been more pragmatic if there had been less uncertainties or hidden agendas. They were dealing with the desire to see the process being genuine and were prepared to contribute to that, but there were many uncertainties and questions which had been in play from when the process started. Don't forget that around the time of the ceasefires you had John Hume and Gerry Adams saying that they had created this process, which made it something very difficult for unionism to embrace. Most of the discussions were about what it was that couldn't be seen, but a big part of the problem was that they were listening to people in their community who were saying we are getting screwed, which made them jittery and reluctant to move ahead.

Because of the different relationship that existed between Adams, McMichael and the UDP on the one hand, and Ervine, Hutchinson and the PUP on the other, there was variation in the flexibility and confidence within the two groups towards the dialogue process. As David Ervine viewed this difference:

> The PUP and the UDP were talking to each other and to a degree were singing off the same hymn sheet. But the UDA and the UVF are structured differently and we very often found ourselves in a situation where, no matter how good these guys were, they would have to leave the room and consult somebody else, whereas we had latitude and could make decisions. This having to check was reflective of the different types of structure. The UDA has a series of autonomous regions, and that's a nightmare putting a single position together. But the UVF is an elitist organisation that is structured like the IRA, therefore there is an elitist group that makes decisions. The UVF is a politically attuned organisation and we just happened to be the vehicle for that. The problem for Gary McMichael and Davey Adams was that because of the autonomous regions, the opportunity for mischief-making was massive, the who was in line with who, that kind of stuff, and it was a nightmare for them both. Remember also that Billy Hutchinson served a double life sentence for the UVF and I served a sentence for possession of explosives, so you could argue that we were of them, and I think that made a substantial difference for us as well. We weren't always politicos.

Gary McMichael affirmed how the lack of a centralised command structure in the UDA created difficulties for supporting the process:

> At brigadier level there is a certain amount of leadership, but essentially they represent their own people. Also, because you tended to have large groups of people in an area who were not challenged by their leadership, so they were allowed to develop this intransigent view and it

became legitimised. Because the leaders wanted to play it safe, they wanted to keep in step with their own people, so you had this cyclical process where one reinforced the other. The leaders were going to the Inner Council meetings and we were giving them briefings about what we were doing in the process. They were telling us that they didn't like this and that, but they were letting it go ahead because it was the only game in town. But then they were going back to their own people and complaining to show that they weren't giving in to this or that. Because there was no attempt to change or develop opinion, you could predict what the membership was going to say and it never changed. Essentially they were taking their analysis from Paisley. It was the opposite with the UVF because there the leaders were actively involved in encouraging debate and they were interested in the process. The people who were taking things forward in the PUP would have been pretty well placed in the UVF, whereas we didn't have that. We were more separate.

This is not to say that the PUP were totally without problems themselves however, for there had been an attempt by two of its representatives, Lindsay Robb and Jackie Mahood, to use the talks process as a platform for declaring their support for UVF paramilitary Billy Wright (who would soon become the leader of the breakaway grouping the LVF). Stephen Leach explained how this intervention came about:

This was really the start of the LVF. The PUP had brought along Robb and Mahood and things were going okay, but then Robb said this is all very well, but I want to protest against the harassment of innocent Loyalists in Portadown, the mid-Ulster command of the UVF, and unless you give me a guarantee that the police will stop this, this meeting won't continue. Obviously, Hutchinson and Ervine did not know this was going to happen. I took a fairly hardline on this and said we would break for ten minutes where they could think about things and come back to me, but I was certainly not going to accept any ultimatum like that and said if that was their position, then we would end the meeting. They seemed to talk the two round and we completed the meeting, but I told Ervine that we didn't want any more of it, and I don't think they reappeared.

The intervention made by Robb and Mahood was an attempt to undermine Hutchinson and Ervine and caused a hostile reaction, as Ervine recalled:

Robb and Mahood read a statement and sabre-rattled on behalf of Billy Wright's group in Portadown, which we were very upset about. I didn't react to it at the time, but I certainly reacted to it afterwards. Mahood was also keen to talk to one civil servant on the potential exchange of guns for prisoners, which was totally alien to the UVF. Gary McMichael and Davey Adams were very angry that the talks were being used in this way and showed it. It looked like there was no control, and that Billy and myself were privy to it, which we were not. I went bonkers afterwards and told the UVF that it was the tail wagging the dog. It was certainly not the honourable or decent thing to do. The whole episode with Wright caused considerable problems. Before the ceasefire he was demanding that we call one quickly and soon after, he was demanding that the ceasefire end.

Although Robb and Lindsay's posturing caused problems, for David Adams of the UDP:

What saved the day then and prevented any long term damage between ourselves and the PUP guys, was the real strong personal friendships that had developed at that stage. Perhaps for Robb and Lindsay it was some attempt to keep their constituency on board by having a say and then things could continue, and perhaps if they could be kept on board by a simple embarrassment, then why not? But it was bounced on us and we were not happy about that. We knew enough about the PUP to see that they were far from happy with it either. But, if we hadn't had the relationship we did, then we would have felt very differently.

Apart from having to deal with such potentially disruptive and unsettling moments, the Loyalist representatives were also working to try and deliver a coherent and consistent approach to the talks in relation to a skilled British negotiating team, who were constantly trying to manoeuvre the Loyalists into particular positions. As Stephen Leach explained it:

If you're engaged in a process which is liable to be misrepresented, or to be the subject of suspicion, you need to have public documents which will lock down what your position is. When you are negotiating on sensitive issues and stretching the parties to go beyond what they are comfortable with, then it could be very damaging if what you were asking them to do is leaked, because their supporters will invariably tell them not to do it and to stop negotiations. We would open up the area with a candid discussion of the issues and realities as we saw them and try to stress how it's in all our interests to move forward, how we all want to achieve peace, but that we need this and this, inclusive government, understanding of the constitutional issues and so on. Then you would explain where that goes to from your perspective, what the commitments needed are. This might not work the first time, but you need to keep going at it on the basis of the relationship which has been established. You may also have to build in some 'negotiating fat', so you might say we want you to say x if x is the absolute minimum, but we would like you to say x and y because we think that's the only thing that will work. They may say both x and y and if they do, that's a success, but if they don't say both, then at least you have secured one move. It's not a good idea to incrementally reduce your requests because that gives the indication that each time you are pushed, you lower a bit more. We tended to make one move and say okay you say you can't do that, but we need to find a way forward here, our bottom line is x and we won't be moving from that. Also, one can make progress by developing linkages between areas. The Loyalists were keen on prisoner issues and we did make some moves on that, which in turn they would reciprocate elsewhere. At the start, it was very much about proving that the British government wanted to have a positive relationship with them and that through this route they would also be able to claim some benefits for themselves. They were very unaccustomed to negotiating on text and that was the less fruitful part of the interaction. I would draft a press release before the meeting and adjust it whilst the meeting was going on, before then asking them to agree what had happened prior to it being released. They were never entirely prepared to put their own views in it, so I would summarise their position and adjust the release accordingly. One should also remember that the representatives of the paramilitary organisations were very keen to stay in dialogue, otherwise it would suggest that the political side of it had failed. Representatives certainly didn't want to be seen walking out and looking bad.

The ability of the Loyalists to maintain the talks at a pace which suited them was not achieved with the same level of skill as was evident with Republicans, who would use stalling tactics to try and hold back the pace of development. Leach provided this example to illustrate the point:

There was a particular time when we put an offer to Republicans which they found too difficult because they saw it as moving forward too quickly, with risks for them. It was a formulation of what they would say about arms in order to meet Ancram in the move from XD to ministerial dialogue. So they engineered a bit of a stunt to take the pressure off. They claimed that a bug had been discovered in their room in Parliament Buildings, which was nonsense, but it was a way of getting them off the hook of responding to what we offered, whilst at the same time appearing to put us in the wrong.

Sir Quentin Thomas, who was the Chairman of exploratory dialogue and Political Director of the NIO, provided overarching control and guidance on the nature of talks and was a key government figure in the drafting of documents and text. Thomas provided this overview of the key issues and motivations which underpinned and sustained the talks:

> Ministers for some time beforehand had been making public statements that if paramilitaries did not come into this process then they were 'going to miss the bus'. We had developed the idea of a three-stranded approach and I remember writing a paper in 1991 talking about 'zones of convergence', working on how people might be brought together and what each strand would end up providing. It was obvious that if there was a government formed in Northern Ireland that both sides would have to be represented, but that it would not happen on a straight majority basis because that leads to one party rule forever, so it's just not tenable. The answer to this problem was the consent principle in all its dimensions. We were never going to accept a timescale for withdrawal as Hume and Adams wanted, because people may never consent to it and once you observe the consent principle that's all there is to it. As regards ending the violence, some people were saying that you have to get to the centre, the constitutional parties, and then pick up the more extreme ends later, whilst others would say it's pointless unless you bring the extremes in first. The truth is we wanted to do both. We wanted a comprehensive deal with the main players, but we also recognised that the people using violence were significant players. Sinn Fein were always much more significant than the Loyalists electorally, but I don't concede that the Loyalists were secondary in the sense that their involvement was part of the dynamic where Northern Ireland's future remained in the UK while the majority wanted it to. One of the worries in dealing with the Loyalists was how far they had standing within their movement and how far they had been licensed to go out and do the talking. They didn't necessarily have a secure power base and they weren't speaking as political leaders. If you talk to Martin McGuiness or Gerry Adams, they are chieftains of their movement and they have a real power base, so they are able to speak with authority. I think that in comparison to mainstream unionism, the Loyalists were more flexible, but then they didn't have an enormous constituency to worry about. Also, they didn't have highly developed political positions that had to be changed. They weren't going to have constituency chairmen giving them a hard time because they lacked a political infrastructure. The Loyalist project and unionism generally, was static in contrast to that of republicanism and nationalism. Their essential posture was that we are going to stop these people with their dynamic project. It seemed to me that their main focus was to defend the Union, and that sometimes could take a more brutal sectarian form. Their political programme, in so far as they had one, was essentially conservative in the sense that they didn't

want Northern Ireland's status within the Union to change. Most of the Unionists and Loyalists took their stand on the consent principle, but their essential programme was to hold the line.

Thomas put considerable emphasis on the use of text as being instrumental for progress and for helping to structure the mechanics of dialogue:

It was a process which was combined as one, with a comprehensive agenda and task list; comprehensive as meaning any serious player who was committed to constitutional methods only. This meant that it was very difficult to get a deal if you didn't look at everything. Nothing could be agreed until everything was agreed and there could be no partial agreement. This was a process about text, and what we called 'single text negotiation'. It started with Peter Brooke's statement on 26 March 1991 [when Brooke had put forward the need for a three-stranded relationship approach as a means for achieving an inclusive Agreement], which came from a shared text that had gone through various drafts and included subordinate clauses to appeal to mainstream unionism, nationalism and the Irish government. In fact, it was a text that had been traded with the participants, where what we did was show others, who would then want certain parts changed and so it would go round and round until it got to a point where we had an agreed text, or something very close to it. We got to the point where everyone in the process played the game by text. I had invented a working rule that if you had a text in play, which might be an agenda, or about rules of procedure, it might take a long time, but you would get a result with it. If you didn't have a piece of paper, you could talk until the cows come home, but nothing would ever be achieved. You can have a process of successive approximation, where you ask everybody to make a bit of paper which sets out the main issues as they see them, and then you can make a composite piece of paper which reflects all positions through different expressions. These variations allow you to play positions back to the participants and eventually create some agreement on the issues. Then you can have a bit of paper you can negotiate with. They would sometimes disagree with the way we put things, so we would then ask them how they would put it. Once there is some agreement on the main issues, you can then look for solutions, taking each in step and asking the players what they think the answer is. All the parties would attend to text with great care and it would focus them into doing business. Everyone was conscious that as long as there is clarity on the points of vital interest, then there was a margin of appreciation for a degree of constructive ambiguity. But that it would only be useful if there had come a point in the process which required what one might call a 'collusive' or, 'collective fudge'. This happened on the question of decommissioning, where if people had stood firm, the process would have ended. Quite a lot of the process did get stalemated on that issue and it occupied a central position far more than it should have done. If the British or the Unionists had stood on that position, and it was plain that it was not deliverable by Sinn Fein/IRA, then there would have been deadlock. So one has to find a form of words to try and carry it forward a bit further, which relied on a collective or constructive ambiguity. At the end, you have got to have an agenda that everyone has ownership of and where they can see that what they feel is being reflected. If you have a text, then on the whole, that is something in the bank. It might only necessarily be a building block, but each bit of paper marked a step forward.

On how he perceived the differences between Sinn Fein and Unionists generally, Thomas commented:

Sinn Fein had a clear script for everything. They had detailed positions for anything under the sun and they had thoroughly worked them through their movement. When there was a shift, they would have endless meetings and caucuses because they are terrified of a split. The Unionists only really had an essential position to defend the Union, whereas Sinn Fein had a policy on education, equal rights, fair employment, on women, on practically everything. This contrasts with the Ulster Unionist Party, whose technique is to play their cards close to their chest. We had a lot of stuff from them in negotiations that the real deal is at the end, so there was this sense of waiting to go down to the wire. That's okay up to a point, but it means that the chaps out in the constituency don't know what's going on. One of the reasons why later on the Good Friday Agreement did not 'bed down' for Unionists, is because there was no process of consensus-building, or of consultation going on. Since the Loyalists did not have a secure base, it's perhaps not surprising that they did not have a very clear position on most things. They did learn about text and the need to consult and to look reasonable, to engage and to move a bit, but that was the people at the table and there was always the risk that they were the 'front of house' people, who could become detached from those behind the scenes, within their respective movements.

For Thomas, the British government's strategy towards exploratory dialogue was one driven by the need to balance the corresponding fears and anxieties of Republicans and Unionists in such a way as to create a non-violent space, where the opposing sides would come to recognise the importance of communicating on the basis of dialogue only:

The only way of ending the violence was through securing a political settlement. A settlement is also the only effective way of delivering and sustaining the end of violence. Without that it was clear that there would be a vacuum which violence would fill. But unless there is a perception that there is political movement towards a settlement, then violence will develop and if the violence develops, this prevents negotiations. If players see that they are going to get their way through violence, there is no way they will want to engage in negotiations, and to get everyone to see that requires a whole lot of things. But a key part of a settlement is to deny people the belief that violence works, because as long as they do think that they will go on doing it. So it's a necessary pre-condition that such a belief is taken away. The second thing to do is to persuade people that although they can't win by violence, they can have a good chance of reaching their objectives without it. That requires a viable political process where all concerns are on the table and no issue is going to be ruled out and that agreement can be found, wherever it is. For the Unionists, this meant getting them out of the mindset where they were convinced the British had already agreed to a united Ireland and that it was part of a conspiracy started by the Anglo-Irish Agreement. And for Sinn Fein, it meant letting them know that they were not going to get a united Ireland tomorrow, but that the British were not the obstacle and that the consent principle can work for them as well as against them. The process was bedevilled by constant suspicions from both sides, each of who saw in every bit of prose a conspiracy. Sometimes, they would say you go and do this bit of work or put together this piece of text, but you knew if you did do that you would be invited into a trap because they would then accuse you of stitching them up and betraying them and this did happen.

But, for Gary McMichael, the main aim of the exploratory dialogue process was essentially about acclimatizing the parties to government officials and developing relations which would support the next stage, leading to ministerial talks:

> The exploratory dialogue process was essentially a quarantine period, where whatever we had talked about would take place within a twelve week period. It was reasonably clear to us that the talking was not really specifically directed, so we decided to talk about the issues we were interested in. We wanted to represent working class Loyalists, so we started talking about working class issues. We felt that they were talking to us as if we were terrorists and that what they were interested in was the equivalency between us and the IRA. We objected to that and stressed that we were there because we had a contribution to make and that there were issues which needed addressing after the guns were gone that effect people on the ground, so we need to talk about them now. They kept wanting to talk about guns and disarmament and about paramilitary

activity and what the tensions were, that kind of stuff. We wanted to talk about what was going on between them and the Provos, what processes there would be, how we could get involved, elections and that kind of thing. We started to get pissed off after a couple of meetings with them coming up with the same stuff, so we started to insist that future meetings would be about education and then agriculture and health issues, community development and so on. They were talking more about what we had to do to come into the political process, but we said no we are in the process, that we had political ideas and we wanted them to understand that. But it soon became clear that they had this set period of time which had to be fulfilled with dialogue and which was about acclimatising us to a point where they were prepared to talk about real issues and take us to the next level of credibility by meeting a minister. What I can say is that we did find it a totally new concept and it gave us some breathing space to discipline ourselves with what negotiation is about.

In relation, Billy Hutchinson of the PUP offered this interpretation of the exploratory dialogue process and the intersection of Loyalist requirements with those of the British government:

They were looking for closure on the paramilitaries, support for the process and for communities to make their own decisions without being threatened. We wanted an end to paramilitary violence, reform of the police, devolved government set up with power-sharing, the release of all political prisoners, to be rid of Articles 2 and 3 designed to give the Irish government jurisdiction over Northern Ireland's affairs, the principle of consent and we wanted the constitutional position of Northern Ireland to be in the hands of Northern Ireland. Although the Irish government were representing the views of nationalism, the British were saying they were representing nobody. We argued that they had an imperative to protect all citizens and especially to ensure that the rights of British citizens were safe. They were trying to resist being seen as Unionists, but we did not accept the idea that they were neutral. We were told that we would not get to see a minister until we had been through a 'decontamination' process and they got round that by putting up these civil service teams. Each team was suited to the kind of people they were talking to. But, it was a stalling and 'smoke and mirrors' process more than anything else, because we were really talking about issues which would then be brought to ministerial level. My argument was that if we were going to be engaged in negotiations with a minister, then it would be better to iron the issues out with the civil servants first, because it would be they who would be briefing him and shaping his stance anyway. Actually, it was more important to talk to the people who would be writing his brief and his papers. When we became involved at ministerial level, there was a continuum and the conversations carried on as before. As far as negotiations were concerned, if you only wanted two things you had to ask for ten, because the chances were that you would get at least two. You always ask for the things you know you are not going to get, and then hope is that you negotiate for the things you want, so you use the things you are not getting to negotiate the things that you want. That's what we tried to do.

Although the Loyalist exploratory dialogue faced relatively few obstructions from the Loyalists, there were major concerns about *The Frameworks Documents*, which sought to present a framework for agreement and was released by both governments in February 1995 (a month before the Loyalists got to meet British minister Michael Ancram). The two-part document underscored the central components of any Agreement by emphasising principles of self-determination, consent, democratic methods and respect for both traditions through parity of esteem and equality of opportunity (Bew and Gillespie 1999: 303–4). Part One of the document was honed from discussions that the British had been involved in about the internal arrangements of Northern Ireland and put forward the concept of an elected Assembly based on proportional representation to reflect the divergent political interests and constituencies in Northern Ireland. Part Two concentrated on the development and conduct of North–South relationships. The relationship between North and South was seen as mutually reinforcing in commitment to the above principles, with the Irish government supporting recommendations for change in the Irish constitution to facilitate the consent principle and structures of engagement (ibid.). The proposition of Irish involvement in the agreement process significantly alarmed Unionists however, particularly where there was talk of harmonising responsibilities in pursuit of common policy (Hennessey 2000: 95). Unionists saw such a move as legitimising 'a process whereby an all-Ireland government could evolve by stealth without a formal transfer of sovereignty from the United Kingdom to the Republic of Ireland' (ibid.: 96). Of the 58-section document, it was section 47 which made Unionists and Loyalists most fearful:

> In the event that devolved institutions in Northern Ireland ceased to operate, and direct rule from Westminster was reintroduced, the British Government agree that other arrangements would be made to implement the commitment to promote co-operation at all levels between the people, North and South, representing both traditions in Ireland, as agreed by the two Governments in the Joint Declaration, and to ensure that the co-operation that had been developed through the North/South body be maintained.

Chris McCabe explained that this created anxieties within unionism and Loyalism because of the perceived possibility that any government within Northern Ireland could be made deliberately unworkable by Republicans, creating a situation where Irish government involvement and interference in Northern Irish affairs would increase:

> The big concern for them was that they envisaged Republicans creating a plot where once an Assembly was up and running, Sinn Fein would engineer its collapse and then paragraph 47 would kick in. They wanted to know that in the event of it not working what steps both governments would take to ensure safety of the constitution. Their major worry was joint authority with Dublin. The Frameworks Document seriously alarmed them and they were convinced that the British government would try and push through change no matter what. They had major fears with the notion of harmonisation and through the three strands, saw that joint authority was a real possibility and liable to be used as a road to a united Ireland. In particular, I recall David Ervine being very condemning of the Frameworks Document. They had to have reassurance from John Major that their fears had no basis in fact, and that the British remained committed to the constitutional status of Northern Ireland until the majority decided different.

The concept of 'harmonisation' in the Frameworks Documents alarmed Unionists considerably and the Loyalists shared those concerns, but there was also an attempt to engage further with the possible connotations of the document and contentious issue of harmonising North/South relations. As McMichael put it:

> The concept of harmonisation was enough to create concerns, without looking at the details, but what we tried to do was to try and get underneath the surface a bit of what this could mean. We undertook to try and establish exactly what the nature of the relationships North and South were already, because even while we were talking about harmonisation and more equity, that could go from devolving elements of power to North/South bodies, which would have an influence in policy and development within Northern Ireland, something we would have difficulty with, to looking at how to harmonise the standards of culpability and traffic laws. We undertook a study with the EU commissioners in Belfast to try and establish how under the EU many of these actual bodies already existed and what the potential might be for them. We thought that there was scope to look at how you might facilitate better working relationships on the North-South basis, but through very practical means. The concept of North-South co-operation was not something that had to be alien. We knew that it had to be there somewhere and that it

was about trying to get something that would give people political cover, but that wouldn't be overtly political and could be benign. Harmonisation was a very poor choice of word and it there was always the problem that North/South harmonisation would be a Trojan Horse for joint rule.

Billy Hutchinson, like McMichael, indicated how the PUP was also trying to adopt a flexible approach to the Frameworks Documents and deal with the problem of harmonisation:

> Harmonisation was the dangerous part of the Frameworks Document because at that time we didn't know what it would deliver. But we knew that if an Assembly was up an running and that people were harmonising on things like health and education and the border that this would be a good thing. We argued about health and about airlifts to hospitals. That if you lived near the border you should go to the nearest hospital with the necessary expertise and that airlifts should be available for this between the two jurisdictions. People were worried about a united Ireland by stealth and people had stereotypical views about the Republic, which they saw as intent on having to harmonise up to Britain rather than the other way around. We argued that harmonisation need not be about that and that there were things happening on both sides of the border in, say, education which needed harmonising. People assumed that departments were going to be harmonised rather than actual pieces of work. But, for example, if Sinn Fein had a minister and they were going to the South and working with that government, there would always be Unionists that went along too. Similarly, if Unionists were meeting the British government, somebody from a Nationalist background would also go. It would have to be transparent and representatives from both traditions were to be present. One couldn't talk about harmonisation and then exclude one side from what was going on, so for us, we knew there would be the potential to shape that process. We didn't react immediately to the Frameworks Document because both David Ervine and I thought that it would be better if we took some time to negotiate with the UVF and others about what it could mean, what we would want in and what we would want out. We knew the Strand Two element and harmonisation was always going to cause trouble, but we decided to work through that rather than react immediately. Although we had the same concerns as other Unionist parties, our tactic for dealing with those concerns was different.

When asked how the UVF responded to Strand Two, Hutchinson said:

> The UVF were worried about where Strand Two fitted into the overall picture and how it would work in relation to Strands One and Three. Strand

One was more important to Strand Two because it was about how you would actually carry Strand Two out and it was evident that Unionists would be involved in Strand Two because of the principle of consent. The PUP felt that any problems here could be picked up at a later date and that we needed to manage this stuff rather than try and resolve it. We discussed with the UVF the most contentious aspects of Strand Two and worked with those concerns over time, but it was also important not to overplay the Strand Two element and underplay Strands One and Three. There were reassurances built in and we worked to try and bring those out. So we concentrated on Strand One and Strand Three and Tried to leave Strand Two until later, when anxieties were less pronounced.

Even though the Frameworks Documents caused great consternation for Loyalists (and indeed unionism generally) because of its perceived significance as a 'green document', there was still sufficient enough progress made by its representatives within the exploratory dialogue to gain access to a British minister, which is what happened on 22 March 1995.

Ministerial dialogue

The British minister who met the Loyalist representatives in March of 1995 was Michael Ancram. Beginning his involvement in Northern Ireland as under-secretary of state in 1993, Ancram progressed to become minister of state for Northern Ireland in 1994 (the post he occupied when he met the Loyalists). Ancram explained the initial stages of his relationship with the Loyalists:

When I arrived in Northern Ireland, nobody was speaking to anybody. The whole process had gone dead and I slowly built it up by going to party leaders at Westminster in order to get some dialogue going. It was official parties only at that stage, but the Loyalists were also making noises that they wanted to be involved. I think it was David Ervine who made the first approach, and Gary McMichael who made the second. When I met them my intention was two-fold. First, to try and examine how much of so-called loyalism was criminal, because there was a strong feeling that loyalism had grown out of the underworld in Belfast and I wanted to see how much of that was genuine and how much wasn't. And the second aim was to assess how much of what they were saying was equivalent to the IRA and whether there might be a balance to any dialogue. To begin with, I thought the Loyalists were fairly naïve. They had well prepared statements, but you had the feeling that they had taken a long time in preparing them. There wasn't an awful lot of give and take in the conversations, it was more about well prepared and cliched phrases. Some of the language was very esoteric and there was talk about understanding the psychology of the people. Their concerns were more about their community and how those communities were poorly represented. The argument they put to me was that official unionism could not represent them because they were working class and official unionism was middle-class. They were saying that if we wanted to talk to unionism we should talk to official unionism [the UUP], the DUP and to the Loyalists themselves. I thought that the Loyalists demonstrated the potential for a pluralist politics which had not existed before. Up until then, the politics of Northern Ireland had been based on whether you were Republican, Nationalist or Unionist, not whether you are left and right. When the Loyalists first appeared they were the first equivalent, if you like, of the Labour Party from the Protestant/Unionist side. They were about a kind of trades unions unionism, a street unionism, and I thought there was great merit in encouraging that. When we started talking to them, we were not talking to them as experienced politicians, but as people who were emerging from a background of paramilitarism.

Ancram saw the Loyalist approach as being underpinned not by the argument for constitutional change, but defence of the status quo:

Their Britishness was anti-Irish and was trying to maintain Protestant supremacy within Northern Ireland. That Britishness was therefore premised on not being dominated by the Catholic south. The paramilitary leaders were tough, but they didn't have any great burning fundamental philosophy which was driving them on. When you spoke to Adams or McGuiness, you felt they were driven by this fundamental vision, whereas for the Loyalist paramilitaries, the approach was generally negative and concerned with not being run by the South. They weren't there to say we are British and the flag, Queen and country is ours etc, but that they did not want to be under the control of Ireland. In that sense, their position was different from that of formal unionism.

Elaborating further about how the British envisaged the purpose and overall aim of talks at ministerial level, Ancram went on:

I was literally trying to draw people out to see where they were coming from and to see how far they were prepared to go. There was a little ground preparing necessary for this, but nothing like to the extent there was with Sinn Fein. With the Loyalists, things were done at a much lower key. I was continually trying to find out whether they were genuine, how much they represented a different brand of unionism, and whether they were able to provide greater 'wriggle room' than the Unionists. That was the assessment I had to make over a period of time. You could talk to those who were politically associated, but not with those who had guns on the table, under the table or outside the door. The moment you are faced with someone who has a gun and doesn't mind using it, you are immediately under duress and so you don't do that. Having said that, there were certain fictions that had to be used and accepted if you wanted the process to work. Some of the people the PUP and the UDP brought with them were UDA and UVF officers and we knew that.

Like Quentin Thomas, Ancram emphasised the creative use of diplomacy and wording to hold positions and keep the possibility for movement in play:

There were some points where you could not have ambiguity and there were others where you needed it. I suppose the best example of that, was that there could be no change until the majority in Northern Ireland wanted it. Republicans wanted that applied to the whole of Ireland and in the end we went for two referendums and both had to be positive. One gave the Unionists the majority in Northern Ireland, but by the definition of two votes North and South, it gave Republicans the majority of the whole of Ireland. Republicans were able to say this is the vote of the Irish people and the Unionists were able to say this is the vote of the people of Northern Ireland. It was the classic linguistic fudge, but it allowed both to positively use the consent principle and to move on.

Consistent with the view of British officials involved in the talks, Ancram emphasised the single-minded approach of Republicans and their commitment to national unity, which stood in contrast with unionism and loyalism:

Republicans were intense fundamentalists. For me, it wasn't a territorial form of terrorism they were engaged in, but a fundamentalist form of terrorism. If you talked to them about decommissioning, they would talk about holding sacred arms in trust for the people of Ireland and that they would never get rid of them, which you never got from the Loyalists. They would say how they were willing to die for their belief in the sanctity and integrity of the whole of the islands of Ireland and nothing less is sufficient. For Republicans, everything was based on the interim. We would say, well if you're not going to compromise on that, then how about an interim solution, where as long as we don't say five years, ten years and so on we could get round problems and that's what brought them round. That was the only way we were going to get them to sign up to anything. There was obviously not going to be a settlement which allowed for no other solution than Brits out. Apart from anything else, there was a constitutional imperative that nothing could happen unless the majority of people in Northern Ireland voted for it. But by talking about interims, they were able to tell their own people that they had not left that goal and that they would be looking for a solution to see them through this meeting period and then, eventually, they would be able to return to the pursuit of a united Ireland. If you had said to them that getting Stormont restored was the endgame, they would say no, it could only be an interim on the way to achieving the sanctity and integrity of the whole of the islands of Ireland. We never had that problem with the Loyalists.

Ancram talked further about the British approach to dialogue in relation to the release of documents, and particularly about how the parties reacted to the Frameworks Documents:

We were of course acutely aware of how the sides had different priorities. The Unionists wanted to talk about safeguards against home rule, demilitarisation and disarmament of the IRA. And of course, Republicans were not too keen on talking about any of these. The first real stage was the Downing Street Declaration and the second stage was known as the 'document of clarification'. The Republicans responded to the declaration by saying they didn't know what it meant and wanted clarification. We would not talk to them at that time because they were a terrorist organisation and there had been no ceasefire, but by a means of 'smoke and mirrors', a document of 'non-clarification' was produced. This was sent to the Irish government as a public document and stressed that if anybody thought such and such meant this or that, we would reassure those people that it meant something else and that was the way it was done. The third key element was the Frameworks Document, which was put together largely without consultation with the parties. Although the concept of harmonisation was not new and we had talked about it in relation to tourism, investment and so on, the Unionists got very concerned about the Assembly being set up with working groups between North and South. They were worried that in the event of an Assembly collapsing Dublin would take over, which was never the intention. Unfortunately, instead of being able to explain to Unionists quietly why it was a Unionist document, it was leaked in such a way that it was seen as a sell-out of unionism and by the time that had happened, it was very difficult to catch up again. It was a Unionist document because within it, the Irish government, for the first time, agreed to remove the constitutional imperative of a united Ireland. Because the media wrote the document up as being anti-Unionist, Republicans saw it as being rather helpful. Looking back this still causes me some amusement, because if anything, it was the other way round. However, the Loyalists were not as negative as the Unionists and were very keen to get into talks, so they produced responses with that in mind.

Formal negotiations with Republicans did not start officially until 27 July, but had been preceded by a meeting between Ancram and Northern Ireland Secretary Patrick Mayhew from the British government and Sinn Fein's Gerry Adams and Martin McGuinness in Derry on 18 July, just a few days prior to the formal announcement of Sinn Fein's entry to ministerial dialogue. Although Ancram commenced talks with the Loyalist teams some months before he met the Sinn Fein team, he had nevertheless met Martin McGuinness in advance of those talks and Sinn Fein's meeting with Mayhew took place before the Loyalists got to meet the Northern Ireland Secretary on 12 September 1995. What these moves indicate, is that even if the Loyalists were given precedence in terms of gaining earlier entry to ministerial dialogue, the British were more preoccupied with Republicans and convincing the Sinn Fein leadership of the benefits they could gain if they made conditional moves that satisfied the British criteria for dialogue to take place. British claims about not talking to Republicans while IRA violence continued also turned out to be false, since communications between both sides had been taking place for some time (Sinn Fein 1994).

Patrick Mayhew, who occupied the position of Northern Ireland Secretary from 1992–7, tended to reinforce the comments of Ancram and the British negotiating team when he spoke about the aims of the peace process and his experiences of loyalism:

> The British government was totally loyal to the principle of consent. There was no question of working more upon one set of enthusiasts rather than another. Both sides had to be persuaded on the consent principle. The key to everybody's actions and reactions in Northern Ireland is fear and what drove most people was the axis of fear for each side. For the Loyalists, there was also a real concern with fighting turf wars as there was in securing a long term political settlement. Our aim was to develop by all means we could a restoration of a state of affairs which would permit the return of devolved government, but this time on a fair basis. Previously, Westminster had turned its head and didn't want to know about the years of Stormont and we paid a price for that. So we were trying to establish a basis of confidence on all sides and to try to get them to see that their fears had little basis in fact.

Highlighting how the British expected loyalism to follow an IRA end to violence, Mayhew commented:

> Loyalist violence was essentially reactive to Republican violence. But there were also people in so-called loyalism who found it very convenient to have strong arms and to demonstrate them. It provided them with money and influence. My hope was that if the IRA showed that they had

abandoned violence and were seeking the political road to get to their objectives, then Loyalist violence would disband.

Mayhew then explained how the relationship between the Unionists and the Conservative Party impacted significantly on the potential for movement and scope in talks:

> Unionists only seem to talk to themselves and if you only talk to each other you find yourself repeating the same mantra and saying the same things. My recollection of the political climate on both sides was that because elected people had been given no real elected responsibilities, except perhaps for a parish council, they tended to make their name by repeating the same trusty old mantras time and time again and that has been how you gained a reputation as someone who was sound and reliable. Unionism was founded on the ethos of 'no surrender', but having said that, there was considerable sympathy in the Conservative Party, and indeed within sections of the greater part of the party, for the Unionist position. There had been a long association and for many influential Conservatives, maintaining the Union was a matter of great importance. The Conservative majority went down to zero in the last couple of years of John Major's administration and there was something like sixty very ardent Unionist sympathisers on our backbenches who were not going to wear anything very adventurous at all. The stumbling block within our administration was the refusal of the IRA to undertake any significant decommissioning. When Blair's government took over, he was able to risk bringing Sinn Fein into talks without any decommissioning of note, which is something we could not accept. We couldn't have done it because the Unionists could not accept it and the government would have fallen. During the latter years of John Major's administration, he would have been told by his own people to not make concessions to the Unionists because they have no majority, they're dependent on you and there are sixty very strong Unionists on the Conservative backbenches, who apart from anything else, want to postpone the onset of a general election because they're going to lose their seat. Because of that, Trimble and Molyneaux had no real scope for flexibility had they wanted to show it. Come the new government everything is different. Instead of a Unionist sympathising government, you now have a government whose official policy until a few years previously had been to encourage the unification of Ireland. So if you're going to cut any mustard with them, you have to show that you are prepared to be flexible and negotiate. It was also evident that amongst the political class in Northern Ireland, there are some extremely able people who don't want to spend the whole of their lives sniping away at direct rule and having no responsibilities worth speaking about.

They wanted to get their hands on the levers and it would be a much healthier position for Northern Ireland if they did.

For Mayhew, the Downing Street Declaration was the starting point in the process because it resulted in Dublin easing pressure on demands for constitutional control of Northern Ireland:

> Remember that the Republicans were being backed by Dublin, whereas the Unionists had no such backing and were to a large extent on their own. Also Dublin had some extremely sophisticated politicians and officials who were actively advancing the single Ireland objective. But, the Downing Street Declaration brought about an important shift. For one thing, American opinion about the Brits started to change and then it became about how many angles there were on the head of a pin. The sticking points for us revolved around the Irish claim for jurisdiction over the six counties, Article 3 of the Irish constitution, and whether they would or could put forward proposals for a referendum to have that repealed in certain circumstances. There was a large majority for abandoning that claim because we had made it clear that we had no selfish, strategic or economic interest in Northern Ireland and that if the majority wanted to end the partition of the UK in Northern Ireland then we would not stand in their way. Once that was accepted, there was room for some relaxation with Dublin and we worked quite well with them.

Talking about how he viewed the negotiation process with the parties and what strategies he favoured, Mayhew concluded:

> It is important to have a clear objective because then you can better survey the options open to you. I used to ask myself what was the biggest obstacle I have to overcome and I was always clear that that obstacle was fear, so it required all sorts of ways to try and diminish that fear. I used the metaphor of it being like trying to get a horse into a horsebox. If you just try and pull a horse into a box, you're not going to succeed. But if you walk round and round the horse starts to get familiar and then if you are lucky he's more likely to come up the ramp with you. Once he does that then get the ramp up quickly behind you. The bottom line was the continuation of UK rule whilst people wanted it. The key phrase I used the whole time was 'It needn't be like this', so you focussed on the point that it could be different and that endless patience would be required. It's no good working to quick timetables. We were always pushing of course, but suspicions were endless from the parties towards us and us towards them. The Unionists always thought that we were in cahoots with the Irish. But ultimately, it was a question of trying to maintain balance.

To further facilitate the possibility of substantive negotiations, the NIO published a 'Building Blocks' document in November 1995 which outlined the necessity of a twin-track approach to multi-party talks (launched publicly a few weeks later along with news that American senator George Mitchell would chair the talks). The twin-track approach, designed to make progress on decommissioning and politics in parallel, was emphasised in the document as based on talks which would be overseen by both governments, and an independent international body to develop and monitor the decommissioning process. The document also stressed that multi-party talks would depend on the parties working to create the necessary conditions for constructive and purposeful negotiations. Significantly, the introduction of an independent monitoring body which would 'advise on how illegal arms could be removed from the political equation' (Bew and Gillespie 1999: 314), also meant that decommissioning could be detached from the substance of political talks and so allow those talks to proceed without being anchored to the decommissioning problem (although a perceived British intransigence and preoccupation with this problem could only have helped those calling for retaliation against government bad faith inside the Republican movement).

The separation of decommissioning issues from political issues was further reinforced by The Mitchell Report released in January 1996, which stressed that if paramilitary organisations would not disarm in advance of talks, then some decommissioning should take place while talks were going on (Hennessey 2000: 100). The report also forwarded six principles which participants would be required to meet. First, political issues had to be addressed through democratic and peaceful means. Second, all paramilitary organisations should disarm. Third, any disarmament should meet the satisfaction of the independent monitoring commission. Fourth, parties should oppose the use of force to try and influence outcomes. Fifth, parties should abide by any agreement reached through the multi-party talks and should only use peaceful and democratic means to change any part of an agreement they don't agree with. And sixth, punishment killings and beatings had to stop (ibid.: 100–1).

Such initiatives were drawn up against a background of considerable hostility and resistance within unionism. The UUP leader James Molyneaux resigned in August 1995, having been accused by party colleagues of being too trusting of John Major (Hennessey 2000: 97). Molyneaux was replaced by David Trimble who used the Orange Order parade stand-off at Drumcree in July of that year to promote the image of his potential qualities as a strong and dependable leader. The stand-off between Orange marchers and the Catholic residents of the Garvaghy Road, along which the march attempted to pass, was also used by Loyalist paramilitary Billy Wright as a platform for resisting what he and others saw as an attack on the liberty and rights of the marchers. For Wright, this was indicative of a general erosion of Protestant culture that had been brought about by the policies and motivations of the peace process (Ryder and Kearney 2001: 155). The Drumcree episode and the actions of Wright, were seen to present evident dangers for derailing the peace process, which David Ervine tried to defuse when he visited Drumcree in order to address Unionists about how their actions would reinforce negative public perceptions of unionism in ways which republicanism and nationalism could only gain from. Ervine's appeal was shouted down and faced accusations from Wright about the UVF leadership and Ervine's own role in the peace process as contributing to undermine the Union and by association, Protestant culture in general (Sinnerton 2002: 189). Talking about the destabilising influence of Wright at this time, the UVF's Number One said:

> The only fracture throughout came from the Billy Wright episode. Essentially we saw it as a bogus and non-political attempt to destabilise loyalism. No doubt that the formation of the LVF, which Wright organised and supervised, was an attempt to split the UVF and represented a direct disobeying of orders. We went to Drumcree and heard that 'the balloon was going up' [an attempt to create civil war]. It was clear then that Wright was trying to form a dissident group and in August 1996, the Portadown UVF unit under Wright's control was disbanded. The mid-Ulster UVF had made it clear that the PUP did not reflect their views. When Wright released his statement which started with something like 'At a meeting today the UVF …' there had been no meeting and Wright had written his statement in a holding centre. He was told to revoke the statement and give another one where he gave full backing to the UVF leadership. He refused and was expelled. We arranged for a new mid-Ulster leadership and Wright made a phoney public show of strength, which the media focussed on. He was told to leave the country on pain of death, but held a rally in Portadown to show his defiance. But we know that he also intimidated people to go to that rally, knocking on doors to demand that people show. There is no doubt that Wright was trying to collapse the ceasefire. He had gained the support of Jackie Mahood and Lindsay Robb, who was arrested in Scotland trying to acquire guns. Wright was also there and it seems as though he set that up. Mahood came into our office and said that the ceasefire was over and that his task was to liaise with mid-Ulster and Billy Wright. We made it known at the time that the UVF was not responsible for this and Mahood was court-marshalled. Senior members of the UDA asked us to deal with the 'Wright problem', but Wright was also being supported by others like Willie McCrea of the DUP. His public profile made him difficult to deal with without risking an escalation.

PUP representative Billy Hutchinson also became involved in the Drumcree saga, and was asked by the UVF leadership to travel to Portadown and dissuade Billy Wright from becoming involved in the stand-off. Hutchinson explained the background to this action and how Wright's movements were exacerbating tensions at this time:

> Billy Wright had been involved in his own talks with the Irish government and was promised an amount of money to build a community centre in Portadown [see Finlay 1998: 205–8 for further verification of Wright talking to the Irish]. He was giving his okay to the Frameworks Document for this and I was tipped off by an Irish civil servant about the meetings. When I told the UVF leadership they thought it was nonsense, but when they questioned Wright about it, he told them it was true. That's when the whole relationship started going downhill. I told the Irish not to believe him because he was causing all sorts of problems and trying to undermine the peace process. His involvement in Drumcree caused particular concern and I was sent to Portadown to advise him to stop his involvement. We went to a house and I told him that that he was not going to be doing Paisley's work and that the PUP and the UVF were quite clear that the dispute was not for us. I told him it was the Orange Order's dispute and it was for them to get out of. He said that he had been in contact with the police and that Paisley was saying if the march was not allowed down the road then the UVF would kill all around them. That was when he let it be known that he was working to his own agenda. I told him that he should tell the policeman that this would not be the case and that it was very dangerous for him to be talking to a policeman in the first place, since UVF men don't talk to policemen, and especially, not on their own. But a couple of days later Wright did get involved, which was a direct disregard for UVF orders. He was certainly fucking everything up in mid-Ulster and was doing things at stages in the peace process to destabilise things. The formation of the LVF was the actual manifestation of these efforts. This also opened up a conduit for people who felt threatened by the UVF, especially if they were involved in drugs or criminal activity, and gave them somewhere to run to.

Against this backdrop of turbulence, dialogue continued to take place and Sinn Fein responded to the decommissioning question by releasing a document *Building a Permanent Peace* in January 1996, which stipulated that decommissioning would only be considered after a political settlement had been reached and within a broader context of 'demilitarisation' (meaning the reduction of British security and military apparatuses in Northern Ireland) (Bew and Gillespie 1999: 318). This was followed a few weeks later by a report *Paths to a Political Settlement in Ireland: Realities Principles and Requirements* produced by the Forum for Peace and Reconciliation in Dublin, which sought to provide an analysis of the underlying problems that sustained division in Northern Ireland and which laid out the principles which would support a lasting political settlement. The report, which resulted from submissions and contributions from a range of parties, significantly, did not include any recommendations from Unionists and Loyalists, who had not taken part in the FPR discussions (except for Roy Garland making a representation as an independent Unionist, which was opposed by the UUP). And, because the policy positions submitted lacked any substantive sense of the Unionist/Loyalist perspective on conflict, or its potential resolution, its value was seriously limited as an inclusive document (*Paths to a Political Settlement in Ireland* 1995). Irish involvement in resolving the Northern Ireland situation was still heavily resisted by Unionists and only four days after the FPR report was released, a PUP delegation visited taoiseach John Bruton (who had taken over from Albert Reynolds in December 1994) and Dick Spring to reiterate that Loyalists would not tolerate the Irish playing a role in the internal affairs of Northern Ireland (Bew and Gillespie 1999: 320).

The contacts and talks between the Loyalists and British government ministers were seen by some as part of a containment exercise, where representatives would be kept in the dialogue process so others could become similarly engaged. Gary McMicheal perceived the exercise this way:

> It was clear that these discussions were moving in the direction of some form of talks. Once we started to talk to Ancram, there was another agenda brought into play. Those talks often followed a holding pattern while the British were trying to sort out between the UUP, SDLP and Sinn Fein and working out the structures that would engage those parties in talks. Debates about mandates, elections and who would not talk ran through until late 1995 and we continued to be part of that holding pattern, whilst also getting closer and closer to relationships with other parties, who we started talking to. At the same time, there was a different level to these discussions taking place which was about how to structure the whole thing. Clinton came in 1995 and that changed things. It created a space for decisions to be made and the governments announced the twin-track process which would separate arms from politics, where there would be one process to deal with military issues and one process to deal with negotiations. But it took two years from the ceasefires to get everyone sitting in a room.

The talks were thrown into crisis however, when the IRA ended its ceasefire on 9 February 1996 with a bomb at Canary Wharf in London. Even though Gerry Adams reiterated a commitment to finding peace, the IRA embarked on a campaign of attempted bombings across London in the days that followed Canary Wharf. Republicans blamed Unionist and British government intransigence for the resumption of violence, although Adams continued to try and put distance between Sinn Fein and the IRA by talking about peace, while the IRA conducted activities in London. Albert Reynolds, who was no longer taoiseach at the time, provided some context to these events:

> John Major and I had an agreement that Sinn Fein would be brought into discussions and the next thing, I was gone. Then it started to look like they were not going to be brought into talks that soon and that the understanding they would, was not going to be upheld. The rules seemed to be changing and then the ceasefire collapsed with bombs in Canary Wharf. I was informed by my connections with the Army Council that the ceasefire would collapse and that this was imminent if John Major did not implement the agreement he had made with me about quickly bringing Sinn Fein into the talks process. I knew that the ceasefire was going to collapse two weeks before, and I sent a note to the British in the 'diplomatic bag' which was the only guarantee that it would reach the right people. And nothing happened.

Gary McMichael summarised some of the tensions within the Loyalist groupings when the IRA ceasefire ended:

> At that time, there was more heavy contact with Alex Reid, Gerry Reynolds and Ken Newell because that was the only way communication could be done. We had a very difficult time containing the UDA and the UVF because they were saying that as far as we're concerned, the people in England are British citizens the same as we are, so how can it be okay to kill people over there as long as it doesn't happen on your own turf. It was challenging their sense of loyalism and unionism and it was very difficult to dissuade them from retaliation. One of the big issues for us was that it was all very well for the IRA to have an infrastructure to be able to do that in Britain and therefore have maximum effect, but at the same time to reignite the conflict locally would be much more uncontrollable and there would be higher casualties which would make it harder to pull back from. In a similar way, the problem for Loyalists was that they didn't have the means to wage war anywhere else and so in order to react, they would have to react in Northern Ireland or else in the Republic, so there was some minor activity in the Republic to let off steam and buy time. We were doing our best to develop some degree of tolerance about what was happening, without reacting as we normally would have.

Intermediary Chris Hudson also highlighted the problems which Canary Wharf created within the UVF:

> When Canary Wharf happened there was a possibility that they were going to return to war. In response to this there was a co-ordinated

campaign to organise public demonstrations against the IRA's decision to end their ceasefire. There were 60,000 on the streets of Dublin and sustained applause when I spoke to the crowd and mentioned the discipline shown by the Loyalists in maintaining their ceasefires and not responding. They also took reassurance that Sinn Fein would be excluded from talks until the IRA re-instated their ceasefire. I said to them that it was important to hold the moral high ground and not descend into violence. Ervine was permanently on the airwaves saying how difficult it was and it was uncertain that the ceasefire would hold. In reality it was very difficult for them to hold that ceasefire because the IRA had ended theirs and so to all intents and purposes they were back at war. But I think there was a lot of internal discussion about the logistics of that and they knew the IRA had ended its ceasefire because it was in a weaker position. They had also made it clear previously that their ceasefire was not predicated so much on the IRA ceasefire, but whether the Union was safe. That was the main concern and the IRA ceasefire was secondary to that. To further help matters, Irish prime minister John Bruton made a statement on a visit to America which highlighted that the Irish were hostile to the IRA's decision to end its cessation. Even so, there was significant pressure for retaliation internally, which had to be met with considerable effort to dissuade such action.

The British reacted to the events of February by announcing a few weeks later that multi-party talks would begin by June 10. This announcement (the timing of which indicates it was a response to IRA violence) put forward a suggestion for 'proximity talks' where the design and agenda for multi-party talks would be worked out, along with a referendum within Northern Ireland and the Republic to measure public support for a negotiated settlement. The announcement also requested that the IRA re-instate its ceasefire as a pre-condition for talks and demonstrate a commitment to non-violence and democratic principles (Bew and Gillespie 1999: 326). Significantly, however, the British continued to maintain contact with Sinn Fein and NIO officials led by Quentin Thomas met Sinn Fein's Martin McGuinness only three weeks after the Canary Wharf bomb; where McGuinness, along with two other representatives, provided assurance that the party were still committed to pursuing a peace strategy (Clarke and Johnston 2003: 238).

The Loyalists reacted with anger to the IRA's resumption of violence, and splinter groups within the UVF and UFF ended their ceasefire in early March, with a threat to target known Republicans. The PUP also boycotted talks that had commenced at Stormont and the CLMC announced that although it would maintain an overall Loyalist ceasefire, it would retaliate against further IRA attacks. Against this uncertainty, the British sent a document *Ground Rules for Substantive All-Party Negotiations* to Northern Ireland parties in mid-March (one month before its public release) which made it clear that the Irish would play a joint role with the British in negotiations. The document, which was sent to parties while Unionist leaders were visiting America (ibid.: 327), was clearly distributed to try and gain some support before Unionist leaders returned and so acquire advance favour as the basis for formal talks. Just two months later, on 30 May, elections for all-party negotiations were held, allowing the 10 most successful parties to win seats for the negotiations Forum (ibid.: 329). Those parties would then take part in the negotiations which led to the Good Friday Agreement of 1998. The PUP and UDP acquired 3.5 per cent and 2.2 per cent of the vote respectively, and each gained two seats for entry to the Forum (Elliott and Flackes 1999: 580).

The inclusion of the PUP and the UDP had been an outcome manufactured partly by the British to make sure that Loyalists were at the table. Quentin Thomas explained how the electoral process was designed to facilitate the Loyalists' inclusion:

> The Unionists, and I think it was Paisley who said it first, said that they couldn't sit down with people who had blood on their hands and that the only reason we do work with these people up and down the country is because they are elected and we have to. This led to the idea that we should have an election to determine who should take part in the process and that also opened the door for the Loyalist parties to become engaged if they could get enough support to get some seats. We then devised a very purist electoral system, one merit of which was that nobody had advocated it, and that was extremely important because one could then avoid accusations of pushing the idea to protect specific interests. Although the condition was that violence would have to be abandoned, this system did allow the Loyalists to join the process and it allowed a number of relatively minor parties to get in as well.

Michael Ancram underlined the view that the Loyalists had to be included in the multi-party talks and added:

> In my mind it was absolutely imperative that we had the Loyalists in the talks. We developed this extraordinary election system from scratch to ensure that whatever happened, we got the two Loyalist parties in. I reckoned that a talks process that didn't have them in wouldn't be complete. We took the Unionist line that they had no mandate to talk and so created an electoral system that allowed them to talk. Through that system ten parties gained access.

The elections paved the way for the start of multi-party talks, which began at Stormont on 10 June as planned. But, it would not be until 10 April 1998 that agreement would be reached.

6
Towards the Good Friday Agreement

Multi-party talks

In his account of the how the Good Friday Agreement was achieved, the talks chairman Senator George Mitchell explained how the first year of multi-party talks was dominated by Unionist opposition to rules and procedure, with weeks given to debates about the potential meanings of rules, and with the DUP and UK Unionist Party (UKUP) walking out (and back in) the talks in protest at attempts to develop a 'sufficient consensus' around voting methods (Mitchell 1999: 46–63). For Mitchell, the DUP and UKUP were trying to undermine Trimble and the UUP and using the negotiations process to fuel 'intra-Unionist conflict' (ibid.: 85). While Sinn Fein remained outside the talks (because of the IRA ending its ceasefire), Unionists did little to develop an agenda in advance of Sinn Fein's possible inclusion (which occurred in September 1997), and on Sinn Fein's entry to the talks, the DUP and the UKUP walked out, not to return. Criticising Unionist (in)activity during the formative year of the talks, Gary McMichael commented:

> Everything was argued about and the parties even argued about what they should be talking about on any given day. We spent months and months listening to people argue about what the rules of negotiation should be, never mind the agenda. Then ground rules had to be set, which were the procedures through which we would discuss how decisions could be reached. It seemed as though for Unionists, everything had to be done to show that nothing had been imposed on us and which we had created. We couldn't reach agreement on anything because we spoke about procedures for a year. The Unionists were constantly talking about Sinn Fein not being allowed into the talks and that there would be no negotiations if they were there. We said that even without them there no negotiations were taking place. The DUP and the UKUP thought that we didn't deserve to be there and were just thugs in suits and because Sinn Fein weren't there, we were the next best thing as a target for their

attacks. We felt that we should be getting down to business and sorting out as much as we could before Republicans came into the process. We knew that Sinn Fein would resist moves towards a middle ground in the negotiations when they came in, and that they would try pulling things towards the more extreme positions. Essentially, what the parties did was hold up talks for Sinn Fein. We tried to get discussion moving on the issues we needed to talk about, but for the Unionist parties the main concern was decommissioning, which they could use to hit Sinn Fein and us over the head with. But, in Sinn Fein's absence, they didn't have any substantive talks about anything, and just spent time arguing over procedure. They failed to take advantage of an opportunity to make agreements which Sinn Fein would then have real problems trying to re-negotiate. I don't think they even expected Sinn Fein to appear at all, so short-sighted were they. And when Sinn Fein did come into the talks, the DUP and the UKUP walked out, so we started all over again. From then on, the DUP and the UKUP set about undermining the process from the outside and did so very successfully.

McMichael's account of the early stages of talks and the role of the Unionist parties was also reinforced by Billy Hutchinson:

People took the decision that they were going to posture and drag this thing out. There was a lot of stupidity and raising procedural issues that took forever to get to. It went from days to weeks to months, talking about the same thing, which was made overly technical in order to frustrate the process. People were trying to outdo each other by being more technical and devising words to frustrate movement. Then the contentions started about what this or that word meant; it was crazy. They were not interested in preparing themselves for Sinn Fein coming into talks and they were so arrogant that they thought it would never happen. Instead of striving to find a Unionist position which was agreed and shared, they just wasted a year. We were very naïve in terms of the politics and we thought that if people wanted peace, we could get it, but that wasn't the case. It was clear that there were people who did not want to move on. We were saying that there's no point the Shinners being outside of this process because if they're part of the problem, they have to be part of the solution, but many were not interested.

Senior NIO representative Stephen Leach further elaborated on the resistant stance taken by Unionists, by referring to their reaction towards those chairing discussions during the initial stages of multi-party talks:

We couldn't start the talks on the timetable set because the Unionists were unhappy about the independent chairs brought in for the talks. We had George Mitchell, a chief of the Canadian defence forces John De Chastelain, and former Finland prime minister Harri Holkeri sitting in Castle Buildings and the Unionists were saying they wouldn't go in. They were always unhappy with what they saw as internationalising the problem, because they saw that as classifying them with other problems around the world, such as with Israel. They saw themselves as having a particular validity to their case and so were opposed to having international chairs. On the other hand, Nationalists wanted international chairs. We certainly put it to the Unionists that Sinn Fein's inclusion was necessary because the trend of the talks was towards inclusivity and it was only going to work if we found the right geometry to include Sinn Fein, but there was resistance. The fact that the Unionists tried to slow things down is politically explicable, because their view was that the longer they deferred from substantive engagement, the longer the IRA had to prove that they had gone out of business and so the easier it would have been with the Unionist electorate.

In particular, the Unionists placed emphasis on the decommissioning of paramilitary weapons; an issue which, according to Gary McMichael, the Loyalists tried to resist:

We maintained our approach which was that primarily it's not the guns which are important, but the motivation behind them and the motivation to use them. We knew that it was an issue that had to be dealt with at some point, but by putting it ahead of everything else, it was actually made impossible to resolve. In order to change the language of the debate, we needed to look at the intentions of those who possessed the guns and that was why we adopted a 'no first strike' policy, which was essentially saying that yes, Loyalists are armed, but what we are saying to the Catholic community is that you have nothing to fear from our guns, provided we are not forced to defend ourselves. In other words, there will be no initiation of conflict, no initiation of violence and there will be no first strike.

However, trying to keep the Loyalists away from conflict proved to be especially difficult when the IRA carried on violence from the end of its ceasefire in February 1996 to the reinstatement of that ceasefire in July 1997 (Sinn Fein signed up to talks on 9 September 1997). Throughout that period, a spate of IRA bombs and attempted bombs threatened to derail the process and draw the Loyalists back into full-scale conflict. In June 1996, the IRA planted a bomb in Manchester which killed two small boys and injured 200 people, and attacked a British barrack in Germany with mortar bombs. The pressure for retaliation from the Loyalists created considerable problems for the PUP and UDP representatives, who were granted a visit to Downing

Street in July 1996 to meet John Major and voice their concerns. Describing that visit, McMichael said:

> To try and resist the pressure, we said to Ancram that we needed to be seen going to meet the prime minister so our people could see that we are being recognised at that level. It was as much about credibility and legitimacy as anything else, so wanting to see Major was in part cosmetic, but also necessary. We used that visit to try and find out where the boundaries were in the process and to make it known that the Loyalist ceasefire was close to collapse.

The situation was made worse still in October when the IRA exploded two bombs at Lisburn barracks in Northern Ireland, killing one soldier and injuring more than 30. Previously, the IRA had concentrated its attacks in England, but by now planting bombs in Northern Ireland itself, the conflict had been (re)localised, creating enormous pressure for retaliation from Loyalists. As McMichael explained:

> With the Lisburn bombing we felt that it was ending and we didn't think it possible to hold off things from there. Indeed, it gradually deteriorated to a point where there was no Loyalist ceasefire, and this was taking place whilst we were still involved in negotiations. Things were made worse by a lack of progress within talks and then the LVF entered the fray with a number of anonymous shootings. Certain things were allowed to happen by the UVF and the UDA, which were just enough to ease internal tension, but not enough to tilt the situation back over the edge. Remember that the default position of these organisations was if the IRA do things, we respond. We were saying that you have to let these guys isolate themselves and not get drawn into the conflict again, because that will mean two social enemies rather than one.

For David Adams, the IRA's actions were also seen as an attempt to destabilise the Loyalist ceasefire, which the UDP representatives used as an argument to try and dissuade retaliation:

> We thought that it was going to be impossible after Lisburn and nobody except the Provos had the capability of doing that. It was very touch and go. Loyalism being on ceasefire was not part of the IRA game plan. I would imagine that the IRA envisaged loyalism would come on board further down the line and that certainly they weren't happy about loyalism being on ceasefire in such a disciplined fashion. Indeed, they did everything they could to try and upset that. But in doing so, it became obvious where they were at and people became determined not to have their agenda set by anybody else, so that worked in our favour.

But, for Billy Hutchinson the PUP position was that the Lisburn bombing needed to be considered in the context of other 'failed' IRA activities and the probability that Sinn Fein would use the pressure from the bombings to re-engage with the negotiation process:

> There's no doubt that Canary Wharf and Lisburn alarmed people and this was because they obviously came off. The problem is that there is a tendency to get carried away with those that get all the headlines. We don't look at the ones that don't come off and it was clear that at that time there were quite a few that didn't. The IRA had a success rate of about twenty per cent, although it was the high profile targets which came off. But a lot of other things didn't and from that we knew that they weren't in a state of readiness and that they needed to work their way back into the process. I think also that a key factor at that time was the Americans. We had a relationship with the Americans who were funding these people and we knew that the Americans could shut them down, or at least make it difficult for them to get off the ground with a campaign. So we met very quickly and separately with the Irish and Americans. We told them not to be thinking that when a Blair government comes in and these people have done all of this, that the Prods are going to sit back and fold their arms, because they are not. They need to see some commitment from you in terms of wanting to withdraw. We started to get statements from people who were saying this is not the way to move forward and that democratic means was the only way ahead. Everyone knew that the Provos couldn't survive without support from America, and we had the American administration coming out against them, the Irish government coming out against them and Irish-America coming out against them, which were three very strong cards to play.

There was still some time to go before the IRA ended violence, however. Throughout 1997 until July, the IRA carried on planting bombs in Northern Ireland and England (one of the most public scares being at the Aintree Grand National in April), while Unionists and Loyalists failed to make progress in talks which remained deadlocked on decommissioning (Mitchell 1999: 103). This deadlock continued until the Conservative government was replaced by New Labour under Tony Blair in May. Then, the dynamic of the negotiations shifted. The British quickly met Sinn Fein, and impressed that a reinstatement of the IRA ceasefire would lead almost immediately to talks. Shortly after this meeting, the decommissioning problem was seen by the governments and Mitchell as better dealt with if isolated from the talks process and monitored through an Independent International Commission on Decommissioning. Along with this recommendation, the proposal also stressed a need for talks which focussed on the three-stranded relationships, to commence in September (ibid.: 104). The IRA recalled its ceasefire on 19 July, and Sinn Fein entered talks under the auspices of a commitment to democratic methods as laid down by the Mitchell Principles on 9 September. Blair quickly tried to develop momentum in the negotiations and formed a productive relationship with Bertie Ahern, who succeeded Albert Reynolds as Fianna Fail leader in 1994 and defeated John Bruton to be elected as taoiseach in June 1997. For Billy Hutchinson, Blair's arrival provided a different political engagement with the peace process, which was less ideologically structured than the approach which had prevailed under the Conservatives:

> Blair would have done anything to get this problem resolved. His administration came in with a different attitude and a commitment to getting a deal. Also important, is that in Blair, Ahern and Clinton, you had three people from similar backgrounds in terms of their politics, which was centre or left of centre, whereas the Tories, who were right of centre were going to see it differently. With the Tories it seemed as though every decision they took was based on ideology, rather than let's solve this problem. Blair, Ahern and Clinton had different attitudes because they were individuals rather than party animals. They saw themselves as world leaders and were going to use their personalities to deal with the issues rather than their political party's ideology. It was always right let's get on with this.

Gary McMichael's impression of Blair's approach, in contrast to the Conservatives, was compatible with Hutchinson:

> His entrance was a signal that we had to move forward and generally this was accommodated. He tended not to deal with detail and let other's deal with that. He worked more as a touchstone, trying to establish where things were set, whether you were in or out, whether you were moving in the right direction, that kind of thing. He didn't want to get too involved in the minutiae of negotiations. But in comparison, I would have trusted the Conservative government more because you knew they were trying to screw you. They had a more honest position and you knew where their values were. With the Labour government, things were more liberal. There were good and bad dimensions to that and it meant that they could exert more influence and be more openminded. But there was also more chance, because they were being pragmatic, that they would undermine you because they were listening to everyone else. It's more comfortable to be faced with someone who is more ideologically rigid because at least you know the boundaries in which you're working.

As David Adams also recalled with the Conservative government:

> They were like ourselves in that they liked everything down in black and white, whereas the Irish were always prepared for ambiguity. When Blair arrived the British began to become more Irish in their approach as the process went on.

Sinn Fein's entry to the talks coincided with the DUP and UKUP's exit, but the Loyalist parties stressed the need to keep the talks going and to move on (ibid.: 110). This left the UUP and the Loyalist parties as the representing voices of unionism in the talks, but facing hostility and criticism from the DUP and UKUP, who now tried to destabilise progress from outside the discussions. Although documents were produced in the initial stages of these talks which sought to address ways of proceeding in relation to constitutional issues, the nature and extent of new arrangements and rights and safeguards (ibid.: 121), it was the one-page document *Propositions on Heads of Agreement* introduced by the British government in January 1998, which provided the framework for a co-ordinated approach to a talks agenda. The document once more reinforced a commitment to the consent principle and advocated change to Articles 2 and 3 which gave the Irish a constitutional claim on Northern Ireland. It also stipulated that there would be an Assembly with devolved powers to six departments and pushed for a Council of the Islands in order to oversee the totality of relationships, and a council to facilitate North–South cooperation, which would oversee Assembly decisions in the context of agreement between the British and Irish (Hennessey 2000: 115–16). As a counterbalance to the document and its British representations, the Irish also produced a document which argued for 'balanced constitutional change', with an Assembly suggested as a possible rather than necessary component of agreement (ibid.). The document was an attempt to underscore the role of the Irish by framing recommendations in terms of an all-Ireland context and collective responsibility (ibid.). Out of these two positions, the British and Irish moved towards a single Propositions document which presented the components of agreement (the substance faced intense contestation), and set out the talks agenda. As such, it enabled inclusive negotiations to begin.

But against these developments, violence from Loyalists (the UFF in particular) and Republicans continued and a series of what appeared to be tit-for-tat killings and attacks undermined the legitimacy of political representation from both sides. Because the continuation of violence breached the Mitchell Principles, which required a commitment to peaceful and democratic means, the UDP were expelled from the talks on 26 January (to return a month later). Gary McMichael explained the background to the expulsion:

> There was continued intransigence in the talks, especially between the UUP and the SDLP and the paramilitaries said fuck this, this is going

nowhere, so they got involved in a spate of murders, as did the IRA. That's why Sinn Fein was booted out of the talks on our return [Sinn Fein were temporarily expelled from 20 February]. Bear in mind that we always had a tiger by the tail. There weren't many moments when people were feeling optimistic and you are dealing with organisations that lack political maturity. It wasn't that there was no capacity there, but that that their most instinctive form of expression was violence and they were under pressure to return to type. The Chief Constable in Northern Ireland was saying that the UDA were behind killings and we were saying they weren't, because that was what they were telling us. It got to a point where I argued with my colleagues to the leadership, that it had become standard to have a no claim, no blame policy, where anyone can do anything they want as long as they don't admit it. We were saying that we should be getting beyond this and that if this was going on and you want to pull back, you need to show your sincerity and try to rebuild trust. You need to admit it and say what you're going to do next. And we got them to put a statement out admitting their involvement in three killings and to say that it was now over and they were committed to making this work, if the space is there for that to happen. When they made the statement, we were in London at the talks and were attacked by the bigger parties, in particular, for being associated with these people. Our response was that we said at the start that we had to be there because we do bring the political voice of Loyalist paramilitarism to the table, and that we were there on the basis of an electoral mandate. We were elected to the talks, so we said how can you sanction us and choose who we represent depending on what suits your morals? These were people who had done nothing to stop violence, while we had been riding the storm and been in a lion's den day in, day out, trying to convince these people to maintain a democratic commitment and not be involved in violence. And when they did slide off the path, we told them to own up, when we could have just denied it. So we went. We knew it was going to be for a fixed period, so we kept going, but things got worse. Once we got thrown out, the UDA were saying what good are you to us now? So we had less control. Being expelled actually put us in a weaker position to be able to maintain control.

Importantly though, another development had occurred which also played some part in moving the UDA Loyalists back towards a ceasefire. A few weeks previous to the UDP's expulsion on 7 January, Northern Ireland Secretary Mo Mowlam had visited Loyalist prisoners in the Maze prison in order to convince them to stay with the process. In her autobiography, Mowlam recalls McMichael travelling to London to ask her to visit the Maze to try and instil come confidence in the prisoners about where the process was heading (Mowlam 2002: 183). Mowlam also acknowledges that the symbolism of this act was helpful in terms of conveying to the prisoners that they were a serious consideration in any future Agreement (ibid.: 187). However, McMichael contends that Mowlam's visit was her idea and not at the request of the UDP:

> The prisoners were saying we have backed all these things and have said do what you need to do, but the politicians are playing games. They saw it as a sham and said we're not supporting it anymore and this created a crisis. We tried to get them to change their mind, but they refused. You had five or six strong personalities in the prison and you had a number of others who tended to react quickly in saying the same thing. It made us powerless and we needed to articulate these concerns, so we asked for a meeting with Mo Mowlam and we went to London to meet her. We wanted to explain why this was happening, what the implications were for us and that the next step might be more physical. We also told her that it was not a stunt, that the power sits with those in the Maze and that we were helpless. We weren't asking for anything except to be saying things that might be assuring, like we believed in the process and that it needed to go forward. Then she said why don't I go and talk to them. We didn't ask for it. It was her idea and we were shocked but she went about two or three days later. We left the meeting and told everybody. Because we didn't want her to backtrack, we went and announced it so she had to go through with it. She told the prisoners she was not messing about, that the British were not backing Republicans, that the principle of consent was central, what the conditions of a settlement were, those kinds of things. It wasn't the substance of what she said, but the recognition of the huge risk she had taken. First of all, it pumped them up because it was her going to them, they had made this happen, but from then on the onus was on them. She was asking for extra time and they couldn't turn their back on the gesture she had made.

Mowlam's visit had not been enough to stop the violence entirely, even though she also spoke to UVF prisoners when in the Maze. And, even when the UDA stated that it had restored its ceasefire on 23 January, just a few days before the UDP were suspended from talks, the LVF continued to carry out sporadic acts of violence up until a few weeks before the Agreement in April.

Final stage negotiations

The Strand Two element of negotiations was by far the most contentious for Unionists and Loyalists, since it was seen as the path to further Irish involvement in Northern Ireland's affairs (ibid.: 126–39). Although the Loyalists were more comfortable with the idea of 'co-determination' (ibid.: 160), the UDP sought an agreed position from Unionists on the role of 'implementation bodies' (ibid.: 160), which raised fears of decisions being made outside an Assembly, as part of an imperative to create a united Ireland by stealth. A series of position papers were created and revised as negotiations took shape. While Strand One discussions attended to how decisions would be taken in a new Assembly, Strand Two concentrated on who would create North–South institutions and the extent of their powers to intervene in Northern Ireland's affairs (Mitchell 1999: 143).

Against the complexities of the mechanisms and structures of the negotiations, parties were jockeying for influence and trying to develop positions which would build negotiating advantage for them. For Billy Hutchinson, this led to the bigger parties striving to augment their influence, which left the smaller parties in a situation of having to work closely so as to not be marginalised:

> The difficulty was that the Unionists wanted to make sure that they wouldn't be shafted, so they were continually looking at the process in terms of what they didn't want, rather than what the Unionist community needed. The PUP, the UDP, the Women's Coalition and the Labour grouping were all pushing in the same direction, but the problem was that the Ulster Unionists, the SDLP and the Alliance were trying to set the thing up from their perspective, which was that they are born to lead and the others were born to follow. They trivialised what we said, so the smaller groups always tried to have conversations so as to not be divided by others. We knew that if we were going to do this, we needed some sort of framework that was going to allow us to share power and that power had to be shared on a sectarian basis, because there was no other way out of it.

But, as David Adams made clear, with the DUP and the UKUP out of the talks, the UUP also required the support of the Loyalist parties for Unionists to operate as a majority presence:

> It was evident that once the DUP and the UKUP walked out of the negotiations, Trimble needed the Loyalist parties to make up a majority within unionism, so we became quite significant then. We also knew that although the Irish wanted to see a united Ireland, they certainly didn't want thousands of recalcitrant Unionists against their will, or a Unionist version of the IRA operating in some thirty-two county context. We believed that if that ever came about it would be because unionism would see it making sense and not being the threat that it had always been perceived to be. But what also happened was that the UUP became frightened by the relentless campaign that Paisley and Bob McCartney were conducting against them, which would eventually turn the Unionist community off the Agreement. In the later stages, the Unionist

community were more prepared to believe Gerry Adams and Martin McGuiness saying it was great for republicanism, than they were prepared to listen to Trimble, Ervine or myself saying it was a good thing for unionism. Because unionism never ran positively with the ball from the outset, it gave the anti-Agreement factions greater influence and this just magnified the problems.

As the talks entered the more advanced phase of providing the blueprint for the final Agreement, the British and Irish tried to delay the Strand Two part of the document in the drafting process because of contentions between the two governments about North–South relations. For talks Chairman George Mitchell, this created problems for the release of a full draft, or 'comprehensive paper', as had been planned, with Ahern and Blair asking Mitchell to push on without decisions having been finalised on the Strand Two formulations (Mitchell 1999: 155). Particularly angry about this request by the two governments was Gary McMichael, who, as Mitchell records, viewed the release of a 'partial document' as unacceptable (ibid.). Recollecting this moment, McMichael went on:

> Essentially what you had was that we were getting to a point where a lot of this stuff was being signed off. Difficult elements of the Agreement were being sorted out, but the one area where there was particular difficulty, was with Strand Two and the North-South relationship bodies. But then the governments adopted a tactic of saying let's agree the bits we can't agree and let's work on the rest. That might have worked to an extent if they were prepared to do the same thing about decommissioning, but they weren't and we found it unacceptable. The reason it was unacceptable was because the only way, and we knew this because it was the unique selling point of the Agreement, to get through this, was to deal with everything at once, so people were buying into a package. You couldn't have elements separated out for people to argue over and find a reason for opposition based on judgements about single dimensions of the Agreement. It would only work if people were able to take the good with the bad in the round. We couldn't have negotiations taking place beyond the negotiations. And at that point this appeared to be what was happening. We were only willing to consider the North-South relationship on the basis of how it fitted into everything else. And there was natural Unionist suspicion, when there was an attempt to take control of Strand Two out of the hands of any Unionist.

Disputations over the meaning and potential for 'cross-border bodies', which would be set up to oversee recommendations made by a new North–South Ministerial Council, caused further problems for Unionists, which the British tried to impose without negotiation or adjustment, but present as the work of Mitchell and his negotiating team (ibid.: 160–1). The Strand Two detail was hastily presented in 'the form of options on key issues, rather than a definitive text' (ibid.: 163), as both governments sought to use a framework of annexes to Strand Two which listed, rather than specified, the purposes of 'executive, harmonizing and consultative' roles (ibid.: 164). As the negotiations entered the advanced stages, parties continued to press for concessions particularly on issues of devolution and North–South relations (Patterson 2006: 338–9).

On the point of differences over the North–South relations, the British tried to emphasise the logic and convenience of co-ordinating services and practices and used agriculture and tourism as two examples of where working together would benefit both sides. As Paul Murphy who was undersecretary to Mo Mowlam at the time of the negotiations (Murphy went on to become Northern Ireland Secretary in 2001–4) put it:

> There were obvious problems with the cross-border bodies being proposed. The Unionists wanted to make them as weak as possible and the Nationalists wanted them to be as strong as possible. What we were proposing was a more logical approach where by using examples we could point out the benefits for all by co-operation. It was clear that agriculture needed to be seen on an all-Ireland basis because that was what was required to deal with the threat of foot and mouth disease at that time. We also stressed that it would be sensible to work together on tourism and were saying that if people were coming to visit Ireland then there was a good chance that they would also visit Northern Ireland. It was obvious that this was an example of a common approach helping to benefit both Ireland and Northern Ireland in a practical way. We also stressed the need to think about all such developments in the context of Europe. We were saying that we are all part of the same club now, working together all the time and seeing borders blurring within the EU. We were emphasising that it was a different world from thirty years before.

In the final three days before the Agreement was finally reached, Blair and Ahern went to Belfast to oversee moves and bring pressure on the need for a deal. As each manoeuvred through Strand Two details, trying to modify positions while keeping Unionists and Nationalists from walking out, both also realised the importance of prisoner releases (especially for Republicans) as an important bargaining tool, which was used alongside efforts to move the Unionists through Strand Two details. Sinn Fein was looking for Republican prisoners to be released as quickly as possible and tried to strike a deal with Loyalists about this (even though Unionists were strongly opposed to an early release programme). As Billy Hutchinson explained:

> I can remember Gerry Kelly of Sinn Fein coming to the door and David Ervine going out to talk to him. When David came back in, he said that

Kelly wanted all prisoners to be released within six months. We decided that we couldn't support six months because people on the ground would need time to adjust to the idea and it would need to be spread out over a period of time. In the end we agreed a time frame of a year.

At this stage, the parties were camped in Castle Buildings at Stormont in Belfast, where the negotiations continued without respite for three days and nights towards their conclusion. The PUP and the UDP were accompanied in their rooms by the UVF and UDA leaderships respectively and communications were relayed to the prisoners in order to keep inmates updated with developments. Through a series of bi-lateral discussions, parties sought clarification and threatened walkouts to try and prise further concessions from the governments (the UUP threatened to walk out on 7 April and Republicans used the same tactic on 9 April). In the final hours, efforts to shape outcomes intensified, where, as Gary McMichael put it:

> The only way you were going to sort anything out was to put everyone in the same building and shoot the first one that walked out and that was what was being done politically. It was made clear that we could talk all day for years and never achieve anything. Basically the UUP and the SDLP were holed up with the governments most of the time and the expectation was that everyone else would fall into line. To some degree influence would shift from time to time, so the doors would become more open to us when the talking moved to policing issues, decommissioning or prisoner issues. You had periodic multi-party meetings where there were at least three parties, maybe all parties, involved in talks and then you had people like Jonathan Powell, Blair's assistant, and others who were basically runners, meeting each party individually. But the governments were particularly concentrating on the UUP and the SDLP to put things together. Powell and others were feeding back to Blair and Ahern, who were then dealing with two or three parties at once to try and pull things together. People would then come out of those meetings and scuttle off to discuss what was said. It was a complex and lengthy process. Blair tended not to deal with detail. He was aware of it, but others were there to sort that out and he didn't want to get into negotiation about that. Really the whole thing was done in forty-eight hours. There were bits and pieces of paper flying about, but in terms of the structures, there weren't any surprises and you could have predicted ninety per cent of it because we had been working on it for the last two years. There were a couple of hot issues like decommissioning and prisoner releases and people were afraid to put anything down on paper because they were so hot. We had the Inner Council in the room with us because you weren't allowed to take anything out of the building, so we had to bring them in to see the documents.

The process of how the negotiations were conducted and the reason why the smaller parties played less of a role was addressed by NIO official Stephen Leach in the following way:

> The negotiations were carried out in a way which is common around Europe, where at summits you have all the players in the same building with their delegations and there would be bartering about text, and then you would have officials moving about from one group to another. That is quite a recognised approach for governments trying to reach multi-lateral agreements. But there wasn't a great master plan in these kinds of negotiations; it just sort of happened. Things centred around the prime minister's office and Jonathan Powell, who did a lot of the final negotiations themselves. There wasn't a huge bunch of officials with them, although we were around. Blair tended to have a lot of discussions with Trimble on a one-to-one basis, so we didn't have a complete picture of what was happening, but there was a lot of information flying around from various sources. It wasn't as if we had a battle plan which we were working through, because the circumstances were too chaotic for that. However, the issues got crystallised through successive texts. To get a deal you had to get the UUP, Sinn Fein and the SDLP and the two governments together. Because those three were the key parties, inevitably you needed to spend a lot more time with them than the others. A certain amount of time, it was necessary to keep the other parties in the picture, but if nothing was moving there was nothing to tell them and because of that there was a lot of downtime. If you have to get lots of pieces into a particular position and you think you have the Loyalists in a particular position anyway, then your focus is obviously going to be on the other elements. It was a very complicated process to run, but it works easier through bi-lateral meetings, rather than trying to deal with everyone at once. You tried to bring the big parties to where you wanted them to be and keep the smaller parties in the picture so they wouldn't leak what was going on, or torpedo the thing inadvertently when it got into the formal negotiations. The round table discussion is a good debating format, but it's difficult to get agreement, because parties are less inclined to make concessions in that environment. That's why the bi-lateral discussion format was so important.

Gary McMichael recalled a particularly difficult encounter with Blair in the late hours, where the UDP were sure that the electoral process which the governments were proposing would lead to their exclusion from any Assembly, and so would create problems for maintaining UDA support:

> The last meeting we had with Blair was 3.30 am on Good Friday and we had all been awake for a very long time. We needed to make our position

clear on the electoral process, where procedures for its implementation had already been drafted and were to be released the following day. We had made the argument that we couldn't get into the negotiations on a constituency seat electoral contest because our support base was spread in small numbers across Northern Ireland. It wasn't concentrated in any one constituency, so to be in competition with the big players, even with proportional representation and with multiple seats, inclusion was very difficult to achieve. That's why, to get the talks process started, we had a top-up system which took the aggregate vote of the top ten parties and provided an additional two seats. It allowed the PUP and UDP to get into negotiations and it needed to happen because our importance to the peace process was less to do with our electoral mandate, and more to do with what we were able to bring to the table. But come the GFA, that was not considered to be necessary. We did not believe, given the fears which had been stoked by the DUP, that we would gain the seats, so we argued that we needed to be in the Assembly because the Assembly itself would be a continuation of the negotiations and the next phase of the peace process. The people who slammed the door on that were the UUP and the SDLP because they calculated that if there was a top-up system it would benefit Sinn Fein, so immediately they were looking at electoral advantage to make up numbers and get hold of ministerial posts. Blair was basically taking his lead from the UUP and the SDLP because he needed them on board and so we were forced to settle for a system which would be likely to exclude us. We also knew that the consequences would be bad, which turned out to be the case. Why should the UDA listen to us when we were out in the wilderness with no linkage to the process? Why should they listen and how would we have influence? We tried to argue for involvement in some kind of management structure which would allow us to be involved in the day to day business of the Assembly, which would give us some inclusion. But, although we were involved in a number of crisis talks after, we got to a point where we did not get asked back and that put the nail in the coffin.

For British negotiations architect Quentin Thomas, not dealing with the UDP's electoral concerns was seen to result more from time pressures than being part of a deliberate move which would lead to their exclusion from the process:

You would like to see the paramilitaries in the process but at a certain point you are up against a hard democratic reality that if the electoral support is not there then they're goners. With hindsight I think there should have been consideration given to that concern, but the way the rules of sufficient consensus worked it meant that for a lot of the time the process was waiting for Trimble. We couldn't get an agreement and we couldn't get sufficient consensus unless we had a majority of Unionists and that meant we had to have Trimble. Also, every time he made a concession he was attacked by McCartney and the DUP, so he had to play out the rope. At the end, a lot of stuff was done in a rush and it would have been better to spend to a couple of weeks dealing with electoral issues rather than decommissioning. Another problem was that people were playing their cards very close to their chest and there was a view, particularly amongst the Unionists, that negotiations would have to go down to the wire. So I think part of the reason the UDP's electoral concerns were not properly addressed was because things were done in a rush at the end. Also, of course, although the Loyalists constituted a powerful paramilitary threat, they had virtually no political constituency. We were all conscious that the electoral system we devised had got their political representatives into the process, but because they didn't have much political standing it was hard to try and do that again. It's not a good case to argue for an electoral scheme to get people in because they have no electoral support.

But for Paul Murphy, consideration of an electoral process which would bring parties like the UDP into the Assembly was taken into account, before being deemed unworkable because of a lack of consensus between the parties and the burgeoning amount of seats which the Assembly would need to cater for:

> An electoral system which would help the UDP was considered but you couldn't get consensus on it. Remember the Assembly would incorporate 108 members representing a population of 1.5 million. The Welsh Assembly which represents a population double that size only has a 60 person Assembly, so we were stretching it with 108 and of course, we did that to ensure that we could get as wide a net as possible to create diversity. There is also a limit to how far you can go, both with size and cost. There wasn't consensus for stretching or manipulating things further because the parties wanted a more straightforward system of voting. We knew that unattached from the process there would be a number of paramilitaries who would lose interest in political developments. The answer really would have been for the two Loyalist parties to become a single party, but for historical reasons that was not to be.

For David Adams however, the UDP's probable exclusion from the Assembly was something which needed to be accepted and considered in the context of other gains and positive outcomes which were advantageous to unionism:

> The was some discussion about whether we should hold out for a different system which would help to guarantee us seats, but I opposed that.

I'm not a believer in contorting democracy in order to get seats. One couldn't really push for even more Assembly members or a top-up system again. I think that some of the smaller parties like the Women's Coalition would have supported us on that, but people had stomached the electoral system being stretched once to get us into negotiations and it didn't seem right to do it again. There was an implementation body idea floated at the time and we said we wouldn't mind being involved in that to oversee the implementation of the Agreement, but it never came about. We had tried to do what we could to bring paramilitarism to an end, but my and Gary's role was running out on that. The constitution was the important thing and we were agreed on that. The real problem was after the Agreement was signed. Republicans sold the Agreement, which was really a defeat for them, as a victory and because of that, unionism must have lost, which was nonsense. Remember that for Republicans the goal was always a united Ireland or nothing. Now they has signed up to an Agreement which dictated that the constitutional future of Northern Ireland would remain in the hands of the people of Northern Ireland, and that will continue as far as the eye can see. The Union was copperfastened, the cross-border stuff was very much about the yes or no of particular issues laying at Stormont, East-West relationships were built on the same terms as North-South, and Articles 2 and 3 of the Irish constitutional claim over Northern Ireland by the Republic was gone. It was as close as we were going to get in those circumstances to having the best political and constitutional agreement. The problem for unionism though, is that it has always been in the position of trying to defend the status quo and, because every little movement from the status quo is a defeat in some way, it's an uphill battle trying to present anything as a victory. Unionism has never really learnt the trick of giving a little so that you can earn a lot. It was always not an inch, which means that when you do give an inch, you lose almost everything.

Talking further about the tensions within the room where the UDP and the UDA congregated (some 40 representatives in all), and the moves made just prior to the announcement of the Agreement by the participants, McMichael added:

> There were about forty of us in the room and a lot of people were getting irate. The problem was that they were taking their analysis from television. There was a lot of inactivity and waiting so the cameras were an obvious magnetic pull. Myself and David Adams thought it better to convey a calm message to our constituency rather than make desperate appeals, which would only increase public anxiety. We made our assessments and discussed them with the leadership. We would also, from time to time go out to the cameras and make it clear if we thought a previous announcement

that a party had made was crap. Everybody wanted to go out and say we demand this and that and we are making a lot of progress, but it was nonsense. The real issue was that nobody wanted to give the impression that they were outside the loop. It wasn't just the media appeals from those inside the building that was making people nervous. You had Paisley outside, as he had been for weeks, saying it was a stitch up, which put pressure on those inside to challenge him. This in turn created pressure to be more positive, because you couldn't agree with him. You had to take the opposite view. But you also had to be measured and make it clear that it was by no means guaranteed that we were just going to agree to whatever was going to be presented. We were interested in everything, but if it looked too much out of shape, it was no go. We were all agreed that just because the pressure was on for us to agree, we would dissent if we didn't believe it could be sold. We also thought that if a deal could be reached that was broadly the right shape, which didn't put us in a position where it would be impossible to deliver, and we felt that the Unionist community would offer support, then we would go for it. We knew that we had to swallow a lot of things, so there was a willingness to be open-minded, but with boundaries. But what didn't help us was the process and dynamic within the building, because we felt isolated. It was okay for me and David Adams, who had a lot of experience of a process which was ninety per cent inaction and ten per cent action. That is how the days were spent, because in a process of bilateral or trilateral meetings, the focus would regularly be only on two or three parties, with the others not involved, so much time would be spent twiddling thumbs. In those final days there was a lot of that. There might have been one or two round table meetings where everyone was involved, but there were large periods of inactivity, which we understood because we were used to that pattern of working. But with bringing people in from the outside who were not used to that, there were inevitable problems. These people were seeing us in rooms for hours with nothing happening and insisted that we were being taken for a ride. They would say to us that we were being treated like shit and that these guys think they've already got our vote in the bag. They also thought it was dangerous because nobody could really see what, if anything, the others were concocting. Their fears were reinforced by the first draft of the Agreement which created problems for us. The electoral system being designed was probably going to exclude us and there were concerns on the decommissioning issue. But at the same time there were positive aspects which enabled us to shift the focus. We were able to send John White into the Maze prison at the eleventh hour to brief the prisoners on the document and the prisoners supported it. This greatly helped because the leadership was always more comfortable when the prisoners were behind them.

Other UDA personnel were kept informed of developments throughout and as senior UDA and UFF commander 'Alan' explained:

> At every move we were being told about what was happening through phone calls. The leader of every area was in contact with certain individuals from that area. Taking south Belfast, for example, there would have been at least six people being updated at any given time and at least four of those would have been battalion commanders.

In the final moments of negotiations, the PUP, like the UDP, also had concerns about the Agreement to deal with. Indeed, Billy Hutchinson walked out of the talks at the last minute because of objections about North–South issues:

> My concern at the end was the cross-border bodies. I wasn't sure that we had got that right and I was also concerned that the Agreement was like a three-legged stool, where if one leg collapses it all collapses. I felt that because of what we had been hearing during the day from the media, that there would be backstabbing of some sort. I can remember going for a walk in the grounds of Stormont at night when it was snowing with the UVF's Number Two, who was trying to convince me that we had got it right, but I wasn't convinced. I supported the Agreement on the basis that it was where we were going, but I had serious reservations. I stayed outside the room for the last hours and wouldn't get involved with our negotiating team. I think that what the UVF's Number Two did, was allow me to communicate my fears to him and the UVF rather than the PUP. What he did do was convince me that I needed to show unity and not create a split in the camp. If I had walked away, it would have left the UVF in a bit of trouble and that needed to be avoided. I had a real fear that we couldn't be sure about what was being said and that we didn't know the thinking of the prime minister. My view was that if the governments were going to do anything it was a deal with the bigger parties, without our knowing. Another fear was that we weren't seeing all the bits of paper. I knew they were showing us bits of paper that they thought we would be alright with, but then we were hearing through the media stuff about Jeffrey Donaldson walking out, which gave me concerns that if Trimble was going to sell this to his party, he would need something from Blair. I was also worried that it would be something which not only could be used against Republicans, but against us as well, as turned out to be the case, because he was given a letter from Blair on decommissioning. When we walked out the door the letter was thrust in front of me by a journalist who said 'What do you think of that?' I said it didn't matter because what had been negotiated was different. But, of course, the letter became the basis for the UUP strapline 'no guns, no government'.

The letter handed by Blair to Trimble that Hutchinson refers to, made it clear that the 'process of decommissioning should begin straight away' and was used both to prevent the UUP walking out of the negotiations (last-minute tensions meant that UUP representatives were making it known to the media that a deal was not possible) and provide Trimble with the assurance that decommissioning would be a prerequisite for political progress. But, although the letter enabled Trimble to persuade the UUP to accept the deal, it had no official import for the paramilitaries and therefore lacked substance as a condition of the Agreement (O'Kane 2007: 95–6). Yet, as NIO official Stephen Leach pointed out, without the letter it would have been unlikely that the Unionists would have accepted the deal:

> The letter was an important element in the UUP decision to go with the Agreement. They did put a lot of weight on it, which ended up being more weight than it could bear, because essentially it was a letter of comfort which ended up not providing much comfort at all. Trimble asked for the letter as an assurance and it was carefully phrased. We were so close and there was such impetus and momentum, that it had to be done really. There is always a risk in a process of multi-lateral negotiations when you give an undertaking to one side, but in saying that, it did reflect what we hoped would happen. I don't remember it being too big an issue for the other parties actually, but I think the Unionists thought that once the Agreement was signed and the new Assembly had started, that it would give them a strong negotiating hand in terms of the next steps, which turned out not to be the case.

Because the decommissioning issue took on such importance for the Unionists and offered negotiating potential for Republicans (less so the Loyalists), it became a major obstruction to movement which both governments adjusted their position towards as time progressed. Explaining how decommissioning came to gain such prominence, Stephen Leach continued:

> The big issue was decommissioning. Sinn Fein wouldn't talk about a permanent end to violence, but spoke about a total end to violence. As one prominent Unionist put it in response to this, you come to a total stop at a red light, but not a permanent stop, so the issue became about whether Republicans would return to violence. In effect, decommissioning was seen to be a hurdle below saying there was permanent cessation of violence. But it became a huge sticking point, the question of whether progress on decommissioning was being made. The initial idea was to decommission all weapons before they went into talks. Then it was to decommission weapons before going into government and ended up being a process leading towards decommissioning and having that independently monitored. Sinn Fein immediately saw that as a bargaining chip. They saw that we needed them in the process and that if they did

nothing at all and were too provocative then Trimble would not be able to stay in, but nonetheless, they did extort a price for every move on decommissioning. Sinn Fein are very good when you try and pin them down and tell them they agreed to do something, because they translate it into further negotiation, in which effectively, you are being asked to pay them again for something they had already agreed to do. As one of my colleagues put it, it was as if you were buying the same horse twice. Significantly, what the decommissioning issue did do was it put the power within the Republican movement into the hands of the hardest men, those who actually controlled the weapons, as opposed to the politicos and that led to other demands which made it a crab-like process.

Quentin Thomas was critical of the importance attached to decommissioning and argued that it acquired a significance which obstructed progress:

Inevitably decommissioning was a key item on the agenda, but it came to achieve a centrality that was not helpful. There were obvious movements in a process of change and we hoped that it was change in a benign direction. Behind the shifts that we observed lay a considered strategic judgement that it was right to abandon the physical force campaign and to commit to political methods. But in any process of change in a political organisation, or any movement at all, it is difficult. It's clearly important to anyone managing a political movement that they bring as many people as possible and that they avoid schisms and splits. So it was understandable to me that those managing that change had some difficulty in saying to their own people, look the game is up and we're not doing that any more. It was also patently in our interest that paramilitary groups should move as a whole, without fracture. But I think one of the difficulties was that there was a mismatch between a sort of static analysis and a dynamic analysis. The static analysis said well if these people say they've given up violence, so they should give up guns and why is there an issue about this since one follows the other as night follows day. If, on the other hand you look at it dynamically and acknowledge that a very difficult process of change is being undertaken, then a bit of imagination and cleverness is needed to assist this process in order to reach the right result. Harping on about the weapons, at points in the process seemed to be the only issue, but I don't think it was necessarily clever, or in our own interest.

Thomas elaborated further on how the decommissioning problem occupied the negotiations and how positions adopted towards that issue tended to overwhelm the process:

Because everyone kept going on about decommissioning, it actually made it difficult for the paramilitary parties to address. If you want a dynamic and creative interaction on negotiations and bargaining, it's deeply unhelpful to everybody because nobody could say let's forget about this and even though it was a real issue, you couldn't do anything with it. In one way you could say that it gave Republicans in particular a bargaining position, but in another it was unhelpful to them and everybody else, by dominating proceedings in a deeply obstructive way. It was very difficult to get off the issue because it wasn't an issue that people could say was of no account, but it also became a problem that was very difficult to get out of. Things were not made better by the tendency of the British government to be slightly too ready a capacity to declare such issues to be matters of principle, when actually they were not and subsequent moves showed that, because they adjusted their position in a way that wouldn't or shouldn't have been done if it really had been a matter of principle. It was stated to be a matter of principle that we should not meet Sinn Fein while a campaign of violence continued, but soon after the Canary Wharf bomb, that principle didn't seem to matter much any more because I was instructed to meet Martin McGuinness within weeks of the bomb. So I think that we should have been less ready to talk about issues such as decommissioning as a matter of principle and to look at the points in terms of those where you have to draw a line and those where you don't.

Hutchinson's concerns about the Agreement in those final moments, as he acknowledged, were eased, to some extent through his communication with the UVF's Number Two. Offering this assessment of developments just before the Agreement was signed, the UVF Number Two recalled:

We were convinced that the Union was safe and that prisoners would be released and that was relayed to the prisoners themselves. We also made it clear that as long as the Union was safe, we would see it through. The prisoners had an equal say on the matter, but no more than that. They, of course, also had a vested interest and a visit was made to brief them on developments at 4.00 am the day before the Agreement was reached. We had seen drafts of the document and had a pretty good idea of what the final document would look like. There were obviously military and political people in the room together and we had been working closely for some time beforehand, meeting three or four times a day in the weeks leading up to the final negotiations. We had been over every detail and processed every sentence, so we were confident there would be no surprises in the final outcome. There was a consensus amongst the entire leadership on this and they were all in the building during those last hours. Although Loyalists should have come out winners with the deal, the Unionist perception was that we had lost. The decommissioning issue became a major obstruction, even though Republicans were also saying it was nonsense. There was a rumour some time before that the UDA were prepared at one stage to exchange weapons for prisoners, but I think that was emanating from the prison rather than the leadership. But we were very clear and had positions which were solid. Everyone knew the ground rules and there had been a long consultation process so we had a policy on everything we needed. David Ervine and Billy Hutchinson would access the leadership and were given the parameters on what could and couldn't be said, how far to go and how far not to go, so there was considerable confidence at both political and military levels.

Continuing to talk about how fears about what was going on behind closed doors with other parties were intensified when journalists and the media passed the PUP information which the governments had not made them aware of, Hutchinson said:

> I was particularly interested in what people were saying when they were talking to the media off screen and that was where we were getting our information from. Participants were careful in telling journalists that they couldn't say certain things because they were supposed to be the only ones who knew. But the media were telling me what was going on. They were repeating what had been said to them and would tell you directly that so and so said this. Essentially, they were telling us things we didn't know, which concerned us. We thought that Blair would have to give Trimble something because of Donaldson [a UUP representative who walked out of the negotiations], but we did not know whether it would be cross-border bodies, a referendum, or decommissioning and this raised tensions. As we know, it turned out to be decommissioning, but all the discussions around the GFA said that decommissioning would never happen. What was said was that we would use our best offices to try and bring that about, but not that it would happen. The problem was that the British stopped behaving as ten parties and started behaving as three, with the UUP, the SDLP and Sinn Fein. We had made the process happen through collective action and we argued that for any Agreement to be sold on the ground, it needed to be done collectively. We knew that if people went off and tried to sell it individually, we were beat. And, that's what Trimble did because he got hooked on the 'no guns, no government' slogan which effectively destroyed him, because that was never going to be delivered in 1998. I think that Blair's letter to Trimble was a big mistake, because what it showed was that there was a flaw in the process, which allowed the DUP to drive the anti-Agreement argument. But, most importantly, it was given when nobody in the talks had promised decommissioning.

The declining level of influence of the Loyalist parties at the final stages of negotiations, which Hutchinson alludes to, was a view also shared by McMichael, who saw the final stages as the beginning of efforts to undermine positive and collective ownership of the peace process:

> Remember that when the IRA ceasefire happened and Sinn Fein re-entered the talks a large proportion of unionism walked out, leaving the UUP with something like forty-seven per cent of the vote. And while the PUP and ourselves only had a few per cent between us, it meant that no decision could be taken without us and that the UUP could not enter negotiations without us, so we had quite a strong hand. If anything our influence in the negotiations became infinitely more critical as a result of that quirk. But with the Agreement negotiations that influence dropped significantly. At the same time, you had Paisley on the outside saying you've all been fooled and he's behind you. You also had various streams of process, with republicanism and nationalism focussed on the British government, the Irish bringing up the rear and the Americans coming from the side. Within unionism you had the UUP and the paramilitaries, who were more pragmatic, and the DUP were trying to pull things back and everybody was concerned with Sinn Fein. There was no commonality between the communities, no common objectives, no agreement or sense of common ownership of the process. This lack of ownership, as political leaders tried to argue it was their own design, made it very difficult to bring the communities and the Unionist community in particular, to accept the consequences of the negotiations. Even the name of the Agreement was disputed to maintain separateness. It was the Good Friday Agreement for some and the Belfast Agreement for others.

In the last moments of negotiations, Mitchell recalled how the details of Strand Two were reworded to address the mutual concerns of Unionists and Nationalist and noted how

> On the crucial issue of authority, a delicate balance was struck. The British and Irish governments made an absolute commitment to establish a North/South Ministerial Council and to create 'implementation bodies' to carry out the council's decisions. The difficult issue of timing and authority was resolved by the creation of a 'transitional' phase, during which the ministerial council, the new Northern Ireland Assembly, and a new British/Irish Council would simultaneously and cooperatively begin to function. Any expansion of these arrangements would have to be approved by the Assembly.
>
> (Mitchell 1999: 175)

Regarding fears about North–South institutions for Unionists and the role of an Assembly for Nationalists, where each was perceived as having the potential to sabotage the role of the other, the governments decided to make the function of the institutions 'mutually inter-dependent', therefore establishing that each would be unworkable without the other. This important modification moved the parties significantly closer towards accepting Strand Two, which had been further streamlined to now incorporate one annex with 12 subject areas (ibid.).

Although the latter stages of negotiations had created problems for the perceived input and influence of the Loyalist parties, for David Ervine, the very presence of the Loyalists acted as a necessary block against Irish exuberance to push through an all-Ireland context and for that reason helped to ensure broader longer term aspirations of political stability and ending violence:

> The conditions we were functioning in at the end reduced our latitude quite a bit. We had an Irish government telling us that there is going to be a secretariat between London and Dublin which was going to be the engine to drive all affairs between Northern Ireland and the Republic, and we were resisting that. We asked them where does the involvement of the Ulster man come into this and where was the democratic imperative here? We also said that had to be changed or we were gone. I think they thought about that and could see it was not a good idea if we went. One also had to realise how governments will often listen to your concerns and then just ignore them, but we also knew that if the UK didn't fancy another Canary Wharf, so the Dublin government wouldn't either. That was never threatened, but I've no doubt it was part of their dynamic. Both governments wanted to protect their respective concerns. In some ways the Agreement was shit, but I was a great advocate of it because it helped to establish a core process, which society was invited to share. It also started to establish a sense of common purpose – which is not the same as a common allegiance – which if realised through a functioning Assembly, would help to reduce fear. Once an Assembly is working which deals with the everyday boring things, then over time, people will become used to its functions and confidence will build. That was why I thought agreement was important.

But for McMichael, the positive outcomes offered by the Agreement were only achievable if sold positively by the parties who oversaw its making and for Unionists, this proposition would turn out to be decidedly problematic:

> I think the weakness of the GFA came down to how the parties approached it and was not necessarily the content. There were always going to be things that you are not going to like, but it covered a lot of ground and was roughly the right shape. There was enough wins and loses for everyone. Basic principles were underpinned and we thought that with a functioning Assembly, there would be enough room and

protection for the democratic system to evolve. We weren't too happy with decommissioning and we knew it would be used as a stick to be beaten with, but actually its looseness meant that we could live with it. The release of prisoners was vital for our constituency, but we decided not to argue for more than we got on prisoners because we knew that we also had to bring the general Unionist population with us, and we didn't want that potential area of interest being turned into a negative. We refused an offer from Sinn Fein to push for an earlier release programme because we knew it would throw the Unionist community offside. We also knew that we were operating in an agreed framework with a sufficient independence that could evolve and we had relationships external to Northern Ireland through the North-South-East-West axis, which we saw as important. As an organisation, we had raised the concept of a British-Irish Council on the basis that we had to find a relationship in a wider context. Those relationships were interdependent and that was the important thing. Everything was subsidiary to the internal relationships, structures and institutions, so for the first time, you had a shift from policy between British and Irish control towards both governments having a limited role. You also had a political framework where British and Irish relationships would be secondary to a Northern Ireland Assembly and where the GFA was in the hands of the Assembly and not the governments, if the Assembly worked. The big problem however, was that unionism couldn't believe that it had the opportunity to work the controls. So paranoid is unionism in its concept of defeat, that it wanted someone else to drive the car. Unionists just didn't realise the massive potential of the Assembly. They didn't seem to grasp that the Assembly could put the people of Northern Ireland in a position where the British and Irish government agendas would be secondary, providing it worked. It seemed beyond their imagination.

McMichael's criticism of unionism, though consistently shared with other Loyalist representatives at the negotiations did however, perhaps fail to properly acknowledge the internal and external stresses and strains that the UUP were operating under. As Stephen Leach pointed out:

One has to remember that the UUP had the DUP over their shoulder, so anything they communicated publicly to their constituents was likely to be used against them by the DUP, who were very hostile to the process and in electoral competition with the UUP. Sinn Fein, on the other had, couldn't be outflanked as it were by a more hardline group, because they were the hardline group on the Nationalist side. So, Sinn Fein did not have to fear attacks from within their own camp, the way the UUP did. A further problem for the UUP was how Sinn Fein managed to present the Agreement as a success, or victory to their people. They had kept open the option of permanent Irish unity, they had changed the aspects of Northern Ireland life which Republicans found unacceptable, policing in particular, and they had a share in a future government. They regarded it as a job well done because they had delivered an Agreement that enabled them to keep their options open, but they also did it by ignoring to some extent those elements of the Agreement which they didn't particularly like. For the Unionists, perceived losses were being used against them by those outside the process, and because of what was happening to the police, the Irish language etc, they had a harder job selling the Agreement.

The final plenary session when the parties voted for the Agreement took place at 5 pm on 10 April, when George Mitchell announced to the media present that a deal had been ratified (except for Jeffrey Donaldson of the UUP who refused to endorse the document and who later defected to the DUP). The overall aim of the Agreement to 'harness cultural and political pluralism within an institutional framework' (Tonge 2005: 36) was underscored by the need to create tolerance for 'co-identity, rather than shared identity' and based on the prospect of developing political consensus through cooperation and support for the institutions (ibid.: 56). Designed to create a reconstitution of Northern Ireland, the GFA was essentially 'attempting to turn the province into a more explicitly binational entity' (ibid.: 58), where peaceful co-existence would be underpinned by the Agreement's recognition of the need for political aspiration and expression to take place without recourse to violence. Although, as we shall see, the Agreement succeeded in creating a 'realignment of the traditional political order' (Tonge 2006b: 86) when disillusionment about the Assembly and lack of trust contributed to its suspension in 2002 (a development which the DUP and Sinn Fein made significant political capital out of), it is nevertheless clear that the Agreement itself, and the resulting referendum which produced Assembly representatives across a range of parties, marked a clear shift towards a public acceptance of power-sharing and democratic politics. Unfortunately, for the Loyalists, and in particular for the UDP, it was the high point of their political influence.

7
After the Good Friday Agreement

The decline of the UDP

Once the Agreement had been signed by the respective parties, a referendum was conducted to reveal the strength of public support for the settlement. For Sinn Fein, legitimising the referendum meant meeting with the Republican grassroots at a specially convened ardfheis in Dublin to change the party's constitution, in order to allow part representatives to take seats in a Northern Ireland Assembly (overwhelmingly endorsed) (Bew and Gillespie 1999: 363). Advanced publicity for the referendum, which took place in May, was supported by a British government campaign which emphasised the positives of the Agreement, while playing down the negatives. As part of this campaign, the British stressed how 'The message is to be reinforced and the public need to be in no doubt about how a deal will improve every aspect of their quality of life'. To successfully convey this image, the government recommended that 'key messages be repeated at every opportunity', and that important figures who gave consent to the Agreement should be used in order to promote 'message credibility among those they represent'. Significantly, the government's propaganda blurb instructed how 'serious consideration needs to be given to the timing and content of any messages, because it could be seen as "big government" imposing its view ... For that and reasons of propriety, the focus should be on selling the concept of an agreed future. The central message will be "It's Your Choice". Initially that choice will be posed as being between the failure of the past and the future towards which we are making progress. Once an agreement is in place, the message will change to encouraging people to vote for this future' (McCartney 2001: 224–6).

The result of the referendum was that 71.1 per cent voted 'yes' (with 94.39 voting 'yes' in the Republic) (Elliott and Flackes 1999: 596), paving the way for an election in June with the allocation of seats for the Assembly as follows: SDLP 24, UUP 28, DUP 20, Sinn Fein 18, Alliance Party 6, UKUP 5, Independent Unionist Group 3, PUP 2 and NIWC 2. Importantly, the UUP vote had fallen 2.9 per cent from the 1996 Forum election and 11.4 per cent from the 1997 Westminster elections (ibid.: 597). The voter turnout for the election among Protestants was only 57 per cent and within that community, unease about the Agreement steadily increased, to the extent 'where Trimble and pro-Agreement Unionists found it increasingly difficult to counter a growing mood of sour cynicism about post-Agreement Northern Ireland' (Patterson 2006: 347). By 2001, only one in three Protestants backed the Agreement and a Unionist refusal to work with the North–South Ministerial Council, coupled with allegations of an IRA spy ring in operation at Stormont, led to the suspension of the Assembly in October 2002 (Tonge 2005: 59–60). An inability by the UUP to contain disputations within the party, along with being unable to positively sell the Agreement (Spencer 2006a), contributed to the rise of the anti-Agreement DUP, which became the dominant Unionist party in Northern Ireland from 2003 onwards. Although realising that Protestants' fears over a united Ireland had declined (Patterson 2006: 347), the DUP also sought to reinforce perceptions that the Agreement had advantaged Nationalists more than Unionists (ibid.: 348) by concentrating attention 'not on creeping unification but rather on the claim that the Agreement had institutionalized a Nationalist agenda and on its supposed marginalization of Protestant and Unionist values and culture' (ibid.: 347).

Growing Protestant unrest with the Agreement, linked to the fact that the UDP were now cut adrift from the Assembly because of a failure to gain seats, meant that although the UDP leaders tried to prevent the party's demise, it became inevitable. Tentative support for the Agreement shown among the UDA leadership quickly dissipated, along with dissent spreading quickly throughout the broader UDA membership. As David Adams recollected on this deterioration:

> The Agreement was endorsed by the UDA leadership on the night it was signed. There were meetings in different brigade areas afterwards to explain the ins and outs of what different parts of the Agreement might mean. But even at that stage, there is no doubt that for some, such as those in north Antrim, there were people who were totally opposed. That area, in particular, had always been leaning towards independence rather than any internal settlement, even though the political representative for that area was also at Stormont when the Agreement was endorsed. One also has to remember that the Inner Council had the major 'Vote Yes' rally in the Ulster Hall, which was attended by thousands and where the whole of the leadership were present. But, both myself and Gary had doubts about whether it would stick and there was a lot of personal stuff in there as well, where individuals started to see that this was going to impact negatively on their own self-interest. There was active undermining of our position and support for the Agreement,

even though at that stage the organisation wasn't anti-Agreement and had the full backing of the prisoners in the Maze. But quite quickly, people started calling it a sell-out and were trying to pick holes in it. Again one has to consider this in the light of the Unionist community not being prepared for compromise and Republicans actively undermining people like Trimble, so the Unionist community would be kept ranting and raving about what they had lost. These factors destroyed moderate unionism's support for the Agreement and we were part of that.

Adams elaborated further on the problem of paramilitaries accepting the Agreement by talking about the need to account for personal self-interest in this process of disparagement, as well as highlighting the difficulty of trying to create consensus in a traditionally fractious organisation:

The UDA is made of 6 brigades which are almost autonomous units and whose leaderships come together to discuss broad strategy and agreements, but within their communities are almost a law unto themselves. You have to filter all the human elements into all of this. It is extremely difficult to argue with some person that for the greater good of the community they need to get a job and leave paramilitarism behind. What you are really asking someone to do is give up being maybe the most influential person in an area, a person who if not respected, is able to create widespread fear in a area and who has enemies the length of your leg. And you're asking them to walk away from all that. That's all very well in theory, but it's difficult for them and for you to argue the need to bring it about. It's a case of paramilitaries reaching a point where they decide to stand down and disappear, or where despite some of the best efforts of the best people, they morph into criminal gangs.

Complementing this view, Gary McMichael offered this assessment of the difficulties faced by the UDP as it travelled across Northern Ireland after the Agreement in an attempt to garner support:

There were two major problems which were that these guys just couldn't get past the concepts of the Irish government having a role or legitimacy in issues that related to Northern Ireland, and Republicans being in power. After the Agreement, we had to go all over the country trying to get the UDA membership on board and address the division which was opening about the Agreement. We argued until we were blue in the face about the balance of the Agreement, about the principle of consent, about the framework within which other relationships existed, about the checks and balances that were in place, about the conflict resolution benefits of the prisoner releases and that in the context of where we had been aiming, the Agreement wasn't a million miles away. But when it came down to it and decisions had to be made, none of that mattered because they just couldn't get beyond the mantra of no Dublin, no involvement.

McMichael also reflected on the issue of not having fully engaged the UDA throughout the later and more crucial stages of the negotiations process in order to try and bring members along (as had been the case between Sinn Fein and the IRA), and spoke about the lack of a consultative framework and demands on resources as entrenching problems:

> Those of us in the negotiations had evolved and shifted in our attitudes and understanding essentially by being involved in those negotiations for two years. But those outside did not follow us and we weren't able to bring them with us. They had not had the opportunity to evolve to that point in the same way we had. A big reason for that was that we didn't have the infrastructure. We were constantly going back into our areas and talking to people, but it was never enough. We were also working against Paisley who was ever present and who had to work a lot less hard than we did in order to change peoples' minds, because they were in his mindset to begin with and he was just holding on to them. We were trying to convert them to do something which was beyond what they conceived in the first place and do the job at the same time, and it just wasn't possible. That was a major flaw on our part, but the UUP didn't fair much better and has a very strong infrastructure. Also, after the election, the peace process moved on and became housed inside the institutions which we were not part of. In other words, we were no longer involved with the peace process. It moved on and we were just left sitting with people from the paramilitary groups who wanted some influence but now had no connection to it. Because we had no influence in the process, so we had no influence or leverage over the paramilitaries, who were saying why should we listen to you? We had no political relevance and no political voice. The UDA was now unanchored from the process and had no political clout. They then started misbehaving and doing things they shouldn't have been doing and we were held accountable by the public, even though we had no influence at all by this time. This quickly deteriorated to a situation where they didn't support either the peace process or us, and we were cut out. But more broadly, the difficulty was that those leaders within unionism involved with the process made decisions that people weren't ready for. Republicanism had to make more ideological adjustments than we did, but unionism didn't believe that it did. The ideology is about maintaining what you have rather than achieving anything, and a strong unionism has tended to be based on those who lose less, more slowly. Unity within unionism, in my experience, tends to arise as unity in opposition to something.

Tommy Kirkham, who was involved with the UDP, but then joined the UPRG on its dissolution, reinforced the argument about the UDA lacking a positive conviction towards the Agreement, adding:

> I think that we failed in not having an endgame. It was always to oppose a united Ireland, to oppose Sinn Fein and always to oppose. You were always in constant opposition without a political goal for yourselves.

But, Kirkham's UPRG colleague David Nicoll was more critical in his assessment of what the UDP had achieved:

> I was one of the agitators against the UDP. David Adams and Gary McMichael were invited by our branch to meet with the Londonderry/ north Antrim area in Ballymoney Town Hall and they were told in no uncertain terms that this part of the organisation could no longer support the political thinking in terms of where they were going. There was no consultation with the organisation, or people on the ground, and we felt that things were being run to a government agenda. I think that the UDA was like rabbits caught in the headlights and became part of a process they weren't prepared for and hadn't prepared for. It was Trimble who did the negotiating and loyalism had become a sideshow. The Agreement was something the UDP signed up to, but it wasn't something the UDA had signed up to. I said that I believed we had a deal with a framework in which political parties can work and nothing more, and if everybody works the system then we will have a future, but it will depend in the long term on how it is played out within communities. If one group is seen to be given more than the other, it will impact on the way forward and that's what happened. The government negotiated with Sinn Fein and made deals on policing which isolated unionism again.

Confirming Nicoll's recollection of the Ballymoney meeting, UPRG representative Frankie Gallagher went on:

> There were over three hundred in the hall and the feeling was very anti-Agreement, partly because the organisation is very DUP oriented there. Gary insisted that the organisation would be going for the Agreement and this didn't go down well. I think it would have helped if he and David Adams had said that there were two processes going on: the peace process and the political process. The political process at the time was right for us but we needed to rededicate to the peace process. The problem was they didn't work on people from the bottom up and there was a lack of consultation.

Reinforcing McMichael's contention that the UDA were unlikely to move away from the analysis provided by Paisley, Nicoll continued:

> One thing that annoyed the UDA leadership was the day Paisley and his supporters were castigated by UVF people in front of the world's media outside the negotiations. Eighty per cent of UDA members would support the DUP and we watched him be humiliated in front of the press. McMichael had brought into that and that turned the rank and file against him. Even though Paisley was outside the talks we understood why he did that and irrespective of his stance, Paisley was seen as someone who for thirty years had stood by unionism and was reading the situation at that point.

Nicoll and Gallagher's responses raise important questions about what the UDA leadership had been doing within their own areas and why they hadn't driven the consultation process themselves. If the UDP had not been able to sign up to the Agreement without the authority and consent of the leadership, then one is left to wonder why the leadership had not led a pro-Agreement dialogue process within the UDA. What this indicates is that the leadership's support for the Agreement was essentially superficial and because of that, not transmitted down through the organisation with any conviction. Indeed, one could argue that the UDA leadership tended to reaffirm the concerns and fears of their respective areas, rather than instigate pro-Agreement positions which were challenging and dealing with those concerns. UDA leader for south Belfast Jackie McDonald, summarised what the main concerns were in his area to the Agreement, which the UDP supported:

> Although the UDP were giving us their political analysis, there were an awful lot of people who were worried they were being sold out and who couldn't understand what the Agreement was about. I was saying let's give it a chance and if we don't like it we can pull the plug. But they were saying we can't pull the plug because once the thing is in place the British government will do what they want. People were asking me how to vote and I was saying give it a chance. But afterwards people were coming up to me saying the Agreement was designed for Sinn Fein, about making more and more concessions to Sinn Fein and they didn't agree with it. The problem then was you had the UDP agreeing with it and the paramilitaries going against it and neither was going to change their position. The paramilitaries were always arguing against the way things were being implemented. It was not possible to reconcile how the membership felt and how the UDP felt and in the end the UDP resigned its position and things fell apart.

Senior UDA and UFF figure 'Alan' intimated that part of the reason why the UDP came to an end was because of the weak linkage between its representatives and the UDA membership and because UDA paramilitaries tend to see the conflict through military rather than political eyes:

> The problem was that the UDP left the foot soldiers behind. They distanced themselves when they got to a certain position. If you look at Sinn Fein, all the top people came through the system and the majority of them have been military men. They have the feelings of the people on the ground. But I also think that one of the reasons why the UDA didn't push the political way forward was because they could see no reason for the existence of yet another Unionist party. Their aim was military rather than political and so it was logical that they would not view the conflict as having moved into a political phase. Their thinking and response was military.

This reaction was also shared by west Belfast UDA commander 'Charlie' who argued:

> When you are engaged in a war of attrition the politics gets pushed aside. We needed to do what Sinn Fein had done which was to develop politically from the bottom up. After the Agreement, the perception was that loyalism had been forgotten and that it was Republicans who were benefiting most. Rhetoric started to fill the gap and Paisley was hitting the mark. I would say that over 90 per cent of the 700 to 800 members in west Belfast would have been for the Agreement, but that this was because many had friends and family who were in jail and the Agreement offered a way out of that. However, pretty soon there was disillusionment about the Agreement and support died quickly.

In contrast to the negative reactions expressed about the Agreement by many within the UDA leadership, its impact was far less corrosive within the UVF leadership. As the UVF Number One explained:

> The UVF did not view the outcome of the Good Friday Agreement as a good deal. There was certainly a feeling of insecurity, but our position was that we had tried to get the best deal possible and we were sure that under the circumstances we had done that. In order to address concerns, the leadership conducted extensive consultations with the various constituencies. The best argument that we could offer was that this was the only show in town and that just as sacrifices had been made in the past, so compromises were necessary now. We weren't coming out as winners and we knew that political manoeuvrability would not be the same again. We didn't really know which way it was going to be

implemented and it was a confusing situation. But we stressed that if you want peace then you have to settle on what is not desirable as well. Although we were satisfied with the constitutional arrangement, the Loyalist community as a whole has no doubt been disillusioned with the implementation and interpretation of the Agreement. But it was never going to be a win situation and the best you can hope for is a draw.

There were also other internal factors which were contributing to the growing isolation of the UDP, which were connected to criminality, drugs and individuals seeking to increase their influence by capitalising on the growing uncertainty which permeated the UDA membership. At the centre of this development was the rise of Johnny Adair (Lister and Jordan 2003; McDonald and Cusack 2004: 310–89; Woods 2006: 226–96), who was supported by UDP representative John White and a small group of paramilitary associates. Billy Hutchinson of the PUP was very uneasy about the role of White and the rise of Adair, whose presence started to dominate the public image of loyalism, particularly from 2000, when Adair co-ordinated a damaging Loyalist feud (Rowan 2003: 205–27):

> From 1994 after the ceasefires, we had the articulate voices of David Ervine and David Adams who were moving loyalism away from the stereotypes of neanderthal criminals and then, all of a sudden, the media moved towards this shaven head, tattooed man with a dog in a t-shirt and you have to ask yourself why. Why did he become the image of loyalism when everybody knew we had articulate voices putting forward a legitimate and intelligent Loyalist case? Adair was basically a criminal that the UDA couldn't control and what they used to do with people they couldn't control was to bring them further into the organisation. Adair rose through the ranks of the UDA very swiftly and within two years he was at the very top of the organisation. When he came out of jail, John White became his mentor and it was White who got Adair all the publicity and who basically used that publicity to keep Adair alive. I had been arguing with Gary McMichael since 1998 that his big problem was being surrounded by people who were up to their necks in drugs and who actually, were driving the UDA agenda. These people were claiming peace whilst behind the backs of McMichael and Adams they were undermining the process at every turn. The problem for the rest of us was that the articulate voices then became associated with criminality, which was made worse by feuds.

Given these problems (the rise of Adair will be examined in more detail later) and the growing lack of support among the UDA leadership towards the Agreement, it was clear that the UDP's position would become increasingly untenable, making its collapse unavoidable. Though the party continued to try and hold its position as political voice of the UDA after the Agreement, its political influence both towards the politics of the peace process and the direction of the UDA became glaringly ineffective as the organisation became embroiled in a series of internal and external feuds. The end for the UDP came in May 2001 elections, when the party fought not as a party, but as a series of independent candidates because it had not registered as a political organisation as required by new electoral laws (reflecting the disarray and growing disaffection) (McAuley 2005: 326). Now, without the UDP, the UDA lacked any sense of political purpose and dissolved into internecine conflict as figures such as Johnny Adair became engaged in power struggles which were devised to recreate the idea of Loyalist resistance and establish a new criminal and sectarian form of leadership within paramilitarism.

Omagh

Before we look at the feuds which emerged in this period, it is important to consider to a key moment in the peace process where political progress was destabilised and where Loyalists came close to re-engaging with military action against Republicans. Some four months after the signing of the Good Friday Agreement on 15 August 1998, dissident Republican group the Real IRA exploded a huge car bomb in the market town of Omagh, killing 29 people and unborn twins and injuring hundreds (many seriously). The bomb had created the worst single act of terrorism in the history of the 'Troubles' (Spencer 2005) and its impact resonated throughout Northern Ireland and beyond. Clearly designed to undermine the peace process and draw public support away from politics, the bombing posed significant concerns for Loyalists, who met immediately to determine a response. At a UVF leadership emergency meeting on the same day as the bombing (a string of subsequent meetings followed), there was 'massive' pressure for retaliatory measures to be taken. The UVF's Number One recalled:

> Those of us who resisted demands for retaliation had real problems 'holding the line'. The meeting was hot and heavy and it was primarily the military thinkers who were pushing for a response. The argument being put forward against retaliation was that this had been carried out by dissidents and that those who had committed this were against the process and so not useful to Sinn Fein. We could see that from the Provisionals' point of view, there was nothing to be gained, although there was some debate about whether it was a tactical move, and that it was a 'dirty bomb' designed to up the ante. There was also evident Catholic anger against Omagh which removed any sectarian argument for revenge. We decided almost to a man that we needed to get a message to the Irish government that those responsible had to be dealt with.

In other words, dissidents needed to be 'jailed on the basis of intent'. The message we sent to the Irish was that if this was not dealt with there would be action and that new legislation would be required, which the Irish introduced soon after. It was important to be seen to be acting and we made it clear that if the Irish didn't act, we would. What we were asking ourselves was if there was a return to violence how was it going to finish? Those around the table had people across the border ready to go and the question of targets did come up. They had McKevitt's [head of the Real IRA] shop targeted and were ready to move.

David Ervine and Billy Hutchinson also met with the UVF leadership in meetings and Ervine commented on how reactions to Omagh were handled:

> I was out of the country when the first meeting occurred and I think that there was one or two in the leadership who used that as a stalling tactic. Although I possess no authority at leadership level, there was a suggestion that the leadership should not respond until they had put questions to me and seen if I could put things to the government. This obstructed immediate reactions which would have been emotionally driven and made out of anger, rather than being considered. What emerged was a response where the Loyalists were saying to governments if you deal with this we will stay out of it. But there were considerable questions and arguments about that. We got the British to react in terms of publicly stating that these people would be hunted down, but it was the Irish who were more active afterwards and that helped ease pressure.

Billy Hutchinson explained how important Ervine's role was at this time and how his contribution helped to defuse the pressure for retalitation which members of the leadership were pressing for:

> I rang David immediately after the bomb and said it was over, but David disagreed. He said we needed to do the same with the Americans and the governments as we had over Canary Wharf, which was to get them to commit to taking action. We had a meeting with the UVF leadership on the Sunday and David put a scenario to them which he sold brilliantly and which he got them to agree to. There were three meetings up to the Wednesday of the week after the bomb and we got them to hold back. David laid out what he thought needed to be done and he also said that he had been talking to people who had been relaying some intelligence information and that people needed to stay calm. He put together his conversations with civil servants and senior police officers and he put forward a very convincing case to not retaliate militarily. Also Sinn Fein helped by the public statements they were making and there was condemnation from the Provos. David was told that the Americans were

going to come out hard against this and that the CIA had been involved and had scanned a few phones to try and catch those who had done it, and all that was relayed to the UVF to try and allay their fears. After a few weeks there was enough action taken against dissidents by the Irish to show people that they weren't going to allow those people to use Irish territory as a boot camp. But the reaction of Republicans was very important here as well. They were concerned that these dissident groups would give their people a platform to jump to, but they were also saying positive things like we're past this period and need to get on with the Agreement. In many ways, there was a determination in people not to let this derail them, but also in a paradoxical way, people were using it as an excuse not to move too quickly and to make sure that it wouldn't derail.

The intermediary who relayed the UVF's message to the Irish government demanding action was Chris Hudson. Here Hudson describes the background to that time:

I had been in hospital with heart trouble and I had just come home when the Omagh bomb happened. I was recovering at home when my wife took a call from the UVF's Number Two, who said he needed to talk to me urgently. She told him I was recovering from a mild heart attack so I was unavailable. He said okay and put the phone down. But thirty minutes later he called back and said he had to talk to me because it was urgent. He told me he could come to Dublin to see me and my wife met him from the train. He apologised, given my condition, for troubling me, but said there was no choice and that they might retaliate unless there was a clear signal from the Dublin government that it was going to take measures against those responsible. From what I understood, the UVF had planned to put a bomb in McKevitt's shop in Dundalk and the Number Two stressed that the Dublin Government had to be clear in its message against these people. I got a message to Martin Mansergh and shortly afterwards the Dublin government made some very tough sounds about the Real IRA 'being given no quarter' and that those who planted the bomb would be dealt with harshly. The Garda would also be given more powers of arrest and it seemed as though the UVF leadership settled for this response.

When talking about the UVF's reaction to Omagh, Hudson also offered an insight into his relations with the UVF's Number Two and gave this evaluation of the Number Two's role within the UVF's political thinking:

Often the Number Two would present other people as hardliners without mentioning names. He would never mention names, but would say things like 'My people think this', or 'the people I am talking to' etc. But over the fullness of time I came to see the Number Two as a hardliner, who would be using himself in the third person. I also knew that in their dispute with the LVF he was the hardliner who wanted them removed from the scene. He would regularly say 'The people I'm talking to are concerned', and that 'there is always a danger that some people could revert back to what they know best', or 'we have to convince certain people that Dublin is serious about this' etc. In interactions of this kind, and from my experience, no single person is going to say 'I'm not accepting this', but if that person positions themselves as somebody else, then you have to try and sell all the arguments for him so he will then sell them to other guys. The case has to be made more effectively and it removes personal likes and dislikes from the exchange.

The intense discussions which took place in the immediate aftermath of the bomb between the UVF and the PUP and the reaction of the Irish Government to the UVF's demands for strong public condemnation and the implementation of clearly recognisable measures against Republican dissidents, contributed to prevent the UVF embarking on a responsive campaign of violence and thereby worked to keep their ceasefire intact. The public reaction to Omagh also significantly demonstrated the end of sympathy for Republican violence and 'offered the leadership of the republican movement the best possible conditions to address the arms issue' (Patterson 2006: 341), as well as supporting arguments which stressed that political violence as a way forward was now counterproductive and so effectively over.

Feuds and intra-Loyalist violence

For Loyalists, more violence was to come in the form of feuds and internecine conflict. A key underlying reason for this descent into violence was the emergence of personality struggles within the UDA and in particular, Johnny Adair's attempts to promote a battle with the UVF, which would satisfy his ambition of becoming the figurehead of Loyalist paramilitarism. Released from prison in September 1999, Adair quickly sought to build relations with the LVF (despised within the UVF) and incite a feud with the UVF in order to try and augment UDA control and affirm his own position as a leading force within the UDA. Working with John White – who had been involved with the UDP – Adair staged provocative gestures of defiance, and in August 2000 organised a UDA march on the Shankill Road alongside LVF members, which incited UVF reaction and led to a murderous feud between Adair's 'C' company of the UDA and the UVF (Rowan 2003: 205–27; McDonald and Cusack 2004: 310–40; Woods 2006: 226–96). Over a period of seven weeks in the summer of 2000, seven men were killed (four by the UVF and three by the UDA) and hundreds were driven from their homes as the feud gained in intensity (Rowan 2003: 206).

Using the Drumcree stand-off and interface rioting in parts of Belfast to stir unrest and shape the conditions for violence, Adair intended (but failed) to embroil the UDA in a battle for Loyalist supremacy. However, his role in co-ordinating murders and sectarian hatred became so obvious, that Northern Ireland Secretary Peter Mandelson revoked his early release licence, returning Adair to jail weeks after the start of the feud (ibid.: 208). Although other UDA units had tried to distance themselves from Adair, his determination to ignite a struggle for internal control within the UDA by way of provoking the UVF into a feud, proved particularly destructive for those who had spent years trying to provide loyalism with a political voice and respectability. Leading figures both within the UDA and the UVF were highly critical of Adair and his attempts to destabilise loyalism and the peace process. For the UVF's Number Two:

> There's no doubt that Adair did a lot of damage to loyalism. His characterisation reinforced problems of perception and identity and loyalism seemed to reinvent itself on the Johnny Adair model of criminality. This man came from nowhere. There had been an attempt to move away from the portrayal of Loyalists as neanderthals and then Adair comes on the scene and becomes an icon. It almost disfigured this community and the bigger issues about his role still rumble on. Our problem was his portrayal by the media and how it was being used. It resulted in young lads flocking to join Adair and in the case of many, going to jail. He essentially parachuted in from nowhere and became a personality. People were saying at the time, if this isn't dealt with, we will end up with him and it resulted in a feud. Both Wright and Adair were used to demonise and criminalise loyalism and the involvement of both in drugs exacerbated the problem. The media contributed to Adair's sense of invincibility and it was difficult to get at him. What helped was that significant elements within the UDA didn't support Adair and they knew he was an egotist. They could also see that Adair was heading for oblivion. The problem for the UVF was that if Adair had been killed the violence would have intensified, so it was necessary to see him further marginalised and isolated. There's no doubt though that Adair undermined political loyalism and created a war situation within the communities.

The view that Adair had quickly emerged as a figure of influence was also stressed by senior UDA and UFF commander 'Alan', who commented:

> I became a paramilitary in 1973 and I never heard of Johnny Adair until 1990. The media said that he was supreme commander of the UFF, but I don't know of him in that role and he certainly never had any idea of the units or the operations I was involved with, nor would he have

known about the targets we were involved in eliminating. The only way he would have had knowledge about the operations would have been from within prison and not because he was directing operations or sending people out. The two key people involved in the UFF kept themselves in the background and wouldn't have sought the publicity that Adair did. He was neither intelligent or a military genius. I came across a lot of people in my five years involvement in the UFF and never heard of him. He surrounded himself with some respected people who allowed him to take credit for things, but as time went on he became a destabilising influence. The criminality, drugs and lifestyle he had did have an impact. Imagine if you're a volunteer struggling to support your family and you see Adair with fancy cars, going on expensive holidays. A lot of people got sucked in by that.

The UDA's east Belfast commander 'Billy', similarly voiced criticism against Adair for his destructive role:

Adair caused more trouble in Northern Ireland in recent years than the Provos did in a long time. He may have been a committed Loyalist when he was fighting the war, but when that stopped all he saw was pound signs and once that happened it ruined everything. Initially young lads looked up to him but after a number of Loyalists were murdered he made a fool out of himself and resentment increased. We have argued that people didn't join the UDA to become drug dealers, but to fight a war. It was just unacceptable.

And the UDA's west Belfast commander 'Charlie' added:

Adair became a megalomaniac. When he came out of jail, White advised him to start talking to the press and he just started feeding all this publicity. He was saying I will do this and I will do that, as if he was bigger than the whole organisation. He was also pulling a lot of young people in through drugs and the status the media was giving him. But as has been shown time and again, once an individual starts to think they are bigger than the organisation, it's the end.

From the south Belfast commander Jackie McDonald, who clashed with Adair on a number of occasions, there was particular criticism:

Adair's campaign was driven by his macho-ego. He particularly hated the UVF and wanted to wipe them out, but he also came on the scene when drugs were becoming more available. He just abused the position he got to and he couldn't cope with the idea of this society moving towards normality. He almost destroyed loyalism and he was obsessed by publicity. In any newspaper article there seemed to be a half page photograph of him, which journalists would put in to increase the sensationalism. He was dominating the image of loyalism and he was the main drug dealer. We had reports from the LVF that he was making £60,000 a week from selling drugs. Loyalism was just a vehicle for him to get to where he wanted to go and his role in the feuds was a very bad time for loyalism.

Adair's role from 2000–3, reveals a systematic and unrelenting attempt to destroy the UVF and remove those elements of the UDA's Inner Council who were resistant to his delusions about becoming an icon of Loyalist paramilitary violence. Although Adair had played some part in raising the need to decommission Loyalist weapons (McDonald and Cusack 2004: 317), it became apparent over time that this move was designed to augment his public image as peacemaker, while behind the scenes Adair orchestrated the murder of those who obstructed his goal of dominance. Indeed, behind Adair's rhetoric about decommissioning, he proceeded to rearm his 'C' Company unit in readiness for an upsurge in internecine Loyalist violence (Lister and Jordan 2003: 283). Essentially, Adair's main aim was to 'lead a realigned anti-Agreement mass Loyalist movement' (ibid.: 323), which meant removing those Loyalists who had played a key part in supporting the Agreement such as the UVF. This strategy was not always about the use of overt violence, but using supportive UDA members to help expel families with UVF links from their homes in order to bring wider areas under his control and influence (ibid.: 335). Adair's hatred for the more pro-Agreement convictions of the UVF and PUP, made them necessary targets in Adair's grand design to present him as the 'true' protector of Ulster's interests and culture, and he was particularly resentful of those within the UDA who did not share the hostility on which this position was based. The divisive nature of Adair's attempt to further fragment loyalism in order to reconstruct it to complement his sectarian worldview, was not unknown to the security forces who had intelligence about his part in interface violence, provocative parades and drug-dealing (Rowan 2003: 209). And it was Adair's involvement in each of these activities which went largely unchallenged by the security services until it had become impossible to ignore them, which most alarmed and frustrated the PUP. To quote Billy Hutchinson:

> Adair not only created uncertainty but he polluted the atmosphere in loyalism further towards a 'them and us' situation. The problem this created was that if you were for the Agreement you were seen as a bad person and if you were against the Agreement you were also seen as a bad person. If you were in the 'yes' camp it was made to look like you were prepared to

do anything to get the Provos on board and give them everything, whilst getting nothing in return. And if you were in the anti-Agreement camp, it suggested that your main task was to stop the Provos from getting anything. People on the ground got sucked in by the anti-Agreement stuff and the feuds in 2000 fed into that business. We had people who were being controlled by the security services, who were anti-Agreement behind closed doors, whilst publicly saying pro-Agreement things. The more they articulated pro-Agreement positions, the more criminality they were involved in and the more sectarian acts they were involved in. This created major confusion about what was going on, which of course was the aim because these people wanted to bring everything down. In August 2000 Adair was teaming up with the LVF and he knew that the UVF were putting pressure on the LVF to get out of the picture. He was telling the LVF that he would support them and together they would strike back. That was why he decided to walk up the Shankill with an LVF contingent in the parade, because it was a deliberately orchestrated provocation which he knew the UVF would not allow. That started the feud which just created the impression that all Loyalists were a bunch of criminals and gangsters and things disintegrated from there.

The feud that began in the summer of 2000, led to a spate of sectarian murders which moved the UDA towards an overwhelmingly rejectionist position for the Agreement by 2001 (ibid.: 210), and the organisation was being drawn further into tensions about area leaders and their ability to either contain, or, live up to the hardline approach being espoused by Adair. Even from within jail (having had his license revoked by Mandelson because of the 2000 feud) Adair continued to direct violence and murder. Indeed, Adair's re-arrest further encouraged his colleagues to accelerate their campaign in his absence. A series of tit-for-tat murders between UVF and UDA members spread throughout Belfast, with UDA members seen as unfaithful to Adair executed on his orders (Lister and Jordan 2003: 299). UDA and senior UFF commander 'Alan' elaborated on Adair's strategy of trying to draw paramilitaries into conflict:

> There were a number of battalions that didn't support Adair and it was brigadiers from outside Adair's area that brought an end to the feud. Adair was being told to stop and sort out the feud he was creating, but he was actually sending people into other Loyalist areas to attack houses and put the thought into peoples' minds that they were being attacked by Nationalists in order to try and draw them back into conflict. In the end it came out that it was members of 'C' Company who were trying to draw other brigades in by saying the attacks were the work of the UVF or the IRA when it was Adair's men.

The sectarian tensions were not only confined to Loyalist organisations, but would also become manifest in interface areas where Protestant and Catholic communities existed alongside each other in tense circumstances. In June 2001, Protestant residents began a 12-week protest against Catholic children and their parents as they passed along the Ardoyne Road to the Holy Cross primary school in north Belfast. The incident came about when Protestants from the adjoining Glenbryn estate were drawn into conflict with Nationalists from the nearby Ardoyne because of efforts by Loyalist sympathisers to raise UDA and UFF flags. The men who were driven at by a car which brought down a ladder and one of the Loyalists, resulted in Ardoyne Republicans chasing the Loyalists into Glenbryn, where they were confronted by other Loyalists. This resulted in Ardoyne Republicans chasing the Loyalists into Glenbryn, where they were confronted by other Loyalists. Both communities were quickly drawn into the confrontation and trouble escalated (McDonald and Cusack 2004: 355). Resentment among Loyalists about the Agreement benefiting Republicans, as well as considerable social disadvantage in the area itself, provided the necessary fuel for Protestant anger, as Catholic children and their parents came under attack when trying to attend the Holy Cross school. Though the extent of the UDA's role in Holy Cross may be open to some speculation, there is little doubt that elements of the organisation sought to manipulate and exacerbate difficulties by issuing a death threat (through the cover name of the Red Hand Defenders) against Catholic school teachers and all staff working in Catholic schools in north Belfast (Troy 2005: 152). There is also some suspicion that UDA members vacated the Lower Shankill and moved to Glenbryn during the 2000 feud in order to avoid the unwelcome attention of the UVF, and orchestrated violence from within (Cadwallader 2004: 201). Other explanations tend to emphasise deteriorating relations between Nationalists and Protestants after the Drumcree stand-offs in 1995–6 and the migration of residents from the area at this time, to be replaced by those less inclined towards friendly inter-communal relations (ibid.: 202). Those who did arrive were seen to have included a number with UDA sympathies, which increased the potential for interface violence between Loyalists and Republicans.

The resulting protests and problems gained international news coverage, which magnified the impression that Loyalists were responsible for the anguish being suffered by Nationalists and Catholic children, and was used by Republican representatives to reinforce general assumptions that Loyalists were ostensibly sectarian and so without legitimate grievance for underlying communal tensions (McDonald and Cusack 2004: 358). Such grievances were made harder to convey when UDA members moved into the area to try and exacerbate the protests and increase the potential for wider trouble by drawing Holy Cross into a campaign of low-level, but concerted Loyalist violence, which took the form of pipe bombing Catholic homes across north Belfast (Cadwallader 2004: 209). For those engaged in this violence, Holy Cross could be used to demonstrate Loyalist resistance to perceived Nationalist advancement and so be presented as a gesture of deterrence and defiance (ibid.: 223). It could also be used to try and incite a larger cross-communal campaign of hatred in order to undermine the peace process and exacerbate conflict (ibid.: 205).

Initially, Adair encouraged the Holy Cross dispute from prison (Cadwallader 2004: 204), but then ordered the protests to end. On the one hand, this was because media images were reinforcing the view that Loyalists were driven by pathological animosity and hostility, but on the other hand, came about because Adair was trying to re-invent himself as an influential Loyalist who was now committed to peace. Released from prison in May 2002, Adair later met with Loyalists on the Glenbryn estate to prevent a reoccurrence of the protests and briefly held ambitions to try and move into politics (McDonald and Cusack 2004: 362). But within four months of Adair's release, security service intelligence had ascertained that he was intending to wipe out the UDA's Inner Council in a bid for total control (Rowan 2003: 221). It took until September for the next feud to begin, which again Adair directed. The feud started with the murder of LVF member Stephen Warnock on 13 September (at the time, east Belfast UDA were suspected of the murder, but it is now believed to have been the work of the Red Hand Commando) which resulted in the attempted murder of UDA Inner Council member Jim Gray three days later by the LVF. Five days after that the UDA's north Belfast leader Andre Shoukri was arrested, charged with possession of a firearm and sentenced to six years in prison (Adair was responsible for Shoukri's rise to leader and the removal of its former leader 'Jimbo' Simpson (Lister and Jordan 2003: 308–9)). In response, the UDA's Inner Council acted on 25 September by expelling Adair from the organisation and Adair retaliated the following day, by making a statement (released by the Red Hand Defenders), that three Inner Council members should publicly stand down or face military action. The Inner Council responded the next day by expelling John White (Rowan 2003: 222–3).

Two further murders followed before the UDA and the LVF agreed to end the feud, with the LVF publicly stating on 5 November that it accepted that east Belfast UDA had no role in the murder of Stephen Warnock (ibid.: 223). The statement made to this effect, was reached as a joint decision by the leaders of both organisations and provided a clear signal that the deadly feud, which Adair had co-ordinated, was over. Soon after this announcement was released, the UDA set about isolating Adair totally. However, this did not occur until south east Antrim UDA leader John Gregg was murdered. Adair was rearrested and sent back to prison on 10 January 2003 (remaining there until January 2005), but his colleagues still remained under his influence, and carried out the murder of Gregg shortly after Adair's incarceration on 1 February. Increasingly at this time, even Adair's closest associates were moving away from the murderous campaign that he had orchestrated and finally waking up to its destructive impact. The murder of Gregg provoked a strong reaction in the UDA and there immediately followed a choreographed sequence of moves and statements by both the UDA's Inner Council and the LVF which led to an ultimatum, where those who wished to remain loyal to Adair would now be regarded 'as the enemies of Ulster' and treated accordingly (ibid.: 225). With Adair in prison, White in hiding and the combined efforts of the Inner Council and LVF working to marginalise those still supportive of Adair, loyalty to his campaign quickly vanished and the UDA moved towards restating a new ceasefire in February 2003 (ibid.: 226).

The impact of the struggle for power and control which Adair had created, dramatically undermined progress towards an articulate Loyalist politics, replacing it with an image of loyalism as being little more than a process of criminality, brutality and self-destructiveness. For those such as David Ervine of the PUP, the actions of Adair, which contributed to the demise of the CLMC and damaged the potential for cross-community co-operation and dialogue, could not have acquired the devastating consequences they did without some external support:

> I would say that the CLMC fell apart because of Johnny Adair and John White. They didn't want it and worked relentlessly to get the UDA to move away from the CLMC, which is what happened. It was tactical and planned, and all kinds of games were being played to undermine the validity of what the CLMC were doing. Both Adair and White were allowed to ply their trade of drugs and allowed to gain all the manifestations of strength and wealth. White saw no contradiction in being a Loyalist and a drug-dealer. They actively talked pro-Agreement language by day and killed Catholics by night. I have to say that the impunity of their actions calls into question the sincerity of the intelligence services. And I would argue that the security services were quite manipulative of elements within loyalism. It was recognised by the government and the security services that it was highly unlikely that you could truck with loyalism and republicanism at the same time because they wanted opposite things. We know that the IRA produced wish-lists, shopping lists. Now if you get a Loyalist shopping list and an IRA shopping list, you will see that they are diametrically opposed. The British Governent's main goal was to get the IRA off the stage, so the impetus was for them to deliver an IRA wish-list and it was this which was causing anti-Agreement sentiment in the Unionist community. If you concede something to Republicans, you couldn't concede it to loyalism and a loyalism that was in disarray was probably a more controllable loyalism. You also diminish the ability of loyalism to derail the process if its anger is internalised into feuds, schisms and other difficulties. What

this did was create a situation where the criminals were politicised and the politicos were criminalised. The attention was then focussed on steroid pumped up men, with dogs in t-shirts and I don't believe that happened by accident. There was a feeding frenzy within the media and all the interest was on the evil and bad things paramilitaries were getting away with.

If Ervine's contention about Adair being unable to gain influence without the security forces seems contentious, one should note that Adair himself confided he was approached by the RUC's Special Branch with offers to work for them. Furthermore, although Adair was apprehended and imprisoned twice (raising questions about him being allowed to tear loyalism apart), his arrest was carried out by the CID, who found Special Branch to be obstructive and unhelpful in bringing Adair to justice (Woods 2006: 316); contributing to later revelations about collusion between Loyalists and Special Branch (ibid.). But, taking these factors into account, it is still necessary to bear in mind that even if Special Branch had used Adair, it would have been impossible for him to gain the influence he did without wider support from Loyalists who were drawn to his campaign. No doubt also, the media increased the attraction, as well as the fears, which surrounded Adair and helped to exaggerate his own sense of importance, which was to be a key motivation in his efforts to become a paramilitary figurehead (Lister and Jordan 2003: 307), and that tensions were magnified by a growing despondency within the wider Protestant community about the peace process and the perception that Nationalists were gaining most from the change taking place (even if alongside this perception there was a broad acceptance of power-sharing and the consent principle among that audience (Mac Ginty 2004)). As Ervine discovered within his own constituency, so entrenched were perceptions about Republican violence and Nationalist manipulation that many were unable to read the changing relationship between Catholic voters and Sinn Fein as a sign of growing support for politics, instead viewing this transformation as developing out of a belief in the successes of violence, rather than a growing resentment for it:

> I debated long and hard with the UVF when their view was that the Catholic population was voting for violence when they are voting for Sinn Fein. My argument was exactly the opposite. I was saying that Catholics are not voting for violence when they are voting for Sinn Fein, they are voting against violence when they vote for Sinn Fein. That what they are doing is bolstering Sinn Fein against the IRA and inviting Sinn Fein to take the primacy of politics over the paramilitaries. That is what the Catholic community is doing.

The Loyalist Commission

In response to the feuds which took place from 2000 onwards, a Loyalist Commission was set up to try and facilitate dialogue between the warring Loyalist factions. The Loyalist Commission, which was devised through the recommendations of David Trimble and Archbishop Robin Eames, consisted of clergy, community workers and paramilitaries from the Protestant community and offered a platform for the UDA which now lacked political representation (Woods 2006: 278). Adair initially joined the Commission to once more present himself as peacemaker, but in all probability, was using the Commission to assess how UDA and UVF representatives were planning to end the feuds and working on a strategy which would obstruct those efforts. For the UVF, the Commission was seen as a possible replacement to the role of the CLMC, in that it offered the possibility of a forum for paramilitary leaders from the UVF and UDA (the LVF were not deemed acceptable to attend) to meet and discuss underlying tensions within respective communities and suggest possible forms of action to diffuse those tensions. The Chair of the Loyalist Commission was Presbyterian minister Reverend Mervyn Gibson, who provided this background to its aims and intentions:

> The big feud of 2000–2001 between the UVF and the UDA was based mainly on the Shankill and was largely internalised in that community. It created the biggest population movement in Belfast since 1968, with UDA and UVF members having to move out. The feud had been more or less sorted out militarily, but there was no sign of a healing process, which was something the church needed to be involved in. I was asked to chair a Commission which had been devised largely through the work of David Trimble and Archbishop Eames, and the paramilitaries wanted me to chair it. So the Commission was formed with church representatives, some politicians and community activists. We got the three Loyalist groups the UDA, the UVF and the Red Hand Commando together, but at first they would not talk to each other, or even sit in the same room, such was the hurt and pain that the feuds had caused. Those who attended were leaders or high ranking members and although attendance would change from time to time, it was always the highest ranking people who were there. The main purpose was to get the groups together to stop any bad blood and a reoccurrence of the feud. There was no set agenda and the aim was to get them talking and build up relationships, which we did quite quickly. We told them at the start that they couldn't go sitting in separate rooms if they had agreed to join the Commission, and once we had overcome that, we put a triple-lock on all three groups in that all three had to agree what to talk about and there would have to be a consensus at the end of each meeting about how

to proceed. It was important that no one group could gain advantage over the other two. We always had clear support from the leaderships and they were also clear that with some things they would need to go back to their own people for reference, which was fair enough. It was no good them agreeing to something which down the line their organisation was going to throw out, so there had to be leeway there as well. Significantly, some of these guys didn't see their own command structures from other areas, so they were seeing the broader picture and could reciprocate accordingly. There was quite a bit of sharing going on. I would say that we had involvement in something like six or seven feuds until the Commission came to an end in April 2006.

Going on to explain the work of the Commission in more detail, Gibson commented:

We stressed that it was the paramilitaries who should determine the issues and that we were there to facilitate that process. Some wanted to take it towards political issues, while others wanted to stress the need to get any ceasefires to hold and it tended to move from one to the other. It was clear that one of the groups was further down the road towards peace than the other and that had created a tension which, some would say, contributed to the first big feud. So we had to get to a stage where they were both at the same point with regard to the peace process. This wasn't a conscious or overt aim, but it soon became apparent that for practical purposes, the success of the Commission depended on getting the groups to some kind of even keel. We always tried to deal with the military side of things rather than the political, since that was what we were there to try and prevent. Initially we met in church halls, but we sometimes met in pubs and clubs and used one community centre. We moved the venue to reflect the different areas and to show that we didn't favour one group or area over another. Significantly, the LVF were not involved and nor would their presence have been acceptable. The meeting consisted of about 25–30 people and we always opened and closed with a prayer, which reflected the church's input. Once the agenda was sorted out, we got settled on the mechanics and the rules of engagement. We laid out the ground rules for how the Commission would meet, as well as security and integrity issues, because many of the paramilitaries did not know Commission representatives. This enabled us to proceed with some degree of confidence. We would sometimes meet in hotels if there was a feud going on and we would try to go over what the feud was about. We would try to get to the bottom of what started it and we would ask them what might help to resolve it and what their bottom line was in resolving it. Sometimes that would mean an organisation wanting a person dealt with, which we wanted no part of. Another organisation might then tell you their position, but stress they did not want to negotiate, so sometimes the Commission conducted negotiations by proxy, where they listened to one side and then went to speak to the other, who would take a certain position. Then both sides would see if it was a starter and we would proceed from there. The meetings would tend to last two to three hours and minutes would be taken. However, no names were attached and the minutes have never been released. We started by meeting every few days and then this went to fortnightly meetings, but the meetings also took place in response to developments as they occurred and which the paramilitaries wanted to deal with straight away. We got church leaders and government figures to come and talk with them directly, but the presence of the clergy would provide the government with a degree of cover so they could say that they weren't just talking to the paramilitaries, but the Commission itself.

Gibson then spoke about how the Commission's first real test came with the Holy Cross dispute and emphasised how the Commission sought to develop a sense of ownership and responsibility among the local Protestant community in order to encourage control of the protest and so provide a space for consideration of alternative action (contrasting with McDonald and Cusack's contention that it was Adair who 'read the riot act' to core protesters to stop (2004: 362)):

The Commission became involved at that time in order to create a framework where it was okay for the Protestant community to express their views. It was also used to enable the paramilitaries to give control of the situation to the community. We went to a local community centre and we had community members and the paramilitary leaders present and it was agreed that the community had a legitimate cause for grievance, but that there were better ways of getting that grievance across. The paramilitaries did however say that they would support a local decision to either continue with the protest, or to call it off. It was clear that the bad publicity being produced was not doing anybody any good, but it was also clear that there was no real ownership of the protest, or any real idea about what else could be done. People were afraid to call for the protest to end in case they were seen as a traitor and the paramilitaries told them that this would not happen. The paramilitary leaders, by being present, enabled the community not to feel threatened by their own paramilitaries and at that time, there was a lot of rumours that paramilitaries were behind the protest and keen to keep it going. The Commission tried to create a sense of confidence that this was not going to happen and put decisions into the hands of local residents. Holy Cross was a moment which was dealt with to some extent like the feuds, where it was important to set up lines of communication so that things didn't get out of hand. That was the aim, to bring the situation under some kind of control so that people could make clearer sense of what was going on and how to respond.

The Commission was ostensibly involved with working to avoid a reoccurrence of feuds *between* Loyalist groups rather than dealing with feuds that took place *within* those groups (hence its lack of impact on the UDA's internal feuds coordinated by Adair). As Gibson explained this interaction:

> The Commission never dealt directly with single organisation feuds, although there was some individual input from members of the Commission in that area. The reason the Commission could not get involved was because it was set up to deal with all three paramilitary groups on issues. If it was an internal UDA feud, the Commission couldn't do anything because it had nothing to do with the UVF, and by the same logic, if it was a feud between the LVF and the UVF, the UDA could not be involved so neither could the Commission. It's also important to say that nothing one can say will stop a feud. All you can do is try to create the climate and space so when organisations are ready to come together you can facilitate that, and make sure that things are ready to go when it comes to that point, or when the signals are evident that it's coming to that point. Often a group would use the Commission to inform another group that things were going to end for 24 hours and the other group would act on that. Sometimes the Commission would be told when things were going to stop and that information was then provided to other groups. This was a way of avoiding accusations that one group was talking directly to another. Apart from the first big feud between the UVF and the UDA, most of the others were internal UDA or UVF/LVF feuds. Sometimes, if a feud was on, meetings would not take place for security reasons because all the leaders did not want to come to one place. We were also told when ceasefires were off and I recall on one occasion being phoned to say this was the case. Within eight hours UDA leader John Gregg was shot.

In order to try and ease tensions, the Commission was thus less concerned with the internal problems and disputes of the organisations and concerned more with preventing wider social fears and anxieties developing which would exacerbate violence:

> We became heavily involved in reducing flags and dealing with the competition about who could fly their flag the highest, which itself was seen as symbolic of strength, territory and tensions. We also brought in protocols to deal with the problem of schools being used to recruit kids

into the paramilitaries and we put together a schools charter to help stop that. We also got the groups access to senior government officials, such as Northern Ireland Secretary John Reid, who we met at a church hall, and we put together an anti-racist campaign. As well as that, we monitored developments and tried to address potentially dangerous situations as they arose. Not all the protocols came through us, because some actions were military, involving weapons and punishments. We made it clear that we wanted nothing to do with that. I remember in the early days, people were still being shot and I had to tell one UDA leader that he could not sit on the Commission if his people continued to kill others. Of course, people may have spoken with forked tongues at times, but overall the leaders were supportive. It wasn't a love-in or a hugging session. Talking was frank, open and often heated. We also tried to get those attending to move away from supporting criminality. The whole political situation was changing and criminality had become a problem, so we worked on debates about that and the damage it was doing. It's also important to point out that although these guys were making life and death decisions and in many cases were ruthless, they also, at times, held the communities back from taking actions into their own hands and had a calming influence. In many instances, when things happened, it was about letting off steam and controlling the situation so it didn't get worse. That doesn't justify what they did, but it's a point that is rarely acknowledged.

Gibson saw the end of the Commission in 2006 as an inevitable consequence of shifts in the political landscape, but also as reflective of how the organisations were beginning to respond more effectively to their own problems:

I think the Commission had served its purpose by then. It had got to the stage where the organisations were starting to work out their own respective approaches to the peace process. The UVF were always that bit ahead of the UDA in that regard and the work they were doing with the Red Hand Commando was well under way. Also it's important that they work out their own approaches for the integrity and culture of their organisation. One size doesn't fit all and the organisations had their own evolution, command structures, memberships and history, so it was necessary for each to evolve a peace strategy which suited that particular organisation. I think the Commission helped to bring them to that point. We offered a platform and opened a few doors with regard to the military end of things. It was a safety valve for things when tensions got high.

The Commission had offered a forum for Loyalist paramilitary leaders to communicate and had played a constructive role in helping to ease tensions, which were contributing to feuds between the organisations. Nevertheless, there was little it could do to address the feuds taking place within organisations, which continued to exacerbate the public perception that loyalism was ostensibly criminal in orientation and unable to break away from its general lawlessness. For the PUP, the feuding had created considerable damage to the development of political loyalism and was seen as the main reason why Billy Hutchinson lost his seat in the 2003 elections (Sinnerton 2002: 230), leaving the PUP with David Ervine as its sole political representative. Ervine himself perceived the feuding to be driven by three interrelated causes. First, British government concessions to Sinn Fein had served to intensify anger in loyalism and provide credence to anti-Agreement positions. Second, ongoing struggles between gangster elements in loyalism were being used to overcome obstructions to drug-dealing, extortion and general criminality. And third, the destruction of the CLMC so as to prevent inter-organisational dialogue and relationships from forming (ibid.: 230). Public fears of social and political developments meant that the more 'extreme' political parties (Sinn Fein and the DUP) were now able to establish themselves as dominant political representatives, while the smaller moderate parties were squeezed out of the political process (Farrington 2004). As part of this transition, the media image of loyalism was now controlled by the criminal behaviour of paramilitaries, which political representatives were being expected to comment on and through perceptible association, increasingly aligned with. Because of this perceived affiliation, the articulation of a progressive political direction for loyalism became increasingly difficult. We now turn to the media's relationship with the peace process and consider loyalism in the context of that relationship.

8
The Media

The role of the media in the Northern Ireland peace process has played a central role in the presentation and interpretation of political change. Former Northern Ireland Secretary Mo Mowlam described how 'the media were always an important dimension to consider' and 'at times seemed like another participant at the talks table' (2002: 80), while talks Chairman Senator George Mitchell saw the media as important both for parties trying to advance their negotiating position, and for increasing hostility among the participants, as each responded to accusations and attacks that were communicated routinely through the press (Mitchell 1999: 62). All the main political players in the peace process have sought to use the media to their advantage and position themselves as credible representatives of their respective communities. Some parties, such as Sinn Fein, have used the media particularly well and have moved quickly to manage the party's profile within the new terrain of policy articulation that the peace process has now created (Spencer 2006b). The media, for Sinn Fein, has been an extension of the party's internal cohesion and discipline and provided the space for its political leaders to portray themselves as respectable political spokespersons. In turn, the media has provided the arena where parties can convey their organisational and presentational skills, and has allowed each to communicate both with a variety of communities and with political opponents. It has been the conduit for megaphone diplomacy, helped to condition audiences for possible developments and been crucial for the choreography of movements and messages which have moved the peace process along. Indeed, for the choreography of statements and moves, the media's role has been and continues to be vital (Dixon 2002). Confirming the importance of choreography as an instrument of change, former Northern Ireland Secretary Paul Murphy stressed:

> Choreography was central all the time to the negotiation process. Everything was worked out to a tightly choreographed timescale and the

planning of statements, down to who would go first and how that was decided or disputed was always there, always.

Perhaps there is no surprise that those who have used the media well in the peace process have benefited most (Spencer 2006b), while those who have failed to exploit the media's communicative potential have benefited least (Spencer 2006a). However, in the case of small parties like the PUP, the UDP and the Women's Coalition (Spencer 2004a), failure to capitalise from the media's coverage of politics cannot be disassociated from a lack of resources and infrastructure, and so should not be seen as evidence of disorganisation or communicative incompetence, as with bigger parties, such as the UUP. The size of the smaller parties in the peace process has meant that they have often been unable to distribute their messages with the skill and persuasion of those such as Sinn Fein and that they were less able, because of this, to manage the news agenda or determine the scope and direction of debate with the same level of success.

News and negotiations

In the build-up to the Good Friday Agreement and particularly in the final hours before its announcement, parties sought to try and use the media to influence negotiations inside Castle Buildings by putting pressure and leverage on their opponents. However, it is instructive to note that the bigger parties such as Sinn Fein and the UUP took a very different stance towards using the news media and communicating their position towards developments at this time, reflecting different attitudes and intentions towards negotiations. The negotiating stance of the UUP had been based on a strategy of trying to hold out until the last moments before making concessions or moderating their position. As Quentin Thomas explained, this caused problems for both the UUP and their constituency:

> The UUP tended to adopt a quite hardline position and maintain it before then making big changes. But they hadn't gone through any process to prepare their own movement for this and that may be why their own movement has suffered politically, because they were lead up the hill and not lead down again. They had this metaphor which their people kept using which is that this thing is 'going to go down to the wire' and they thought that you were not going to get real movement until the end, because that was what they thought tough negotiations were about. The trouble is that you don't always know where the wire is. Although George Mitchell had set the Easter deadline, it was clear that if you tried to leave key negotiating decisions to the end there would be too much left to be done and you would run out of time. The cleverer parties would use the media to prepare the ground and condition expectations,

so that their people were not surprised and knew that a settlement was in the air. But I would say that the UUP did not use the media cleverly because they constantly tried to talk up their firmness of purpose, when it was obvious that in the end, if there was going to be a deal, it would involve compromise.

This negotiating strategy was in contrast with Sinn Fein, who had consulted their grassroots throughout and had prepared their people for the concessions which would need to be made. This consultative process clearly gave the party some confidence with regard to the final stages of the negotiations, which was apparent in the way they dealt with the media. Unlike the UUP, who would regularly use the news media to try and convey a sense of disappointment and anxiety about the way negotiations were going, Sinn Fein would routinely walk around the car park next to Castle Buildings smiling to each other and maintaining an image of control. By not rushing and appealing to the cameras, which conveyed an air of desperation, as the UUP did, Sinn Fein used the magnifying power of the news lens to project a sense of positive ease about the proceedings which was transmitted to all audiences simultaneously. Not surprisingly, as the Loyalist representatives made clear, whereas Republican audiences took the body language and calmness of Sinn Fein representatives as a sign that things were proceeding well, Unionist audiences read such signs as evidence of things going badly, and so took the view that the negotiations were failing to protect Unionist interests (Republican perceptions of Unionist desperation would similarly reinforce confidence that their own interests were not threatened) (Spencer 2004b: 48). Though Republicans did not have hardline Nationalists outside the talks exerting pressure through accusations of selling out, as the UUP did with Rev Dr Ian Paisley and the DUP, the UUP's way of dealing with the news media, in comparison to Sinn Fein, still highlights a failure to understand its communicative significance and magnifying power. As Stephen Leach put it when talking about the media's presence outside the negotiations:

> The media was another dimension to the negotiations. Often you would think that something had been gained in negotiation and then someone representing those you had negotiated with would go outside and give an interview and it would all unravel. The parties got quite savvy about this and it became part of the process. Sometimes a person you had just been speaking with would give an interview for the world to see and this did create problems, even if you could also decode it in ways which were more or less helpful. Of course, the parties were trying to reassure their electorate because they were getting phone calls all the time from party members outside asking if they were going to be sold out and what was happening. Communicating a reassuring message was part of the political strategy in trying to dampen down or remove misconceptions that

were flying around and allowed the parties to say that they were not going to agree to x, y and z. Sinn Fein were especially good at realizing what image would play well with their people and what would be photogenic. Their message was to look relaxed, whilst the Unionists would tend to come over as under pressure. But then they were agreeing to go into government with Sinn Fein and this was more of a stretch for the Unionists than it was for Nationalists.

Former Northern Ireland Secretary Paul Murphy viewed the media similarly to Leach, but also pointed out that ultimately, news coverage did not make that much difference to overall outcomes:

There was always a temptation for the parties to try and publicly communicate their case and that was why it constantly happened. The proximity of the press meant that within seconds the parties had access to the national and international networks. This might have had some leverage, but I don't think that what people said to the press would have materially altered the way in which negotiations went on. The main problem was that it could clutter up time and not only in terms of having to respond to statements, but because at times people would lock themselves into positions which they then had real trouble getting out of. If you tell the world something and have to go back and change your mind, that doesn't look good. But since all the parties were intent on getting the best deal for themselves, it is understandable that they should seek to use the media as best they can. The difficulty is because everybody wants that, there can be a tendency to end up popularising and this is problematic. Having said that, you had to put up with it because it was part of the process and although at times it was counterproductive, it was never destructive because things worked out in the end.

Murphy's contention that the media did not make that much difference to the substance of negotiations and the final outcome of the Agreement, raises interesting questions about what the media's involvement with the participants actually did bring about. For those who were reporting the negotiations, the media's presence helped to create a 'pressure-cooker' atmosphere, which the parties could not avoid being part of. Moreover, the media's involvement was an integral part of the momentum towards agreement, and brought pressure to bear in the sense that none of the participants wanted to be seen by the world's media as responsible for failing to try and bring about peace (Spencer 2004c: 611). The media's impact was therefore ostensibly connected to the expectations surrounding the possibility of a deal and used by the parties to express their positions towards that possibility. Since the substantive detail of the Agreement had been known for some time, it is clear that the media's main role was in conveying how near or far parties were from accepting a deal. In that sense, the media's negotiating influence was more about how the parties acted out their concerns and played up or down what they thought needed to be done in order to bring a settlement about. And the ability of party representatives to use the media in this way relates to the level of persuasive skill and presentational awareness, rather than articulating critical evaluation of the detail which the Agreement consisted of. The media's influence and power was therefore emotive rather than academic.

For David Ervine, the media was used ostensibly to restate and reinforce known negotiating positions rather than used to deliberate new ones, and helped to establish markers for positions, rather than revealing possible flexibility:

> I think the media is important to lay down your negotiating position, but I don't think it's important for negotiating. That is about people declaring their wants and hopefully achieving their needs. Often there are stated negotiation positions, but contained within those has been movement. Clearly with the DUP and Sinn Fein, there has been a massive shift from their previously stated positions, but the direction and goal of their project is primarily about protecting their negotiating position as much as possible. The media's role in that is important when you are not engaging with your enemy beyond megaphone diplomacy, but once opponents start dealing with issues and concerns directly together in an Assembly, the media's role for dialogue will reduce greatly. Then, you need only go along to the office of your opponents and can talk to them there.

Ervine's contention that the media are used to lay down stated positions suggests that the public communication of politics in a negotiations process is primarily about adopting a harder line towards opponents so as to reduce the possibility of appearing weak, uncertain and without conviction. Indeed, unlike private assurances, which can be retracted, public statements, which cannot, are a clear sign of conviction and thus operate as an important mechanism of pressure and commitment within formative negotiations (Spencer 2004c: 613) But Ervine's point about positions also indicating the potential for movement is also an important factor for consideration here. Nuanced shifts in language from 'no' to 'unacceptable', or 'not in that form', for example, present the possibility for movement and bargaining which the media was used constantly for in the early phases of the peace process (ibid.: 612), even though such shifts, were often embedded within a context of apparent intransigence, and even though the appearance of entrenched positions has been repeatedly used as a starting point (rather than an end point) for negotiation. But we should also add here that even if the media has demonstrable ability to exert pressure and through it demand a reaction from opponents, thus setting in motion a form of dialogue, it remains largely ineffective towards the substance of policy, and in terms of impact on policy outcomes is tangential (even if requiring consideration as part of how that process is pursued and presented) (Gowing 1994; Strobel 1994: 19; Strobel 1997).

With regard to the Loyalist parties, it became apparent that for some, the reactive tendency of loyalism acted as a hindrance to those seeking to initiate progressive positions. As media strategy tends to be a continuation of political strategy, there are obvious problems for those whose political strategy has been historically characterised by reaction. As the UDP's Gary McMichael recalled when talking about this difficulty:

> Consistently we spent the first two hours of every day talking about what had happened the day before, so it was always reactive and looking at immediate consequences and the immediate atmosphere, rather than thinking beyond that and looking strategically at things. Not seeming to get beyond day-to-day issues is a common feature within unionism. But not developing strategically means that positions are regularly established on the basis of what is going on now and that seems to be how problems are interpreted. This is an obvious frustration for those seeking to get beyond that. In the early stages, for us the main problem we faced was trying to make the most of events, whether we were at government meetings, reacting to what the British and the Irish were saying, or trying to read what Sinn Fein were saying. Because of those pressures we found it very difficult to project an image of leadership and pragmatism.

The reactive approach to situations, which McMichael mentions, is handled differently depending on the mechanisms of control which operate in varying organisations, however. Although the overall propensity is towards reaction, interviews conducted with those Loyalists attending the Good Friday Agreement negotiations indicate that the UVF was less prone to the negative consequences of reaction than the UDA, and is both representative of the way that organisation is controlled (centralised) and how communications take place within it (greater emphasis on consensus building and managing change than the UDA). The presence of the UVF leadership at Castle Buildings was able to ease tensions and offer insight into media reports in ways which the UDA leadership was not, precisely because the UVF, unlike the UDA, had been working on how to handle negotiations and interpret public party positions for some time. Political understanding is therefore an important factor in how a party reacts, or indeed, whether it reacts at all. For the UVF's Number Two:

> Media pressures were largely ineffective because the substance of the settlement was already decided. Because of this, there were no real surprises

and we knew pretty much what the outcome would be. Don't forget we had been going over this for some time so we were well versed on the details. Problems only really arise when there are unexpected surprises. The only real difficulty we had was on the timescale for prisoner releases. We had about sixty to seventy people there with us in the room at that time and that number did swell to about one hundred because people were watching things unfold on the television and wanted to be part of it. Other than that, things went pretty much how we thought they would.

Media as conduit and platform

It is clear that the media's importance within the peace process should not be underestimated, since particularly during the formative stages of that process it performed a vital conduit for communications between parties who would not talk directly. It also allowed the British and Irish governments to send synchronised signals to the varying communities about potential change (Spencer 2003) and enabled issues such as prisoner releases, to be publicly discussed (thus also preparing audiences for the likelihood of this move) (Spencer 2004c: 611). Public comments made to the media were taken as a sign of commitment (or not) to the process and helped to hold the participants to positions, which could easily be broken and with reduced negative consequences if kept private. The media has been used for leaking information in order to shift logjams in the talks parties, as well as obstruct momentum and interrupt the speed of choreography, and has provided a forum for debate which had been historically largely absent from Northern Ireland politics because of a refusal by each side to engage face-to-face with the other. In that instance, the media can connect parties in dialogue and help form 'space bridges' between opponents (O'Heffernan 1991: 37).

On the subject of the media providing a forum for debate, Gary McMichael recalled an early example of trying to use television in order to confront Republicans about the issue of prisoners during the period of multi-party talks:

> I appeared on a current affairs programme in early 1996 to try and address the issue of prisoner releases, because within the prisons themselves there was heated debate about what would be done and Republicans were saying things which were causing tensions. It was clear that Republicans were manipulating the issue and that they needed to be confronted on this. After gaining clearance from the UDA leadership, we made contact with UTV and stressed that it was important for us to debate this with Republicans directly. Previously, Ken Maginnis of the

UUP had taken part in a televised debate with Adams and McGuiness in America, so because it had been done before, this made it easier to sell to the leadership. The Republican that was put up to debate with me was very soft spoken and pragmatic. Sinn Fein did not put up Adams or McGuiness because that would be making an equation in terms of importance and credibility and they wouldn't do that. They had learned from the encounter with Ken Maginnis that the best way to deal with attack is by putting a dove forward, which exaggerates the apparent hostility and unreasonableness of opponents. The figure they put forward was a progressive thinker within republicanism and he was put there, I think, to help magnify an image of intransigence from our side. However, the debate drew out a number of common points of interest and in that sense it was constructive. But the main intention of this dialogue was to get the taboo broken that Unionists and Loyalists should not be talking with Republicans. We wanted to get across to Republicans that we too had sufficient cause to argue a strong Unionist case and to force them to defend their position. We also felt that by unionism not agreeing to confront Republicans, it was just letting them get away with things and gain the upper hand on issues.

The concern of prisoner releases found resonance in the media well beyond the odd television debate, and continued to present Loyalist political leaders with difficulties in terms of trying to manage the significance of early release. As Billy Hutchinson of the PUP put it:

Very early in the talks the media were saying to me you just want to get all the prisoners released, as if that was the only thing that mattered. But what was interesting is that even at that time and we're talking not long after the exploratory dialogue phase, there were over three hundred lifers out on licence anyway. Although people were shocked about that, the media just didn't run the story. We were trying to get it across that because most were out, this was obviously not the only reason we were going into the process and we had other issues we wanted dealt with. At that point, there were probably only thirty or forty who would benefit from the early release scheme, but the media just kept running with the story.

In relation, Hutchinson continued to give this assessment of the media's propensity to focus on negative and sensationalist stories:

The media never wanted to talk about the positive stuff. Even when we were in the Assembly, I was doing stuff on education and working on legislation about trading rights, but they just didn't want to know. But as soon as an argument over decommissioning or the constitutional position arose, they would be there. Yet if somebody puts down a motion about a hospital in Bangor, they're not interested.

Although Hutchinson also stressed how the media tend to 'represent you as you are', he went on to provide this account of the difficulties in trying to control representation:

> Of course when you try and make a point in the media you have to exaggerate it to gain maximum effect. But the problem with that is when it gets interpreted or comes across as a threat. I have done many interviews where the headline did not match what I said, 'Hutchinson agrees with so and so', 'Hutchinson threatens' and so on. The thing with that is that it is the headline which people hear. I have given interviews where people have phoned me afterwards asking why I took such and such a position, when in fact the interview I gave was about the problems of taking such a position. It's always about looking for the sensationalist angle and the stereotype. That is why the media reacted so quickly to covering Johnny Adair, because he fulfilled the stereotype Loyalist as a neanderthal with knuckles dragging on the ground. The articulate voice of loyalism was just not interesting enough for them.

Signalling and advancing positions

It has been mentioned before that differences in how Unionists and Nationalists view the political world can be attributed to a tendency towards literal and metaphorical interpretation, which of course, creates a distinction in how messages are used and experienced. For Arthur Aughey, the delivery of the Good Friday Agreement was a clear indication of the success of political lying, because trust in the language of politics 'here is the very thing that is missing' (Aughey 2002: 14). Aughey, who appears to apply a literal rather than metaphorical appreciation of the Agreement's significance, argues that the Agreement represents not agreement itself but the illusion of agreement. Aughey contends that 'there may be (although this is still uncertain) broad understandings, implicit acknowledgements and unwritten assurances amongst the leading players (elites), but that these are not the stuff upon which public confidence is likely to be sustained' (ibid.). And that this has emerged because of the apparent irreconcilable positions of republicanism, which uses the concept of peace process to serve the ideological conviction of working towards a united Ireland (ibid.: 7), and unionism, which tends to rely on the stoicism of reputation (ibid.: 11) and adopts a 'detestation of official rhetoric' (ibid.: 13). Both these approaches, which might be seen as oriented towards the imagination on the one hand and the intellect on the other, have implications for media performance. And if that is the case, and the

Agreement is illusory, then it would appear that it is those who are able to apply imaginative and metaphorical interpretations who would be able to manipulate meanings more successfully. This invariably relates to differences between ambiguous and literal understandings towards the Agreement and representations made about it.

If we translate those differences towards media performance we can see that ambiguity opens up the possibility for interpretation, whereas literal interpretation limits possibility and even though both positions are needed within a negotiations process, it is evident that those who overwhelmingly apply a literal reading of events and language tend to come across as static, unappealing and defensive, while those who overwhelmingly apply an ambiguous reading of events and language come across as adaptable, reflexive and more reasonable (generally speaking). Although both approaches came into play to some extent when dealing with the substance of negotiations, it is clear that excessive reliance on literal interpretation not only hinders the potential for flexibility, but it makes known the immediate weakness of a position and therefore provides opportunity for exploitation among opponents. Because of this, it is not a coincidence that Republicans have used and benefited from the media much better than Unionists throughout the peace process (taking into account that the projection of this image is also a reflection of internal cohesion, consistency, planning and discipline) and that it is the communication of ambiguity, rather than the communication of certainty, which has facilitated this benefit. Furthermore, in terms of adopting a politics of evasion, which symbolises the modern political tendency to avoid detail by relying on the feeling or emotion which surrounds an issue, Sinn Fein have been the quicker to realise the importance of this approach (Spencer 2006b: 356).

Highlighting how the different approaches taken by Unionists and Republicans with the media reflect how each of the traditions interacted with negotiations and documentation, former Northern Ireland Secretary Paul Murphy explained:

> The Nationalist/Irish side would tend to write in a more elaborate way when drafting documents, but the Unionist/Protestant side liked it as point after point, bang, bang, bang, and much clearer, which was a difficulty. It would sometimes take a week to decide where a comma would go and whatever example you take, it's all about words and the way you express words to try and help consensus and compromise. Of course it was often necessary to have deliberate ambiguities because if you had precise things, you wouldn't have got an Agreement. Also, you sometimes had to be vague in order to give yourself wriggle room which would allow you to negotiate further and overcome whatever problem it may be. Remember the Good Friday Agreement was not a legal document, but a

political document and a lot of the process that created it was built on constructive ambiguity.

Stephen Leach of the NIO also gave attention to these differences and contributed:

> The Unionists clearly wanted to nail down what was happening and particularly in relation to decommissioning, ending violence and North-South bodies, all of which they wanted to pin down firmly. Whereas the Nationalists, Republicans and the Irish wanted to leave more scope for development, so they were happy with ambiguity. This was not in all areas, but they saw how they could benefit and use ambiguity and this was often the basis of tensions. What the Unionists wanted clarity on, Republicans tended to make ambiguous. When the Agreement was released it stated that the participants should reaffirm their commitment to the total disarmament of all paramilitary organisations and to achieve decommissioning through working with the Independent Commission within two years in the context of the implementation of the overall settlement. The Unionists took that to mean that there would be total decommissioning in two years, but Sinn Fein claimed that they would work constructively and in good faith to try and use their influence to achieve total decommissioning, but they weren't signing up to total decommissioning in two years. And that different interpretation is indicative of how the two sides worked. It was also a source of great contention.

Using the media to underscore these conflicting interpretations, was something the British and Irish governments did with some regularity during the early years of the peace process. At that time, the two governments were engaged in a struggle not only over definitions of what the peace process would mean, but the pace of developments and control of the news agenda. This could result in contradictory briefings to the media about the detail of policy and the British government (which was inclined to move slower because of Unionist resistance) in particular, at times seeking to confuse positions in order to slow progress so as to exert greater control over momentum (Spencer 2003: 67). There was also a tendency for each government to try and wrong foot the other so as to invite defensive positions and introduce views or concerns which had not been forthcoming in face-to-face talks (ibid.: 69). In turn, the governments would seek to confront the intransigence of each other by trying to use the media as a forum for asking questions which could act as a lever of pressure on the government most resistant to comment (ibid.: 73).

Although at the level of direct and confidential talks between the Irish and the Loyalists there was a deliberate aim to keep interactions away from the media for fear of losing both cover and confidence, at ministerial level, where direct meetings did not take place, the media was regularly used. Dick Spring, for example, would communicate alternative messages to Republicans and Loyalists, but often did so indirectly, while addressing his own constituency:

> Sometimes when you are trying to address a meeting of your party you have to speak over their heads to reach a wider audience and we were doing that with the Loyalists. That was done regularly and especially in the build up to the Downing Street Declaration because it was important that things were being picked up in the Loyalist community. This was also necessary to try and reduce the concerns and anxieties that community had about where the peace process was going. It was vital to reach out to these people and the media enabled us to do that.

The Irish were particularly vigilant against the likelihood of the media undermining or destabilising fragile contacts, and as Fergus Finlay pointed out, were highly aware of how journalists tend to interpret developments through the paradigm of confrontation and divisiveness:

> The only time I recall being involved with the media was right at the end of my involvement with the Loyalists. From our point of view, we were anxious to keep things out of the papers, because the media in Northern Ireland has a full-time obsession with one story which is the constitutional one. And, if you say a word out of turn it gets stuck to you forever, so we tried to keep away from journalists and leave that for ministers to deal with. It was vital that my relations with them be kept as confidential as possible, and not only for our benefit but for theirs as well. News of Loyalists talking to the Irish government could easily have got people killed at that time. I think that the main media message which was being driven home was that an Agreement would threaten nobody and that the Loyalists could support it was easily and readily as anybody else.

Framing and interpretation

The media's propensity to construct developments through a framework of conflicting positions can be unsettling for promoting peace because such a framework tends to exaggerate the severity of problems and ignore less obvious nuances and subtleties, which might be more or less significant (Wolfsfeld 1998: 220). Moreover, since the media favours simplistic coverage of negotiations which may be highly complex, there can be a distorting effect in terms of evaluating possibilities and connections. Given that news tends towards the dramatic, there is invariably an exaggeration in the more conflictive and sensationalist aspects of a situation, which emphasises the polarised rather than the integrative. Drama relies on the intensification of possible differences and this, quite obviously, poses difficulties for a process which is trying to encourage the opposite, or at least shift opposing sides towards some kind of consensus. Even if attention on the apparently irreconcilable or the antagonistic might not make situations worse, it is certainly the case that such attention will not help reduce such irreconcilability or antagonism either. By stressing the conflictive aspects of scenarios, the media shift thought away from the more constructive interactions between protagonists, where common ground may exist (however tentatively) towards that which destabilises, hinders and divides. Furthermore, by depicting the peace process as a series of disjointed episodes, lurching from breakthrough to breakdown, the media neglect to provide narratives which reflect the complexity and shifting nature of peace negotiations and tend to construct its trajectory as little more than a somewhat random sequence of reactions and responses to situations which lack detailed analysis, or discernible coherence. There are of course, significant political advantages to a lack of detailed analysis, which the media reinforce through an obsession with sound bites and simplistic explanation. It means, for one thing that the magnifying power of media attention can allow participants to correspondingly exaggerate positions (whether it be an ambiguous or literal position) and augment the emotive potential of situations for political gain. If a party wishes to commit fully to a message and stress its importance, then the media can enable that to happen. If however, participants wish to downplay the relevance of a position or statement, then the media's role becomes more problematic. Here, the parties with a more sophisticated understanding of the media will be able to initiate rebuttal positions or promote divisionary tactics to distract public attention, but for those who adopt a more direct and literal engagement with issues and prefer to read scenarios in black and white terms, such an approach is far less likely to be used, creating a disadvantage in publicity terms.

There have been occasions during the peace process, and especially during the formative stages, where messages have been publicly released through unconventional modes of address so as to try and avoid selective or distorted representations through the mainstream media which could damage relations and trust. An example of this would be Peter Brooke's now famous 'no selfish, strategic or economic interest' Whitbread speech in 1990, which was directed at Republicans. Brooke chose to deliver this speech at a meeting of select business and food importers in order to avoid making it in a context where its political interpretation and reception would have found greater immediate resonance and been likely to cause greater consternation among Unionists. But, in this case, what is less well known is that the ability of the speech to attract media interest was not as anticipated, resulting in

British anger and concern that the signal had not been transmitted as planned (Spencer 2004c: 612). That the message was not picked up as desired, again indicates the integral role of the media in political communications and its centrality in political planning as well as, from time to time, its unpredictability.

The example of the Brooke speech and the sending and receiving of signals through controlled conduits of communication, was integral to the information-gathering intentions of all those engaged in the peace process. To what degree Republicans were aiming messages at the British, Unionist or Loyalist parties through their own media outlets is debatable, but for the Loyalists and particularly the UVF, Republican News was a valuable source of information about Republican thinking. As the UVF Number Two explained when asked about drawing from the media for information:

> Republican News and the annual Sinn Fein ardheis were very important for picking up vibes and allowed us to look at possible options about where we needed to be thinking next and what we should be seriously considering. We also looked at the local press such as the Anderstown News for letters and columns to give us a sense of the desire for peace. One could say that this enabled us to suss others out to some extent.

However, as the Number Two went on to explain, using information in this way was only one of a number of sources which were being collated to try and substantiate understanding of credible positions:

> We knew how good Sinn Fein were at using the media so it was important that we used a host of information sources and were taking signals from clergy and community workers as well. One could not rely on media reports alone, but through cross-checking and talking to others, one could then more reliably validate what was said and consider the possible intentions with greater confidence.

David Adams of the UDP reiterated the importance of looking beyond the signalling and gesturing which was carried through the media and was notably critical in his evaluation of Sinn Fein when asked about how the UDP responded to messages being sent:

> It was gauged, taken on board and factored in but I have to say that by and large we didn't trust a word they said. One always had to wait for solid proof for what was said. There were many times when we were right to not trust what they communicated, because soon after murders and shootings were deliberately developed to support a Republican agenda. There was a lot of game playing by Republicans and even to this day, they will consider nobody else's position except their own. They work on the

basis that if for a period of time, your agenda happens to dovetail their own, then all well and good, but there's no way that they would go outside to accommodate others unless absolutely forced to.

As has been suggested earlier, the UUP were somewhat constrained in their approach to negotiations and developments by the constant condemnations of the DUP. The PUP and the UDP, on the other hand, offered the UUP the scope to be more imaginative and less bound by the expectations of Unionist anxiety and intransigence. But, it should also be recognised, as previously suggested, that the political risks for loyalism were much reduced in comparison to the UUP because the base of electoral support was much smaller. And it was this lack of electoral support which perhaps enabled the Loyalists to be more daring in their communications, allowing leaders like Billy Hutchinson to meet Republicans and discuss background issues (Spencer 2004b: 44) without facing expansive media coverage, which would have had damaging consequences for the UUP (made worse by DUP accusations of talking with the enemy) had they done the same. There are also other reasons why the UUP were unable to capitalise on media coverage which are pertinent to unionism generally. First, the disjointed and divisive nature of Unionist politics along with a dominant perception of intransigence to change holds little interest for journalists. Second, Unionists have been unable to communicate their centrality within the Irish problem effectively. Third, Unionists have not adequately made the case for the relevance of the Union, allowing British politicians to control that debate. And fourth, successful control and management of the media by Republicans has contributed to unionism's detachment from key political debates (Parkinson 1998: 161–5). Consistently throughout the process, the Loyalists sought to challenge these apparent weaknesses, often promoting positions which unionism was unaccustomed to and indeed unprepared for, and perhaps the demise of political loyalism after the Good Friday Agreement was a reflection of this attempted moderation, with constituencies unready for the direct challenges which would unsettle the security and fixedness of traditional unionism.

Loyalist leaders have faced dangers by the media exposing the location of secret meetings (Spencer 2004b: 51) and paramilitary leaders reserve strong criticism for sections of the tabloid press in Northern Ireland, which is accused of naming paramilitaries who were subsequently murdered and carrying stories which deliberately distort paramilitary activities for sensationalist reasons. Indeed, the UDA once advocated a boycott of the *Sunday World* newspaper because its reports were undermining the leadership's efforts to convey a more positive and constructive image for the organisation (Woods 2006: 300). The UDA's concern about the media's ability to exaggerate tensions and negative imagery, of course, indicates that the media's magnifying presence can also have the opposite effect, in providing a public image of confidence, consensus and control, but that this can only occur if the party or organisation being scrutinized is able to project such an image. Clear differences in the public portrayal of Sinn Fein and the UUP derived from how that image was controlled, or uncontrolled, but also revealed very different attitudes and realizations about the potency of the media's role in communicating modern politics. After the Good Friday Agreement the UUP, would regularly use the media to comment on disputes and contestations in the party about leadership and direction, which had a negative and disruptive impact both publicly and internally. Unlike Sinn Fein, who has been conscious to project a single line of communication to the media and avoid public disagreements which might be interpreted as signs of splits and presented as some form of internal crisis, UUP representatives would routinely promote differing positions on issues and use the media to undermine aspects of leadership and decision-making. And, once the media becomes the terrain for such contestation, the party responsible is seen as disjointed, unreliable and ultimately unable to adequately defend or protect constituency interests. In effect, that party becomes a liability, a danger, and is seen as contributing to the demise of the very things which it purports to be defending. It is not surprising, given this tendency that the UUP lost ground after the 2003 elections and has since failed to regain that ground.

Although the political representatives of the Loyalist parties admit that around the time of the Good Friday Agreement they were given considerable access to the media, which exceeded the expectations of access for political parties with such small constituencies, it is apparent that this access was more to do with their connections to paramilitary loyalism than because of their pluralist approach, or advocating progressive politics. As Paul Murphy explained:

> The Loyalist parties were small and yet they were given access to prime ministers and presidents in the U.S. in an unparalleled way. Even heads of state in the U.S. have to wait a long time to meet the president and yet these Loyalist representatives who were councillors in the Assembly, would be give access to the most powerful man in the world, let alone the prime minister who they would see on a regular basis. We saw this open door policy as very important to ending conflict and because of that we had to grant them parity of esteem. It was also necessary to do because it was through them that we were able to communicate to the Loyalist paramilitary groups.

It is because of the different relationship between political representatives of loyalism and the paramilitaries compared to the relationship that exists between Sinn Fein and the IRA, as well as how Loyalist paramilitary organisations are constructed and managed, that Loyalist politics has so far failed to cohere or expand with any real significance (indeed it has shrunk, with the PUP's Dawn Purvis now the only elected Assembly representative). Unlike Sinn Fein, Loyalist representatives have been unable to articulate their position with the same underlying support. Partly, this is because the communicative skills of those who have acted as political representatives in loyalism are not typical of those within Loyalist communities generally, where education and confidence to engage in debates with opponents is lacking. As Jackie McDonald of south Belfast UDA explained this problem:

> Most people I know speak from the heart and I would be like that as well. I couldn't sit down with the likes of Gerry Kelly from Sinn Fein and have a conversation in front of a television camera, because he would destroy me. We might both be explaining the truth as we saw it, but he would come across much better and that's the problem we have. Loyalists are not able to articulate themselves in the same way and much of this comes back to education. Because of this inability to articulate things, the media has focussed on the more sensationalist aspects of loyalism, which is mainly to do with criminality and the image of the balaclava. If Loyalists are going to address this, they have to stop playing to this media stereotype and get educated about the threat this poses. When Loyalists appear in the press on a regular basis but in ways not related to criminality, then we will have turned the corner. But in order to do that we work through an education process.

The consultation and sophistication of the Republican movement in relation to the Sinn Fein leadership and the trajectory the party is trying to take towards the peace process is reflective of an internal debate and adjustment to the merits of politics over violence. Whereas Loyalist violence has tended to reinforce the perceived inadequacies of politics, Republican violence throughout the peace process has paralleled a deep appreciation for politics. And that is why, potentially damaging occurrences such as the alleged IRA involvement in the Northern Bank robbery of December 2004 and the murder of Robert McCartney by IRA members in January 2005 (followed by a public statement that the IRA was prepared to take internal action against those involved), were used by Republican reformers to illustrate the damaging role of such actions in relation to electoral development, which is bearing significant fruit. For loyalism, the possibility of political advancement was never likely to be realised given the absence of such support. Debates about change have effectively been controlled by military rather than political thinkers (although there is a notable consistency of political and military strategy between the PUP and the UVF), and a resistance to republicanism, which tends to facilitate oppositional attitudes and reactions, and has obstructed the need to follow a comparably substantive education process about change. The tendency within loyalism to exert itself as an oppositional and reactive force against republicanism means that conviction is often measured by difference, with similar or comparable political strategy seen as a sign of selling out, or conceding to the enemy. The setbacks this creates for loyalism (taking into account the institutional, cultural and historical differences), which are reflective of educative deficiencies as highlighted by those such as Jackie McDonald (and indeed throughout much of the interview commentary by those within the UDP), also bring us to a not-unrelated contention that ideology within such communities has a tendency to be populist oriented, 'internally contradictory and built on incomplete forms of thought'. From this vantage point there are clearly problems developing a coherent approach to political change since, as McAuley points out, it is 'within these frameworks of thought that everyday political calculations and decisions are made' (1996b: 143). It is the difficulties which arise when trying to develop an educative process within loyalism in response to the demands of the peace process and how to address the problems and discontentment inside Loyalist communities which now concern us in the final chapter.

9
Recent Developments and the Way Ahead

Political background

Widespread Unionist disillusionment and falling confidence, which was made manifest in the local election results of 2003 (Tonge 2006b: 73), did little to assist efforts by the political voices within loyalism to find a constructive way of moving ahead in the peace process. For Unionists, the most prominent reaction to the political process at this time, as personified by the DUP, lay in shifts between outright rejection of the Agreement and demands to renegotiate it in order to try and impose some obvious signs of Unionist influence (ibid.: 75). The political landscape had now moved towards a discernibly traditional configuration of political divisions, with the more extreme DUP and Sinn Fein emerging as the dominant representatives of the peace process (ibid.: 86). Having gained overall control in the elections, the DUP and Sinn Fein became the focus for where the political process was heading and the issues of contention between the two parties now occupied the attention of both governments, who sought to push both towards tentative compromises. Initially such attempts failed, as demonstrated by the discussions which took place at Leeds Castle from 16–18 September 2004. Here, the two governments conducted talks aimed at resolving deadlock over the IRA's continued existence and power-sharing at Stormont. Along with addressing the problem of the IRA's continuation, the talks were also concerned with decommissioning, policing and whether Unionists (essentially the DUP) intended to make the institutions work. The DUP, who raised concerns over the running of Stormont, the accountability of ministers and the authenticity of decommissioning, were notably trying to get Sinn Fein to agree to decommissioning in advance of an Assembly (re)forming, but the outcome of the talks was that discussions on delivering the Agreement would need to take place in advance of the arms issue being properly dealt with. Apart from seeking to reconcile the DUP's request that decommissioning take place before institutions were up and running with Sinn Fein's request for institutions to be up and running before decommissioning takes place, the primary aim of the two governments was to make sure that the fundamentals of the Good Friday Agreement remain unchanged and that the three strands remained intact so the concept of inclusivity would remain the foundation of political progress. The talks ended without agreement between the parties and disputations would not be effectively overcome until the parties met again at St Andrews in Scotland in October 2006.

An extremely significant move which took place before the negotiations at St Andrews was the decommissioning of IRA weapons, announced by the IRA on 28 July 2005 and completed with formal ratification by the Independent International Commission on Decommissioning (IICD) on 26 September. Supervised by the IICD and the two churchmen, Catholic priest Alec Reid and ex-Methodist president Rev Harold Good, the IICD confirmed at a press conference and in their subsequent report, that large quantities of arms had been 'put beyond use' and that these quantities, as consistent with inventories, were deemed to be the entirety of the IRA's armoury. In removing a major obstruction to the DUP's arguments against power-sharing, Sinn Fein and the IRA had effectively moved to meet the DUP request for decommissioning before an Assembly was up and running, therefore increasing pressure on the DUP to now show support for an Assembly and the devolved institutions. Initial reaction about decommissioning from the DUP was sceptical, with accusations that without transparency the validity of the act was questionable. However, the party also knew that by doubting the actuality of decommissioning they were also bringing into doubt the character of those officials involved and by association the integrity of the two governments. To offset such criticisms and offer some positive response, figures in the DUP such as Peter Robinson acknowledged the scale of the act and its political importance. Senior figures in the UVF expressed particular amazement that the IRA had made such a gesture and given up arms to the satisfaction of, among others, a British government.

The decommissioning of IRA weapons gave an impetus to the three-day multi-party talks at St Andrews in October 2006 and was seen as a major step towards achieving a political settlement. The outstanding problem for the DUP however, was Sinn Fein's lack of commitment to policing and the criminal justice system. Moves towards endorsement of both were well advanced within Sinn Fein, but perceived uncertainty at St Andrews on the issue provided Sinn Fein with further negotiating advantage. The outcome of the talks was significantly positive enough for the two governments to announce a timetable date of 26 March 2007 for an Assembly to be up and running, along with a series of intermediary dates for responses to proposals from the parties, the nomination of First and Deputy First Minister, electoral support for the Assembly and nomination of the executive, and a series of modifications on how the political institutions would operate. The St Andrews Agreement, which was seen as more of a tactical rather than strategic document by the British because of the emphasis on time frames, drew up a ministerial code to guarantee cross-community participation and increase accountability, tightened interdependence between First and Deputy First Minister, devised review bodies to monitor Strand One implementations and introduced a network of forums and councils to oversee North–South and East–West relations. The document also reiterated a commitment to peaceful and democratic methods to achieve political goals, underlined Irish involvement in Northern Ireland and effectively tied the parties to a deadline for devolution.

Removal of the last main obstruction to devolution came about on 28 January 2007, when at an ardfheis in Dublin, Sinn Fein overwhelmingly endorsed the Police Service of Northern Ireland (PSNI), committing support to the criminal justice system and the rule of law. Some 90 per cent of the 982 delegates in Dublin consented to this motion, thereby meeting the obligation to support institutions of law and order as specified in the St Andrews Agreement. A few days later, Sinn Fein appointed three party members to be representatives of the Policing Board in Northern Ireland which itself consists of nine independents, ten politicians and is scheduled to meet from early June 2007.

The DUP decided to reserve public comment on Sinn Fein's endorsement until after the Assembly elections which took place on 7 March 2007. The outcome of those elections showed clear public support for the two extreme parties working together in an Assembly with the result of the voting as follows: DUP 36 seats, Sinn Fein 28 seats, UUP 18 seats, SDLP 16 seats, Alliance Party 7 seats, Green Party 1 seat, PUP 1 seat, Independent 1 seat. This clear endorsement, which increased pressure on the parties to formally accept that conditions were set for devolution, provided the DUP and Sinn Fein with the necessary confidence to commitment to power-sharing and facilitated a sequence of moves and interactions which culminated in a joint statement released by Ian Paisley and Gerry Adams on 26 March. The statement announced that a start date for the Assembly would be 8 May. The media image of Paisley and Adams sitting alongside each other at tables which were positioned at right angles to each other (initial arrangements ruled out all participants at one table as over friendly and facing tables as too confrontational) captured the spectacle of the two parties working together, with each statement avoiding past recriminations and hostilities by concentrating on the need for a stable future and articulating the possibilities of parties working together for the public good. The DUP, by setting the start date on 8 May rather than 26 March as the governments had stated, had tried to create the perception that the party was exerting control over the pace of events and therefore shaping the agenda to its own benefit, but this extra time also provided further space for the parties to condition audience expectations about power-sharing. The Assembly was formally opened with historic grandeur at Stormont on 8 May, with speeches of support from prime ministers Blair and Ahern and declarations on working for the common good provided by Paisley as First Minister and Martin McGuinness as Deputy First Minister. The image of Paisley and McGuinness sitting side by side and laughing together was given widespread media attention and created a symbolic resonance which reinforced the magnitude of the event. Subsequent reports about congeniality and respect between Paisley and McGuinness served to create further positive atmosphere around the new Assembly and its ability to facilitate effective cross-party co-operation.

Internal consultation and change in the UVF

Against this backdrop of developments, the paramilitary organisations were working on an internal consultative process to consider what paramilitarism would mean in a non-violent society. The UVF tried to begin internal consultations from early 2004, but encountered problems because of feuds, which set the process back and undermined the possibility of moving ahead with confidence. The consultative process within the UVF was put together by the PUP, the UVF leadership, and included major contributions from EPIC and LINC. Given the title of the 'Roadshow', the discussion process consisted of two parts, with each taking a year to work through. Talking in 2007, the UVF's Number Two explained the intent behind the Roadshow:

> Effectively there were two roadshows. The first was about discussing where we needed to go and the second was about getting agreement on how we would get there. Each part took about a year and the overall mechanics for how we would proceed were drawn up in 2006. The leadership left the country in order to work out, without interference, how to put the structures for change in place and then we went back into the constituencies to explain what we were going to do. It was crucial for us that Northern Ireland remained secure and that there was no discernible threat. The consultation process was driven by the leadership and middle-management and went right down through the organisation to all volunteers. It was the leadership who put down the recommendations, but it was middle-management who tended to develop communications in local areas. We met in community centres and were addressing the same kinds of issues and concerns throughout, which were inevitably about how to deal with a resumption of Republican violence and what role there may or may not be for the organisation in the context of peace. We were saying that it's desirable to move towards peace and that it's the only show in town and that out of the discussions there would be a Code of Conduct drawn up to reflect that.

David Ervine described the consultative process in the following way:

> Billy Mitchell of LINC developed a slide programme which included internal conversations about change and it was taken all over the country.

It was pointing out that in the context of changing conditions there is a need to build policy and that the policy of 1970 could not be the policy of 2006 because circumstances were different. So the policy change was how to set about creating a very rigorous Code of Conduct to meet the new challenges and that was agreed around the summer of 2006. It was important that the UVF leadership moved away from feeding off the process and made it clear that it was working through its own process of change. It was also obvious that people needed confirmation about the way things were moving and needed to be considered in that process. The Roadshow enabled all those concerns to be addressed and dealt with and also enabled some of the populism that paramilitaries tend to feed off to be neutralised. In the early stages, the UVF made two attempts at the Roadshow but it was derailed by the LVF and feuds. The key question was what the UVF's purpose would be when the IRA leave the stage. It was apparent that this was going to happen and so it was important that each volunteer thought about the consequences of that. There was also acknowledgement in the consultations that regarding issues of criminality, it might be better to disband and let criminality be dealt with by the security forces. Ultimately though, the Roadshow was about the realisation that things are changing and getting the membership of the UVF to come to terms with that.

Billy Hutchinson elaborated further on the consultation process:

The consultations within the UVF have been about where they will go and where they fit into a society where Republican violence is absent. Basically the first round of consultations was a presentation in terms of where the UVF have come from, where they are at and what the challenges and threats are for the future. And the second round of consultations was about dealing with the threats and working out how to meet the challenges. The third step is then to make the outcome of the consultations public, but after the Assembly is running and the first and second ministers are in place. What has made the debate harder is that the Loyalist voice has tended to be determined by events on the streets with guns rather than being shaped by discussion. It was clear that the conversations needed to happen almost on a daily basis and that they have to keep going until the UVF have worked their way out of this. It is likely that the UVF will continue to exist in some form like the Provos, but the question will be how they exist and what they exist for. There is also the problem of what the UDA will do, but it seems clear now that the moves taking place within loyalism generally are about isolating the destabilising elements. A lot of people accept the need for change but more needs to be done and some have problems with that. The difficulty is always about what needs to be protected and how to move on.

There also needs to be a parallel process where people learn community based skills, because some of them want to work in their local areas and it's about how you stop people with a paramilitary mindset from taking over and giving orders in those communities; something we have to get away from. You have to have a core group of people to decide what to do here though. There will be a small group who will make sure that people are protected from those seeking to settle old scores and there may be Somme associations to keep community spirit intact, but it is clear that if there is criminality then the police should deal with that. Up until recently the UVF had a Code of Conduct, but it's a bit like the magna carta, it's a constitution and unwritten. The consultation process has changed that, everything has been settled and agreed and it's now about how that will be implemented. It's about making sure that people move away from violence and guns, but that they still have something to belong to.

The UVF had made known a number of concerns to the Irish government throughout the consultation process and used Chris Hudson to convey those concerns. They varied from fears of IRA profiling, which in 2003 the UVF leadership claimed to involve the detailed tracking of individuals' movements and running into 'four figures', fears over the secondment of senior Irish police into the PSNI, anger at the Irish government's refusal to meet the Loyalist Commission, which was taken as a snub, inadequate measures to deal with dissident Republican groups and potential misunderstandings which would be likely to occur if the Irish continued to take the PUP to be the voice of the UVF, rather than listening to the leadership itself. Because of conflicting messages from the Irish at this time, the UVF were also raising the issue of trust and making it clear that if the Irish government did not trust the UVF, as they thought, then there would be no real grounds for the organisation trusting the Irish government either. The leadership stressed that the UVF had been honourable in all dealings with the Irish government and its contacts and so the basis for mistrust from the Irish, was groundless. In order for the UVF leaders to assuage fears among the membership about the aspirations and intentions of the Irish government, it became clear that clarification was necessary which would address the problems outlined above, in return for which the leaders would make positive moves and gestures towards opening links with the IICD and developing a timeframe for the organisation to end as a paramilitary movement and become an 'old comrades association'.

Although the fear of IRA targeting eased significantly when IRA decommissioning took place in 2005, there was still notable anxiety within the UVF about Irish government comments which talked of representing the interests of Nationalists. Public statements made by the Irish at this time were seen by the UVF to signify a 'greening' of Irish politics, which took on greater potency given that such comments had been made after the UVF Number Two had been to Dublin to articulate UVF anxieties over Irish references to 'joint management'. The Irish government publicly communicated that its role was to serve the Nationalist community and this caused considerable tension within the UVF, who saw such comments as in contradiction to the idea of governmental neutrality in the peace process. The British had announced its neutrality some time before (from Brooke on), but this had not been reciprocated by the Irish and since the Unionists did not have the British openly talking about representing Unionist interests, and Nationalists through the Irish did, it was evident that there was a disparity which would disadvantage Unionists. Through Chris Hudson, who formally outlined the need for clarification of such issues, a paper was drawn up which highlighted the potential problems this created for the UVF, and how talk of an obligation for the Irish to provide Nationalists with some form of government had incited discussion of retaliatory action among the UVF leadership. In the event of an Assembly not (re)forming (remember this was 2005) and the Irish using a political stalemate between the parties to play a greater role in governing Northern Ireland, the UVF leadership planned to bring thousands of Unionists to Dublin in order to carry out non-violent actions of civil disobedience and protest.

The DUP's decision to accept power-sharing and to work in an Assembly alongside Sinn Fein, effectively removed the need for civil disobedience and other forms of resistance. An acceptance by the DUP to now work in the political process in line with the demands and responsibilities as outlined through negotiations and the Good Friday Agreement, meant that paramilitary loyalism now had no role and so no validity. The likelihood of this eventuality had been seen by the UVF leadership for some time and a PUP delegation, accompanied by UVF representatives visited Dublin to speak with taoiseach Bertie Ahern on 25 April 2007 to announce that the UVF would be soon delivering a statement which made clear that the organisation would be stood down. But in order for this to happen the delegation wanted Ahern to reassert and make explicit that the Irish were committed to the principle of consent. That assurance was provided and on 3 May 2007, Gusty Spence made the following statement to the media from Fernhill House in west Belfast:

> Following a direct engagement with all units and departments of our organisation, the leadership of the Ulster Volunteer Force and Red Hand Commando today make public the outcome of the three year consultation process.
> We do so against a backdrop of increasing community acceptance that the mainstream Republican offensive has ended; that the six principles upon

which our ceasefire was predicated are maintained; that the principle of consent has been firmly established and thus, that the Union remains safe. We welcome recent developments in securing stable, durable democratic structures in Northern Ireland and accept as significant, support by the mainstream Republican movement of the constitutional status quo. Commensurate with these developments, as of twelve midnight, Thursday May 3 2007, the Ulster Volunteer Force and Red Hand Commando will assume a non-military, civilianised role.

To consolidate this fundamental change in outlook we have addressed the methodology of transformation from a military to civilian organisation by implementing the following measures in every operational and command area:

All recruitment has ceased;

Military training has ceased;

Targeting has ceased and all intelligence rendered obsolete;

All Active Service Units have been de-activated;

All Ordnance has been put beyond reach and the IICD instructed accordingly.

We encourage our volunteers to embrace the challenges which continue to face their communities and support their continued participation in non-military capacities. We reaffirm our opposition to all criminality and instruct our volunteers to cooperate fully with the lawful authorities in all possible instances.

Moreover, we state unequivocally, that any volunteer engaged in criminality does so in direct contravention of Brigade Command and thus we welcome any recourse through due process of law. All volunteers are further encouraged to show support for credible restorative justice projects so that they, with their respective communities, may help eradicate criminality and anti-social behaviour in our society.

We ask the government to facilitate this process and remove the obstacles which currently prevent out volunteers and their families from assuming full and meaningful citizenship.

We call on all violent dissidents to desist immediately and urge all relevant governments and their security apparatus to deal swiftly and efficiently with this threat. Failure to do so will inevitably provoke another generation of Loyalists towards armed resistance.

We have taken the above measures in an earnest attempt to augment the return of accountable democracy to the people of Northern Ireland and as such, to engender confidence that the constitutional question has now been firmly settled.

In doing so we reaffirm the legitimacy of our tactical response to violent nationalism, yet reiterate the sincere expression of abject and true remorse to all innocent victims of the conflict.

Brigade Command salutes the dedication and fortitude of our officers, NCOs and volunteers throughout the difficult, brutal years of armed resistance. We reflect with honour on those from our organisation who made the ultimate sacrifice; those who endured long years of incarceration and the loyal families who shared their suffering and supported them throughout.

Finally we convey our appreciation for the honest exchange with officers, NCOs and volunteers throughout the organisation over the past three years which has allowed us to assume with confidence the position we adopt today.

For God and Ulster

Captain William Johnston; Adjutant.

Earlier that day Billy Hutchinson and senior UVF representatives met the IICD to explain how weapons would be stored and to guarantee that they would not be used again. Though General John De Chastelain communicated concerns and reservations about the storage of weapons not meeting the requirement of weapons being 'put beyond use' to the satisfaction of the IICD, it is likely that further meetings between UVF leaders and the IICD will take place, and that should the act of decommissioning occur, it would take place only after further extensive consultation and at the time of writing is deemed to be unlikely. The UVF leadership realise that IRA decommissioning could only be delivered because of prospective political gains, which are unavailable to Loyalists and that the moral argument cannot be won without significant advantage becoming a distinct possibility. Senior figures in the UVF intimate that if decommissioning were to be realised it would take some considerable time to bring about, and that the circumstances in which the debate is conducted would have to become more favourable in order to sell the argument convincingly.

The Code of Conduct, which provided the necessary confidence for the UVF to proceed with its 'statement of intent' stipulates a series of rules designed to prevent recourse to military activity and criminality and is clear that any actions deemed to be in violation of the Code will result in expulsion from the organisation. In effect, the Code of Conduct attempts to prevent volunteers engaging in behaviour which may be detrimental to peace and stability and at the time of writing, has been successfully implemented; a sign of internal discipline and a commitment by volunteers to the general direction of the consultation process.

The issue of Loyalist criminality had been highlighted again just prior to the 3 May announcement, appealing to those who argued that the continued existence of Loyalist paramilitarism could now only be justified and explained by its associations with crime. Published just a few days before Spence spoke about the UVF moving towards a 'civilianised' role, on 25 April, the Fifteenth Report of the Independent Monitoring Commission stated that from January 2003 until February 2007 Loyalist shootings had numbered 289 compared to 101 by Republicans. Over the same period Loyalist 'paramilitary style assaults' were recorded at 278 compared to 133 for Republicans. As regards the UVF, the report concluded, 'Since the developments in republicanism, the political alibli Loyalist paramilitaries claimed has gone, and they cannot make any argument for paramilitary activity and the retention of weapons. Unless the leadership can deliver results in the very near future we will be forced to the conclusion that they are either unwilling or unable to bring about real change' (p. 28). What was becoming increasingly obvious, at this time in the peace process, was that the continuing prevalence of criminality was now undermining any legitimacy in the contention that Loyalist paramilitary groups existed to defend their respective communities. Indeed, such actions were demonstrating the opposite, that Loyalist groups were being used as a cover to exploit and destroy those communities and so acting in total violation of their founding principles. As the IMC report also stressed on this point, Loyalist paramilitaries can no longer argue that they act on behalf of their communities when 'they extort money from local businesses, drive away investment, poison young people with drugs and intimidate citizens' (ibid.: 29). This realisation is particularly important for the UVF since the organisation risked becoming a growing hindrance to any aspirations that the PUP might wish to articulate with regards to political progress or independence.

A further problem for Loyalist paramilitarism in its associations with criminal activity, remain the ongoing revelations about collusion between individual paramilitaries and the security forces. A report *Statement by the Police Ombudsman for Northern Ireland on her investigation into the circumstances surrounding the death of Raymond McCord Junior and related matters*, which set out to address allegations that a senior UVF man had murdered the son of Mr Raymond McCord and which discovered failures in the investigation that 'significantly reduced the possibility of anyone being prosecuted for the murder' (p. 9) produced by the Northern Ireland Police Ombudsman in January 2007, once more brought to light the role of paramilitary informants and their ability to carry out known crimes without apprehension. The report, which was an investigation into the murder, other murders and attempted murders of named persons, detailed how one individual (Informant 1) was linked directly to ten murders and implicated in five others and yet allowed to continue carrying out armed robbery, assault and grievous bodily harm, punishment shootings and attacks, possession of munitions, criminal damage, drug dealing, extortion, hijacking, intimidation, conspiracy to murder and threats to kill (p. 8). The report also highlighted how the majority of Special Branch and CID officers who were asked to explain 'internal practices' during the period examined (from early 1990s to 2002) failed to assist and of those that did, 'some serving officers, gave evasive, contradictory, and on occasion farcical answers to questions'.

The report went on to state that numerous responses by officers 'indicated either a significant failure to understand the law, or contempt for the law', and stated at on 'other occasions the investigation demonstrated conclusively that what an officer told the Police Ombudsman's investigators was completely untrue' (ibid.: 6). Of particular interest to the enquiry was the 'blocking by Special Branch of searches during a pre-planned CID operation intended to disrupt the activities of the UVF' (ibid.). Though the report acknowledged that the PSNI had since adopted new working practices to confront the perception that sources were being protected, there was evidence that in 1997 'detailed information was received by CID about the location of weapons, ammunition and explosives and also a list of intended murder targets for the UVF' (ibid.: 98). At that time, CID intended to 'frustrate the UVF by seizing a large quantity of their munitions, and arresting individuals in possession of them', and although Special Branch gave clearance to allow searches of some locations, it refused the CID permission 'to search four locations including the two locations used by Informant 1 and the alleged site of the UVF arms hide'. Importantly, 'the searches of the other properties went ahead, resulting in the recovery of some munitions, but they did not significantly undermine the UVF' (ibid.: 98–9).

Stories which emanate from reports such as those provided by the IMC and the Police Ombudsman, do little to assist the political credibility of paramilitary representatives, but perhaps what should also be noted here, as the UVF Number Two highlighted in interview, is that associations with the security forces tend to be represented differently by those who reveal them. Thus whereas for Loyalists, the term 'collusion' is quickly applied, for Republicans (who have also experienced informant relations with the security forces, and made known through revelations about Sinn Fein representative Denis Donaldson and IRA member Freddie Scappaticci, along with others, in the 'Stakeknife' affair (Ingram and Harkin 2004)) 'infiltration' appears to be used as a more appropriate definition of involvement. Perhaps also, recognition of such distinctions is necessary when considering the nuances of perceived successes and failures of the security forces in relation to Loyalist and Republican groups, each of which has been heavily implicated in criminality and the actions of state violence.

Internal consultation and change in the UDA

The consultative process which has taken place within the UDA about how to best respond to the challenges of the peace process since the end of the UDP, had its roots in an announcement made by the leadership in November 2004. Working with the UPRG, the leadership attempted to outline a programme for change and named this programme the 'John Gregg Initiative' in memory of the south east Antrim leader who was murdered in 2003 in a feud inspired by Johnny Adair. Consisting of a four-pronged approach, the initiative set out to '(a) work towards the day when there would no longer be a need for the UDA and the UFF; (b) desist from all military activity; (c) develop a strategy for the organisation which would be one of community development, job creation, social inclusion and community politics; and (d) work diligently with other political parties and the two governments to create an environment which would secure a lasting peace' (Hall 2006: 7). The announcement formally set out that there would be an ongoing dialogue process with the UDA membership in relation to these points, which would also seek to assess the extent of feeling within the organisation about the need for change and to consider attitudes about a conflict-transformation process.

The dialogue process began formally in 2005 and was carried out across all areas in Northern Ireland. It was lead by UPRG representatives along with senior UDA personnel. Frankie Gallagher elaborated further on the intentions behind the process:

> When the UDP collapsed a vacuum was left which needed to be filled quite quickly. What became apparent was that there was no real interest in politics, but there was a very real interest in social development and addressing the social needs which had been to a large extent created by the conflict. It was about trying to consolidate all the work that was being done with volunteers on the ground and to make the case that circumstances had changed. It was also important to hammer home the point that because of those changes we could no longer afford to be reactive and had to become proactive. There is a very weak community infrastructure generally throughout most areas, with low skills levels and low educational attainment levels and this makes people vulnerable to exploitation. It was this which we began to address.

Among others, the consultations grappled with such questions as what the new Republican politics would mean for loyalism, how to respond to the decommissioning issue, how to deal with IRA dissidents, how to adapt from a military war to a political war, whether to develop politically, how to engage with the social initiatives being proposed, how to address the problem of criminality, how to maintain identity and culture and how to develop debates and discussions about transformation and change (Hall 2006). The consultations were also designed to gain support for a Conflict Transformation Initiative (CTI), which would provide a comprehensive package of measures aimed at moving the UDA away from conflict towards a process of reconciliation and through collaboration with the British government, attempt to confront the range of social and economic problems that are endemic to many Loyalist communities. UPRG representative David Nicoll summarised the relevance of the CTI:

> From the start of the conflict the very first community association was a defence association, which was established to protect various Unionist areas. The CTI was a return to those roots in the sense that it is designed to work for communities and address the social effects of conflict. We need to associate and coalesce around the safety and preservation of the Union, but also to bring people together in community based politics rather then electoral politics. We need to lobby for change and to influence where we can on social needs through locally elected parties, politicians, local development partnerships and the councils. We also need to deal with the criminality. The next phase is reconciliation and the problem of how we get people there. We need to break down the sectarian mindsets and the bigoted stuff between communities and that requires building partnerships and relationships with government agencies and other communities that we fundamentally disagree with. The key issues now for us are jobs, social and economic advancement, better healthcare, education and working with district partnerships and associations in order to address disadvantage.

The need to avoid seeing the CTI as part of a strategy to move into electoral politics, was also highlighted by fellow UPRG representative Tommy Kirkham, who added:

> The Protestant community will not accept another political party. But if we could capture the support of some of the 10,000 and the wider 30,000 potential UDA members, we could become the largest lobbying group within unionism. We don't need to be elected to Stormont, but if we object to what the elected members of the Assembly are doing then we can exercise some influence by not voting for them at the next election. So although we have no intentions to be party political, we still see ourselves as being able to exert significant political clout. We will also carry out lobbying activities and will teach people how to lobby.

Frankie Gallagher further outlined the social problems within Loyalist communities that the CTI is designed to address:

> In our communities there is a clear social deficit. We don't have the training or investment that most modern societies have. In education, it's normal to be taught mediation or negotiation skills at an early age and how to become a responsible member of civic society, but since we've always lived in crisis, under fear and been defensive, those things have

been extremely neglected here. And it's been ingrained. A couple of years ago anybody going on a mediation course would have been seen as an idiot, but we have started to convince Inner Council leaders that they need to be on those courses more than anyone, because they are leading. We now have a situation where at least three of the leaders are doing courses on leadership dynamics etc and they are implementing those skills with their own people. This is just a small part of working towards a three year programme on conflict transformation. We also asked UDA members why they joined the organisation to begin with and tried to get them to recognise that since it was a community response to political instability, they can continue to put that energy into the community, but instead of violence use it to work on community development, citizenship and trying to help people make something of their lives. The crucial point here is that to do that, the bar of expectations for our communities must be raised and the CTI is about doing that.

The efforts of the UPRG to bring about conflict transformation, has also meant confronting the UDA's acceptance of criminality and this issue drew a broadly consistent response from those interviewed. One of the ongoing problems for the Inner Council, particularly during the early stages of the CTI initiative, had been in reaching a consensus on moving ahead when three of its members were effectively working to destroy progress and using their collective weight to block the organisation confronting criminal activity. Those three members, who were removed over a period of time, were Johnny Adair, Jim Gray and Andre Shoukri. Adair was expelled because of his involvement in the feuds, Gray was stood down in March 2005 and murdered in October of that year and the influence of Shoukri, which extended to his brother Ahab who ran north Belfast while Andre was in prison, effectively ended in November 2006. Frankie Gallagher described the background to this change and the consequences it created for the organisation:

> The defining moment was when Jim Gray was ousted because once that happened people started to get over their fears and stand up. The symbolism of Gray was massive. Even the statutory agencies, the government and the community organisations said that these people were too powerful and could not be moved, but once they were toppled it was like a domino effect. Part of this was the realisation that paramilitaries have outlived their use and that there are elements who have exploited and surpressed their own communities. It is now clear that people are not prepared to let the organisation become the oppressor of its own people. In the case of Jim Gray, he had moved people into powerful positions and leadership roles in order to protect him, but it soon became clear that there were hundreds of people in that area who wanted

to stay in the mainstream, stay with the ruling body, and who didn't want anything to do with people like Gray. The big thing about the consultation process was that it made evident to everybody that the organisation was changing and that it would not oppress its own people, because that was not what people joined up for. The Shoukri brothers would also try to bully people into supporting them and ruled by fear, but there also the tide was changing. Even though they would order everybody to go to meetings to try and promote the image of support, out of 700, perhaps only 100 would show. There were also numerous meetings behind the scenes in north Belfast with the ruling body and people made it clear that they didn't want the likes of the Shoukris and that they would not tolerate their ways. So there is an intention to close these people down, which we call 'creating a narrow ground'.

What this process highlights is that the UDA is now trying to move towards a centralised structure, which is enabling the leadership to deal with problems in different areas and end the running of individual, autonomous fiefdoms that operate outside and against the emerging consensus. Gallagher continued:

It was quite obvious that there were leaders who relied on the shape of unwritten rules to benefit themselves and knew that because you could not look into the business of another area, they would be able to get away with criminality. A further problem was that others in that area, who were against the criminality, had nowhere to go to for help. In the case of at least two leaders there was big money criminality, which locked the people in that area into the trouble and the other Inner Council members had to just sit and watch that happening. That taboo has now been broken and was an understanding rather than a rule anyway. There is a process of trying to give ownership back to the members who should decide what shape things are in. The view now is that participation rather than exclusion is vital for changing attitudes and that this is more likely when fears are reduced. It's also clear that to do this properly, the governing body has to become more centralised. The paradox is that the UDA has to get stronger to move away because until there is control, consensus and agreement on how and where to move, it can't go anywhere. So strengthening is needed for transformation and that means the UDA becoming more centralised. Without that, the confidence to move on will not be there and the collective importance of the initiatives to address community and social problems will founder. We envisage that it will take at least three years to create the conditions for change and the CTI has been initially put together as a three year programme.

The UDA's west Belfast leader 'Charlie' underlined the direction being taken and stressed the importance of support for the emerging consensus:

> Previously, units would have sorted out problems militarily. Now our discipline has changed and we are encouraging each area to distance themselves from rogue elements. If such people don't want to go, then we will work to ostracise them. All areas know that it will not be tolerated for people to be intimidated and a statement has been made to that effect. But it's a difficult process because people have traditionally used force to deal with issues and we are trying to go down a different road because the last thing anybody wants is a feud. In certain estates and parts of the Shankill people have been working at this doggedly. Although we haven't a political party to represent us, we are getting our views across and we've had meetings with Northern Ireland Secretary Peter Hain and NIO officials. There's no doubt that not being attacked gives you room for manoeuvre and this is necessary to bring about change. Nobody wants to go back to the bad days and the emphasis has now moved from defending communities to mending communities. It's not the conflict which is the war now, but drugs and criminality.

UDA and UFF commander 'Alan' went on to reinforce the importance of the criminality problem and its tendency to impact on disillusioned members:

> If we leave our constituents behind there is no doubt that many will find themselves involved in criminality and that's a particular problem with conflict coming to an end. In south Belfast there is now a zero tolerance to drugs and if people are caught with drugs they are expelled. There is also a unity on the Inner Council about this. What we are now saying to people is that if they are caught with drugs and expelled it will be for the police to deal with them. We cannot take actions into our own hands, as we have done in the past. Consensus is the way ahead. Without a shot being fired, north Belfast has been transformed because they want to be like everyone else. There was a small minority of people there who were dictating to everyone else what to do. I was at meetings and listening to people who had spent long years in jail, or who had lost family members killed in action, who were being told that they had to deal drugs. But the situation is improving. I have been at debates with over 3,000 people and the questions raised would have never been raised in the past. This is a sign that confidence is rising. I would say that about 95 per cent of the organisation is now on board with where we are going and if the 5 per cent who are not decide to take a different route, the police will sort them out. The emphasis now is less on who is orange and green and more on education, health, housing and employment.

We are saying to those who developed reputations as hard men to keep that status, but through community development and helping people in their area. We are also trying to give the young people lessons about the danger of trying to pursue the Johnny Adair lifestyle and pointing out that the realities of a paramilitary lifestyle are to end up with no family, spending the best years of your life in prison and coming out to sleep in a car, which is what happened to me. Not running around in flash cars flaunting gold jewellery and selling drugs. And this requires constant discussion, saying the same things over and again and keeping to the same story.

Commenting in more detail about the CTI and how it was put together, 'Alan' went on:

The process of conversation picked up from the summer of 2005 and into 2006 and over a period of six to eight weeks some of us were at that 24/7, speaking to every unit and bringing the results of those conversations back to the leadership, so we were building a process from the bottom up. That information was collated and used to plan the next stage of the transformation process. We spoke to hundreds in community centres, tin sheds, houses, pubs and clubs and we were saying that changes in republicanism had brought them huge benefits which we need to bring about as well. It was held back through certain elements, but in October 2006 we were given a small grant from the government which allowed five areas [south east Antrim to date has been kept out of the initiative because of criminality and the organisation is currently looking at how to 'reform' that area] to work on the ground with the membership through a series of workshops. We put out evaluation sheets and reported the feedback from those workshops to the Department of Social Development in the NIO. We are hoping for financial support to start a three year programme which will also be accompanied by eight publications to chart 'loyalism in Transition'. That money will help us to employ key workers who will work with people on the ground and help people find employment etc. We have 10,000 members and their families, so you're talking about 60,000–70,000 people, which is a big constituency. This also gives us some political influence and a stronger say in how communities should be treated. Importantly, one also has to remember that there are generations of people here without an education. Fathers and sons fought this war and didn't get an education and there are even third generation kids who are also without an education. Until that is addressed, not only will they lack the skills necessary to gain employment, but they won't be able to see beyond the sectarianism and will remain susceptible to all the fears which surround that.

Jackie McDonald leader of south Belfast UDA also strongly emphasised the necessity for change if loyalism is to successfully address the social deficit effecting communities:

> Previously with the UPRG we were bouncing ideas of each other but were going in different directions and that has changed. The recognition is now clearly here that if the military campaign is over then political activity is the only way forward and Republicans have proved that. Sinn Fein teach their people how to fill out forms for housing benefit and are actively involved in improving the conditions for their communities and we need to do that. Progress is down to dialogue and achieving some sort of political representation which is credible. The organisation has to leave criminality and criminality has to leave the organisation and most people know that now. Different people have started to talk about their fears and some of the problems they face and they have seen us try to help them with those problems. Fears about paramilitaries are now beginning to fade and the realization is growing that nobody can frighten others into supporting them. The more people are frightened, the more enemies one makes and this has been a historical problem which needs confronting if we are to prevent future young people losing out. There are people who have an interest in keeping the violence going because they have been making a fortune out of it, but the vast bulk of the organisation are not part of that and many struggle to exist day to day. But we have argued that we can either live together or die together and it's better to live together, even if you disagree. Mainstream unionism has done little to help us in that regard and this is because they are afraid of being embarrassed by Sinn Fein accusing them of talking to us. Even though that is starting to change, we still need to prove that we are not thugs and it's in our hands to do that.

On the possibility of cross-community dialogue with Sinn Fein and working to develop cross-community relations generally, McDonald reiterated the importance of education:

> Remember that Sinn Fein have many people who are schooled, coached and educated in community issues and Loyalists have tended to be frightened of that. There's no doubt that Loyalists haven't been bothered with education in the same way. For the many Catholics I have spoken to the importance of education was ingrained very early on and the outcome of that is a confidence, which loyalism lacks. People are also worried about talking to others who they think are winning and in a stronger position, which is how many people see Republicans. They see Republicans as being in the ascendancy and automatically recoil from that. What is needed is a complete change of attitude towards education

and what it can bring, because only then will people feel they have the necessary confidence to engage and deal with their opponents on a comparable level intellectually. So the issue of education is not only central to improving the lot for Loyalists generally, it is central for helping to develop better cross-community relations as well.

The problem of educational achievement and social improvement in Loyalist communities was also recognised as important by former Northern Ireland Secretary Paul Murphy who stated:

> There are some genuine grievances and obstacles for a number of people living in Loyalist areas and especially with ex-prisoners who face considerable problems gaining employment. It is also extremely significant that opportunities for young people are seriously limited without a good education, and for many young people on the Shankill hardly anybody would go to university. Then there is the added complication of support for selective education, which the two main Unionist parties strongly support. Northern Ireland has the world's best and worst schools, but as yet, there is little sign of improving the chances of young deprived people through education. There are still seriously disadvantaged Loyalist areas, in a part of the world, which on balance, is pretty prosperous. At this point in time though, the education argument is still essentially a middle-class one. We should also remember that on the side of financial development and getting access to grants, Nationalist communities are much better at drawing down money from various organisations and creating community development than Loyalists. There is an emphasis on the individual in Protestantism and unionism, whereas for Nationalists, the community is a focal point of social life. We had to teach Loyalist communities how to fill in the forms, how to get the applications and how to get grants because they had no experience at all in doing that kind of thing, which was a real disadvantage to them.

The CTI was put as a proposal to the Department of Social Development on 6 April 2006 and was devised in close co-operation with NIO officials and government representatives. The comprehensive document worked from the starting point that the war was over and set out a detailed list of points which needed to be addressed in order to help transform deprived Loyalist areas. A key point of interest related to identifying domestic, religious, national and other influences which might be seen as causes for conflict and designing acceptable methods for dealing with each. Other areas of concern focussed on helping communities to acquire the necessary skills to help bring about the end of paramilitary activity, the reduction of crime and criminality, creating the conditions where violence is no longer seen as a viable option for expression and developing the educational skills to find employment and improve immediate areas. By taking an approach based on movement 'from defending to mending', Loyalists are being asked to concentrate on their own internal difficulties and work to overcome those difficulties from within, without recourse to violence. Guiding principles particularly relate to accepting responsibilities, adopting an inclusive approach to communal problems and disadvantage and taking holistic, integrated approach to issues (2006: 10). According to the CTI, priorities in relation to all these areas are specifically tied to 'growing as a community' and 'targeting social need'. With regards to the former, the aim is to 'embed equality of opportunity, human rights, mutual trust and respect as core values', while for the latter, a commitment to dealing with problems of unemployment, health, housing and education is stressed (ibid.: 12). Broken into a variety of sections, with attention to quantitative statistical data (necessary to satisfy government criteria for measurements and targets) the CTI document provides a detailed breakdown which relates to costs and value for money and outlines the methodology of 'good practice' in relation to social development.

But, although costing and devising targets may be essential for accessing government money, how effective or relevant those targets are in relation to changing attitudes and dealing with decades of sectarian hatred is questionable. Here, the targets of the CTI need to be weighed against the perpetual conversation and consultation which is required to unpack the emotional and historical myths that bind communities to a divisive worldview. Talking further on this process and the CTI, Frankie Gallagher went on:

> This process of change we call bringing the people over from the dark side to the light side. We need to talk to people one on one, as well as hundreds of people all together, and this has to be done constantly. We certainly plan to have 3 conversations in every area each year and to broaden these conversations to include church-based organisations and community groups. The biggest enemy now is staying still. You have to have movement to show that things are changing. The proposal stands to employ 16 people and remember that is across 6 geographical areas dealing with tens of thousands of people. The main problem with this, so far, is that there are gatekeepers who think you have to speak to them first before you can speak to others and sometimes those gatekeepers will try and prevent you from addressing the people in that area. That is happening in south east Antrim at the moment, where there is a core of 12 who are trying to stop a community of 2500 from getting involved. But there are other ways of addressing that and creating a different environment for people to communicate in, such as through email and phone. These people are also starting to find out that they can't stop others from communicating, which is a powerful thing for the person who feels oppressed. This also means an end to corner boy

politics, because it now means equal opportunity to speak and be heard. Those who try to obstruct this process have all been given ultimatums and put in a position where they can go the easy way, or the hard way. They're not seen as Loyalists because they have no political aspiration and are only interested in self-gain. Ultimately, they will be moved aside and will probably form into armed criminal gangs and then the police and state forces will have to deal with them. There's no doubt that now, the new battlefield is about politics, education and putting your message across in an organised, disciplined and confident way and confronting those you disagree with through peaceful means. It's important to remember that when one community is destabilised we are all destabilised and that if we are going to live together social cohesion is important.

As is evident, the biggest obstacle to the kind of change envisaged by those working on the CTI is the ongoing criminality which permeates Loyalist communities. And as 'Alan', indicates in this final comment, it is how this problem is dealt with which exercises the efforts of the leadership most of all at the time of writing:

The problem is and will be getting the few people who have got a good lifestyle through criminality to give that up. But what we are asking people is to think about whether such individuals became paramilitaries because of a desire to protect Ulster, or to be criminals. Yet, we cannot sort these people out through violence, which will only reinforce another form of criminality. Previously, with north Belfast, those people would have been dealt with through violence, but now we are encouraging areas to vote with their feet and move away of their own accord. It's vital we don't go back to settling differences with guns. There is no threat from Republicans anymore, the threat is internal. We're not talking about a lot of people here, but they need to be dealt with. Until all this has been sorted out and things are stabilized, I don't see the UDA disbanding.

Though there are signs that criminality is being reduced in the UDA, which is acknowledged by security agencies, the IMC's fifteenth report, published in April 2007, states that the UDA remained 'heavily engaged in violence and other crime, although not in terrorism' (p. 14). The report also talks of shootings, believed to have occurred 'as a result of friction within the organisation or as a response to perceived anti-social behaviour' (p. 13). While recognising that there has been a decline in the level of drug dealing and extortion in some areas, the report stresses that members have 'continued to be engaged in serious crime, including drug dealing, extortion, the sale of contraband and counterfeit goods and loan sharking'. Moreover, although the leadership is recognised as having made efforts to address issues of criminality, such efforts do not appear to 'amount to an effective strategy for dealing with criminality generally'; nor has there been any progress on the issue of decommissioning (ibid.: 14). The work of the CTI is welcomed, but viewed primarily as a first step for dealing with such problems.

A significant difficulty for the UDA is that although individual members may decide to commit acts of crime of their own accord, without organisational knowledge or consent, this action will inevitably be seen as paramilitary crime. Criminal acts which in any city within the UK would be attributed to individuals, or gangs, in the case of those acts being carried out by paramilitaries become attributed to the paramilitary organisation to which they belong. One way for the UDA to address this is for the organisation to disband (as the UVF appear to have done), so this association no longer has legitimacy or validity. One also needs to recognise the considerable problem of trying to keep an organisation of up to 10,000 people under control and trying to transform those people into responsible law-abiding citizens when the history and culture of the organisation has been the complete opposite (another reason for disbanding). Ironically, the CTI may be seen as a commendable first step towards change, but its effectiveness may ultimately rest on whether the UDA continues to exist or not.

Conclusion

The testimony used in this book reveals a range of points in relation to how loyalism has adapted to the demands of the peace process. The influences of nationalism and religion still impact on the Unionist imagination, and the social and political world continues to be witnessed through the literal interpretations of an individualistically determined worldview. A tendency for Loyalists to pursue violence throughout the peace process, but more especially against each other, can also be seen as an expression of this imagination and its existential nature, where responsibility is tied to individual experience and where community defence has all too often been manipulated for individual gain. But, alongside this tendency, there have been some notable shifts in how the political and social world is being understood which appear to parallel changes brought about by the peace process. The orthodoxy of extreme religious belief and its association with paramilitarism, for example, is no longer as certain or pervasive among paramilitaries. Indeed, for many, there is considerable criticism towards the use of fundamentalist religious rhetoric, as well as a growing cynicism and suspicion towards its social and political relevance.

The political transformation of Paisley and the DUP is no doubt a response to this critique, along with the realisation that the religious world view is no longer the primary vantage point to deal with the political challenges faced. Many people interviewed in this book view the importance of Paisley and the DUP not so much in terms of security provided by religious articulation (although the traditional stance taken and displayed through such articulation may be seen to be part of this), but because of an ability to confront the advance of republicanism and nationalism by political skill and an appeal to the moral dilemmas which are likely to arise through the process of change. Though Paisley's historical tendency to talk of resistance to change is a prominent reason for his perceived reliability among many Loyalists and Unionists, it should also be noted that for a number interviewed here, that reliability is seen as too often aligned with intransigence, a position no longer tenable in relation to a shifting political climate, regardless of claims about defence and preservation. Indeed, for many, such a position is not only unrealistic, but actually destructive towards reinterpretation of identity and tradition in a world which is increasingly being absorbed into the fluid and interdependent realities of European life and globalisation (consider arguments for such a defence against the Celtic Tiger, Irish introduction of the Euro and a broad consensus towards European integrative practices). The promotion of the DUP as the biggest Unionist Party in Northern Ireland and the decision by the DUP to accept power-sharing is far removed from the traditional 'no surrender' and 'not an inch' stance for which Paisley became famous. His strength among Unionist and Loyalist voters comes from the expectation that he will translate his perceived dependability into the political realm, but that he will do so by facilitating rather than blocking the sharing of power, and will be more inclined to concede ground from a position of strength rather than weakness (as appeared to be the case with the UUP). Moreover, the sectarian attitudes taken by the DUP while outside negotiations were notably absent when the party was faced with the problem of actual political responsibility and decision-making inside negotiations. Paul Murphy mentioned in interview that at the Leeds Castle talks which took place after the 2003 elections, when the DUP had become the dominant Unionist party, there were no sectarian attitudes or positions evident as the DUP focussed ostensibly on the issues surrounding violence and a commitment by both Republicans and Loyalists to accept democratic and peaceful means in the pursuit of political aspiration. What was also noticeable after those talks is that public criticisms about Sinn Fein and the IRA were based on the motivations of those groups as being Republican and not Catholic. The discourse and public conduct of Paisley and the DUP shifted markedly once its position of dominance was attained and the party was forced to confront directly the dilemmas of power-sharing and political control.

The shift from violent to non-violent society in Northern Ireland has been arduous and problematic for Loyalist paramilitary organisations. And as with mainstream unionism, until recently, there have been antagonisms and schisms which have been disruptive for the development of a coherent political project. However, the transition from violence towards tentative peace has nevertheless occurred, even if disjointedly and with certain trepidation. For the UVF, this transition has been conducted with more confidence and greater control than the UDA, with the UVF's recent decision to stand down an indication of that confidence. But here, there is another factor of influence which requires some attention. In the build-up to the 2007 elections, the PUP were advocating 'A New Dawn' as the party's electoral message (a play on words with the party's representative Dawn Purvis), but was facing criticism that such a message was not actually possible given the PUP's close association with the UVF. In order for the PUP to deliver on the aspiration which was implicit to the slogan, it became reasonably obvious that political growth and independence would be hampered by involvement with the UVF and that paramilitary association would become a burden for the party. The UVF's exit from the stage is both recognition of this problem and a response to it. By moving away from the PUP (at least as far as the public image is concerned), the UVF is effectively allowing the PUP to develop and gain political credibility on its own terms, rather than being seen as anchored to the UVF and acting as its mouthpiece. Criticisms of the PUP by mainstream unionism that the party is merely articulating what the UVF wants, take on an unconvincing, accusatory tone, given the UVF's withdrawal from the political scene, and it is this withdrawal which may allow the PUP to develop a voice for working-class loyalism in ways which its previous leaders were not able to bring about. Crucial though those leaders were in bringing political loyalism to the fore in the peace process, it has been only recently that a broad consensus has emerged about the conflict being effectively over (remembering the obstructions and divisions within loyalism and unionism which remained until at least 2003 because of a lack of consensus about the conflict being at an end) and that Loyalist paramilitarism no longer has a role. In turn, political development may be able to flourish better without suspected affiliation to paramilitary interests.

This is a particular dilemma for the UDA, which at the time of writing, is neither advocating a political front which can transform into electoral political representation, or pushing the need to disband as a paramilitary organisation. One might argue that the lack of a political front explains why for those interviewed here, the UDA will continue to exist for some time, since without direct party-political representation the organisation is less subject to direct political pressure for disbandment. But there is a further problem here in that because the UPRG sees itself as effectively a lobbying group without electoral aspirations, it may be unable to exert the kind of political influence it thinks it can. True, that by staying outside of electoral politics the UPRG does not have to establish political credibility, as a political party does, and does not face the prospect of removal by being voted out because of that, but on the other hand, attempting to have concerns addressed through parties who represent other constituencies and protect different interests makes the idea of exerting political clout decidedly contentious. Without transforming into a political party at some point, the UPRG may find that the momentum it seeks to develop will stall. There are, of course, grounds to argue that the Unionist community would not be interested in another party, but by looking at the 108 seats which are available in the Assembly rather than the number of parties, future political progress may be likely to become established less on how a broad range of political issues are dealt with and more on how specific community concerns are met. In turn, as voters become less concerned with the preservation of Unionist identity, traditions and culture, and more with education, housing and social development, it will be those more closely involved with the latter issues who will be likely to gain votes. The transition towards 'normalisation' will highlight the need to confront challenges which are less to do with traditional arguments and postures and more to do with involvement at local level and helping specific groups to overcome problems as they arise. The UPRG has already identified the importance of working at local level to gain public support, and if that support grows, political transformation and growth will emerge as distinct possibilities. This may be some way down the road, but as long as Northern Ireland continues to face political and social stability and power-sharing continues to become entrenched, the UPRG could find its social aspirations strengthened from transformation into party political representation. If that happens, the existence of the UDA will then become a liability and any political party that may form, will be up against the same criticisms as those which faced the PUP, namely that the party is a mouthpiece for paramilitaries.

The UPRG are looking at the role of community development as crucial for providing paramilitaries with a sense of purpose and conviction, which is made particularly uncertain in the event of paramilitarism coming to an end. It is also important to note that the purpose of striving to develop a sense of cohesion around social themes and concerns by the UPRG is also designed to make a return to violence by rogue elements less likely. Many people who were interviewed admit that ending violence is much harder than starting violence in that although the arguments for peace may be more compelling, the sense of emotional excitement and social empowerment is less tangible. Being involved in paramilitarism has given many a sense of identity, value and status which is hard to replace by the mundane, laborious and long-term efforts of community development and social regeneration. To enable this transition to work, leaders must continue to invite constant debate and keep members close to the benefits of social change, which are manifestly hindered and destroyed by violence.

On the point of structural difference between the UVF and the UDA, it is clear that the centralised structure of the UVF has enabled the leaders of that organisation to control consultations and moves towards disbanding with some degree of confidence. To put it another way, the centralised nature of the UVF has enabled the process of dispersal to be handled with greater attention and purpose and has been made from a position of lengthy and detailed communication. The leaders of the UVF have made it clear than any illegal action taken by ex-members must be viewed as criminality and as such, dealt with by the forces of law and order. For the UDA however, a lack of centralisation means that moving towards disbandment runs a greater risk of factions developing and pockets of resistance re-forming into other violent groups. A recognition of the UDA needing to centralise much more before the organisation is able to confidently move towards a position where disbandment becomes the next inevitable step (at least as a paramilitary force), is also recognised by some of its representatives. Only when the consensus is clear and there is confidence, is the UDA likely to follow the UVF. Without such confidence, the UDA risks fragmentation, further episodes of violence and a return to power-struggles between areas. Because of this, it may be a while yet before the UDA effectively ceases to exist as a paramilitary organisation. The current process of developing consensus and a centralised structure to deal with the challenges of transformation is a sensible step and is essential to avoid past mistakes. But, although there is a developing cohesion and agreement among the Inner Council and the UPRG about the way ahead, that agreement, as yet, does not extend to south east Antrim, which is currently ostracised because of criminality, drugs and a resistance at leadership level to the changes being proposed through the Conflict Transformation Initiative.

What is clear across both organisations is that the biggest problem now facing loyalism is loyalism itself. That without the threat of Republican violence (apart from dissent groups which are being further marginalised by the clear public support for power-sharing), there is no case for politically motivated violence and because of that no justification for the continuation of Loyalist paramilitarism. This realisation was emphatic among all those interviewed for this book. As such, this marks a significant step forward which has taken a long time to reach. One might perhaps discern that loyalism has moved on when the term loyalism itself becomes absent from the lexicon used to describe Northern Ireland politics, and that those currently seen as Loyalists may, over time, become viewed as working-class Unionists. Once the expressions and articulations around tradition and culture are no longer threatening, but offer cross-communal potential for celebration and understanding, then intimidating aspects of Loyalist culture (towards Republicans and Nationalists) may give way to a more constructive and educational interpretation of meaning and exchange. What is reasonably certain though is that this position can only be realistically achieved from a position of confidence and a shift away from the constant perception of loss which has pervaded the Unionist imagination. At the end of his autobiography, the paramilitary Johnny Adair, reminiscent of Arnold Schwarzenegger's character in Terminator (and similarly reflecting that character's robotic and unimaginative tendencies), states 'Make no mistake: I will be back' (Adair 2007). For those seeking to end violence and contribute to peace, the return of the pathologically driven appeal of violence in pursuit of individual status and gain would risk returning loyalism to the destructive ways of the past and would be nothing short of a catastrophe. Whether this turns out to be the case or not, only time will tell.

Afterword

In July 2007, as a result of ongoing tensions between south east Antrim and the mainstream UDA, a police officer was shot while attending to a dispute in Carrickfergus, County Antrim. This incident was followed on 1 August by riots on a housing estate in Bangor, County Down, when petrol bombs were thrown at police and live rounds were fired. Such action was seen as serious enough for the Minister for Social Development of the new Assembly, SDLP member Margaret Ritchie, to threaten the withdrawal of £1.2 million of Conflict Transformation Initiative money if the UDA did not commence decommissioning within 60 days. The deadline for the 60 days was 9 October 2007. Although faced with a range of objections from within the Assembly (mostly from the DUP), statements from senior officials that the UDA had commenced 'meaningful engagement' with General John de Chastelain's decommissioning body, and requests from a range of senior clergy for Ritchie to reconsider her deadline, progress at the 60-day deadline was deemed to be insufficient by Ritchie and CTI funding was subsequently withdrawn. The UPRG continue to challenge the removal of CTI funding on legal grounds.

Within days of this development news of a Special Agent informant working in south east Antrim was released to the media. This revelation followed reports that south east Antrim had decommissioned a small amount of weaponry which had been badly received within the UDA mainstream. Exposure of the informant also reinforced ongoing suspicions among the UDA leadership that state intelligence services continue to influence internal divisions and that this intervention should also be considered in the light of efforts by the leadership to unsuccessfully get the police to arrest drug-dealers and confront criminality in south east Antrim. Claims of the intelligence services allowing illegal activity to carry on in order not to expose informants are widespread within the UDA and contribute to the popular view that political instability is being underscored by state agencies and others who wish to see the UDA remain destabilized (one must also take into account here however that the history of the organisation has tended to be one of disharmony and fragmentation anyway).

Against these background events, after a concentrated process of internal consultation and dialogue and in response to changed political events in Northern Ireland, the UDA leadership through a co-ordination of speakers released its 'Remembrance Day Statement' on 11 November 2007. The statement effectively followed a similar pattern to the UVF statement of May in terms of language and intent and outlined a commitment to established principles and history while advocating the importance of pursuing aspirations through non-violent means. Stressing the role and importance of community action, the statement also asserted a conviction to eradicate criminality as a necessary requirement for organisational stability. The statement said:

> The Ulster Defence Association believes that the war is over and we are now in a new democratic dispensation that will lead to permanent political stability, but we believe the political parties and the political institutions are themselves in a period of transition. In that context, the organisation intends to contribute through a process of transformation that will ultimately achieve a Northern Ireland based on equality, justice and exclusivity, where no sections of our people are left behind regardless of religion, politics or identity.
>
> We believe that to secure our British identity and maintain the Union we must play a positive role in achieving political stability here in Northern Ireland. This means developing the skills and increasing the confidence of our community so they can play an active role in building and shaping the future, but be able to defend ourselves through non-violent means when our rights are taken from us, or if our identity is being eroded and our place within the United Kingdom is threatened. The ballot box and the political institutions must be the greatest weapon.
>
> At present up to 60 per cent of our community do not vote or do not register to vote and languish in the top 10 per cent of the most socially and economically deprived communities in the country. This leaves our people isolated, marginalised and open to exploitation and not able to defend ourselves from politicians who would seek to improve their political careers and represent us as criminals, in particular drug-dealers.
>
> If we are able to create a society where citizens feel they should not be defended by paramilitaries, then we must have political structures that protect all the citizens, where politicians can not jump in and out of those political structures when it suits them to further their own political aims. The people must have confidence in the political structures and feel they will be defended if wronged. That feeling does not exist in our community.
>
> We feel that some Irish Nationalist politicians, along with others, are intent on excluding our people from the new shared future that is the over-arching principle of the new Assembly. They are working at every turn to erode our British identity and undermining the Union. What we do recognise is that we must face these challenges within the law and

through non-violent means. What compounds this situation is that we feel the majority of Unionist politicians are unable to defend our rights at present, but recognise that politics in the new Assembly are very much in transition.

Under these difficult conditions the organisation has agreed a number of actions that it can implement over a period of time in the belief that they will bring about positive change, add to a greater political stability and if our communities are given the right support, so they can become equals in the new political dispensation and shared future, achieving a lasting and sustainable peace.

These series of actions cannot achieve peace, justice and equality on their own, they require recognition that loyalism needs a process and that process requires support. The length and duration of achieving these actions depend on that recognition and support. The Ulster Defence Association is committed to achieving a society where violence and weaponry are ghosts of the past.

Action 1

It is our intention as a result of the ongoing consultations with our members to go back to our roots and direct all our energies into developing our communities. The Ulster Defence Association will remain the parent organisation but will establish an umbrella organisation titled the Ulster Defence Union to facilitate the continued transformation of members and the needs that will affect them.

In this spirit we the members of the Ulster Defence Association 2007 reaffirm our commitment to maintaining the Union now as our fore fathers did during the political instability of the home rule crisis and resisted the passing of the first home rule bill when on the 17 March 1893 the then Unionist leaders saw fit to call on all Loyalists of Ulster to form a new organisation titled the Ulster Defence Association; who would then select an assembly of 600 delegates and having then convened, nominated an executive council of 40. This executive would then form an umbrella organisation titled the Ulster Defence Union where all sections of unionism could come together regardless of their social class to stand united against any proposals for an all-Ireland parliament.

Our members have from 1893 gone forward and paid the ultimate sacrifice and given their lives in the defence and freedom of small nations on Flanders fields at the Somme during the First World War, Africa, Europe and the Middle East during WWII. We continue that struggle for freedom in the present theatres of war in Afghanistan and Iraq.

Action 2

Acknowledging that the military war is over and the struggle to maintain the Union is on a new and more complex battlefield. In consideration of this new reality, all active service units of the Ulster Freedom

Fighters will as from midnight tonight stand down with all military intelligence destroyed and as a consequence of this all weaponry will be put beyond use.

It must be recognised with honour that it was through the sacrifice of these brave men, who were the cutting edge that took the war to the enemy, why we enjoy a relative peace and stability and an opportunity to build a new future. It was these Freedom Fighters who brought the enemy to the peace table and established the first ceasefires in 1994. Many of these men served long prison sentences and many lost their lives. We must also acknowledge the sacrifice of their families, wives and children who suffered through no fault of their own. The battle flags of the Ulster Freedom Fights will be furled in a sincere hope that they may never have to see the light of day again, but stand in readiness. We will not forget what they did or why they did it, nor will we forget who called them to arms in the defence of Ulster.

Action 3

All Ulster Young Militants will be re-directed towards education, personal development and community development. It is acknowledged that the youth stood ready to face the enemy when called and feel that they have lost out on their opportunity, but through education they will learn that there are many ways to do battle and that it can be done without firing a shot. They are our country's future and we will be in their hands soon enough.

Action 4

A general order to all members not to be involved in crime or criminality. It is the duty of every member to understand that to be involved in crime or criminality is to undermine the cause. We have had those who joined our ranks for political reasons; these men went on to give great sacrifice and brought honour to the organisation and gained the respect of their comrades. But there have been those who joined our ranks for crime and self-gain. These people must be rooted out and never allowed to breathe in our ranks. These people have been involved in drug-dealing and this must be stamped out. Drugs destroy our children and our children are our future. These people are not Loyalists; they are criminals. There is no place in the organisation for such people.

Our loyal members in south east Antrim continue to face up to their responsibility to defend the community against criminals and criminality. The organisation pledges support to those loyal members, who, despite threats, intimidation and attack from a small criminal gang, stay committed to the direction and policies of the organisation. It was this criminal gang who carried out the recent act of decommissioning. This was not an act of decommissioning. This gimmick was an attempt to try and undermine all of loyalism. We believe that there are a number of police informants involved at the highest level in south east Antrim who are the key organisers of the crime and criminality, in particular drugs. We encourage all out genuine members in south east Antrim to take courage from those who have stood up to these criminals at personal risk and call on them to join these brave men.

The Ulster Defence Association is committed to supporting the building of communities and encourages all our members to participate at all levels of regeneration and social development. Our people and our country will face many challenges in the future, we must stand ready to do battle, but we must be on the right battlefield and we must train in the skills that will enable us not just to defend our community, but also to improve our community. We must be able to face the challenge to create a better future for our children. The majority of our community do not participate in activities related to social and economic regeneration; the majority of our community do not have a voice. We must develop ways of getting a voice so we can speak for ourselves and learn to speak with one voice. We are a sleeping giant. Above all we must stick together and let no one separate us.

Quis Separabit.

At the time of writing, both the UVF and the UDA show no sign of decommissioning weapons and argue that given the potential for fragmentation and disorder if such a move were to be imposed, it would not only be profoundly damaging for organisational cohesion, but would run the risk of re-igniting conflict. In that context, the imposition of such a move is seen as irresponsible and not responsible as official bodies imply. This does not mean, however, that there are not senior paramilitary figures seeking to facilitate such an outcome in the long term and who perhaps see moving towards this conclusion as an inevitable and necessary step towards total de-militarization. But to achieve this outcome there is another factor to be considered apart from resistance to change within the organisations themselves, which is that they are not connected to a wider political process which could systematically help them facilitate complete transformation. Without this level of engagement the Loyalist organisations remain detached from a dynamic of change beyond what they can manage and create themselves. As can be seen in the UDA statement, feelings of communal isolation and detachment are inextricably linked with the motivation to change. All the while this perception endures, it is highly unlikely that the Loyalists will decommission as governments and public opinion desire. Indeed, the longer such perceptions endure the harder it will be to create any momentum around this problem and the more likely that frustrations will manifest as criminality and wider communal tensions. If not addressed, this risks an escalation of instability which will feed into growing demands for retaliation and exacerbate the conditions from which violent reaction springs. Of course, the overriding obligation and responsibility for supporting peace and ending violence rests with the organisations themselves, but it is very difficult for such groups to move in this direction when they are only talking to themselves and not part of a broader political interaction process where underlying tensions can be more effectively comprehended and addressed.

What I am suggesting as a final point is that to bring about decommissioning, it seems important to deal with a range of underlying issues first in order to weaken internal arguments for it to not take place. For, as long as Loyalists see decommissioning as a step without perceived advantage, either organisationally or politically (unlike Republicans who were able to relate pressure for decommissioning to clear political gain), the reasons being used to prevent it taking place will not be challenged with confidence or persuasiveness. Communal problems which derive from feelings of detachment from a wider process of social change seen as beneficial for most should not be seen as incidental to that process, but rather integral to its progression. Indeed, the benefits of change also depend on addressing the difficulties which contribute to perceptions of loss and lack of connection to wider society if underlying conditions which could contribute to a return to violence are to be removed. What is required therefore, is for official bodies to re-engage with the Loyalists in order to create a dynamic which re-connects them with the political process.

Through such engagement, a multi-dimensional approach to dialogue and action could systematically work to address the fears and anxieties (social, economic, cultural, historical and political) which make steps such as decommissioning so difficult to contemplate. It is improbable that Loyalists will be able to reach this position by themselves without any high-level political help and support. Recognition that resistance to decommissioning is also symptomatic of Loyalists seeing themselves as detached from the advantages of social change (especially the UDA) highlights the need to create a process which will re-attach them to those advantages. Until this happens, obstructions to transformation will not only remain, but probably grow, risking a reversal of potential gains already made in the process. Political pressure for change without political support for that change will in all probability merely serve to compound the growing sense of marginalisation and frustration which reinforces resistance to steps such as decommissioning. A commitment to achieve this end should not therefore be seen as the sole responsibility of the organisations themselves (vital though that is), but the responsibility of those who claim to represent the political and social interests of wider society and the transition from conflict to a post-conflict Northern Ireland.

Bibliography

A Citizens' Inquiry: The Opsahl Report on Northern Ireland (Dublin: The Lilliput Press, 1993).
Adair, J. *Mad Dog* (London: John Blake Publishing, 2007).
Anderson, B. *Imagined Communities* (London: Verso, 1983).
Aughey, A. *Under Seige* (Belfast: Blackstaff Press, 1989).
———. 'Recent Interpretations of Unionism', *Political Quarterly* 61 (1990) 188–99.
———. 'The Art and Effect of Political Lying in Northern Ireland', *Irish Political Studies* 17, 2 (2002) 1–16.
Aughey, A and McIlheney, C. 'Law Before Violence – The Protestant Paramilitaries in Ulster Politics', *Law Before Violence?* 19, 2 (1984) 55–74.
Bairner, A. 'The Battlefield of Ideas: The Legitimation of Political Violence in Northern Ireland', *European Journal of Political Research* 14 (1986) 633–49.
Bew, P. and Gillespie, G. *Northern Ireland: A Chronology of the Troubles 1968–1999* (Dublin: Gill and Macmillan, 1999).
Beyond the Religious Divide (Belfast: Ulster Defence Association, March 1979).
Billig, M. *Banal Nationalism* (London: Sage, 1995).
Bloomfield, D. *Political Dialogue in Northern Ireland* (Basingstoke: Macmillan Press, 1998).
Boulton, D. *The UVF 1966–73* (Dublin: Gill and Macmillan, 1973).
Bourke, R. *Peace in Ireland* (London: Pimlico, 2003).
Bowyer Bell, J. *Back to the Future* (Dublin: Poolbeg, 1996).
Brewer, J. *Anti-Catholicism in Northern Ireland, 1600–1998* (Basingstoke: Macmillan Press, 1998).
Brown, T. 'The Whole Protestant Community: the making of a historical myth', *Field Day* 7 (1985) 5–24.
Bruce, S. 'Authority and Fission: The Protestants' Divisions', *The British Journal of Sociology* 36, 2 (1985) 592–603.
———. *God Save Ulster* (Oxford: Oxford University Press, 1986).
———. 'Ulster Loyalism and Religiosity', *Political Studies* 35 (1987) 643–8.
———. 'Northern Ireland: Reapprasing Loyalist Violence', *Conflict Studies 249*, Research Institute for the Study of Conflict and Terrorism (March 1992a).
———. 'The Problems of 'Pro-State' Terrorism: Loyalist Paramilitaries in Northern Ireland', *Terrorism and Political Violence* 4, 1 (1992b) 67–88.
———. *The Red Hand* (Oxford: Oxford University Press, 1992c).
———. *The Edge of the Union* (Oxford: Oxford University Press, 1994).
———. *Conservative Protestant Politics* (Oxford: Oxford University Press, 1998).
———. 'Terrorists and Politics: The Case of Northern Ireland's Loyalist Paramilitaries', *Terrorism and Political Violence* 13, 2 (2001) 27–48.
Building a Permanent Peace (Belfast: Sinn Fein, 1996).
Cadwallader, A. *Holy Cross: The Untold Story* (Belfast: Brehon Press, 2004).
Carroll, J. *Puritan, Paranoid, Remissive* (London: RKP, 1977).
Cash, J.D. *Identity, Ideology and Conflict* (Cambridge: Cambridge University Press, 1996).
Clarke, L. and Johnston, K. *Martin McGuinness* (Edinburgh: Mainstream, 2003).
Cochrane, F. *Unionist Politics* (Cork: Cork University Press, 1997).
Common Sense (Belfast: Ulster Political Research Group, 1987).

Coogan, T.P. *The Troubles* (London: Hutchinson, 1995).
Cooke, D. *Prosecuting Zeal* (Dingle/Co Kerry: Brandon, 1996).
Coulter, C. 'The Character of Unionism', *Irish Political Studies* 9 (1994) 1–24.
Crawford, C. *Inside The UDA* (London: Pluto Press, 2003).
Cusack, J. and Taylor, M. 'Resurgence of a Terrorist Organisation – Part 1: The UDA, a Case Study', *Terrorism and Political Violence* 5, 3 (1993) 1–27.
Cusack, J. and McDonald, H. *UVF* (Dublin: Poolbeg, 1997).
Delaney, E. *An Accidental Diplomat* (Dublin: New Island Books, 2001).
Dillon, M. *God and the Gun* (London: Orion, 1998).
Dixon, P. 'Political skills or lying and manipulation? The choreography of the Northern Ireland peace process', *Political Studies* 50, 4 (2002) 725–41.
——. *The Northern Ireland Peace Process: Choreography and Theatrical Politics* (London: Routledge, 2008).
Drake, C.J.M. 'The Phenomenon of Conservative Terrorism', *Terrorism and Political Violence* 8, 3 (1996) 29–46.
Duignan, S. *One Spin on the Merry-Go-Round* (Dublin: Blackwater Press, 1996).
Dunlop, J. *Precarious Belonging* (Belfast: Blackstaff Press, 1995).
Dunn, S and Morgan, V. *Protestant Alienation in Northern Ireland: A Preliminary Survey* (Centre for the Study of Conflict: University of Ulster, 1994).
Elliott, M. 'Watchmen in Sion: The Protestant Idea of Liberty', *Field Day* 8 (1985) 28.
Elliott, S. and Flackes, W.D. *Northern Ireland: A Political Directory 1968–1999* (Belfast: Blackstaff Press, 1999).
English, R. *Armed Struggle* (London: Macmillan, 2003).
Farringdon, C. 'The Northern Ireland Assembly Election 2003', *Irish Political Studies* 19, 1 (2004) 74–86.
——. *Ulster Unionism and the Peace Process in Northern Ireland* (Basingstoke: Palgrave Macmillan, 2006).
Fifteenth Report of the Independent Monitoring Commission (London: HMSO, 25 April 2007).
Finlay, A. 'Defeatism and Northern Protestant "Identity"', *The Global Review of Ethnopolitics* 1, 2 (2001) 3–20.
Finlay, F. *Snakes and Ladders* (Dublin: New Island Books, 1998).
Finlayson, A. 'Nationalism as Ideological Interpellation: The Case of Ulster Loyalism', *Ethnic and Racial Studies* 19, 1(1996) 88–111.
Finlayson, A. 'Loyalist Political Identity After the Peace', *Capital and Class* 69 (1999) 47–75.
The Frameworks Documents – A New Framework for Agreement (London: HMSO, 1995).
Gallagher, E. and Worrall, S. *Christians in Ulster 1968–1980* (Oxford: Oxford University Press, 1982).
Gallagher, T. 'Religion, Reaction, and Revolt in Northern Ireland: The Impact of Paisleyism in Ulster', *Journal of Church and State* 23 (1981) 423–44.
Ganiel, G. 'Ulster Says Maybe: The Restructuring of Evangelical Politics in Northern Ireland', *Irish Political Studies* 21, 2 (2006) 137–55.
Garland, R. *Gusty Spence* (Belfast: Blackstaff Press, 2001).
Gowing, N. 'Real-time Television Coverage of Armed Conflicts and Diplomatic Crises: Does It Pressure or Distort Foreign Policy Decisions?', Joan Shorenstein Barone Center on the Press, Politics and Public Policy, Working Paper 94-1 (1994).
Graham, B. 'The Past in the Present: The Shaping of Identity in Loyalist Ulster', *Terrorism and Political Violence* 16, 3 (2004) 483–500.

Hall, M (ed.) *A New Reality? Loyalism in Transition 1* (Belfast: Farset Community Think Tanks Project, 2006).
Hennessey, T. *The Northern Ireland Peace Process* (Dublin: Gill and Macmillan, 2000).
——. *Northern Ireland: The Origins of the Troubles* (Dublin: Gill and Macmillan, 2005).
Ingram, M. and Harkin, G. Stakeknife (Dublin: O'Brien Press, 2004).
Jordan, G. *Not of This World* (Belfast: Blackstaff Press, 2001).
Kennaway, B. *The Orange Order* (London: Methuen, 2006).
Lister, D. and Jordan, H. *Mad Dog* (Edinburgh: Mainstream Publishing, 2003).
MacIver, M.A. 'Ian Paisley and the Reformed Tradition', *Political Studies* 35 (1987) 359–78.
Mac Ginty, R. 'Unionist Political Attitudes After the Belfast Agreement', *Irish Political Studies* 19, 1 (2004) 87–99.
Mallie, E. and McKittrick, D. *The Fight for Peace* (London: Heinemann, 1996).
——. *Endgame in Ireland* (London: Hodder and Stoughton, 2002).
Mandle, J. *Global Justice* (Cambridge: Polity Press, 2006).
Mason, D. 'Nationalism and the Process of Group Mobilisation: The Case of 'Loyalism' in Northern Ireland Reconsidered', *Ethnic and Racial Studies* 8, 3 (1985) 408–25.
McAllister, I., Hayes, B.C. and Dowds, L. 'The Erosion of Consent: Protestant Disillusion with the Agreement', *Research Update* 32, January 2005, www.ark.ac.uk.
McAuley, J.W. 'Cuchullain and an RPG-7: The Ideology and Politics of the Ulster Defence Association', in *Culture and Politics in Northern Ireland 1960–1990* ed. E. Hughes (Buckingham: Open University Press, 1991).
——. '"Not a Game of Cowboys and Indians" – The Ulster Defence Association in the 1990s', *Terrorism's Laboratory* ed. A. O'Day (Aldershot: Dartmouth) 1995.
——. 'From Loyal Soldiers To Political Spokespersons: A Political History Of A Loyalist Paramilitary Group in Northern Ireland', *Etudes Irlandaises* 21, 1 (1996a) 165–82.
——. '(Re) Constructing Ulster Loyalism? Political responses to the "peace process"', *Irish Journal of Sociology* 6 (1996b) 127–53.
——. '"Very British Rebels": Politics and Discourse within Contemporary Ulster Unionism', in *Transforming Politics* ed. P. Bagguley and J. Hearn (Basingstoke: Macmillan Press, 1999).
——. 'Many Roads Forward: Politics And Ideology Within The Progressive Unionist Party', *Etudes Irlandaises* 25, 1 (2000) 173–92.
——. 'Redefining Loyalism – An Academic Perspective', *Redefining Loyalism*, IBIS working paper no. 4 (Dublin: Institute for British-Irish Studies, 2001) 8–24.
——. 'Unionism's Last Stand? Contemporary Politics and Identity in Northern Ireland', *The Global Review of Ethnopolitics* 3, 1 (2003) 60–74.
——. '"Just Fighting to Survive": Loyalist Paramilitary Politics and the Progressive Unionist Party', *Terrorism and Political Violence* 16, 3 (2004) 522–43.
——. 'Whither New Loyalism? Changing Loyalist Politics after the Belfast Agreement', *Irish Political Studies* 20, 3 (2005) 323–40.
McCartney, R. *Reflections on Liberty, Democracy and the Union* (Dublin: Maunsel and Company, 2001).
McDonald, H. and Cusack, J. *UDA* (London:Penguin) 2004.
McGarry, J. and O'Leary, B. *Explaining Northern Ireland* (Oxford: Blackwell, 1995).
McGrath, A.E. 'Protestantism – the Problem of Identity', in *Protestantism* ed. A.E. McGrath and D. C. Markes (Oxford: Blackwell Publishing, 2007).
McLaughlin, M. 'The Irish Republican Ideal', in *The Republican Ideal* ed. N. Porter (Belfast: Blackstaff Press, 1998).
McMichael, G. *An Ulster Voice* (Boulder/Colorado: Roberts Rineharts Publishers, 1999).

McSweeney, B. 'Identity, Interest and the Good Friday Agreement', *Irish Studies in International Affairs* 9 (1998) 93–102.
Miller, D.W. 'Presbyterianism and "Modernization" in Ulster', *Past and Present* 80 (1978) 66–90.
Mitchel, P. *Evangelicalism and National Identity in Ulster 1921–1998* (Oxford: Oxford University Press, 2003).
Mitchell, C. 'Protestant Identification and Political Change in Northern Ireland', *Ethnic and Racial Studies* 26, 4 (2003) 612–31.
Mitchell, C. *Religion, Identity and Politics in Northern Ireland* (Aldershot: Ashgate, 2006).
Mitchell, G. *Making Peace* (London: William Heinemann: London, 1999).
Mitchell, C. and Tilley, J.R. 'The Moral Minority: Evangelical Protestants in Northern Ireland and Their Political Behaviour', *Political Studies* 52 (2004) 585–602.
Moloney, E. *A Secret History of the IRA* (London: Penguin, 2002).
Moloney, E. and Pollak, A. *Paisley* (Dublin: Poolbeg Press, 1986).
Morrissey, M. and Smyth, M. *Northern Ireland After the Good Friday Agreement* (London: Pluto Press, 2002).
Morrow, D. 'Suffering for Righteousness' Sake? Fundamentalist Protestantism and Ulster Politics', in *Who Are 'The People'?* ed. P. Shirlow and M. McGovern (London: Pluto Press, 1997).
Mowlam, M. *Momentum* (London: Hodder and Stoughton, 2002).
Nelson, S. *Ulster's Uncertain Defenders* (Belfast: Appletree Press, 1984).
O'Brien, B. *The Long War* (Dublin: The O'Brien Press, 1995).
O'Dowd, L. '"New Unionism", British Nationalism and the Prospects for a Negotiated Settlement in Northern Ireland', in *Rethinking Northern Ireland* ed. D. Miller (Harlow/Essex: Longman, 1998).
O'Heffernan, P. *Mass Media and American Foreign Policy* (Norwood, NJ: Ablex Publishing Corporation, 1991).
O'Kane, E. 'Decommissioning and the Peace Process: Where Did It Come From and Why Did It Stay So Long?', *Irish Political Studies* 22,1 (2007) 81–101.
O'Malley, P. *The Uncivil Wars* (Boston Massachusetts: Beacon Press, 1997).
Paisley, I. 'Peace Agreement – Or Last Piece in a Sellout Agreement', *Fordham International Law Journal* 22 (1999) 1274–5.
Parkinson, A.F. *Ulster Unionism and the British Media* (Dublin: Four Courts Press, 1998).
Paths to a Political Settlement in Ireland (Belfast: Blackstaff Press, 1995).
Patterson, H. *Ireland Since 1939: The Persistence of Conflict* (Dublin; Penguin Ireland, 2006).
Pollak, A. 'Towards a Magnanimous Unionism: An Interview with Gusty Spence' *Fortnight*, Issue 225, 1985.
Porter, N. *Rethinking Unionism* (Belfast: Blackstaff Press, 1998).
Power, M. *From Ecumenism to Community Relations* (Dublin: Irish Academic Press, 2007).
Principles of Loyalism: An Internal Discussion Paper (Belfast: Progressive Unionist Party, November 2002).
Roshwald, A. *The Endurance of Nationalism* (Cambridge: Cambridge University Press, 2006).
Rowan, B. *The Armed Peace* (Edinburgh: Mainstream Publishing, 2003).
Rowan, B. *Paisley and the Provos* (Belfast: Brehon Press, 2005).
Ruane, J. and Todd, J. 'Diversity, Division and the Middle Ground in Northern Ireland', *Irish Political Studies* 7 (1992) 73–98.
——. *The Dynamics of Conflict in Northern Ireland* (Cambridge: Cambridge University Press, 1996).
Ryder, C. and Kearney, V. *Drumcree* (London: Methuen, 2001).

Sharing Responsibility (Belfast: The Progressive Unionist Party, September 1985).
Sharing Responsibility 2000: Into the new Millennium (Belfast: The Progressive Unionist Party, December 1997).
Shirlow, P. 'Fundamentalist Loyalism: Discourse, Resistance and Identity Politics', in *Landscapes of Defence* ed. J.R. Gold and G. Revill (Harlow/Essex: Prentice Hall, 2000).
Silke, A. 'The Lords of Discipline: The Methods and Motives of Paramilitary Vigilantism in Northern Ireland', *Low Intensity Conflict and Law Enforcement* 7, 2 (1998a) 121–56.
——. 'In Defense of the Realm: Financing Loyalist Terrorism in Northern Ireland – Part One: Extortion and Blackmail', *Studies in Conflict and Terrorism* 21 (1998b) 331–61.
——. 'Ragged Justice: Loyalist Vigilantism in Northern Ireland', *Terrorism and Political Violence* 11, 3 (1999) 1–31.
Sinnerton, H. *David Ervine* (Dingle/Co Kerry: Brandon, 2002).
Sinn Fein. *Setting the Record Straight: A Record of Communications between Sinn Fein and the British Government, October 1990 – November 1993* (Belfast: Sinn Fein, 1994).
Smyth, C. 'The DUP as a Politico-Religious Organisation', *Irish Political Studies* 1 (1986) 33–43.
——. *Ian Paisley: Voice of Protestant Ulster* (Edinburgh: Scottish Academic Press, 1987).
Southern, N. 'Ian Paisley and Evangelical Democratic Unionists: An Analysis of the Role of Evangelical Protestantism within the Democratic Unionist Party', *Irish Political Studies* 20, 2 (2005) 127–45.
Spencer, G. 'Pushing for Peace: The Irish Government, Television News and the Northern Ireland Peace Process', *European Journal of Communication* 18, 1 (2003) 55–80.
——. 'Reporting Inclusivity: the Northern Ireland Women's Coalition, the News Media and the Northern Ireland Peace Process', *Irish Journal of Sociology* 13, 2 (2004a) 43–65.
——. 'Constructing Loyalism: Politics, Communications and Peace in Northern Ireland', *Contemporary Politics* 10, 1 (2004b) 37–54.
——. 'The Impact of Television News on the Northern Ireland Peace Negotiations', *Media, Culture and Society* 26, 5 (2004c) 603–23.
——. *Omagh:Voices of Loss* (Belfast: Appletree Press, 2005).
——. 'The Decline of Ulster Unionism: The Problem of Identity, Image and Change', *Contemporary Politics* 12, 1 (2006a) 45–63.
——. 'Sinn Fein and the Media in Northern Ireland: The New Terrain of Policy Articulation, *Irish Political Studies* 21, 3 (2006b) 355–82.
Statement by the Police Ombudsman for Northern Ireland on her Investigation into the Circumstances Surrounding the Death of Raymond McCord Junior and Related Matters (Belfast: Police Ombudsman, 22 January 2007).
Stewart, A.T.Q. *The Narrow Ground* (London: Faber and Faber, 1989).
Strobel, W.P. 'TV Images May Shock but Won't Alter Policy', *Christian Science Monitor* 14 December (1994).
——. *Late-Breaking Foreign Policy* (Washington: United States Institute of Peace, 1997).
Taggart, N.W. *Conflict, Controversy and Co-operation* (Blackrock/Dublin: The Columba Press, 2004).
Taylor, P. *Provos* (London: Bloomsbury, 1997).
——. *Loyalists* (London: Bloomsbury, 1999).
Thomson, A. *Fields of Vision: Faith and Identity in Protestant Ulster* (Belfast: Centre for Contemporary Christianity in Ireland, 2002).
Todd, J. 'Two Traditions in Unionist Political Culture', *Irish Political Studies* 2 (1987) 1–26.

———. 'The Limits of Britishness', *The Irish Review* 5 (1988) 11–16.
———. 'History and Structure in Loyalist Ideology: The Possibilities of Ideological Change', *Irish Journal of Sociology* 4 (1994) 67–79.
Tonge, J. *The New Northern Irish Politics?* (Basingstoke: Palgrave Macmillan, 2005).
———. *Northern Ireland* (Cambridge: Polity Press, 2006a).
———. 'Polarisation or New Moderation? Party Politics since the GFA', in *A Farewell to Arms?* ed. M. Cox, A. Guelke and F. Stephen (Manchester: Manchester University Press, 2006b).
Troy, A. *Holy Cross* (Blackrock/Co. Dublin, Currach Press, 2005).
U.V.F. Policy Document (UVF, Belfast, November 1974).
Volkan, V.D. 'The Need to Have Enemies and Allies: A Developmental Approach', *Political Psychology* 6, 2(1985) 219–47.
Walker, G. *A History of the Ulster Unionist Party* (Manchester: Manchester University Press, 2004).
Wallis, R. Bruce, S. and Taylor, D. 'Ethnicity and Evangelicalism: Ian Paisley and Protestant Politics in Ulster', *Comparative Studies in Society and History* 29, 2 (1987) 293–313.
Weber, M. *The Protestant Ethic and the Spirit of Capitalism* (London: Routledge, 1930; 2005 ed).
Wells, R.A. *People Behind the Peace* (Grand Rapids/Michigan: William B. Eerdmans Publishing, 1999).
Whyte, J. *Interpreting Northern Ireland* (Oxford: Clarendon Press, 1990).
Wolfsfeld, G. 'Promoting Peace through the News Media', in *Media, Ritual and Identity* ed. T. Liebes and J. Curran (London:Routledge, 1998).
Woods, I.S. *Crimes of Loyalty: A History of the UDA* (Edinburgh: Edinburgh University Press, 2006).

Index

'abject and true remorse' (CLMC statement), 114–15, 118–19, 231
accountability, 109, 183, 226, 231
Adair, Johnny, 187, 191–5, 197–200, 202, 214, 235, 237, 240, 250
Adams, David (UDP), 21, 23, 42–3, 70, 72–3, 181–2, 184, 187, 219–20
 in peace talks, 77, 81–2, 84, 105, 110, 112, 116–19, 121, 126–7, 156, 162, 168–71
Adams, Gerry (Sinn Fein), 50, 74–6, 79–83, 121, 127, 143, 149–50, 163, 213, 226
'agreed Ireland,' 110–11
Ahern, Bertie, 158, 163, 165, 230
'Alan' (UDA/UFF), 37–8, 56–7, 67–8, 171, 186, 192–3, 195, 239–40, 244
Alliance Party, 180
all-Ireland context, 136, 159, 164, 177
ambiguity, 133, 141, 159, 215–16
American involvement, 74, 145–6, 157
Ancram, Michael (NIO), 121, 139–43, 149, 152, 156
Anderson, B., 8–9
Angel paper, 103–4
Anglo-Irish Agreement, 55, 57, 69, 72, 95, 134
anti-Agreement positions, 162–3, 175, 178, 181–2, 184, 194–5, 198, 205, 224
anti-Catholicism, 27, 30–1, 33–8
anti-state terrorism, 54–5, 60
Articles 2 and 3, 135, 145, 159
Assembly, 126, 136–8, 159, 162, 166–9, 172, 210, 213, 221–2, 232, 236
 collapse (2002), 49
 (re)formation of, 142, 224–8, 230
 role of, 176–9
 see also elections
Aughey, A., 7–9, 28, 54, 214–15
authority, mistrust of, 18, 42
autonomy in UDA, 65–7, 127, 182, 238

Bairner, A., 56
Ballymoney meeting, 184

Barr, Glenn (UDA), 70
Bell, Bowyer, 23
belonging, sense of, 11, 17–18, 26
betrayal, fear of, 14, 20, 29–31, 35, 39, 202
Bew, P., 111–12, 136, 148–9, 151, 180
Beyond the Religious Divide (UDA), 43
bi-lateral meetings approach, 165–6, 169–71
bill of rights proposal, 43, 72
Billig, M., 10
'Billy' (UDA), 57, 193
Blair, Tony, 144, 157–8, 163, 165–7, 171
 letter to Trimble, 172, 175
Bloomfield, D., 76, 78
Boulton, D., 61
Bourke, R., 27
boycotting of talks, 151, 154–5, 159
Brewer, John, 27, 33–5, 52
British governments
 cf Irish government, 103–5, 109
 Conservative *cf* Labour, 144, 157–9
 distrust of, 35, 72
 'no selfish interest' statement, 115, 218–19
 peace talks, 74; Loyalists, 77, 85, 87–90, 97, 99–100; Republicans, 75–6, 79–80, 83 *see also* exploratory dialogue; final stage negotiations; ministerial dialogue
 see also individual departments and ministers
British identity, 24, 45, 140, 150
British intelligence services, 50, 65, 113
British-Irish Council concept, 178
British nationalism, 8, 26
Brooke, Peter (NIO), 75–8, 132, 218–19
Brown, T., 9, 14
Bruce, S., 11, 14, 16, 29, 35–6, 39, 54, 61–2, 67, 71
Bruton, John, 149, 151
B-Specials, 48

Building a Permanent Peace (Sinn Fein), 148
'Building Blocks' document, 146

Cadwallader, A., 196–7
Calvinism, 13, 15, 31
Campbell, Gregory (DUP), 29–30
Canary Wharf bombing, 149–51, 157, 174
Carroll, John, 32
Catholics, 9–11, 14–19, 23, 41, 43–5, 48, 59, 61–3
  during the peace process, 81, 87, 113, 140, 146, 155
  post-Agreement, 188, 196, 198–9, 241
  see also anti-Catholicism; interaction with Catholics
ceasefires
  1992, 50, 61, 76–9
  1994, 84, 87, 89, 91–2, 96–7, 102, 107–9, 112–19, 147–51
  1997, 155–8
  2003, 198, 201, 203, 231
certainty, 14–18, 20, 23, 28, 32–3, 37, 39, 215
change
  and containment, 19–28
  engagement with, 37–8, 43, 51, 71, 77; UDA, 234–45; UVF, 227–34
  resistance to, 11–13, 15, 18, 21, 27, 32
'Charlie' (UDA), 8, 38, 57, 186, 193, 239
Chastelain, John De, 155, 232
choreography for media, 206–7, 212–13
CIA, 190
CID, 199, 234
citizenship, 7–9, 25–6, 237
civic model, 16, 23, 25–6, 34
civil disobedience, 230
civilianisation, 227–34
Clarke, L., 121, 151
class issues, 28, 32, 39–53, 62, 97, 103, 134, 140, 242, 248, 250
clergy, 39, 59–60, 79–89, 109, 200–2, 219
Clinton, Bill, 149, 158
CLMC (Combined Loyalist Military Command), 78–9, 85, 91–2, 100–1, 106, 112, 114–16, 151, 198–200
Clonard priests, 79, 81, 84

CLPA (Combined Loyalist Political Alliance), 77–8
Cochrane, F., 7–8, 19, 21
Codes of Conduct, 228–9, 232
co-determination concept, 161
Common Sense (UDA), 43, 57, 70–3
community work, 19, 38, 41, 46, 51, 57–8, 64–5, 229, 232, 236–7, 240–1, 249
compromise, resistance to, 14–17, 20, 23, 31, 33
confidentiality, 96, 107, 202, 217
consensus, 70, 179, 211, 237, 239
  Loyalist, 66, 88, 115, 174
  Unionist, 23, 28, 43, 133, 168
consent principle, 182, 199, 230–1
  in peace talks, 95, 111, 131, 134, 136, 139, 141, 143, 159, 161
Conservative Party, 144, 157–9
conspiracy theories, 33–4, 40, 72, 134
constitutional issues, 21, 25, 70, 88, 135, 159, 213
consultation, 114–15, 118, 127, 133, 142, 164, 175, 183–6, 208, 222
  UDA, 234–45
  UVF, 227–34
contractual obligations, 18, 25, 30, 34–5
Cooke, D., 35
counter-terrorism, 59, 62
covenantal view, 15, 30–1, 34–5
Crawford, C., 66–7
crime and security issues, 47, 122, 124–5, 225, 231–2
criminal activity, 56, 63–7, 71, 139, 148, 182, 187–8, 192–6, 198–9
criminality, 50, 55, 63, 66, 68, 122, 222
  post-Agreement, 187, 192–3, 195, 198, 204–5, 228–9, 231–42, 244–5, 249–50
cross-border bodies, 163–4, 171, 176, 181
cross-community dialogue, 213, 220, 241–2
cross-community relations, 43, 49, 52, 57, 69–70, 89–90, 115, 198, 226
CTI (Conflict Transformation Initiative), 235–8
cultural issues, 66, 147, 179, 181, 194, 204, 223, 235, 245
  and identity, 8–12, 16–17, 19, 24–5, 28, 39, 44–5, 49, 53
Cusack, J., 61–3, 65–6, 70–1, 90–1, 194, 196–7, 202

Index   265

death threats, 196, 234
decommissioning, 17
  in the peace talks, 122–4, 133,
    141, 144–8, 154–7, 163–5,
    168, 170–5, 178, 213,
    216
  post-Agreement, 194, 224–5, 229,
    232, 235
Defence Associations, 58, 65
defensive positions, 7, 11–12, 16, 24–5,
    56–9, 61–4
  and identity, 30, 32, 38–9, 42,
    45–6
  in peace talks, 88, 99, 140
Delaney, Eamon, 102–3, 111
demilitarisation, 148, 227–34
democratic positions, 14–15, 27,
    178–9, 231
deniability, 106, 110
destabilisation of loyalism, 113–15,
    192–3
devolutionist perspectives, 12–13, 43,
    70, 143, 159, 164, 225–6
DFA (Department of Foreign Affairs),
    102–3, 105, 107
difference, 10, 16–20, 25
Dillon, M., 39
disadvantaged communities, 236–7,
    240–3
disbandment, 228, 245, 248–9
discipline, paramilitary, 62–5, 118,
    129, 148, 150–1, 156,
    188–9, 191
dissident Republican groups, 229, 231,
    235
diversity, 11–12
Dixon, P., 206
Donaldson, Denis, 234
Donaldson, Jeffrey, 171, 175, 179
Downing Street Declaration, 97, 99,
    104, 107, 110–12, 114–15, 136,
    142, 145, 217
Drake, C. J. M., 55
drug-running, 65, 187, 192–4, 198, 205,
    233, 239, 244
Drumcree stand-offs, 146–8, 192,
    196
Dublin campaign plan, 93
Duignan, Sean, 104–7
Dunlop, J., 16, 80
Dunn, S., 23

DUP (Democratic Unionist Party), 13,
    15–16, 22, 208, 210, 220
  Paisleyism, 29–30, 35–9
  and paramilitarism, 39–52
  during peace talks, 97, 100, 147,
    153–4, 159, 162, 167–8, 175–6,
    178–9
  post-Agreement, 180, 184–5, 205,
    224–6, 230, 246–7
dynamic analysis, 173–4

Eames, Archbishop Robin, 85–9, 105–6,
    108–11, 200
East-West relations, 169, 178, 226
education, 10, 46, 83, 94, 115, 125,
    133, 222–3, 235–7, 240–4, 248
elections, 26, 36, 70, 180–1, 224, 226
electoral issues, 38, 70, 166–70, 220,
    222
Elliott, M., 14
Elliott, S., 70, 152, 180
endgames, 75, 78, 184
Engagement with Republicans (UVF), 52
English, Joe (UDP), 74, 117, 121
EPIC (Ex-Prisoners' Interpretative
    Centre), 47–8
Ervine, David (PUP), 19–20, 44, 69–70,
    187, 189–90, 198, 205, 210, 227–8
  in peace talks, 90–2, 94, 96, 106–9,
    115–19, 121, 127–9, 137–9, 147,
    151, 163–5, 175, 177
Evangelism, 29, 35–40, 52
exclusion, Loyalist fear of, 71, 75, 87,
    90, 92, 108, 183–4
exclusivity, 9, 14, 17, 27, 35, 70
exploitation of communities, 233, 237,
    243
exploratory dialogue, 125, 130–4
  Frameworks Documents, 136–9, 142,
    148
  negotiating strategies, 123–4,
    126–36
  preliminary meetings, 119–21
expulsions, 55, 159–60
external influences, shift from, 74–5
extortion, 56, 205, 233, 244

Farrington, C., 36, 205
fear, exploitation of, 30–1, 33, 42–6,
    48–9
Fernhill House statement, 230–2

feuds, 50, 55, 64, 67, 187–8, 191–9, 227–8, 235, 237
  resolution of, 200–5
  final stage negotiations
    bi-lateral meetings approach, 165–6, 169–71
    decommissioning, 171–5
    electoral issues, 166–9
    prisoner releases, 164–5
    strand two, 161–4, 176–9
Finlay, A., 24
Finlay, Fergus, 90–4, 96–8, 100, 103–4, 108, 217
Finlayson, A., 11, 30
Fitzgerald, Brian, 94–6
Flackes, W. D., 70, 152, 180
flag-flying, 38, 196, 203
flexibility, 16, 26, 34, 98–9, 109, 123, 127, 131, 138, 144, 210, 215
forgiveness, Protestant attitudes, 32–3
'For God and Ulster' slogan, 29–30
formation of paramilitary groups, 61, 65, 71
Forum election, 152, 181
FPR (Forum for Peace and Reconciliation), 148–9
fragmentation, 20–2, 24, 28, 35, 67, 98, 147, 151, 168, 173, 194, 250
Frameworks Documents, 136–9, 142, 148
fundamentalism, 10, 12, 15–16, 18, 29–30, 33, 35–7, 39–40, 49, 52, 246

Gallagher, Frankie (UPRG), 12, 41–2, 67, 184–5, 235–8, 243–4
Gallagher, T., 35
Ganiel, G., 37
Garland, R., 77, 106–7, 149
Gibson, Rev. Mervyn (Loyalist Commission), 200–4
Gillespie, G., 111–12, 136, 148–9, 151, 180
'God and Ulster' slogan, 51
Good Friday Agreement, 17, 26, 72–3, 133, 152, 176–7, 180–90, 194–5, 207–11, 214–16, 224–5, 230
  opposition, 33–4, 36–8, 49–51
Good, Rev. Harold, 225
government grants, 240, 243
Gowing, N., 211
Graham, B., 52

Gray, Jim (UDA), 197, 237–8
Gregg, John (UDA), 197–8, 203, 235
Greysteel killings, 86
Ground Rules for Substantive All-Party Negotiations, 151

Hain, Peter (NIO), 239
Hall, M., 235
Harkin, G., 234
harmonisation concept, 137–8, 142
Hennessey, T., 35, 111, 136, 146, 159
historical context, 18–19, 30–1, 41, 52–3
Holkeri, Harri, 155
Holy Cross incident, 196–7, 202
Hudson, Chris, 90–4, 150, 190–1, 229–30
Hume, John (SDLP), 74, 80, 105, 127
Hutchinson, Billy (UVF/PUP), 19, 44–5, 60–1, 189–90, 194–5, 205, 213–14, 220, 228–9, 232
  in peace talks, 109, 117, 121, 127–8, 135–9, 148, 154, 157–8, 162, 164–5, 171, 174–5

identity, 7, 15, 18, 27
  and culture, 8–12, 16–17, 19, 24–5, 28, 39, 44–5, 49, 53
  national, 8, 13, 24, 26, 45, 140, 150
  negative, 23–4, 28
  and Paisleyism, 29–39
  paramilitary, 40–3, 46–8, 50–3
ideology
  Conservative, 158
  liberal, 12, 25, 31
  Loyalist, 20, 24, 30, 47, 52–3, 67
  Republican, 183, 214
  Unionist, 8–12, 16–17, 183
IICD (Independent International Commission on Decommissioning), 157, 225, 229, 231–2
image of loyalism, 57, 65, 71, 187, 192, 194–7, 205, 220–2, 245
imagined communities, 8–10, 23
IMC (Independent Monitoring Commission), 232–3, 244
inclusivity, 39, 70, 167, 243
Independent Unionist Group, 180
individualism, 13–23, 28, 32, 242, 246

informal peace talks, 80–9, 95, 97
informants, 233–4
Ingram, M., 234
initial developments in peace process, 74–80
INLA (Irish National Liberation Army), 39
insularity, 22, 28, 36, 93
integrationist perspective, 12–13
intensification of violence, 66, 78–9, 86, 92, 113–14
interaction with Catholics, 35–6, 43, 51–2, 57, 69–71
interface areas, 57, 66, 196
interpretation, 214–15, 217–23
intra-communal violence, 56, 191–9, 203
intransigence, 21, 32, 37, 69, 127, 146, 150, 159, 210, 213, 216, 220, 246–7
intra-Unionist conflict, 153
introspection, 14, 32
IRA (Irish Republican Army), 47, 57–61, 63, 90, 181, 198–9, 222, 224–5, 228–9, 234
 in peace talks, 112–13, 115–16, 144, 149–51, 155–8, 160, 176
 see also dissident Republican groups; PIRA (Provisional IRA); Real IRA
Irish governments, 65
 cf British government, 103–5, 109
 and Omagh bombing, 188–90
 peace talks, 74–5, 79; Loyalists, 85, 88–100, 102–11, 216–17, 229; Republicans, 80–1, 83
 see also individual departments and ministers
isolation, 17–18, 33, 184
'It's Your Choice' slogan, 180

John Gregg Initiative, 235–45
Johnston, K., 121, 151
Johnston, William, 232
Joint Declaration, 97, 99, 104, 107, 110–12, 114–15, 136, 142, 145, 217
joint statement (Paisley/Adams), 226
Jordan, H., 195, 197, 199
journalists, 171, 175, 217

Kearney, V., 147
Kelly, Gerry, 124, 164

Kennaway, B., 29, 39
Kirkham, Tommy (UDP/UPRG), 64, 71, 121, 184, 236
'Kitchen Cabinet,' 77

Labour Party, 144, 157–8
law and order, 46, 48, 55
Leach, Stephen (NIO), 123–6, 128–30, 154–5, 166, 172, 178–9, 208–9, 216
Leeds Castle talks, 224, 247
legitimation, 54–6, 58–9, 69, 231
liberal ideology, 12, 25, 31
liberty, individual, 7, 15–17, 34
LINC (Local Initiatives for Needy Communities), 46, 227–8
Lisburn bombing, 156–7
Lister, D., 195, 197, 199
lobbying groups, 236, 248
loss, perception of, 48–9, 55, 169, 178–9, 181–2, 185–6, 199, 250
Loughinisland killings, 92
'Loyalism in Transition,' 240
Loyalist Commission, 200–5, 229
LPA (Loyalist Political Alliance), 110
LVF (Loyalist Volunteer Force), 39–40, 128, 147–8, 156, 161, 191, 194–5, 197–8, 200–1, 203, 228

McAllister, I., 49
McAuley, J.W., 24, 52–3, 63–5, 67, 69, 71, 188, 223
McCabe, Chris (NIO), 119–24, 137
McCartney, Bob, 162, 168, 180, 222
McCord, Raymond (junior), 233
McCrea, Rev. William, 39, 147
McDonald, H., 61–3, 66, 90–1, 194, 196–7, 202
McDonald, Jackie (UDA), 49–50, 66, 185, 193–4, 222–3, 241–2
McGarry, J., 8–9, 12–13
McGrath, A. E., 14
McGuiness, Martin (Sinn Fein), 75, 121, 143, 151, 163, 174, 213, 227
McLaughlin, Mitchel (Sinn Fein), 74, 113

McMichael, Gary (UDP), 20, 42, 58, 70–2, 182–5, 187, 211–13
  in peace talks: exploratory, 119–21, 126–9, 134–5, 137–8; final stage, 163, 165–7, 169, 176, 178; ministerial, 139, 149–50; multi-party, 153–6, 158–60; preliminary, 77–9, 81, 84, 112, 116–18
McMichael, John (UDA), 71
McSweeney, B., 36
MacIver, M. A., 30–1
Mac Ginty, R., 39
Magee, Rev. Roy, 84–7, 100, 106, 110, 120
Maginnis, Ken (UUP), 212–13
Mahood, Jackie (PUP), 121, 128–9, 147
Major, John, 87, 104–5, 107, 120, 137, 144, 150, 156
Manchester bombing, 155–6
Mandelson, Peter (NIO), 192
Mandle, J., 10
Mansergh, Martin, 85, 105–7, 190
marches, 66, 146–7, 191, 195
marginalisation, sense of, 23, 49, 52, 181
Mason, D., 11
Mayhew, Patrick (NIO), 96, 120–1, 143–5
media, 169–70, 172, 175, 192, 196–7, 199, 205–7
  as communications conduit, 212–14
  framing and interpretation, 217–23
  and negotiating process, 207–12, 214–17
mediation courses, 236–7
mending communities, 239, 243
MI5, 50, 113
military perspectives, 91, 93, 186, 201, 222
military strategies, 62, 66–8, 78–9
Miller, D. W., 15
ministerial dialogue
  disruptive tactics, 145–51
  Michael Ancram, 139–43
  Patrick Mayhew, 143–5
  towards multi-party talks, 151–2
Mitchell, Billy (UVF/LINC), 46–7, 227–8
Mitchell, C., 32, 39
Mitchell, George (American Senator), 146, 153, 155, 157–9, 162–4, 176, 179, 206–7

Mitchel, P., 16–18, 39
Moloney, E., 35, 74
Molyneaux, James (UUP), 104, 144, 146
moral certainty, 14–15, 17, 20, 32–3, 37
Morgan, V., 23
Morrissey, M., 86
Morrow, D., 15
motivation, paramilitary, 45, 54–61, 90–4
Mowlam, Mo (NIO), 124, 160, 206
multi-party talks, 151–61, 212–13
Murphy, Paul (NIO), 164, 168, 206–7, 209, 215–16, 221, 242, 247

Nally, Dermot, 106
nationalism, 7–8, 10–11, 26, 181, 195–7, 199, 208–9, 214–16, 229–31, 242
  and Loyalist identity, 29, 33–4, 40–1, 43, 46–9
  and the peace process, 74–5, 77, 81, 90–1, 95, 99, 105, 109–11
  and the peace talks, 113–14, 125, 131–2, 135, 138, 140, 147, 155, 164, 176, 178
  and political violence, 56–7, 59, 63, 68, 70
  and unionism, 8–12, 16, 25–7
Nationalist interests, 74, 229–30, 242
negativity, 19–22, 27, 44, 47–50, 91, 140, 162, 183
negotiating process, 131–2, 137–9, 158, 161–6, 169–71, 207–12, 214–17, 226
negotiating strategies, 202, 207–8, 210
  exploratory dialogue, 123–4, 126–36
  and media, 206–7, 212–17
  ministerial dialogue, 141–2, 145
Nelson, S., 61–2
neutrality, 135, 228, 230
Newell, Ken, 81–4, 150
New loyalism, 52
news coverage of negotiations, 207–12
New unionism, 26
Nicoll, David (DUP/UPRG), 40–1, 184–5, 236
NIO (Northern Ireland Office), 112, 119–21, 151, 166, 239–40, 242–3
NIWC (Northern Ireland Women's Coalition), 162, 169, 180, 207
no claim, no blame policy, 160

'no first strike' policy, 155
'no guns, no government' slogan, 171, 175
'no selfish interest' declaration, 115, 218–19
'no surrender' slogan, 34, 144
Northern Bank robbery, 222
North-South relations, 135–8, 142, 159, 161–4, 171, 176–8, 182, 216, 226
nuanced communications, 93, 99, 102, 172, 210, 217, 234
NUPRG (New Ulster Political Research Group), 70

obstructionism, 19–20, 22, 26, 50–1
O'Dowd, L., 8, 26
O'Heffernan, P., 212
O'Kane, E., 172
O'Leary, B., 8–9, 12–13
O'Malley, P., 9, 27, 31–2, 34
O'Neill, Captain Terence, 35, 44–5, 61
Omagh bombing, 188–91
oppositional concepts, 8, 39, 49, 184, 222
Orange Order, the, 39, 146–8
orange sceptics, 22

Paisleyism, 29–39
 and working-class Unionists, 39–53
Paisley, Rev Dr Ian, 15–16, 29, 61, 65, 148, 162, 170, 176, 185–6, 208, 226–7, 246–7
paramilitarism, 19–20, 37–8, 56, 126, 159–60, 167, 173, 185, 200, 240
 and communities, 57–9, 61, 233, 237, 239, 243
 dialogue with clergy, 80–9
 discipline, 62–5, 118, 129, 148, 150–1, 156, 188–9, 191
 motivation and structure, 45, 54–63, 65–8, 90, 94, 127–8, 182, 238, 249
 in a non-violent society, 227–34, 248
 psychology of, 90–4
 recruitment, 54, 57–8, 62, 64, 68, 203–4
 secrecy, 60, 64, 68, 93
 and security agencies, 64, 233–4
 and unionism, 39–53
 see also individual organisations
Parkinson, A. F., 220
particularism, 7, 10, 17

Paths to a Political Settlement (FPR), 148–9
patrols, paramilitary, 56–8
Patten Report, 38
Patterson, H., 164, 181, 191
pipe bombings, 196
PIRA (Provisional IRA), 74, 78, 87–8, 98
pluralism, 9–10, 13, 25, 29, 36–7, 43–4, 53, 69, 71, 140
polarities, religious, 15, 17–18, 31
Police Ombudsman Statement, 233
Policing Board, 226
policing issues, 122, 148, 165, 184, 190, 225, 229, 233–4, 239, 244
political issues, 146, 148, 178, 199, 201
political representation, Loyalist, 200, 205, 239, 248
 see also individual parties
political strategies, 22, 24, 49, 208
 Loyalist: development of, 52, 65, 68–73, 77–9, 84, 93; lack of, 45–51, 55, 60–2, 235
 Republican, 74, 78, 88–9
 Unionist, 30–1, 33, 42–6, 48–9
politicisation of loyalism, 52, 65, 68–73, 77–9, 84, 93, 198
politics and religion, 34–5, 37–8, 40, 43, 51–3
Pollak, A., 35, 77
popularism, 209, 223, 228
Porter, N., 25
Powell, Jonathan, 165–6
power-sharing, 43, 49, 57, 65, 69–70, 72, 135, 162, 179, 199, 224–6, 247
power struggles, 55, 65–6, 147, 188
pragmatism, 22, 37, 158
Presbyterianism, 13–14, 16, 20, 33
Principles of Loyalism (PUP), 40
prisoners, 83, 95–6, 115–18, 124, 130, 135, 160–1, 170, 174, 186, 242
 releases, 164–5, 178, 182, 212–13
 sentences, 58, 60, 197, 199
proactivity, 57, 235
pro-Agreement Unionists, 181
procedural issues in talks, 153–5
propaganda, 180–1
proportional representation, 70, 72, 136, 167
Propositions on Heads of Agreement, 159
proscription, 65
pro-state terrorism, 54, 56, 61
protection concept, 31, 57–9, 61

Protestantism, 9, 12–19, 31–3
  see also Calvinism; Evangelism; fundamentalism; politics and religion; Presbyterianism; Puritanism
PSNI (Police Service of Northern Ireland), 226, 229, 234
psychology, paramilitary, 90–4
publicity, 91, 118, 180, 187, 193–4, 202
punishment, paramilitary, 55, 204, 233
PUP (Progressive Unionist Party), 13, 19, 24, 26, 69, 77, 79, 82, 89, 94, 108
  and the media, 207, 213–14, 220, 222
  and paramiltary identity, 40, 44, 46–8, 50, 52–3
  in peace process, 113–14, 119–23, 127–9, 135, 139, 141, 148–52, 155–7, 162, 165–7, 171, 175
  post-Agreement, 180, 191, 194, 198, 205, 227, 229–30, 247–8
Puritanism, 32–3
Purvis, Dawn (PUP), 222

racketeering, 62, 65
radicalism, 15
reactivity, 47, 55–61, 86–9, 93, 102, 106, 118, 143–4, 150, 155–6, 189, 222
Real IRA, 188–90
reconciliation, 28, 31, 43, 57, 71, 236
recruitment, 54, 57–8, 62, 64, 68, 203–4
Red Hand Commando, 68, 115, 196–7, 200, 204, 230–1
referendums, 141, 145, 151, 180
Reid, Father Alec, 74, 79, 81, 84, 105, 109–10, 115, 150, 225
Reid, John (NIO), 204
religion and politics, 13–19, 34–5, 37–8, 40, 43, 51–3
Republican News, 76, 219
Republicans, 19, 44, 58, 61
  cf Loyalists, 97–8, 102–3, 122–3, 130–1, 133, 140–1, 183, 186, 207–9, 214–16, 221–2, 241–2
  dissident, 191, 229, 231, 235
  in peace talks, 75–6, 79–81, 83
  political strategies, 74, 78, 88–9
  targetting of, 63, 78, 92, 151
responsibility, 69–70, 72, 118, 243
restitution to victims, 55
revenge killings, 86, 92, 101

Reynolds, Albert, 85, 97–8, 104–8, 110, 150
Reynolds, Father Gerry, 81–2, 84, 150
rigidity of belief, 14–16, 32, 39
riots, 58, 64, 192
Roadshow, the, 227–34
Robb, Lindsay (PUP), 121, 128–9, 147
Roberts, Tom (UVF/EPIC), 48, 64
Robinson, Peter (DUP), 225
Roshwald, A., 11
Rotary Club Speech (Brooke), 76
Rowan, B., 52, 191, 194, 197
Ruane, J., 27–8
RUC Special Branch, 199, 234
Ryder, C., 147

Scappaticci, Freddie, 234
schools charter, 204
Scottish Presbyterianism, 30–1
'script factory,' 102
SDLP (Social Democratic & Labour Party), 74, 81, 83, 109, 149, 159, 162, 165–7, 175, 180
secrecy, 60, 64, 68, 90–1, 93, 106–7
sectarianism, 62–71, 84, 86, 188, 192, 194–8, 236, 240, 247
Section 47 of Frameworks, 136–7
secularism, 31, 36–40, 50–2
security agencies, 54–5, 83, 195, 197–8, 228, 232, 244
  and paramilitaries, 64, 233–4
  perceived failure of, 55–6, 59
self-determination, 8, 29, 136
self-interest, 181–2, 238, 244
sensational reportage, 218, 220, 222
Shankill bombing, 63, 86, 92, 100–1
Sharing Responsibility (PUP), 69–70
Shirlow, P., 40
Shoukri, Andre (UDA), 197, 237–8
siege mentality, 15, 18, 31, 40
Silke, A., 55–6
simplification in the media, 217–18
Simpson, 'Jimbo,' 197
Sinnerton, H., 77–8, 147, 205
Sinn Fein, 17, 38, 44, 47, 50, 61
  and the media, 206–10, 219–20
  in peace talks, 74–5, 80–2, 90, 112, 124–5, 134, 143–4, 148–51, 153–60, 164–6, 172–5, 178
  post-Agreement, 180, 184, 189, 199, 205, 224–6, 230, 234, 241–2

siren systems, 59
Six Principles, 97, 100–1, 105–6, 110, 230–1
slide programme, 227–8
Smallwoods, Ray, 77, 81, 84, 86, 103, 114, 116, 119
Smith, William 'Plum' (UVF/EPIC), 47, 117
Smyth, C, 16, 30
Smyth, Hugh (PUP), 117, 119–21
Smyth, M., 86
Snodden, Martin (UVF), 45, 59
Social Development Dept (NIO), 240, 242–3
socialism, 48, 52–3, 69
social issues, 37, 41–2, 47, 51, 62, 135, 138, 213, 232, 235–7, 239–43, 248
social solidarity, 10, 40, 46, 244
Southern, N., 37
Special Branch, 199, 234
Spence, Gusty, 61, 79–80, 96, 106–9, 117–19, 230–1, 233
Spencer, G, 22, 26–7, 181, 188, 206–10, 212, 215–16, 219–20
Spring, Dick, 89, 91, 93–4, 96, 98–101, 105, 149, 217
stalemate, military, 74, 76, 80
St Andrews Agreement, 224–7
Steele, John (NIO), 123–4
stereotypes, 20, 31, 57, 187, 214, 222
Stevens Inquiry, 65
Stewart, A. T. Q., 15
storage of weapons, 232
Stormont *see* Assembly
street violence, 58, 64
strikes, 65
Strobel, W. P., 211
structure of paramilitary organisations, 54–63, 65–8, 127–8, 182, 238, 249
Sunday World boycott, 220
Sunningdale Agreement, 65
superiority, sense of, 14, 31, 33, 70

Tartan Gang Youth Wing, 58
Taylor, M., 65, 70–1
Taylor, P., 74, 77
television, 52, 170–1, 212–13
'terms of engagement,' 122
territorial interests, 29
texts, negotiation around, 166, 171
theological interests, 14, 29, 35, 52

Thomas, Quentin, 123–4, 130–4, 151–2, 167, 173–4, 207–8
Thomson, A., 29–30, 36
three-stranded approach to talks, 131–2, 137–9, 158, 161–4, 226
Tilley, J.R., 32, 39
Todd, J., 9, 11–12, 27–8
Tonge, J., 22, 24, 65–6, 179, 181, 224
'totality of relationships,' 110–11, 159
tradition and unionism, 12–13
training of paramilitaries, 61
tribalism, 50
Trimble, David (UUP), 21–2, 26, 44–5, 181, 184, 200
  in peace talks, 144, 146, 153, 162–3, 166–8, 171–3, 175
Troy, A., 196
truth, notion of absolute, 23, 29–31, 35
twin-track approach, 146, 149
Tyrie, Andy (UDA), 70

UDA (Ulster Defence Association), 8, 12, 20, 37–8, 41, 43, 49–50, 52–3, 56–61, 72–3, 220
  autonomy within, 65–7, 127, 182, 238
  cf UVF, 109–10, 127–8, 211–12
  history, 64–8
  during peace talks, 79, 116–19, 123, 126, 141, 150, 156, 160; talks with clergy, 81, 83–6, 89; final stages, 161, 165–7, 169, 171, 175
  post-Agreement, 181–5, 187–8, 191–8, 200, 204, 228, 233–45, 247, 249–50
UDP (Ulster Democratic Party), 13, 20–1, 24, 26, 40, 42, 58, 70–3
  and the media, 207, 211, 219–20, 223
  in peace talks, 78–9, 81–2, 112–14, 119–23, 126–7, 129, 141, 152, 155–6, 159–62, 165–9, 171
  post-Agreement, 180–8, 191, 234–5
UFF (Ulster Freedom Fighters), 37–8, 56–7, 65, 67, 77, 86, 151, 159, 171, 193, 195, 235
UKUP (UK Unionist Party), 153–4, 159, 162, 180
ULDP (Ulster Loyalist Democratic Party), 70
'Ulster says no' slogan, 49–50
Ulster Unionists, 40–1

Ulster Young Militants, 57
uncertainty, 39, 88
undermining of peace process, 153–7, 159, 176, 181, 187–8, 192, 195, 197, 199
unionism
  containment and change, 19–28
  and nationalism, 8–12
  and paramilitarism, 56, 59–62, 65, 69–73
  and peace talks, 74–83, 91, 112–15, 126–7, 131–42, 144–7, 149–50, 152; Irish government, 94–9, 101–5, 107–11; multi-party and final negotiations, 153–5, 157, 159, 161–4, 168–70, 172, 174, 176–9
  post-Agreement, 180–6, 198, 208–9, 211, 213–16, 218–20, 224, 230, 236, 241–2
  religious tradition, 12–19
  see also Paisleyism
Union, the, 7, 12–13, 23–5, 33–5, 47, 49–50, 57, 59–62, 220, 231
  and peace talks, 88, 90, 114, 131–3, 144, 151, 169, 174
united Ireland concept, 8, 27, 31, 34, 37–8, 47, 50, 58, 181, 184, 214
  and peace talks, 84, 88, 99, 111–12, 134, 137–8, 142, 145, 162, 169
UPRG (Ulster Political Research Group), 12, 40–2, 52, 58, 64, 67, 71, 184, 235–7, 248–9
UUP (Ulster Unionist Party), 21–2, 38, 46, 49, 51, 180–1, 183, 207–8, 220–1
  in peace talks, 133, 146, 149, 153, 159, 162, 165–7, 171–2, 175, 178–9
UVF (Ulster Volunteer Force), 19, 29, 45–9, 53, 56, 68–9, 73, 219, 222
  cf UDA, 109–10, 127–8, 211–12
  consultation and change, 227–34
  history, 61–4
  Number One, 50, 59–60, 63, 77–8, 84, 113–15, 147, 186–9

Number Two, 50–2, 60, 90, 92, 101, 171, 174–5, 190–2, 211–12, 227, 230, 234
  during peace talks, 79–80, 85–6, 106–7, 116–19, 129, 138–9, 141, 148–51, 156, 161, 165
  in peace talks, 89–94
  post-Agreement, 185, 194, 196, 199–200, 203–4, 225, 247–9
U.V.F. Policy (UVF), 62
UWC (Ulster Workers' Council), 65

vigilantism, 55–7, 59, 204
violence, 54–5, 58, 60–2, 64–7, 69, 71–3, 133–4, 233
  intensification of, 66, 78–9, 86, 92, 113–14
  intra-communal, 56, 191–9, 203
  and nationalism, 56–7, 59, 63, 68, 70
  during peace talks, 81, 159–61
  see also feuds
Volkan, V. D., 11
VPP (Volunteer Political Party), 69

Walker, G., 26
Wallis, R., 9
Warnock, Stephen (LVF), 197
Weber, M., 13–14
Wells, R. A., 80
Whitbread Speech (Brooke), 76, 218–19
White, John (UDP), 117, 121, 170, 187, 191, 197–8
Wolfsfeld, G., 217
Women's Coalition, 162, 169, 180, 207
Woods, I. S., 65, 67–8, 199–200, 220
working-class unionism, 24, 26, 28, 39–53, 62, 97, 103, 248, 250
Wright, Billy 'King Rat' (LVF), 39, 50, 128–9, 146–8, 192
written constitution proposal, 72

Youth Wing, Tartan Gang, 58

zero-sum approach, 44, 49